AMC'S BEST BACKPACKING IN
NEW ENGLAND

A GUIDE TO 37 OF THE BEST MULTIDAY TRIPS
FROM MAINE TO CONNECTICUT

MATT HEID

SECOND EDITION

Appalachian Mountain Club Books
Boston, Massachusetts

AMC is a nonprofit organization, and sales of AMC Books fund our mission of protecting the Northeast outdoors. If you appreciate our efforts and would like to become a member or make a donation to AMC, visit outdoors.org, call 800-372-1758, or contact us at Appalachian Mountain Club, 5 Joy Street, Boston, MA 02108.

outdoors.org/publications/books

Distributed by The Globe Pequot Press, Guilford, Connecticut.

Front cover photographs: top © Caleb Kenna, calebkenna.com, bottom all © Jerry and Marcy Monkman, EcoPhtography.com
Back cover photographs © Carey Kish, editor of AMC's *Maine Mountain Guide*
Interior photographs © Matt Heid, unless otherwise noted.
Maps by Larry Garland © Appalachian Mountain Club
Cover design by Matthew Simmons
Interior design by Eric Edstam

Library of Congress Cataloging-in-Publication Data

Heid, Matt, 1975-
  AMC's best backpacking in New England : a guide to 35 of the best multi-day trips from Maine to Connecticut / Matt Heid. -- Second edition.
      pages cm
  ISBN 978-1-934028-90-2 (pbk.)
  1. Backpacking--New England--Guidebooks. 2. Hiking--New England--Guidebooks. I. Title. II. Title: Best backpacking in New England.
  GV199.42.N38H45 2014
  796.510974--dc23
                        2013048617

The paper used in this publication meets the minimum requirements of the American National Standard for Information Sciences-Permanence of Paper for Printed Library Materials, ANSI Z39.48-1984. ∞

Outdoor recreation activities by their very nature are potentially hazardous. This book is not a substitute for good personal judgment and training in outdoor skills. Due to changes in conditions, use of the information in this book is at the sole risk of the user. The authors and the Appalachian Mountain Club assume no liability for accidents happening to, or injuries sustained by, readers who engage in the activities described in this book.

Interior pages contain 30% post-consumer recycled fiber.
Cover contains 10% post-consumer recycled fiber.
Printed in the United States of America,
using vegetable-based inks.

10 9 8 7 6 5 4 3 2 1   14 15 16 17 18 19 20

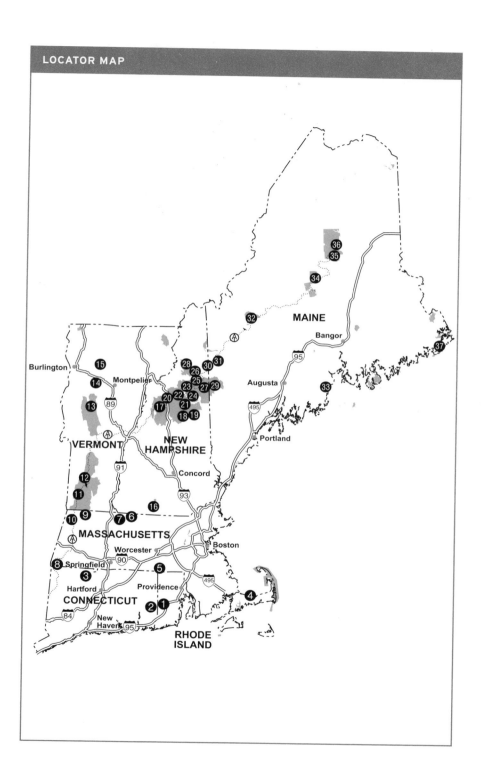

LEGEND

————	Backpacking Route
··············	Connecting Trail
═══════	Highway
══════	Improved Road
════════	Unimproved Road (4WD)
——··——	Stream
🏠	Lodge, Cabin, or Hut
◭	Campground
⊏	Shelter
◩	Tentsite
🅿	Parking
Ⓐ	Appalachian Trail
▲	Peak or Summit

CONTENTS

SECTION 1: SOUTHERN NEW ENGLAND: MASSACHUSETTS, CONNECTICUT, RHODE ISLAND

SECTION 2: VERMONT

SECTION 3: NEW HAMPSHIRE

SECTION 4: MAINE

AT-A-GLANCE TRIP PLANNER

#	Trip	Page	Location	Difficulty	Distance and Elevation Gain
	1. SOUTHERN NEW ENGLAND				
1	Arcadia Management Area	2	Exeter, RI	Easy	0.6 mi, 50 ft
2	Pachaug State Forest	5	Voluntown, CT	Easy	0.8 mi, 160 ft
3	Tunxis State Forest	9	Hartland and Barkhamsted, CT	Moderate	9.8 mi, 1,650 ft
4	Sandy Neck	15	Barnstable, MA	Easy	7.9 mi, 50 ft
5	Douglas State Forest	19	Douglas, MA	Easy	4.8 mi, 500 ft
6	Tully Trail	24	Royalston, MA	Moderate	20.6 mi, 3,300 ft
7	New England National Scenic Trail, Section 17	32	Northfield, MA	Moderate	10.4 mi, 1,800 ft
8	The Taconics	39	Northwestern CT, southwestern MA	Challenging	16.9 mi, 4,600 ft
9	Monroe State Forest	50	Monroe, MA	Moderate	2.0 mi, 300 ft
10	Mount Greylock State Reservation	55	Williamstown, MA	Challenging	11.0 mi, 3,050 ft
	2. VERMONT				
11	Glastenbury Mountain Wilderness	63	Woodford, VT; southern Green Mountain National Forest	Challenging	22.7 mi, 4,700 ft

Estimated Time	Loop, Car Shuttle, or Out-and-Back	Fee	Dogs Allowed	Dispersed Camping	Trip Highlights
1-2 days	Out-and-Back		🐕		Quiet backcountry base camp
1-2 days	Out-and-Back				A hidden shelter, CT's backpacking potential
2 days	Car Shuttle		🐕		Woodlands so wild even moose live here
1-2 days	Loop	$			Dune camping
1-2 days	Loop	$	🐕		Secluded backcountry shelter, geographic novelty
2 days	Loop				Surprising wilds of north-central MA
1-2 days	Car Shuttle		🐕		Explore Shenandoah's dark hollows and high peaks
2-3 days	Car Shuttle		🐕		Summits, ravines, waterfalls, vistas, old-growth forest
1-2 days	Loop		🐕		Old-growth forest
1-2 days	Loop		🐕		The highest mountain in MA
2 days	Loop		🐕	△	The most remote summit in the Green Mountains

Estimated Time	Loop, Car Shuttle, or Out-and-Back	Fee	Dogs Allowed	Dispersed Camping	Trip Highlights
2 days	Loop		🐕	⛺	Streams, ponds, Prospect Rock, VT's highest waterfall
1-2 days	Loop		🐕	⛺	Forested heart of the Green Mountains
1-2 days	Loop		🐕		Highest never-developed peak in VT
1-3 days	Loop	$	🐕		Tallest mountain in VT, gnarly trails
2 days	Car Shuttle	$	🐕		Ridgeline backpacking less than 50 miles from Boston
1-2 days	Loop	$	🐕	⛺	Riveting brookside ascent to an alpine summit
2 days	Loop		🐕	⛺	Sweeping summits, easy access, minmal crowds
2 days	Loop		🐕	⛺	Rocky peaks, quiet streams, remote mountains, challenging trails
2 days	Loop		🐕	⛺	Quiet trails, a wild ascent, prime viewpoint from summit
2-3 days	Loop	$	🐕	⛺	Easy cruising, remote waterfall, five 4,000-footers, alpine ridgeline
2-4 days	Loop	$	🐕	⛺	Four 4,000-footers, Thoreau Falls, classic backcountry experience
2-3 days	Out-and-Back	$	🐕		Alpine peaks, continuous views, four 4,000-footers, including Mount Washington
2 days	Car Shuttle	$	🐕	⛺	The least-traveled ridge in the Presidential Range
3 days	Loop	$	🐕		A yawning chasm, alpine ridgeline, a challenging big mountain adventure
2 days	Car Shuttle	$	🐕	⛺	Ravines, cliffs, ridgelines, alpine scenery, New England's second highest summit
2-3 days	Loop		🐕	⛺	Streams, rivers, mountains of NH's newest Wilderness Area

Estimated Time	Loop, Car Shuttle, or Out-and-Back	Fee	Dogs Allowed	Dispersed Camping	Trip Highlights
2 days	Loop		🐕	⛺	Wild and empty northern White Mountains
1–2 days	Loop		🐕	⛺	ME's quiet, scenic White Mountains
2–3 days	Car Shuttle	$	🐕		Rugged mountians, alpine bogs, views, Hardest Mile on the AT
3–5 days	Loop or Car Shuttle		🐕		Rugged mountains of western ME
2 days	Loop	$	🐕		A mountainous ridge with maple-cloaked flanks
1–2 days	Loop	$	🐕		Coastal mountain views, diverse forest
5–10 days	Car Shuttle		🐕	⛺	The most remote section of the AT
1–3 days	Loop	$			Grand alpine amphitheater, base camp, mile-high Katahdin
2–4 days	Loop	$			Ponds, peaks, ME's grandeur
2 days	Loop		🐕		Coastal backpacking

PREFACE

WELCOME TO THE SECOND EDITION OF *AMC's Best Backpacking in New England*! Fully updated and revised, it features several significant additions and improvements over the first edition—and continues to reflect my enduring fascination with the wonders of the New England backcountry.

Four new trips have been added to this edition: a long-distance adventure on Maine's Grafton Loop Trail (Trip 31), a scenic sample of the New England National Scenic Trail in Massachusetts (Trip 7), a dramatic overnight excursion in New Hampshire's Pemigewasset Wilderness (Trip 20), and a visit to a hidden shelter in Douglas State Forest in southeast Massachusetts (Trip 5).

Also new in this edition are GPS coordinates to precisely locate trailheads, backcountry shelters, designated camping areas, and major summits. This will help aid in trip planning and navigation, and make it easier to locate starting points and key destinations throughout each hike.

Every trip in this book was field-checked to ensure accuracy and reflect current conditions. Since the first edition was released, several backcountry shelters have been removed, sections of trail have been relocated or closed, trail signs have been added or lost, and other important changes have occurred. (The effects of Hurricane Irene in 2011 also significantly impacted New England's trails.) With this comprehensive and completely updated resource in hand, you can head out with confidence on your next adventure.

I hope that you will find the wilds of New England to be remarkable, exciting, and endlessly enticing. From the lush and diverse woodlands of southern New England to the sky-scraping views of New Hampshire's alpine peaks, from wave-lapped shorelines to remote wilderness areas, from roaring rivers to mellifluous streams, New England offers a little bit of everything. No matter what you love, you can find it here in New England—and you can find a trip within these pages that takes you there.

ACKNOWLEDGMENTS

MANY PEOPLE HELPED MAKE this second edition a reality. I would like to thank: Victoria Sandbrook Flynn, who successfully shepherded this book through many a stressful challenge; Dan Eisner, for his copyediting skills; Athena Lakri for turning computer files into printed reality; Sally Manikian, for her early rising emails and invaluable help in coordinating several of the White Mountain updates; Kimberly Duncan-Mooney, for getting this project off the ground in the first place; my wife, Gretchen, for accommodating this taxing project; my extended family, especially Mimi and Grampy, for always being there to help; and especially my mom and dad, who have always encouraged and supported my passion for the great outdoors.

But I would most like to acknowledge and recognize the people who joined me on this project as part of The Best Backpacking in New England Group. Collectively, this dedicated and passionate group of people field-checked and rehiked nearly every mile of trail in this book—and I couldn't have completed this project without their invaluable assistance. You can learn more about this wonderful group of people in the back of the book.

Finally, I would like to particularly thank all the stewards of the New England backcountry, who work to maintain and keep it open and accessible to us all. Thank you from all of us who hike the great trails of New England.

Dedicated to my boys, Kieran and Rohan. May you always love and cherish Nature.

Matt Heid
October 2013

INTRODUCTION

WELCOME TO THE TOTAL NEW ENGLAND backcountry experience. This guidebook tours the wildest, least touched landscapes in a region known for its dramatic terrain, majestic forests, and exhilarating mountaintops. Virtually every outdoor highlight can be found in these pages—roaring waterfalls, alpine summits, sweeping views, old-growth forest, idyllic swimming holes, airy cliffs, tranquil ponds, burbling streams, abundant wildflowers, radiant foliage, intense isolation . . . the list goes on.

The 37 featured trips range in length from less than a mile to nearly 100 miles. They visit nine Wilderness Areas, thirteen state forests, four state parks, two national forests, and a variety of other protected landscapes. Though many can be completed in a day, they all provide opportunities for overnight adventure. Most are two- to three-day trips, perfect for a weekend outing. Trips were selected with two goals in mind:

- The routes should be loops.
- The trails should cross roads as infrequently as possible.

Loop hikes are convenient, do not revisit scenery, and avoid the hassle of arranging a car shuttle. Road crossings detract from the wilderness experience and are avoided whenever possible. There are a few exceptions—a handful of trips are out-and-back or point-to-point journeys, most notably the 100-Mile Wilderness, a one-way hike through the wild heart of Maine and the longest trip featured in this book.

So what are you waiting for? Go discover. Go explore. The wilds of New England await.

HOW TO USE THIS BOOK

THIS BOOK DIVIDES NEW ENGLAND into four geographic areas and sections—southern New England, Vermont, New Hampshire, and Maine. Maps at the beginning of each section locate trips in each area.

To prepare for your adventure, read *Trip Planning and Safety*. Those unfamiliar with the outdoor world of New England or unsure about where to go should consult the section *Where Should I Go Hiking?* For those looking for a specific feature, review the *At-a-Glance Trip Planner*. Otherwise just evaluate each adventure based on the information provided.

BACKPACKING TRIPS

Each trip is described using a standard, easily understood template. The template is divided into two parts: the Header and Hike Description.

THE HEADER

Icons. These indicate if the trip has any associated fees (including entrance fees, parking fees, and any fees for camping at established backcountry campsites or shelters), whether dogs are allowed, and whether dispersed camping is permitted outside of established campsites and shelters.

Location. The town or specific destination where the trailhead is located.

Difficulty. This book rates hikes from Easy to Epic.

Easy. Short and level, these hikes can be done by nearly anybody and have less than 500 feet of elevation gain.

Moderate. Longer hikes with 500 to 3,000 feet of total elevation gain per day along good, easy-to-follow trails. Suitable for any reasonably fit hiker.

Challenging. Difficult hikes with 1,000 to 3,000 feet of elevation gain per day on more challenging trails. Good fitness required.

Strenuous. A very strenuous hike involving considerable elevation gain and loss on challenging trails. Higher mileage can also increase the difficulty to this rating.

Epic. Extended adventures with considerable and constant elevation gain and loss, often in remote regions on challenging trails. Experienced backpackers only. Maine's 100-Mile Wilderness (Trip 34), the Great Gulf Wilderness in New Hampshire (Trip 25), and Baxter State Park (Trips 35 and 36) are the only destinations featured in this category.

Distance. The total mileage of the hike.

Total Elevation Gain/Loss. The amount of climbing and descending on the hike, measured in vertical feet. It can be significantly greater than the difference between the hike's lowest and highest points.

Trip Length. The recommended duration of the trip; ranges listed account for differing paces. Be aware of your physical capabilities and limitations when selecting a hike and setting your pace. A reasonably fit hiker can expect to cover 2 to 3 miles per hour over level ground and on gradual descents, 1 to 2 miles per hour on gradual climbs and steep descents, and only about 1 mile—or 750 to 1,000 feet of elevation—per hour on the steepest ascents.

Recommended Map(s). Some hikes can be completed using only the maps in this book, but greater safety and enjoyment comes with more detailed and comprehensive knowledge—especially on lesser-known hikes that venture into more remote areas. Acquire a good map of the area; the best are listed here, followed by publisher if applicable.

Highlights. What makes the trip special, unique, and impossible to resist.

HIKE DESCRIPTION

Following an introductory paragraph, the hike description is broken down into six sections:

HIKE OVERVIEW

A general overview of the hike, including trail highlights and route, seasonal considerations, and other key information.

OVERNIGHT OPTION(S)

A detailed description of established campsites, lean-tos, and other overnight options, including mileages and GPS coordinates, natural setting, amenities such as water sources, reservations, and crowds.

TO REACH THE TRAILHEAD

Concise driving directions to the trailhead. This book assumes you have a basic highway map of New England. Latitude and longitude are also provided. Every car's odometer is different, so please note that mileages may vary slightly between those listed here and in your vehicle.

HIKE DESCRIPTION

A detailed narrative of the hike itself. Parenthetical notations such as (3.2/1,450) are included in the text at all trail junctions and important landmarks. The first number represents the total distance traveled from the trailhead in miles; the second identifies the elevation of the location in feet. A third, if given, indicates latitude and longitude. Occasional notations of peaks such as (3,849) indicate elevation in feet.

INFORMATION

Address, phone number, and website.

NEARBY

Local points of interest, including nearby dining and interesting destinations ideal for short, convenient visits on the way home.

A NOTE ABOUT GPS COORDINATES

GPS coordinates are included for trailheads, established campsites and shelters, and occasional landmarks or water sources. They are listed in latitude/longitude format using the WGS84 datum and included in the relevant parenthetical notations. These coordinates were taken with a range of handheld devices with varying levels of accuracy; use your best judgment when navigating and always carry a trustworthy map and compass for safety.

THE MAPS IN THIS BOOK

A basic reference map is included with each trip to help you plan. Important landmarks are marked—including trailheads, designated camping areas, summits, and bodies of water—but these maps are not intended for navigation purposes. Purchase the recommended maps highlighted at the beginning of each trip, which will include more detailed topographic information and other elements crucial for a safe and enjoyable trip in the backcountry. The legend for these maps is on page iv.

WHERE SHOULD I GO HIKING?

NEW ENGLAND GEOGRAPHY

New England is a jigsaw of mountain ranges. From the low-lying terrain of Massachusetts, Connecticut, and Rhode Island, north to the mountainscapes of New Hampshire, Vermont, and Maine, the region offers an inspiring diversity of landscapes, ecosystems, and backpacking excursions.

Southern New England (Trips 1–10)

This region can be divided into roughly three sections, which become increasingly mountainous to the west.

The densely populated east section—which includes Rhode Island and the eastern third of Massachusetts and Connecticut—is dimpled by hills and small parcels of open space. Backpacking opportunities are limited, though Arcadia Management Area (Trip 1) in southwestern Rhode Island and Pachaug State Forest (Trip 2) in southeastern Connecticut protect a large swath of land. Cape Cod provides a rare seaside backpack along Sandy Neck (Trip 4); Douglas State Forest (Trip 5) offers a quiet forest retreat at the junction of Massachusetts, Connecticut, and Rhode Island

Further west in central Massachusetts and Connecticut east of the Connecticut River, the landscape begins to rumple and roll, defined by a low-lying collection of hills and small mountains. Elevations climb above 1,000 feet in many locations, capped by the prominent bulge of 2,006-foot Wachusett Mountain in north-central Massachusetts. Open space increases, though it remains a patchwork of small parklands. Nevertheless, a sense of wildness begins to grow. The population density is low in many areas. Moose live in the region, some as far south as Tunxis State Forest (Trip 3) in north-central Connecticut. In north-central Massachusetts, 22-mile Tully Trail (Trip 6) explores conservation lands through the lush forest that blankets most of the region.

The northern section of the long-distance New England National Scenic Trail (Trip 7) stretches from southern Connecticut to the New Hampshire border; some of the region's wildest and most rugged terrain can be found here.

The western portion of southern New England encompasses western Connecticut and Massachusetts, including the Berkshires and Taconic Range. The terrain starts to exceed 2,000 feet. Lush and diverse forest cloaks ridges and valleys. In Massachusetts, the Berkshires—a hilly range highlighted by several stands of old-growth forest—rise west of the Connecticut River. Monroe State Forest (Trip 9) protects one of the most remarkable old-growth forests in New England. Near the New York state line, the Berkshires drop into deep valleys bordered to the west by the Taconic Range. The Appalachian Trail (AT) weaves between the two ranges, running along a unique high-elevation plateau in northwestern Connecticut and southwestern Massachusetts (Trip 8), and later clambering over the singular massif of Mount Greylock (Trip 10)—the highest point in Massachusetts—in the state's northwestern corner.

Vermont (Trips 11–15)

The Green Mountains span the length of Vermont on a north-south axis. The entire length of the 272-mile Long Trail runs along their spine and is the state's primary hiking and backpacking artery.

Elevations in the Green Mountains generally rise above 2,000 feet, and exceed 3,000 feet in many locations. Forest veils most of the range, and hiking here is defined more by woodlands than by dramatic above-treeline views. The Green Mountain National Forest protects much of the range and is divided into two sections. The southern portion is less mountainous and less traveled than points farther north. At 3,748 feet, Glastenbury Mountain (Trip 11) crowns the southern region, protected within the Glastenbury Mountain Wilderness. The Lye Brook Wilderness (Trip 12) encompasses a high-elevation plateau dissected by streams and ponds north of Glastenbury. The northern Green Mountain National Forest is more rugged, though still densely forested. The Breadloaf Wilderness (Trip 13) epitomizes the experience.

The Greens continue north past the national forest to the Canadian border, marked by two landmark peaks: Camel's Hump and Mount Mansfield. The summits offer alpine views in all directions. Camel's Hump (Trip 14) is the highest peak with an undeveloped summit in the state. Mount Mansfield (Trip 15) is the state's tallest peak, with a long alpine ridge with wild trails.

The landscape east of the Green Mountains is lined with ridges, incised by valleys, and flush with pastoral scenery. Backpacking options, however, are essentially nonexistent.

New Hampshire (Trips 16–28)

The 700,000-acre White Mountain National Forest defines New Hampshire's backpacking scene. In the north-central portion of the state, the Whites are a rugged collection of peaks laced by hundreds of miles of trails. Forty-eight summits exceed 4,000 feet. Five designated Wilderness Areas protect vast swaths of the landscape. Hiking and backpacking opportunities are almost without limit.

A variety of smaller ranges compose the overall topography. The Sandwich Range (Trips 18 and 19) rises as the Whites' southern front, one of the area's most accessible—yet least traveled—collection of trails. To the west, the isolated massif of Mount Moosilauke (Trip 17) looms. North of the Sandwich Range is the 45,000-acre Pemigewasset Wilderness, the largest in New England. The Pemigewasset River drains its peaks, including fifteen taller than 4,000 feet, which offer some of the deepest and longest adventures in this book (Trips 20–22). The most remote summit in the Whites—Bondcliff—can be found here, more than 10 miles from the closest trailhead.

Then there is the Presidential Range (Trip 23)—capped by 6,288-foot Mount Washington, the highest mountain in New England—which boasts more than a dozen miles of alpine zone, the largest alpine area east of the Rocky Mountains.

Deep valleys score the mountain flanks. The Great Gulf (Trip 25), the wildest chasm, curves below the Northern Presidentials to a 2,000-foot headwall beneath Mount Washington. The Dry River valley drains the Southern Presidentials, a significant watershed hemmed to the east by little-traveled Montalban Ridge and the Davis Path (Trip 24). Beyond Mount Washington are the towering peaks of the Northern Presidentials: Mounts Jefferson, Adams, and Madison. Their northern flanks are dissected by streams, deep valleys, and a remarkable density of trails. King Ravine (Trip 26) is the deepest gorge, a sheer bowl gouged from the mountainside.

The Wild River Wilderness (Trip 27), the newest Wilderness Area in the White Mountains, is located east of the Presidential Range and encompasses most of the Wild River watershed. It is a self-contained world of forest, streams, and few people.

The White Mountains also include two outlying areas. The Pilot Range (Trip 28) is located north of the Presidential Range and disconnected from the rest of the national forest. A mountain range in miniature, it is capped by 4,170-foot Mount Cabot. The second is Speckled Mountain (Trip 29), just over the state line into Maine and protected within the Caribou–Speckled Mountain Wilderness.

Outside of the White Mountains, New Hampshire boasts multitudes of smaller ranges and summits, but limited backpacking opportunities. The diminutive Wapack Range (Trip 16) is an exception, straddling the state's southern border with Massachusetts.

Maine (Trips 29–37)

Maine is larger than the five other New England states combined. A mountainous backbone runs northeast from the White Mountains in New Hampshire to the north-central portion of the state. The Appalachian Trail (AT) travels the length of it—more than 280 miles—passing over a collection of peaks and small ranges en route to its terminus atop Katahdin in Baxter State Park.

From New Hampshire's White Mountain National Forest, the AT travels across the Mahoosuc Range—arguably the most rugged ridgeline in New England. In the middle of it is Mahoosuc Notch (Trip 30), a boulder-strewn cleft rightly dubbed the Hardest Mile on the AT. Nearby, the 39-mile Grafton Loop Trail (Trip 31) loops around the steep and dramatic topography on either side of Grafton Notch. A hundred miles later, the AT travels across the Bigelow Range (Trip 32), a prominent east-west mountain ridge capped with exceptional views.

Near its end, the AT enters the 100-Mile Wilderness (Trip 34), the most remote section of the entire trail. The route does not cross a paved road for its entire length as it visits open ridgelines, massive lakes, and rushing rivers on a grand tour of the Maine backcountry.

Baxter State Park borders the 100-Mile Wilderness to the northeast. Its centerpiece is 5,268-foot Katahdin. New England's only true arête, the Knife Edge, crowns a headwall rising more than 2,000 feet above placid Chimney Pond (Trip 35). Crowds tend to congregate around Katahdin, but the vast landscape of lakes and hills to its north, centered on Russell Pond (Trip 36), receives much less use.

Most backpacking opportunities in Maine center on the AT, rather than along its sinuous coastline, though there are two exceptions. The low-lying Camden Hills (Trip 33) bulge above Penobscot Bay, a few miles from the ocean. And at the farthest end of the Maine coast, the soggy Cutler Coast Public Reserved Land (Trip 37) protects a rare example of maritime forest.

BEATING THE CROWDS

Hikers in New England are attracted to views like moths to a flame—areas above treeline are usually heavily traveled. These areas are popular for a reason—the scenery is exceptional—and shouldn't be skipped just to evade crowds. Avoid weekends and visit these places midweek to enjoy them with a modicum of solitude, or plan a trip after mid-September, when hiking traffic markedly diminishes.

Many hikes in this book also travel along portions of the Appalachian Trail. A pulse of thru-hikers moves north as the summer progresses, filling trailside shelters and campsites. In Massachusetts and Vermont, June and July are peak travel times. In New Hampshire, July and August. In Maine, August, September, and early October.

In the White Mountains, a disproportionate number of hikers head to the Pemigewasset Wilderness and Presidential Range. Areas outside of these regions receive much less visitation, particularly the Sandwich Range (Trips 18 and 19), Pilot Range (Trip 28), and Speckled Mountain (Trip 29). In the Presidential Range, Montalban Ridge (Trip 24) provides the best opportunities for solitude.

A SEASON-BY-SEASON PLAYBOOK

This is a three-season guide, designed to cover the period from spring through fall (April–October). The trips can be completed in the winter months as well, but this guide does not describe how snow and ice conditions may affect trails or camping areas. Be prepared and know what you're doing if you head out between November and March!

April. It's springtime in southern New England. The snow is gone in southern areas. Trees are bare and leafless, but plants in the understory begin to emerge by the middle of the month. The season's first wildflowers bloom in Arcadia Management Area in Rhode Island (Trip 1) and adjacent Pachaug State Forest in Connecticut (Trip 2). The beaches of Sandy Neck (Trip 4) warm up for the first time, but don't have summer crowds. The weather remains fickle and highly variable. Expect anything from freezing temperatures to comfortable sunny days that can reach into the 60s and even 70s, depending on location.

May. Spring creeps northward and upward. Wildflowers are at their peak. Painted trillium and hobblebushes flower prolifically in northern New England forests, peaking around Memorial Day. In southern New England, trees have fully leafed. It is an ideal time for midelevation hikes such as the Wapack Trail (Trip 16), the Tully Trail (Trip 6), the Tunxis Trail (Trip 3), Monroe State Forest (Trip 9), the Taconics (Trip 8), and Camden Hills (Trip 33). In northern New England, April and May are also known as Mud Season: the ground is soggy underfoot and trails are easily damaged—some locations close their trails entirely during this period. This is also the time of year when blackflies swarm. Depending on the season, snow may linger at higher elevations well into May. Wait until the end of the month before heading north. Crowds are minimal until Memorial Day weekend, at which point they pick up markedly.

June. By the middle of the month, the last trees in northern New England leaf, and summer arrives across the region. School is in until around the middle of the month, which keeps the traffic factor low. It's hard to go wrong when selecting a destination, though blackflies and mosquitoes can be fierce, especially in wet and low-lying areas.

July–August. July and August are perhaps the two most similar months of the hiking season. Temperatures and humidity are at their peak, with many sweltering days. Summer crowds are at their maximum, and thousands of people visit the backcountry. It is the time of year for swimming holes and lesser-traveled destinations. Soak your sweaty self in the Wild River Wilderness (Trip 27). Beat the crowds by visiting the Sandwich Range Wilderness (Trips 18 and 19), Speckled Mountain (Trip 29), or Vermont's southern Green Mountains (Trips 11–13). This is also a good time of year to tour the alpine zones of the Presidential Range (Trips 23–25), when you're more likely to enjoy hospitable weather.

September. In September, fall foliage erupts in northern New England and marches south over the next four to six weeks. Colors first appear early in the month. High-elevation paper birch leaves are the first to change color, followed by the northernmost regions of New England. By late September, the Kilkenny (Trip 28), Mahoosucs (Trips 30 and 31), and Baxter State Park (Trips 35 and 36) peak in a radiance of color, followed in short order by Mount Mansfield (Trip 15), Camel's Hump (Trip 14), and the Bigelow Range (Trip 32). Expect warm crisp days and cool nights that dip below freezing later in the month.

October. Fall completes its sweep across southern New England. Peak foliage occurs in early October at most locations and then rapidly moves south. For the best leaf peeping, head for the White and Green mountains during the first and second weeks of the month. Lye Brook Wilderness (Trip 12) and the Pemigewasset Wilderness (Trips 20–22) are particularly nice. Color lingers at lower elevations and farther south through the third week of October, but by month's end, the leaves are down across the region. Expect cool days and cold nights. The season's first snowfall usually dusts the higher elevations by the end of the month. Hiking season winds down, the days get short, and soon it's winter.

TRIP PLANNING AND SAFETY

SAFETY

Venturing into the outdoors entails a degree of risk. Preparation, fitness, and knowledge help mitigate this risk.

WILDLIFE HAZARDS

Moose. As a general rule, New England's largest land animal poses little threat on the trail, and you should consider yourself fortunate if you see one in the backcountry. They avoid people for the most part, and in most close encounters, your best view will be of the animal fleeing the scene. But they are not harmless. Bull moose can act aggressively during the fall mating season, and a female moose will defend her young if she feels they are threatened.

An agitated moose may present the following warning signs: Its ears lay back, the hair on its back stands on end, it kicks or stomps the ground, walks directly at you, makes threatening noises, or licks its lips. Give the moose a wide berth—at least 100 feet—and do not try to scare it off. If it does charge, *run*. Do not stand your ground. Moose are interested primarily in scaring you off. Once it perceives that you are no longer a threat, it will leave you alone.

Black Bears. Black bears are common in New England, but the odds of seeing one in the backcountry are remote. (The author did not see a single bear while researching this book.) Wildlife biologists estimate that 30,000 bears live in New England, with roughly 21,000 in Maine, though New Hampshire and Vermont also have healthy populations—New Hampshire's White Mountain National Forest is thought to have one bear for every 1.1 square mile.

Black bears feed mostly on nuts, berries, dead animals, and other plants, and rarely kill anything themselves. They almost never attack humans and usually flee at the first sight of an approaching hiker. If a bear does confront you, *do not* run. Make yourself look as large as possible and slowly back away. A loud noise—a whistle, banging pots, or shouting—can help scare off the animal. Always avoid a mother with her cubs. At night, place your food in a bag or stuff sack and hang it from a tree branch at least 8 feet off the ground (or place it in a bear box if available). Never keep food in the tent with you.

Ticks. These parasites love brushy areas and are common throughout southern and coastal New England until the season's first hard freeze. Always perform regular body checks when hiking through tick country. If you find a tick attached to you, *do not* try to pull it out with your fingers or pinch the body; you will likely leave the mouthparts embedded under your skin, which increases the risk of infection. Using fine-point tweezers or another appropriate tool, gently pull the tick out by lifting upward from the base of the body where it is attached to the skin. Pull straight out until the tick releases and do not twist or jerk, as this may break the mouth parts off under your skin. A range of lightweight and effective tick removal devices are available.

Ticks are known for transmitting Lyme disease, but only one tick species found in New England is capable of transmitting it—the diminutive deer tick. The deer tick has a two-year life cycle and ranges in size from a pinhead to a poppy seed, depending on its age. It is typically dark-colored, though adult females appear red. An infected tick must be attached for a minimum of six hours to transmit the disease. Caused by a spirochete bacteria, Lyme disease can be life threatening if not diagnosed in its early stages. Common early symptoms include fatigue, chills and fever, headache, muscle and joint pain, swollen lymph nodes, and a blotchy skin rash that clears centrally to produce a characteristic ring shape 3 to 30 days after exposure. If you fear that you have been exposed to Lyme disease, consult a doctor immediately. Note that most people infected with Lyme disease never see the tick that bit them.

Giardia. *Giardia lamblia* is a microscopic organism occasionally found in backcountry water sources. Existing in a dormant cyst while in the water, it develops in the gastrointestinal tract upon being consumed and can cause diarrhea, excessive flatulence, foul-smelling excrement, nausea, fatigue, and abdominal cramps. Although the risk of contraction is slight, the potential consequences are worth preventing. All water taken from the backcountry should be purified with a filter, with a chemical treatment, or by boiling for a minimum of 60 seconds. Be especially vigilant about water sources near shelters, camping areas, and other heavily used locations.

Raccoons, Skunks, Porcupines, Mice, and Foxes. Although not a threat to humans, these mostly nocturnal varmints are a major hazard for food supplies and have learned that lean-tos and campsites are prime locations for free meals. Never leave food unattended, and always store it somewhere safe at night. Food lockers are occasionally provided at established camping areas; otherwise hang food from a nearby tree or on a mouse-proof line. (These common shelter accessories usually feature a small can or other obstacle that prevents mice from shimmying down the line.) Do not bring food inside your tent with you.

Blackflies, No-see-ums, and Mosquitoes. These biting insects aren't dangerous, but they certainly can be aggravating. The wet landscape of New England provides ideal breeding grounds, and bugs flourish in the millions, especially during May and June. Avoid low-lying and wet areas during this period, if possible. Use an insect repellent as needed. DEET and picaridin are the most effective repellents; concentrations of 20 to 30 percent provide four to six hours of coverage. Consider carrying a head net if the bugs are severe or your tolerance is low.

PLANT HAZARDS

Poison Ivy. Poison ivy grows throughout southern New England and is abundant anywhere with adequate sunshine, such as meadows, field margins, open trail corridors, and abandoned pastureland. A low-lying shrub or climbing vine, its glossy leaves grow in clusters of three and turn bright red in the fall, before dropping off in winter. Other key identification marks are its terminal leaf, which always has a stem, and its hairy vines, which climb trees and other structures. Both the leaves and branches contain urushiol oil, which causes a strong allergic reaction in most people and creates a maddening and long-lasting itchy rash. Wash thoroughly with soap after any exposure, and clean clothing that may have come into contact with the plant. Residual oil on pets and clothing can cause a rash as well.

Danger Berries. Berries are abundant in New England, and many of them—blackberries, blueberries, cranberries, raspberries, and huckleberries—provide delightful trailside snacks. But many other berry species are poisonous and potentially dangerous. Be 100 percent sure before you start snacking.

PHYSICAL DANGERS

Hypothermia. This occurs when your core body temperature begins to drop. Typically caused by exposure to the elements, hypothermia is a life-threatening condition whose initial symptoms include weakness, mental confusion, slurred speech, and uncontrollable shivering. Cold, wet, and windy weather—conditions commonly encountered above treeline in New England—pose the greatest hazard. Fatigue reduces your body's ability to produce its own heat, wet clothes conduct heat away from the body roughly twenty times faster than dry layers, and wind poses an increased risk because it quickly strips away warmth.

Immediate treatment is critical and entails raising the body's core temperature as quickly as possible. Get out of the wind, take off wet clothes, drink warm beverages, eat simple energy foods, and take shelter in a warm tent or sleeping bag. *Do not* drink alcohol because this dilates the blood vessels and causes increased heat loss.

Heat Stroke. The opposite of hypothermia, this occurs when the body is unable to control its internal temperature and overheats. Usually brought on by excessive exposure to the sun and accompanying dehydration, symptoms include cramping, headache, and mental confusion. Treatment entails rapid, aggressive cooling of the body through whatever means available—cooling the head and torso is most important. Stay hydrated and wear some type of sun protection on your head if you expect to travel along a hot, exposed section of trail.

Sunburn. The New England sun can fry you quickly, even if the sky is overcast with light fog or clouds. Always wear a broad-spectrum sunscreen to block out both UVA and UVB rays and consider wearing a hat or visor to shield your face from the sun. The SPF rating refers only to protection from UVB (which causes sunburn), not UVA (which causes long-term damage, including premature wrinkles and premature aging of the skin). Read the label closely to ensure you are fully covered from both types of UV.

Rivers. Be careful crossing rivers and streams, and be selective when choosing a spot to ford. Look for broad, slower-moving shallow sections, and remember that any current reaching above your thighs will wash you off your feet. When crossing, undo your backpack's waist belt so that your pack won't drag you under in the event of a fall. Trekking poles or a walking stick are invaluable aids for river crossings.

HIKING SAFETY

HikeSafe is a joint effort between the White Mountain National Forest and New Hampshire Fish & Game to educate hikers on the inherent risks of hiking and how they can become better prepared before beginning any hike. Their Hiker Responsibility Code may have been developed in New Hampshire, but it is wise to follow its tenets on any hike.

THE HIKER RESPONSIBILITY CODE

You are responsible for yourself, so be prepared:

1. **With knowledge and gear.** Become self reliant by learning about the terrain, conditions, local weather, and your equipment before you start.
2. **To leave your plans.** Tell someone where you are going, the trails you are hiking, when you will return, and your emergency plans.
3. **To stay together.** When you start as a group, hike as a group, end as a group. Pace your hike to the slowest person.
4. **To turn back.** Weather changes quickly in the mountains. Fatigue and unexpected conditions can also affect your hike. Know your limitations and when to postpone your hike. The mountains will be there another day.
5. **For emergencies.** Even if you are headed out for just an hour, an injury, severe weather, or a wrong turn could become life threatening. Don't assume you will be rescued; know how to rescue yourself.
6. **To share the hiker code with others.**

GEAR

Always have the following essentials with you:

- **Water.** Carry at least one liter of water (preferably two), drink frequently, and have some means of purifying backcountry sources (chemical treatment or filter).
- **Fire and Light.** Bring waterproof matches, Vaseline-coated cotton balls, or other easy-to-ignite kindling for starting an emergency fire, and a headlamp or flashlight in case you are still hiking at night.
- **Survival Gear.** Pack heavy-duty garbage bags to use for emergency rain protection, shelter, and warmth, and a whistle to signal for help.
- **First Aid Kit.** At a minimum this should include an over-the-counter painkiller/swelling reducer such as ibuprofen; a 2- to 4-inch wide elastic (ACE) bandage for wrapping sprained joints; and the basics for treating a

bleeding wound: antibiotic ointment, sterile gauze, small bandages, medical tape, and large Band-Aids.

- **Map and Compass.** These will help you find your way home. Even the simplest compass is useful. ·
- **Knife.** A good knife or all-in-one tool can be invaluable in the event of a disaster.
- **Extra Clothes and Food.** Warm clothing can be critical in the event of an unexpected night out or a developing fog. A few extra energy bars can make a huge difference in morale and energy level if you are out longer than expected.
- **Sun Protection.** Carry sunscreen and sunglasses for protection from the blazing sun.

FOR YOUR FEET

Your feet are your most important piece of gear. Keep them happy, and you will be even more so. Appreciate them. Care for them.

Footwear. The appropriate hiking footwear stabilizes and supports your feet and ankles while protecting them from the abuses of the environment. Most trails in New England are rough, rocky, and root-crossed. A pair of lightweight boots or trail-running shoes may be adequate for hikers with strong ankles, but most people will want to opt for stiffer midweight hiking boots.

When selecting footwear, keep in mind that *the most important feature is a good fit*—your toes should not hit the front while going downhill, your heel should be locked in place inside the boot to prevent blister-causing friction, and there should be minimal extra space around your foot (although you should be able to wiggle your toes freely). When lacing, leave the laces over the top of your foot (instep) loose, but tie them tightly across the ankle to lock the heel down. Stability over uneven ground is enhanced by a stiffer sole and higher ankle collar.

All-leather boots last longer, have a good deal of natural water resistance, and will mold to your feet over time. Footwear made from synthetic materials or a combination of fabric and leather are lighter and cheaper, but less durable. Many boots include Gore-Tex, a waterproof-breathable layer, recommended for the wet conditions found on many New England trails. Be sure to break in new boots before taking them on an extended hike.

Socks. After armpits, feet are the sweatiest part of the human body. Unfortunately, wet feet are much more prone to blisters. Good hiking socks wick moisture away from your skin and provide padding for your feet. Avoid cotton socks, as these become quickly saturated, stay wet inside your shoes, and take a long time to dry.

Most outdoor socks are a confusing mix of natural and synthetic fibers. Wool provides warmth and padding and, although it does absorb roughly 30 percent of its weight in water, is effective at keeping your feet dry. If regular wool makes your feet itch, try softer merino wool. Nylon, polyester, acrylic, and polypropylene (also called olefin) are synthetic fibers that absorb very little water, dry quickly, and add durability. Liner socks are a thin pair of socks worn underneath the principal sock and are designed to wick moisture away more effectively than thicker socks—good for really sweaty feet.

Blister Kit. Blisters are almost always caused by friction from foot movement (slippage) inside the shoe. Prevent them by buying properly fitting footwear, taking a minimum of one to two weeks to break them in, and wearing appropriate socks. If the heel is slipping and blistering is occurring, try tightening the laces across the ankle to keep the heel in place. If you notice a blister or hotspot developing, stop immediately and apply adhesive padding (such as moleskin) over the problem spot. Bring a lightweight pair of scissors to cut the moleskin.

OUTDOOR CLOTHING

The Fabrics. Cotton should be generally avoided for outdoor activities. It absorbs water quickly and takes a long time to dry, leaving a cold, wet layer next to your skin and increasing the risk of hypothermia. Jeans are the worst. Polyester and nylon are two commonly used, and recommended, fibers in outdoor clothing. They dry almost instantly, wick moisture effectively, and are lighter weight than natural fibers. Fleece clothing (made from polyester) provides good insulation and will keep you warm, even when wet. Synthetic materials melt quickly, however, if placed in contact with a heat source (camp stove, fire, sparks, etc.). Wool is a good natural fiber for hiking. Even though it retains up to 30 percent of its weight in water, it still insulates when wet.

Raingear/Windgear. Three types are available: water-resistant, waterproof/breathable, and waterproof/nonbreathable. Water-resistant shells are typically (very) lightweight nylon windbreakers with a water repellent coating that wears away with use. The seams will not be taped. They will often keep you dry for a short period but will quickly soak through in a heavy rain. Waterproof/breathable shells contain Gore-Tex or an equivalent layer or coating and effectively keep liquid water out while allowing water vapor (i.e., your sweat) to pass through. They breathe reasonably well until the outer fabric becomes saturated, at which point the breathability is lost and you will still get sticky and wet on the inside. Waterproof/nonbreathable shells are typically coated nylon or rubber and keep water out but hold all your sweat in. Seams must be taped for them to be completely waterproof. Although wearing these on a strenuous hike causes a hot and sticky experience, they are cheap and often very lightweight. All three options effectively block the wind.

Keeping Your Head and Neck Warm. Your body will strive to keep your torso, neck, and head a constant temperature at all times. Without any insulation, the heat coursing through your neck to your brain radiates into the air and is lost. Warmth that might have been directed to your extremities instead replaces the heat lost from your head. A thin balaclava or warm hat and neck gaiter are small items, weigh almost nothing, and are more effective at keeping you warm than an extra sweater.

Keeping Your Hands Warm. Hiking in cold and damp conditions will often chill your hands unpleasantly. A lightweight pair of synthetic liner gloves will do wonders.

BACKPACKING EQUIPMENT

Backpack. For overnight trips, a pack with 40 and 50 liters (roughly 2,500 to 3,000 cubic inches) capacity is generally necessary, though dedicated ultralight hikers with the most compact and lightweight gear can get away with less. For longer trips, a pack with 60 liters (approximately 3,700 cubic inches) or more is recommended.

Just like footwear, the most important feature of a pack is a good fit. A properly fitting backpack allows you to carry most of the weight on your hips and lower body, sparing the easily fatigued muscles of the shoulders and back. When trying on packs, loosen the shoulder straps, position the waist belt so that the top of your hips (the bony iliac crest) is in the middle of the belt, attach and cinch the waist belt, and then tighten the shoulder straps. The waist belt should fit snugly around your hips, with no gaps. The shoulder straps should rise slightly off your body before dipping back down to attach to the pack about an inch below your shoulders—no weight should be resting on the top of your shoulders, and you should be able to shrug them freely. Most packs will have load stabilizer straps that attach to the pack behind your ears and lift the shoulder straps upward, off your shoulders. A sternum strap links the two shoulder straps together across your chest and prevents them from slipping away from your body.

Keep your pack's center of gravity as close to your middle and lower back as possible. Heavy items should go against the back, becoming progressively lighter as you pack outward and upward. Do not place heavy items at or below the level of the hip belt—this precludes the ability to carry that weight on the lower body.

Sleeping Bag. Nighttime temperatures in New England vary dramatically depending on weather and seasons. In July and August, it is not uncommon to have overnight temperatures in the 50s or even 60s. In May, early June, mid- to late-September, and October, freezing temperatures can occur at any time, especially at higher elevations. A sleeping bag rated to 20 degrees is recommended for all-purpose use, though a model rated to 0 degrees is often a better option in the colder seasons or for people who are always cold at night. During the sweltering height of summer, a lightweight bag rated to 35 degrees or higher is often adequate and helps reduce pack weight.

Down sleeping bags offer the best warmth-to-weight ratio, are incredibly compressible, and will easily last 5 to 10 years without losing much of their warmth. However, untreated down loses all of its insulating ability when wet and takes forever to dry—a concern during long rainy spells. Some sleeping bags now offer water-resistant down, which helps reduce this risk considerably. Synthetic-fill sleeping bags retain their insulating abilities even when wet and are cheaper, but weigh more and are bulkier. Keep in mind that synthetic-fill bags lose some of their loft and warmth after a few seasons of use.

Sleeping Pad. Sleeping pads offer vital comfort and insulation from the cold ground. Inflatable, foam-filled pads are the most compact and comfortable to sleep on, but expensive and mildly time-consuming to inflate and deflate. Basic foam pads are lightweight, cheap, and virtually indestructible. For three-season hiking, virtually all versions provide adequate insulation from the ground. Comfort makes the call.

Tent/Shelter. Though you can get by without one during spells of good weather or by staying at shelters, a lightweight, three-season tent is usually recommended. These days, a two-person backpacking tent typically weighs between 3.5 and 5 pounds. As a general rule, the lighter they are, the less spacious they are.

A rainfly that extends to the ground on all sides is critically important for staying dry. Leaks are typically caused by water seeping through unsealed seams or contact between a wet rainfly and the tent body. Seal any untaped seams that are directly exposed to the rain or to water running off the fly, paying close attention to the floor corners of the tent body. Pitch the tent as tautly as possible to prevent a wet and saggy rainfly from touching the tent body.

Stability in wind is enhanced by pole intersections—the more poles and the more times they cross, the stronger the tent will be in blustery conditions. Placing a tarp between the tent floor and the ground will protect the floor from ground moisture, wear and tear, and will increase the lifespan of your tent. Most tents these days have an optional footprint with dimensions that exactly match the floor—a nice accessory.

Ultralight floorless shelters are a weight-saving option and often use trekking poles for support. They can save a pound or more of weight, but come with some sacrifices, including decreased bug resistance and the need to pitch them in an appropriate site that will not allow rainwater to run underneath.

Cooking Equipment. A stove is necessary if you want hot food on the trail. Three types are available. Canister stoves run on a pressurized butane/propane blend. Simply attach the stove burner to the fuel canister, turn the knob, and light. Such stoves are simple, safe, cheap, and have an adjustable flame. Their safety and simmer-ability make them a good choice for summer backpacking. However, the canisters can be hard to purchase outside of outdoor equipment stores, are more expensive, hard to recycle, do not work below freezing, and heat very slowly when less than a quarter full. Alcohol stoves are compact, extremely lightweight, and a popular choice for long-distance hikers. The fuel is readily available, but burns much less hot than butane/propane blends or white gas and takes much longer to boil water. Liquid fuel stoves run on white gas contained in a self-pressurized tank or bottle. White gas is inexpensive, burns hot, is widely available around the world, and works in extremely cold conditions. However, you must work directly with liquid fuel to prime the stove, adding an element of danger. Liquid fuel stoves are also more expensive and produce flames that are prone to flaring up and may not be adjustable. Liquid fuel stoves are a good choice for those interested in winter camping or international travel.

A simple 2- to 3-quart pot is all that is usually needed for backcountry cooking. A black, or blackened, pot will absorb heat more quickly and increase fuel efficiency. A windscreen for the stove is invaluable in breezy conditions. The only dish needed is a plate with upturned edges, which can double as a broad bowl—a Frisbee works particularly well. Don't forget the silverware! Lastly, bring an insulated mug to enjoy hot drinks.

Other Good Stuff. Nylon cord is useful for hanging food, stringing clotheslines, and guying out tents. A simple repair kit should include needle, thread, and duct tape. A plastic trowel is nice for digging catholes. Insect repellent keeps bugs away. Sandals or running shoes are a great relief from hiking boots after reaching camp. A pen and waterproof notebook allow you to record outdoor epiphanies on the spot. Extra sealable plastic bags or garbage bags always come in handy. Compression stuff sacks will reduce the bulk of your sleeping bag and clothes by about a third.

LEAVE NO TRACE

THE APPALACHIAN MOUNTAIN CLUB (AMC) is a national educational partner of Leave No Trace, a nonprofit organization dedicated to promoting and inspiring responsible outdoor recreation through education, research, and partnerships. The Leave  No Trace program seeks to develop wildland ethics—ways in which people think and act in the outdoors to minimize their impact on the areas they visit and to protect our natural resources for future enjoyment. Leave No Trace unites four federal land management agencies—U.S. Forest Service, National Park Service, Bureau of Land Management, and U.S. Fish and Wildlife Service—with manufacturers, outdoor retailers, user groups, educators, organizations such as AMC, and individuals.

The Leave No Trace ethic is guided by these seven principles:

1. **Plan Ahead and Prepare.** Know the terrain and any regulations applicable to the area you're planning to visit, and be prepared for extreme weather or other emergencies. This will enhance your enjoyment and ensure that you've chosen an appropriate destination. Small groups have less impact on resources and on the experiences of other backcountry visitors.
2. **Travel and Camp on Durable Surfaces.** Travel and camp on established trails and campsites, rock, gravel, dry grasses, or snow. Good campsites are found, not made. Camp at least 200 feet from lakes and streams, and focus activities on areas where vegetation is absent. In pristine areas, disperse use to prevent the creation of campsites and trails.
3. **Dispose of Waste Properly.** Pack it in, pack it out. Inspect your camp for trash or food scraps. Deposit solid human waste in catholes dug 6 to 8 inches deep, at least 200 feet from water, camps, and trails. Pack out toilet

paper and hygiene products. To wash yourself or your dishes, carry water 200 feet from streams or lakes and use small amounts of biodegradable soap. Scatter strained dishwater.

4. **Leave What You Find.** Cultural or historical artifacts, as well as natural objects such as plants and rocks, should be left as found.

5. **Minimize Campfire Impacts.** Cook on a stove. Use established fire rings, fire pans, or mound fires. If you build a campfire, keep it small and use dead sticks found on the ground.

6. **Respect Wildlife.** Observe wildlife from a distance. Feeding animals alters their natural behavior. Protect wildlife from your food by storing rations and trash securely.

7. **Be Considerate of Other Visitors.** Be courteous, respect the quality of other visitors' backcountry experience, and let nature's sounds prevail.

AMC is a national provider of the Leave No Trace Master Educator course. AMC offers this five-day course, designed especially for outdoor professionals and land managers, as well as the shorter two-day Leave No Trace Trainer course at locations throughout the Northeast. For Leave No Trace information and materials, contact the Leave No Trace Center for Outdoor Ethics, P.O. Box 997, Boulder, CO 80306; 800-332-4100 or 302-442-8222; lnt.org. For a schedule of AMC Leave No Trace courses, see outdoors.org/education/lnt.

1

SOUTHERN
NEW ENGLAND:
MASSACHUSETTS,
CONNECTICUT, AND
RHODE ISLAND

TRIP 1
ARCADIA MANAGEMENT AREA

Location: Exeter, RI
Difficulty: Easy
Distance: 0.6 mile round-trip
Total Elevation Gain/Loss: 50 feet/50 feet
Trip Length: 1–2 days
Recommended Map: *Hiking Trails, Footpaths, and Roads in Arcadia WMA* (Great Swamp Press)
Highlights: A quiet backcountry base camp in Rhode Island's largest protected landscape.

In the southwestern corner of Rhode Island lies a vast rolling landscape of streams, forests, ponds, open fields, wildflowers—and few people. The only backpacking option in Rhode Island, Arcadia Management Area encompasses more than 14,000 acres, beckons with more than 30 miles of trail, and provides an ideal early-season destination for those chomping at the spring bit.

HIKE OVERVIEW

To call this hike a backpacking trip is a bit of a stretch—the designated camping area is only 0.25 mile from the trailhead—but the site feels surprisingly remote and provides an ideal base camp for exploring the network of trails that lace the park. The short hike strolls through lush and diverse forest along one of the state's most pristine waterways. Note that the park requires hikers to wear hunter's orange for safety during the fall hunting season (roughly September–December).

The hike visits the Falls River, a tributary of the trout-filled Wood River, one of the state's best examples of a scenic and wild river. Animal life is healthy in the surrounding woods. Foxes and mink hunt cottontails. White-tailed deer and gray squirrels skitter through the trees. Birdlife includes ruffed grouse, wild turkey, ring-necked pheasant, and bobwhite. Fish, including trout, bass, and pickerel, fill several warm-water ponds scattered throughout the property.

OVERNIGHT OPTION

Stepstone Falls Backpack Area (0.3/260/41° 36.511′ N, 71° 45.581′ W) perches on forested slopes just above murmuring Falls River in the northwestern cor-

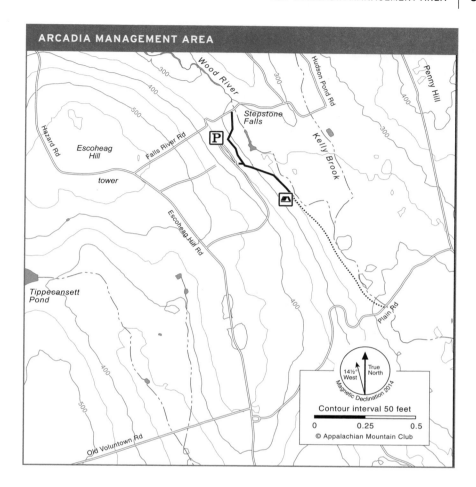

ner of the park. The broad area features a large open-air shelter, plus a clearing beneath red maples and white pines suitable for numerous tents. Reservations are required and can be made by calling 401-539-2356; pick up your permit at the park office before heading out. The site is free and open year-round. Campers are limited to a three-day stay, with a minimum seven-day break between visits. Water is available from Falls River.

TO REACH THE TRAILHEAD

Take Exit 5A from I-95 and take RI 102 south. Go 0.1 mile and continue straight to follow RI 3 south for 1.2 miles to RI 165. Turn right (west) and drive 5.3 miles to Escoheag Hill Road, located 2.0 miles past the main park entrance, and turn right. Proceed 2.4 miles along the twisty road, and turn right onto unpaved

The banks of the Falls River are hospitable to moisture-loving plants such as this skunk cabbage.

Falls River Road. In 0.6 mile, look for the small parking area (41° 36.745′ N, 71° 45.632′ W) by the creek, signed for the Tippecansett and Ben Utter trails.

HIKE DESCRIPTION

Near the parking area, sugar and red maples, white pines, hickories, and the triangular leaves of gray birches overshadow tumbling Falls River, which quickly drops over 3-foot high Stepstone Falls.

From the trailhead (0.0/290), yellow and blue blazes mark double-track Ben Utter Trail. Smooth-barked beech trees line the trail, which passes a path on the left that leads down to an open, rocky area by the creek. Continue straight, following yellow and blue blazes across a rivulet and away from the stream.

Spot hazels and false Solomon's seal in the understory, and beeches and some large red oaks rise overhead. The path rises gently along the slope to the Stepstone Falls Backpacking Area by a large fire pit and small trickling brook (0.3/260). Ben Utter Trail continues for another mile, passing through a lush and diverse forest along murmuring Falls River.

INFORMATION

Division of Forest Environment, Arcadia Headquarters, 260 Arcadia Road, Hope Valley, RI 02823, 401-539-2356, riparks.com/Locations/LocationArcadia.html.

NEARBY

Several excellent eateries can be found along the stretch of RI 3 between RI 165 and RI 102.

TRIP 2
PACHAUG STATE FOREST

Location: Voluntown, CT
Difficulty: Easy
Distance: 0.8 mile round-trip
Total Elevation Gain/Loss: 160 feet/160 feet
Trip Length: 1–2 days
Recommended Map: *Connecticut Walk Book East* (Connecticut Forest and Park Association)
Highlights: A hidden shelter, Connecticut's backpacking potential.

More than 700 miles of trail lace through Connecticut, creating a vast hiking network that encompasses the full spectrum of the state's diversity. Known as the Blue-Blazed Trails, this network consists of 15 long-distance pathways and many other shorter trails. Sprinkled among them are a handful of designated overnight backpacking areas. In southeastern Connecticut, 23,000-acre Pachaug State Forest shelters one of the nicest, and provides a tempting introduction to the state's backpacking potential.

HIKE OVERVIEW

This short out-and-back hike visits the secluded Dry Reservoir Backpack Area, tucked within a rustling beech-hickory forest, which serves as a backcountry base camp for exploring adjoining Pachaug and Nehantic trails. It makes an excellent early- or late-season excursion. At the trailhead, a short climb leads atop Mount Misery for a view of the region's iconic forested landscape.

Few settlers considered this rocky landscape to have potential for farming and agriculture; consequently the land was never extensively developed. During the Great Depression, the federal and state governments bought out many of the private landowners here as part of an economic relief effort, relocating them to more productive farming land elsewhere. The Civilian Conservation Corps then moved in, creating a network of roads, trails, and facilities. The landscape then passed on to the state as a working forest.

Today, Pachaug State Forest includes more than 50 miles of trails and roads, two campgrounds, several large ponds, and four backpacking areas.

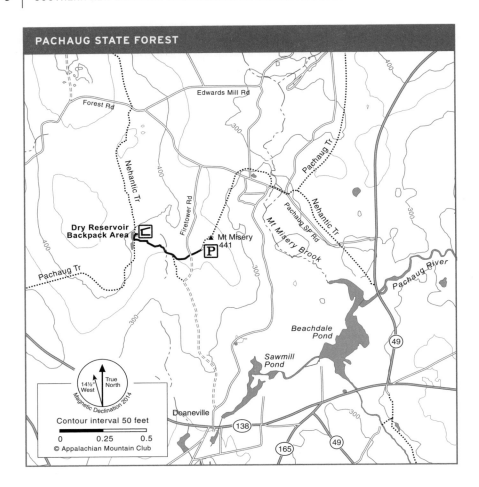

PACHAUG STATE FOREST

Contour interval 50 feet

0   0.25   0.5

© Appalachian Mountain Club

14½° West / True North

Magnetic Declination 2014

OVERNIGHT OPTION

Dry Reservoir Backpack Area (0.4/400/41° 35.432′ N, 71° 52.881′ W) features a small lean-to, a large fire ring, and numerous tenting sites beneath the surrounding beeches, hickories, and red oaks. Located a short distance from the closest trail, this quiet spot is unposted and all but invisible if you don't know where to look.

The Connecticut Department of Energy and Environmental Protection (DEEP) manages the free site. Reservations are required, can only be made through the mail or by fax (860-344-2941), and must be made at least two weeks in advance. The mailing address is DEEP—Eastern District Headquarters, Attn: Backpack Camping, 209 Hebron Road, Marlborough, CT 06447. The request needs to include the following: (1) camping area (Dry Reservoir), (2) date of planned visit, (3) trip leader's name, address, email, and phone number, and (4) number of people in the group and their ages. Overnight stays are limited to one night only. Campfires are permitted. Pets are not. For more information, or to check availability, call 860-295-9523.

TO REACH THE TRAILHEAD

From the North. Take Exit 88 from I-395 and follow CT 14A east for 3.5 miles. Turn right (south) onto CT 49, proceed 8.0 miles, and turn right at the Pachaug State Forest entrance. Follow the park road for 0.3 mile, go left at the fork, and left again 0.5 mile farther by the Mount Misery Brook picnic area. Cross over the brook and bear left at the next fork. The road becomes unpaved and passes by the entrance to Mount Misery Campground on your left. Continue straight on signed Cutoff Road for 0.3 mile, and turn left onto signed Firetower Road. Proceed 0.7 mile to the road's end at a large loop (41° 35.301′ N, 71° 52.460′ W).

From the South. Take Exit 85 from I-395 and follow CT 138 east for 6.5 miles to CT 49. Turn left (north) onto CT 49, proceed 0.6 mile to the state forest entrance, and turn left. From here, follow the directions above.

HIKE DESCRIPTION

From the trailhead (0.0/350), tag the summit of Mount Misery (41°35.339′ N, 71° 52.369′ W). Follow the blue blazes upslope from the parking area, quickly curving right over rocky outcrops to the summit. Views look east over the seemingly endless forests of southeastern Connecticut and western Rhode Island.

To head to the shelter from the trailhead (0.0/350), briefly follow the blue blazes back down the road beneath white and red oaks. Hay-scented and bracken ferns grow in the understory. The well-blazed route—here the combined Nehantic and Pachaug trails—cuts left off the road and narrows to single-track.

The trail soon reaches an open area, with stumps and other evidence of past logging activity, then drops down a slope beneath beeches and oak trees. Look for polypody ferns sprouting from a moss-covered boulder by the trail. The trail meets a T-junction with a wider path (0.1/290).

Go right, passing an obviously named shagbark hickory on the left, across the trail from the lacy needles of a hemlock. Tiny blue-white bluets dot the trail in spring as you approach a gurgling brook, where witch hazels, black birches (also known as sweet birches), and skunk cabbages appear. Cross the stream, noting the false Solomon's seal and Christmas and cinnamon ferns that grow in the lush surroundings. The diamond-patterned bark of white ash—a water-loving tree—also appears. The forest becomes somewhat older past the stream, with some nice beeches and red oaks, and you reach the posted junction where Pachaug and Nehantic trails split (0.4/370). The large embankment here was once a dam, but today holds nothing but a dry reservoir.

Go right onto Nehantic Trail, crossing a bridge over a small outlet stream emerging from beneath the old dam. Spicebushes, jack-in-the-pulpits, yellow birches, and red maples grow in the damp streambed. Approximately 50 feet past the bridge, look for faint and unposted spur trails heading off to the right, which lead a short distance to the otherwise invisible Dry Reservoir Backpack Area (0.4/400).

Retrace your steps to return to the trailhead (0.8/350)

INFORMATION

Pachaug State Forest, CT 49, P.O. Box 5, Voluntown, CT 06384, 860-376-4075, ct.gov/deep.

NEARBY

Refuel after your hike by continuing south on CT 49 and heading west on CT 138 (Beach Pond Road), where several eating establishments and pubs stand ready to refresh.

TRIP 3
TUNXIS STATE FOREST

Location: Hartland and Barkhamsted, CT
Difficulty: Moderate
Distance: 9.8 miles one-way
Total Elevation Gain/Loss: 1,650 feet/1,500 feet
Trip Length: 2 days
Recommended Map: *Connecticut Walk Book West* (Connecticut Forest and Park Association)
Highlight: Woodlands so wild even moose live here.

Sheltering the rumpled terrain and crashing streams above Barkhamsted Reservoir adjacent north-central Connecticut's border with Massachusetts, Tunxis State Forest is one of the state's least visited parcels of protected land. In its east section, a long portion of Tunxis Trail travels through a wooded landscape of solitude and quiet natural highlights.

HIKE OVERVIEW

This 9.8-mile, point-to-point route on Tunxis Trail undulates along a high plateau that rises parallel to out-of-sight Barkhamsted Reservoir below to the west. The area's abundant laurels bloom in May and June. The following north-bound description involves less overall elevation gain than a southbound trip. Dogs are allowed on the trail, but not at the designated camping area.

OVERNIGHT OPTION

There is a designated overnight camping area 2.8 miles from the trailhead (41° 57.268′ N, 72° 55.815′ W), about a quarter of the way along the trail. Situated on either side of tumbling Roaring Brook, it offers several good tentsites beneath the shade of young hemlocks and white pines. A fire pit is available and water can be taken from the stream. There is no privy. Camping is prohibited elsewhere in the forest.

While the site is free, the Connecticut Department of Energy and Environmental Protection (DEEP) requires reservations be made at least two weeks in advance. Include the following information in your request by mail (to DEEP—Western District Headquarters, Attn: Backpack Camping, 230 Plymouth Road, Harwinton, CT 06791) or fax (860-485-1638): (1) camping area

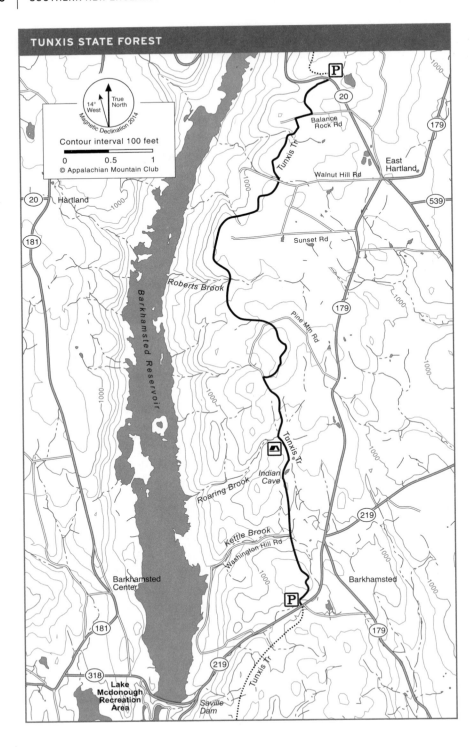

TUNXIS STATE FOREST

(Roaring Brook), (2) date of planned visit, (3) trip leader's name, address, email, and phone number, and (4) number of people in the group and their ages. Overnight stays are limited to one night only. Campfires are permitted. Pets are not. For more information, call 860-485-0226.

TO REACH THE TRAILHEADS

To Reach the Northern (Ending) Trailhead. Take CT 20 to the CT 179/20 junction in north Granby. Continue on CT 20 west for 1.4 miles to a small parking area (42° 00.964′ N, 72° 55.202′ W) on the right, signed for Tunxis Trail.

To Reach the Southern (Starting) Trailhead. Head to the CT 219/179 junction in Barkhamsted. Proceed south on CT 219 for 0.9 mile to a small dirt parking area (41° 57.268′ N, 72° 55.815′ W) on the left, signed for Tunxis Trail.

HIKE DESCRIPTION

From the southern trailhead (0.0/950), cross the busy road and over a guardrail to follow blue-blazed Tunxis Trail up into hardwood forest. Look for the pointy leaves of red oak trees and the telltale red fissures in their trunks. Also watch for the distinctive diamond-patterned trunks of white ashes, the smooth boles of beech trees, the lacy evergreen foliage of hemlocks, and a few scattered paper and yellow birches, unusual so far south. Laurels fill the understory, blooming profusely from late May through June.

Roots protrude in the initially faint trail, which quickly crosses an overgrown woods road and passes through a thicket of witch hazels. Coarsegrained boulders bulge from the ground in spots, and you soon cross a stone wall guarded by a massive white oak nearly 4 feet in diameter. Note the rounded lobes of its leaves, which distinguish the tree from the more common red oak. One side of the tree has broken off and lies crumpled on the ground. Old, spreading trees such as these are known as wolf trees, which were left uncut along stone walls by early settlers to provide shade for grazing livestock. Left in open sunlight, their branches spread outward unencumbered by surrounding vegetation.

The trail slowly rises, passing blueberry bushes as it winds past a mixture of white and red oaks. As you traverse along a rocky hilltop, chestnut oaks also appear in abundance, a less common species that can be identified by its extremely knobby bark and wavy leaf margins. The trail then bends right and drops slightly, traversing through dense patches of laurel. The route steepens and curves left in a semi-open clearing of three types of birch. Paper birch trees are known by their white bark, which peels in large sheets; yellow birches by their silvery-golden bark peeling in thin ribbons; and black birches by their dark, smooth bark, fissuring into large plates with age. From here, slowly descend, cross Kettle Brook in the shade of hemlocks and white oaks, and reach Washington Hill Road (1.1/890), lined with some large and gnarled sugar maples.

Cross the road, travel a short distance through dense white pines, and reach a woods road by a substantial creek. Turn right onto the road, walk about 100 feet, bear right at the fork in the road, and then take an immediate left to continue on the single-track trail. Blue blazes clearly indicate the route.

As you resume climbing through open oak woodland, look for a beaver pond and dam below to the right. Cross another woods road, and make a slow, curving rise to the left, winding past thick laurels to top out at a small ledge. The trail runs along solid rock outcrops and passes an overlook from Indian Council Caves with a few limited glimpses of a pond down below—there's no sign of humanity. Drop steeply past a 40-foot-high overhanging rock face, and take time to explore the extensive cracks and crevices in this giant boulder pile (2.2/1,050).

Beyond the caves, you soon reach another woods road by an inactive beaver pond. Turn left onto the road to head through an area of past settlement. Rock walls, stone enclosures, cellar holes, and large, gnarly sugar maples by the roadside all provide evidence of past human lives. The road forks by another cellar hole (2.5/1,040)—bear left to stay on the continuing route.

After passing another swampy field and former beaver habitat, the trail splits just before reaching Roaring Brook (2.8/990). Bear left to reach the designated camping area; tentsites can be found on both sides of the brook. The short loop to the camping area rejoins the main trail at a nearby outlet stream, spanned by a boardwalk-style bridge.

From the split, the main trail rock-hops the brook and curves right. After crossing the outlet stream, the trail follows a woods road—the southern end of Pine Mountain Road—through an open forest of ashes, black cherries, and increasing oaks. The path next enters a clearing, where the road widens markedly. Remain on the now-drivable road as it steadily climbs past young red oaks and paper birches. As the road crests, the route turns right onto a single-track path (3.6/1,220). The trail briefly climbs and then runs level over bedrock outcrops to emerge into a clearing—a false summit of Pine Mountain. The trail drops briefly before rising to a small clearing on the actual summit (4.2/1,391), which offers a view east-northeast toward Springfield, Massachusetts.

From the peak, descend past oaks and hemlocks. After crossing Pine Hill Road (4.6/1,250), you soon cross a smaller woods road and then almost immediately turn left onto another. The easygoing road winds slowly downward and eventually forks (5.1/1,160)—bear right onto the lesser-traveled option. After a long, steady cruise past extensive hemlocks, the trail passes some large beech trees and then drops more steeply to cross Roberts Brook, a pleasant stream murmuring over rocks and boulders (5.6/1,100).

The route parallels the stream downward, traveling a short distance above and away from the babbling watercourse. The trail then narrows to single-track and curves left before descending into a hemlock ravine and crossing a small brook. The faint trail winds along the lip of dripping stones above steepening slopes, offering a sense of the depth of Roberts Creek gorge. Extensive downed wood indicates the relative maturity of the surrounding forest.

The trail next travels along the state forest boundary, indicated by yellow paint and some occasional rusting barbed wire. For the first time, the reservoir is faintly visible through the trees more than 500 feet below. After making a slow rise, the route crosses a stone wall and undulates along a ridgeline cloaked with young beeches. The well-blazed, faint trail crosses a small creek (7.1/1,080) and enters a dense hemlock grove. A half-mile farther, a sign describes a problem common throughout southern New England: "White pines are being favored in anticipation of hemlocks succumbing to the woolly adelgid, recently discovered in the area."

The microscopic woolly adelgid is an invasive insect that feeds at the base of hemlock needles, slowly defoliating the tree and killing it over time. Common in southern New England, it is slowly marching north, though there is some debate about whether colder temperatures farther north will prevent it from establishing a foothold.

Past the sign, the trail heads left and follows a woods road that soon curves right through a mixed hardwood forest—navigate carefully as there is no double blaze indicating this turn. The trail bears left at a fork—continue to watch for blazes—then quickly crosses old Route 20, paved but in disrepair (8.0/980). The trail next follows a flat woods road, immediately passes over a brook, turns right, then bears right again at a fork. The route then almost immediately turns left away from the woods road, detouring briefly around a giant fallen hemlock. The trail returns to single-track and passes some nice red maples as it descends into the Morey's Brook drainage. Once you reach the pleasant stream (8.7/1,000), take a moment to appreciate the murmuring water as it rushes over rocks and boulders; some pleasant cascades are just upstream.

The trail turns right immediately after crossing the stream and resumes climbing, ascending some rock steps past pleasant little falls. Parallel the stream briefly, then bear left and climb to reach young, recently cut woods. After some level cruising, the trail encounters unpaved Balance Rock Road

(9.1/1,150). Follow the road right about 50 yards, then turn left in a grassy clearing—a tree blaze marks the spot. On the final stretch, the trail crosses several small brooks and winds through dense hemlock stands. After one final quick descent, you cross a stream and reach CT 20. Cross the road and turn left to reach the parking area (9.8/1,100).

INFORMATION
Tunxis State Forest, 860-379-2469, ct.gov/deep.

NEARBY
Saville Dam and its impressive spillway are located at the southern end of Barkhamsted Reservoir and provide excellent fall foliage viewing opportunities. To reach the dam from the southern trailhead, continue south on CT 219 to Saville Dam Road. Turn right onto Saville Dam Road, leave your car in a parking area on the eastern edge of the reservoir, and enjoy a relaxing and scenic stroll across the dam.

TRIP 4
SANDY NECK

Location: Barnstable, MA
Difficulty: Easy
Distance: 7.9 miles round-trip
Total Elevation Gain/Loss: 50 feet/50 feet
Trip Length: 1–2 days
Recommended Map: *Map of Sandy Neck* (Town of Barnstable)
Highlight: Dune camping.

A 6-mile-long spit of dunes lines the south shore of Cape Cod Bay, stretching along its northern margin. Beach grass and twisted pitch pines grow inland between rolling swales of sand, separated from the mainland by a large saltwater marsh.

HIKE OVERVIEW

The hike loops first along the beach, then inland past the camping area before returning along the marsh via wide Marsh Trail. (You can also return on the beach, which reduces the round-trip journey by 1.3 miles.) Trails continue all the way to the east end of Sandy Neck, located 3.0 miles past the camping area.

Try to visit in spring or fall as vehicles are allowed on the beach during the summer and dozens of RVs and truck campers stay along its entire length, significantly detracting from the wilderness experience. A number of small cottages are also speckled throughout Sandy Neck, mostly on the south side. Vehicle access to these weather-worn structures (residents only) is along Marsh Trail, which can become flooded during wet periods. Dogs are prohibited on Sandy Neck from May 15 to September 15 and in the camping area year-round.

Throughout the trip, please remain on the beach and designated paths. The dunes may be tempting to explore, but are fragile and easily damaged.

OVERNIGHT OPTION

Year-round, camping is permitted only at the designated tenting area (3.3/ 41° 44.051′ N, 70° 19.314′ W), which consists of five small sites in a grove of twisted pitch pines, just inland from the beach. Camping elsewhere on Sandy Neck is punishable by a $100 fine. A privy is available. Before heading out, you must obtain a permit for $20 from the Sandy Neck gatehouse, which is open from 8 A.M. to 7 P.M. from Memorial Day to Labor Day and 9 A.M. to

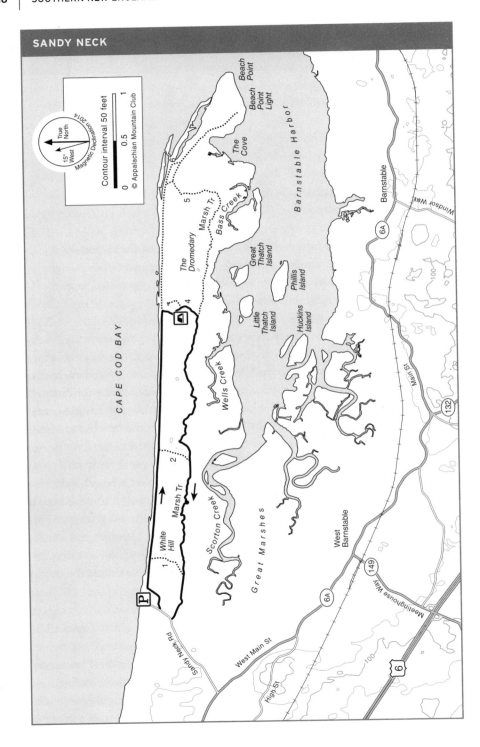

SANDY NECK

4 P.M. Labor Day to mid-October; during the off-season, call in advance (508-790-6272) to arrange a permit. Arrive as early as possible to secure a site and parking spot (fee required), especially during the height of summer. The park provides five gallons of water for each site per night; no water is otherwise available at the tenting area. Campfires are prohibited within the camping area, though open fires are permitted on the nearby beach. Park staff will even deliver wood for a small fee.

TO REACH THE TRAILHEAD

Take MA 6 to Exit 5, turn left (north) onto MA 149, and turn left on MA 6A. Follow MA 6A for 2.0 miles to Sandy Neck Road. Turn right onto Sandy Neck Road, and follow it 0.9 mile to the gatehouse; the main parking (41° 44.299′ N, 70° 22.877′ W) lot is 0.3 mile farther, by a snack stand and bath house.

HIKE DESCRIPTION

From the parking lot (0.0/20), descend to the beach, and head east. Views northwest look up the coast toward Plymouth, Marshfield, Scituate, and beyond. Footing is generally good along the sandy beach, lined with tire tracks and speckled with rounded cobbles of all colors and sizes.

Cape Cod was bulldozed into position by the massive ice sheet that smothered New England during the last Ice Age. As the glacier moved southward, it pushed massive piles of sand and stones before it. Streams and rivers poured from its face, adding to the sediment. As it receded, it left an arc of sand marking its farthest reach south—today's Cape Cod. (Nantucket, Martha's Vineyard, and Long Island were also formed in similar fashion.)

The scenery changes little down the dune-backed strand. Crowds diminish as you pass Connector Trail 1 and gain distance from the parking area, though vehicles continue intermittently along the shore. Pass posted Connector Trail 2 on the right (1.6/10), and continue along the unchanging beach, eventually reaching signed Connector Trail 4 on the right (3.2/10).

Turn inland onto Connector Trail 4, which immediately enters the dunes and encounters a mature stand of pitch pines. Easily recognized by their twisted architecture and needles in clusters of three, these gnarly trees are well adapted to survive in dry soil (or sand) environments. Small black oaks complete the unusual forest mosaic. The tenting area is just ahead (3.3/20).

Continue inland to Horse Trail on the left (3.4/30). (Horse Trail heads east to reach Marsh Trail, which then proceeds out to the (off-limits) lighthouse near the end of Sandy Neck. The round-trip excursion to the lighthouse is about 6 miles.) Bear right to remain on Connector Trail 4 as it winds through

The dunes of Sandy Neck are often walkable even on sunny, winter days like this one.

a rolling dunescape to Marsh Trail (3.6/10). Marsh Trail also heads east toward the lighthouse, but turn right to begin your return journey to the trailhead.

The wide, sandy road occasionally passes dense woods on the right, populated by white and black oak, juniper, and holly trees. The open Great Marshes on the left divide Sandy Neck from the mainland. Cottages appear intermittently on your right as you proceed. Eventually you encounter a house perched in the nearby dunes, just before the inland junction with Connector Trail 2 (5.6/10). Trees diminish past this point, and the rolling, sandy route makes walking tiresome. Pass Connector Trail 1 on the right (7.1/10). Marsh Trail transforms into a dirt road, and you can see an osprey platform in the marshes to your left. Reenter a dune oak forest and emerge adjacent to the gatehouse (7.6/30). Turn right; follow the road back to the parking area (7.9/20).

INFORMATION

Sandy Neck Beach Park, Town of Barnstable, 425 Sandy Neck Road, Barnstable, MA 02668, 508-362-8300 (gatehouse), 508-790-6272 (main office/off-season), town.barnstable.ma.us/sandyneckpark.

NEARBY

A multitude of eating establishments and shops line nearby MA 6A.

TRIP 5
DOUGLAS STATE FOREST

Location: Douglas, MA
Difficulty: Easy
Distance: 4.8 miles round-trip
Total Elevation Gain/Loss: 500 feet/500 feet
Trip Length: 1–2 days
Recommended Map: *Douglas State Forest Trail Map* (Massachusetts Department of Conservation and Recreation)
Highlights: A secluded backcountry shelter and geographic novelty.

In southeastern Massachusetts, directly adjacent to both Connecticut and Rhode Island, 4,600-acre Douglas State Forest offers pleasant and diverse woodlands, a hidden trail shelter, and a backcountry site where Massachusetts, Connecticut, and Rhode Island intersect. A portion of this loop hike travels along Midstate Trail, a 95-mile long-distance route spanning central Massachusetts. This is one of Midstate Trail's more remote and peaceful sections.

HIKE OVERVIEW

This loop begins at popular Wallum Lake, a swimming and boating destination that attracts droves of people during the hot summer months. Crowds diminish radically in the woods, where a surprising amount of solitude can be found.

Beginning on Coffeehouse Loop Trail, the hike heads to Midstate Trail and follows it south to a quiet backcountry shelter. From there, it walks the Massachusetts–Rhode Island border, encounters the stone marker that indicates the three-state junction, and then continues along the Massachusetts–Connecticut border before looping back toward the lake. Though views are absent, the landscape is an interesting mix of rocky terrain and diverse southern New England forest.

Avoid the park on summer weekends when it typically reaches capacity by midmorning. Spring, fall, and summer weekdays are much better options. Note that the area can be quite buggy; bring mosquito repellent, especially in the summer months.

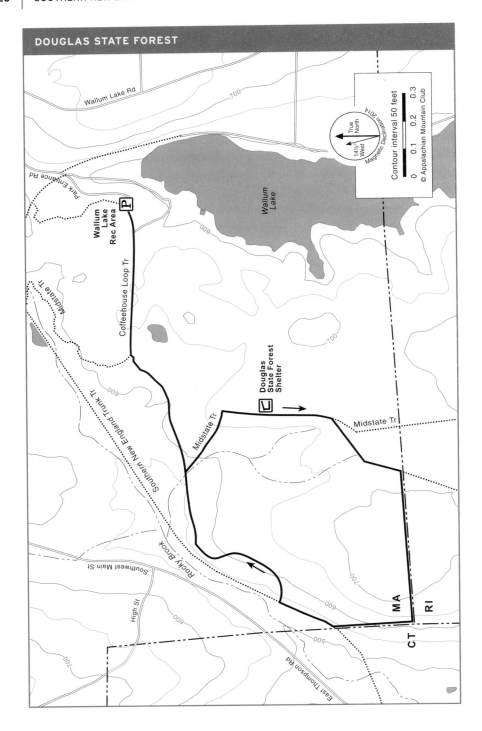

DOUGLAS STATE FOREST

OVERNIGHT OPTION

Douglas State Forest Shelter (1.5/650/42° 0.899′ N, 71° 47.008′ W) is located on the edge of a quiet clearing and shaded by a collection of tall white pines. Constructed in 1999 by SCA AmeriCorps, the solid lean-to also offers several picnic tables and a large fire pit and metal grill. An ample number of tentsites can be found in the surrounding level terrain, as well as some old building foundations and other stone structures. No water is available nearby—the closest source is a half-mile away on your hike in; bring an ample supply with you. The shelter is free to use and no reservations are required. Overnight use is generally light, due at least in part to the fact that it is completely unmarked on park maps and signs—you have to know it's there to find it.

TO REACH THE TRAILHEAD

Take I-395 to Exit 2, proceed east on MA 16 for 5.4 miles, and turn right onto Cedar Street. In 0.8 mile, at the four-way intersection with SW Main Street, continue straight on Wallum Lake Road for 0.9 mile, and turn right at the state forest entrance. Reach the entrance station in 0.7 mile. (A fee is charged from Memorial Day to Labor Day.) Bear right past the entrance station; the trailhead (42° 1.360′ N, 71° 46.235′ W) is at an unpaved park service road (signed for authorized vehicles only) near the back of the first parking area you encounter. Potable water is available down by the lake.

Note that overnight parking is *not* permitted in the main parking area or near the boat launch area. Before you visit, make arrangements with park staff to leave your vehicle overnight; you may need to park by the headquarters building on Wallum Lake Road, adding a mile walk to the trailhead.

HIKE DESCRIPTION

At the trailhead (0.0/630), note the diverse forest around you: look for the rounded lobes of white oak leaves, serrated leaves of red maples, reddish fissures in the bark of red oak trees, platy bark of older gray birches, and lacy needles of hemlocks. The shrubby undergrowth of witch hazels and huckleberries is interspersed with waving fronds of fern.

Sharp boulders are strewn about as the road curves left by a lumpy and mowed lawn area. Turn right on Coffeehouse Loop Trail, a wide, shady trail lined with evergreen azaleas. Cross Cedar Swamp Trail (0.2/620), a short interpretive loop that visits an unusual stand of Atlantic white cedars (see the brochure at the park entrance station on this unique ecosystem). Continuing straight, the trail undulates along, marked by a few blue blazes, and reaches

Midstate Trail (0.5/670), prominently signed with the route's distinctive yellow triangles.

Turn left to follow double-track Midstate Trail as it parallels an old rock wall and slowly loses elevation to reach the next junction (1.0/550). Your return route joins from the right—and the hike's best water, a short distance away—but bear left to remain on Midstate Trail.

Midstate Trail climbs briefly, passes lush collections of cinnamon and interrupted fern, and encounters an old stone foundation, where the trail turns to the right; a yellow birch and dogwood now grow from within the former structure. After passing some adjoining stone wall enclosures on the left, Midstate Trail turns left off of the old woods road, narrows slightly, and reaches the short spur trail to the shelter (1.5/650).

Beyond the shelter, Midstate Trail quickly returns to the woods road you passed earlier. Turn left, entering a wetter area, where ferns once again proliferate. After passing through chest-high shrubs, the trail forks (1.7/670). Midstate Trail continues left to its terminus at the Rhode Island border, but turn right instead.

Winding past more old foundations and cellar holes, the trail drops and passes a wet area on the left. Watch for pitch pines, identified by their platy bark, smaller cones, and needles in bunches of three. Pass the first of several stone markers indicating the location of the Massachusetts–Rhode Island border. Soon thereafter the trail forks. Straight continues into Rhode Island, but instead bear right to travel directly along the border.

The rocky double-track route passes two more border posts before dropping steeply to the tri-state marker (2.5/610), a chest-high stone obelisk etched with the year it presumably was placed here (1883). A multitude of paths converge on this point, including a series of obvious and interlacing tracks that head steeply downhill from here. Turn right to follow a narrow single-track trail that parallels the Connecticut–Massachusetts border.

Regular blue blazes help navigate this less-used path descending over rocky and root-laced terrain to Southern New England Trunkline Trail (2.8/520), an unpaved 22-mile rail-trail that extends from here to its northern terminus in downtown Franklin.

Turn right and soon reach a gate, beyond which the road narrows. Approximately 0.2 mile past the gate, an unposted (but apparent) single-track trail heads right. Follow this track as it climbs, first quickly and then more gradually, through a mixed oak forest flush with an understory of huckleberry shrubs. After running level for a while, the trail then gradually descends to another old woods road (3.6/570).

Turn right, cruising near open wetlands on your left, and cross over a small, flowing stream that burbles through a jumbled collection of sharp rocks. Soon thereafter you encounter the earlier junction with Midstate Trail (3.8/550). Turn left and retrace your steps to the trailhead (4.8/630).

INFORMATION

Douglas State Forest, 107 Wallum Lake Road, Douglas, MA 01516, 508-476-7872, mass.gov/eea/agencies/dcr/massparks.

NEARBY

An extensive complex of facilities can be found by the lakeshore below the main parking area, including a lifeguarded beach and swimming area, drinking fountains, an ice cream truck, dozens of picnic tables and grilling stations, restrooms, and more. Some are open only during summer season; call ahead for current information.

TRIP 6
TULLY TRAIL

Location: Royalston, MA
Difficulty: Moderate
Distance: 20.6 miles round-trip
Total Elevation Gain/Loss: 3,300 feet/3,300 feet
Trip Length: 2 days
Recommended Map: *Tully Trail Map* (Trustees of Reservations)
Highlight: The surprising wilds of north-central Massachusetts.

North Quabbin country is a region of exceptional conservation land in north-central Massachusetts. Small mountains bulge above the landscape, crystalline streams tumble over bedrock, and numerous ponds shimmer within a vast and continuous forest. This ten-town area, located between the Quabbin Reservoir and the New Hampshire border, is one of the least densely populated parts of the state and home to 94,000 acres of protected parkland. This trip visits nine of these parcels on one of the region's most picturesque paths: Tully Trail.

HIKE OVERVIEW

This broad, counter-clockwise loop passes through a mix of conservation land, visiting three Trustees of Reservations properties, three state forests, two state wildlife management areas, and property managed by the Army Corps of Engineers. The hike's low elevation makes it an attractive early- or late-season option, and is particularly good for fall foliage, which typically peaks in early to mid-October. Several natural gems can be found on the hike—including Royalston Falls and the summit of Tully Mountain—but its primary appeals are its proximity to Boston and the light use much of the trail receives. Still, much of this hike may not feel wild. Although some sections follow remote single-track trails, many other portions travel along wide woods roads and one long stretch follows a paved secondary road.

On day one—the shorter of the two—follow the East Branch of the Tully River north, climbing above it to visit pattering Spirit Falls and a pair of viewpoints. The watershed narrows as you follow Falls Brook into Royalston Falls Reservation past its namesake falls and reach Royalston Falls shelter. Day two undulates through forested terrain along a mix of single-track trails, woods

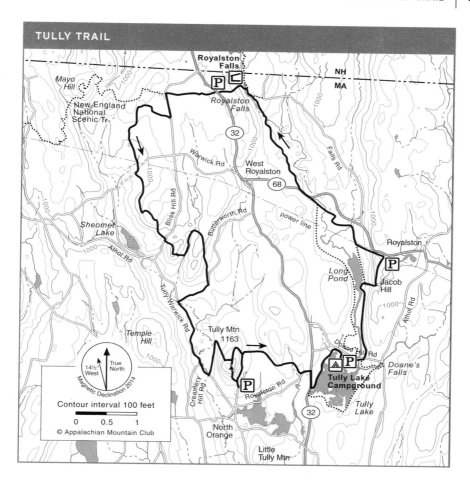

roads, and a 1.5-mile section along paved Warwick Road. The final highlight is 1,163-foot Tully Mountain, which offers the hike's best views.

Tully Trail was completed in 2001 as the first project of the North Quabbin Regional Landscape Partnership—a collection of state agencies, local land trusts, and environmental groups working to protect and promote the North Quabbin Region—and was designed to tour some of the region's highlights. Today it is managed by The Trustees of Reservations.

OVERNIGHT OPTIONS

The hike offers only one overnight option: Royalston Falls shelter. Camping is prohibited elsewhere, though Tully Lake Campground is available for drive-up use at the trailhead.

Royalston Falls Shelter (6.5/960/42° 43.158′ N, 72° 14.901′ W) is located in a grove of hemlocks and young beeches, a short distance above Tully Brook. The cabin-like structure features a sheltered porch, four double bunks, and a loft, and can hold as many as 12 people. The free shelter is first-come, first-served, and receives light use. Camping is permitted around the shelter, though the sloped terrain provides limited options. Tully Brook provides water, though it is usually brown and tannin-soaked. Campfires are allowed in the fire ring in front of the shelter. There is no privy.

Tully Lake Campground (0.0/680/42° 39.017′ N, 72° 12.587′ W) is situated by the trailhead along the shore of its namesake lake and features more than 30 sites. The only campground managed by The Trustees, it is open daily from mid-June through mid-September, weekends only mid-May to mid-June and through mid-October. Hot showers and canoe rentals add enticements to this pleasant location. Reservations are recommended for any weekend visit (978-248-9455, tullylakecampground.org).

TO REACH THE TRAILHEAD

Take MA 2 to Exit 17 in Athol and follow MA 32 north for 6.5 miles. Watch for highway signs as the route meanders substantially. Turn right onto Doane Hill Road (signed for Tully Lake Campground), and proceed 0.8 mile to the campground entrance on your right. Park in the free outer lot (42° 39.017′ N, 72° 12.587′ W) and let campground staff know you're leaving your car there.

HIKE DESCRIPTION

From the lot (0.0/680), head back toward Doane Hill Road and look for purple Tully Trail signs that indicate your route, which bears right to cross over the sluggish Tully River. After passing a boat launch and parking area on your left, bear left onto Tully Trail at the yellow gate. Initially marked by a combination of yellow (hiking route) and orange (biking route) blazes, the broad trail begins in a young hardwood forest displaying a classic southern New England mix of white pines, red maples, beeches, hemlocks, and red oaks. In the understory, blueberries, hazels, witch hazels, and royal, interrupted, and sensitive ferns fill the forest with lush greenery.

The trail parallels Tully River, to your left, and soon passes a red house on the right labeled Whispering Wilderness. Past the building, the route curves left and closer to the adjacent wetlands. Undulating briefly, the trail leaves the Army Corps of Engineers property, enters The Trustees' Jacob Hill parcel, and heads toward the southern end of Long Pond (1.4/640). Views look north to the nearby hills. After passing another lakeside clearing, the trail curves right, narrows to single-track, and crosses a brook on a small bridge.

Here Tully Trail turns right and climbs past white pines and yellow birches. After crossing a stone wall, the path drops briefly toward the brook and stops by Spirit Falls, a little slider that spatters 20 to 30 feet down the rocks. The route ascends a rock staircase along the hissing creek and reaches an unposted four-way junction (1.6/970).

Tully Trail turns left here, but consider dropping your pack and heading right to check out The Ledges, one of the hike's best views. The 0.5-mile side trip travels along an increasingly narrow trail through a ridge-top community of beeches and paper birches. From the aptly named viewpoint, Tully Lake is visible to the south, the round hump of Tully Mountain rises to the southwest, and 1,621-foot Mount Grace appears on the west horizon.

Back at the junction, follow Tully Trail and continue straight at the posted junction (2.0/1,110), climbing to the forested summit of Jacob Hill and a three-way junction. To reach another pleasant view, head straight and briefly follow circle blazes to reach an overlook of Long Pond, Mount Tully, and Mount Grace.

Return to the three-way junction and follow Tully Trail's square blazes down to a wide dirt road. Turn left and immediately cross a power-line corridor. Bear left on the far side and follow the power lines downhill through a brushy corridor, filled with blackberry canes and head-high rhododendrons. The route crosses a dirt access road and steepens. The path becomes difficult to discern as it drops through goldenrod and young birch trees, with loose footing in places. The route generally remains on the right (north) side of the corridor, but crosses over to the opposite side shortly before reaching the bottom. Keep an eye out for a few blazes and small cairns that indicate your route, but use your best judgment in finding the easiest way down. At the bottom is a posted junction for the bike path on the left (2.6/680). Turn right to remain on Tully Trail.

Your route now enters and soon reaches an old building foundation on the right. The route winds down to Boyce Brook and crosses it on a boardwalk (3.0/690). Pass through a sunny area marked by past beaver activity and dead trees and then abruptly reach a wide woods road. Turn right to immediately reach another major woods road near some residences. Paved Warwick Road is visible roughly 10 yards ahead to the right, but bear left to follow the signed trail.

The wide, grassy trail crosses the East Branch of the Tully River on a rickety bridge (3.5/620). Pass the final junction with the bike path, which splits off to the left. Remain on Tully Trail, cross a yellow gate, and reach paved Warwick Road (3.9/690). Turn left, follow the road briefly, and then turn right just before the next curve to continue on Tully Trail—watch for the signs and blazes. Encounter a wide woods road and curve right. Several other woods roads join in—keep going straight. The trail eventually descends to the upper reaches of Tully River; here it has become Falls Brook, a nice gravelly stream. Cross it on a rustic bridge (5.6/710), then immediately ascend along a single-track trail in a small hemlock-shaded ravine.

The trail climbs steeply, then makes a traverse on a rocky and root-laced trail. Nearby Royalston Falls becomes audible before the path drops to reach a fence-protected view of Royalston Falls (6.1/850), which sheets downward into an inaccessible grotto.

The trail continues past the falls and along the now-placid creek. Pass a dark pool fed by a diminutive cascade, travel along the stream, and reach the junction with white-blazed Metacomet–Monadnock (M–M) Trail (6.5/940), a 114-mile long-distance trail that runs from the Connecticut border to Mount Monadnock in southern New Hampshire. (It's also part of the larger New England National Scenic Trail, which extends from the New Hampshire border to southern Connecticut.) Turn left to cross the brook on a basic bridge and reach Royalston Falls shelter (6.5/960).

For the next 1.4 miles, Tully Trail overlaps with M–M Trail. The double-track trail departs the shelter, curving uphill to the left. After a brief drop, it begins a steady rise until the gradient eases near the top; a gently rising traverse leads you to the Royalston Falls parking area on MA 32 (7.0/1,180).

Turn right on MA 32, follow it about 20 feet, and then turn left to follow the single-track trail. The well-blazed trail passes through a grove of red pines, readily recognized by their 4- to 6-inch needles in bunches of two.

Pass through a swampy area, cross a stone wall, and reach unpaved Bliss Hill Road by a driveway (7.9/1,180). M–M Trail continues up the driveway, but follow the road left to reach the property boundary for Warwick State Forest (8.3/1,130). A hundred yards farther, the trail turns right off Bliss Hill Road and onto another broad woods road. When it reaches a fork, proceed straight. Note how the woods on the right feature an open understory and intact overstory of red oaks and red and sugar maples, whereas the area on the left is a more cluttered world of young trees. Foresters have thinned the woods on the right to allow fewer trees to obtain more sunlight, producing a larger and more economically valuable forest.

The road passes a massive red maple as it slowly descends through hardwoods to reach the power-line corridor you traversed earlier in the hike

Doane's Falls awaits near the Tully Trail. (Photo courtesy of Kim Foley MacKinnon)

(9.9/930). Cross the corridor and bear right at the next woods road (10.1/930). Watch for blazes as the route next turns left onto a smaller woods road (10.2/920). The grassy road soon crosses a small stream and climbs past an increasing number of beeches and oaks on a traversing ascent of Bliss Hill. A palpable sense of height culminates at a ledge with a narrow view west of Mount Grace (11.0/1,090).

The blazes here are confusing. The path to the ledge is only a side trail; the main route forks left uphill just before reaching the viewpoint. The continuing trail narrows and becomes faint as it climbs past paper and black birches and curves right. Crest the hill by a wall of flat rocks (11.2/1,180). The trail wraps around the wall and begins a steep descent. After a steady drop, the gradient eases and passes among thick hemlocks to reach the battered pavement of Bliss Hill Road (11.7/960).

Cross the road and climb briefly to reach another woods road by an old rusting vehicle frame. Turn right to immediately reach a four-way junction— go straight, parallel to the rock wall on your left. The trail returns to single-track, tours an area rife with stone walls, climbs over a small rise, and then makes its steepest drop yet, curving left near the bottom to join an overgrown woods road. The trail immediately bears right off the road and enters the small hemlock-shaded gorge of Fish Brook. The route curves down to reach the rushing stream (12.5/850), a mossy rocky streambed lined by a stone wall. The darkness and seclusion make this one of the trail's highlights.

The route follows an overgrown woods road upstream and soon turns away from the brook on a single-track path, climbing briefly to cross a small feeder brook before returning to the main stream. The trail crosses the brook by some pleasant riffles on a plank bridge (13.1/960) and climbs again on a thin trail, which levels out and begins descending along another stone wall. The traversing drop is occasionally steep, but the gradient eases and reaches unpaved Butterworth Road (14.2/700).

Go right and follow the road past roughly a dozen houses. Just before you reach paved Warwick Road (14.8/610), you pass a nice view of Tully Mountain—your continuing route—beyond somebody's backyard. Turn left on Warwick Road and follow it for the next 1.5 miles. Vehicles zip by, but focus instead on the intermittent views across the Tully River to Tully Mountain, and watch for a roadside rock engraved with a 2002 dedication to the establishment of the North Quabbin Bioreserve, another recognition of the region's ecological value. Pass Creamery Hill Road on the right after 1.3 miles and a short distance later over Tully River on a bridge. On the opposite side, Tully Trail immediately cuts left on a grassy woods road (16.3/580).

The wide trail runs level, offering glimpses to the right of adjacent Tully Mountain's steep slopes. The grass disappears as the trail winds along the mountain's lower slopes and climbs through denser forest. The trail cuts sharply away from the road to the right (16.9/600), The trail gains 250 feet of elevation, switchbacks left, passes some nice boulders, and then wraps around the ridge to reach a posted junction (17.5/1,030). Tully Trail goes left here to Tully Lake, but instead turn right to make the 0.1-mile side trip to the summit and the best view of the hike. Climb along the double-track trail through a dense group of hemlocks and cross the forested summit, then descend a short distance to reach several ledges with unrestricted views east.

Tully and Packard ponds are apparent nearby to the southeast, and Tully Lake is visible to the east. The Wapack Range (Trip 16) lines the east-northeast horizon. The summit of Wachusett Mountain peaks over the horizon to the east-southeast. Mount Monadnock, the most glamorous of them all, punctuates the landscape to the northeast in full profile.

Return to the earlier junction and continue on Tully Trail as it traverses gently downward. The trail becomes more of a woods road as it descends to another posted junction (17.9/790). Go left to continue toward Tully Lake (right leads to a trailhead parking area for Tully Mountain). The trail returns to single-track, descends through even-aged white pines, and crosses a dribbling brook. It continues straight across a grassy woods road, makes a brief climb, and then curves right to begin a traverse. After winding past some car-sized boulders, the route crosses another woods road, drops briefly to cross a rock-strewn stream, and then heads through a brushy corridor to reach yet another woods road. Turn right here and drop down to reach Royalston Road (19.1/660). Turn left and follow the road, which becomes paved just before reaching MA 32. Turn right and follow the highway about 50 yards to a parking area by Tully Lake on the left (19.4/680).

From the parking area, the trail follows a root-covered single-track path toward the lakeshore. Curving left, the route runs parallel to the lakeshore about 30 feet inland and reaches the posted junction for Interpretive Trail. Continuing straight, cross a small brook and follow some rocky terrain on a well-trod single-track trail.

Winding around a small inlet, the route passes several unmarked spurs leading down toward the water. The trail crosses a brook, approaches within 5 feet of Doane Hill Road, and curves right to travel along a berm separating a wetlands area from the lake. More spurs run to a small peninsula in the lake, but the trail turns left to cross the wetlands outflow on a small plank bridge. Green circle blazes appear, the path cuts left and widens, and soon you emerge at the campground parking area and hike's end (20.6/680).

INFORMATION

Trustees of Reservations, 572 Essex Street, Beverly, MA 01915-1530. For information on the Tully Trail, 978-249-4957 (seasonal), 978-248-9455 (year-round), tullylakecampground.org.

NEARBY

Doane's Falls, a delightfully frothing cascade, is located a half-mile from the campground parking area along Lawrence Brook and well worth a visit. To reach it, follow the Tully Lake Loop Trail from its intersection with Doane Hill Road; find it just past the boat launch and adjacent parking area.

TRIP 7
NEW ENGLAND NATIONAL SCENIC TRAIL, SECTION 17

Location: Northfield, MA
Difficulty: Moderate
Distance: 10.4 miles one-way; 5.8 miles round-trip to Richardson-Zlogar Cabin
Total Elevation Gain/Loss: 1,800 feet/2,400 feet one-way; 600 feet/600 feet round-trip to cabin
Trip Length: 1–2 days
Recommended Map: *New England National Scenic Trail Interactive Map* (available at newenglandtrail.org)
Highlights: Lush and diverse woodlands, a ridge-top cabin, and two exceptional views along a remote section of the New England National Scenic Trail.

The New England National Scenic Trail (NET) stretches for 215 miles from the shores of Long Island Sound in Connecticut to the New Hampshire border in north-central Massachusetts. In its northernmost section, the NET travels across the hilly sylvan terrain of Northfield and Mount Grace state forests, where lush and diverse forests—plus a pair of superlative views—welcome the handful of hikers who explore this region.

HIKE OVERVIEW

Designated in 2009, the NET utilizes a collection of long-existent trails along the majority of its route. In Massachusetts, it follows Metacomet–Monadnock (M–M) Trail, which was established—and is still maintained by—AMC's Berkshire Chapter.

This point-to-point hike travels through a quiet, rolling landscape and utilizes a mix of little-traveled single-track trails, old woods roads, and one long stretch of a snowmobile corridor. It begins in Northfield State Forest on a delightful new section of trail that winds through a remote vale before ascending to the ridgeline of 1,285-foot Stratton Mountain, where a recently constructed cabin offers overnight accommodations with a remarkable view of the surrounding landscape, including the distinctive profile of nearby Mount Monadnock.

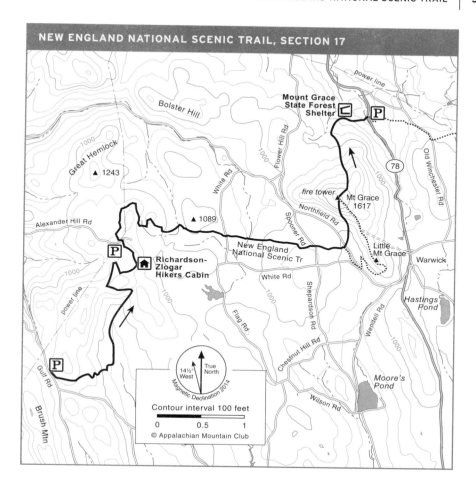

NEW ENGLAND NATIONAL SCENIC TRAIL, SECTION 17

Bolster Hill

Great Hemlock

1243

Alexander Hill Rd

1089

Mount Grace
State Forest
Shelter

power line

Flower Hill Rd

White Rd

fire tower

Mt Grace
1617

Northfield Rd

Spooner Rd

New England
National Scenic Tr

Little
Mt Grace

Warwick

78

Old Winchester Rd

P

Richardson-
Zlogar
Hikers Cabin

White Rd

Shepardson Rd

Hastings
Pond

power line

Flag Rd

Wendell Rd

P

Gull Rd

Chestnut Hill Rd

Moore's
Pond

14½°
West

True
North

Magnetic Declination 2014

Wilson Rd

Brush Mtn

Contour interval 100 feet

0   0.5   1

© Appalachian Mountain Club

The route then descends a faint and little-used path, following a long, mostly straight stretch of snowmobile corridor to Mount Grace State Forest. From there, ascend the rounded hump of 1,617-foot Mount Grace, where a fire lookout offers a 360-degree view from its staircase. The final section drops down the mountain flanks to reach a run-down trail shelter immediately before ending on MA 78.

Note that a car shuttle is required to complete this point-to-point journey. Alternatively, you can leave a bike at the ending trailhead to return to your car, though be aware that the final 2.0 miles back to the starting trailhead are steep and very strenuous. Completing the shorter out-and-back hike to the cabin is another option, though it precludes a visit to Mount Grace.

OVERNIGHT OPTION

Richardson-Zlogar Hikers Cabin (2.9/1,230/42° 40.825′ N, 72° 24.061′ W) perches in an open clearing near the summit of Stratton Mountain and offers a sweeping 180-degree view east. Completed in 2012, it is named for Sam and Barbara Richardson, local landowners who purchased the 38-acre site and donated a conservation restriction to ensure permanent protection of the NET corridor here, and Mike Zlogar, one of the AMC Berkshire Chapter volunteers whose dedicated efforts helped make this cabin a reality. (The cabin exists through the cooperation and partnership of many interested parties, including AMC and the National Park Service, volunteer builders, Mount Grace Land Conservation Trust, the landowners, and the Town of Northfield.)

The enclosed cabin offers a loft sleeping area and can comfortably accommodate up to 10 people. A few twin-size mattresses are available, though visitors will need to bring sleeping bags; larger groups will need sleeping pads as well. Two large tent platforms and a privy can be found nearby. A water source is usually available about a five-minute walk from the cabin, but it can go dry in late summer; you will need to filter or treat it. (You can get an update on its status and exact location when you make your reservation.) It's generally worthwhile, however, to bring enough water with you to meet your minimum overnight needs.

The cabin is available only by reservation and is free to use, though donations are encouraged. Only one group per night is permitted in the cabin, though additional parties can make use of the tent platforms. There is a two-night limit. A combination lock on the door prevents unregistered visitors from entering. To make a reservation, call 413-695-6764 or email srichardson19623@gmail.com.

Mount Grace State Forest Trail Shelter (10.1/740/42° 42.477′ N, 72° 21.086′ W) is located 0.25 mile from MA 78 at the hike's end. Conveniently situated by a babbling brook, with a large fire pit and adjoining grill, it offers an alternative overnight option. As of 2013, however, this lean-to was in a state of disrepair, with a prominent hole through the sagging roof. Camping is possible in the area surrounding the lean-to. It is free to use and no reservations are required.

TO REACH THE TRAILHEADS

To reach the ending trailhead to establish a shuttle, take MA 2 to Exit 13 (no sign), which is marked for MA 2A East and Erving State Forest. Follow MA 2A east for 2.1 miles, turn left (north) onto MA 78, and proceed for 8.3 miles. Watch for the small signs indicating where the NET crosses the highway (1.3 miles north of the main Mount Grace parking area), where a small and informal parking area (42° 42.026′ N, 72° 20.800′ W) can be found on the west side of the road.

To reach the starting trailhead, take MA 2 to the town of Erving, and turn north onto Church Street; the intersection is located next to the fire station and across the highway from Freight House Antiques. In 0.2 mile, Church Street merges into Gulf Road, which you follow for 4.3 miles to reach a small trailhead parking area on the left (42° 39.579′ N, 72° 25.130′ W) at Brush Mountain Conservation Area. ·

To reach the Alexander Hill Road trailhead and shorter access to the cabin, continue from Brush Mountain Conservation Area for an additional 2.1 miles, make a hard right onto Alexander Hill Road, and proceed uphill for 1.9 miles to the road's end, where the NET crosses a clearing. Note that most of the road is unpaved and rough, but readily passable in a low-clearance vehicle.

To reach the starting trailhead from the ending trailhead, drive south on MA 78 for 1.8 miles to Warwick Center, turn right onto Northfield Road, and proceed 7.2 miles to a five-way intersection in Northfield. Turn left onto St. Mary's Street, which reaches Gulf Road in 0.4 mile. Turn left onto Gulf Road, and proceed 4.4 miles to the parking area on the right.

HIKE DESCRIPTION

An information kiosk at the trailhead (0.0/1,210) highlights the area's flora and fauna and also tells the story of Calvin Swan, an African American who home-steaded here in the early to mid-nineteenth century; the site, a short distance to the west of the highway, is open to the public. To begin the hike, cross the road and head north on the NET, passing a large, mature red maple on the left just past the trailhead mileage sign. Numerous white blazes clearly indicate the way here and throughout the hike.

The route quickly reaches the junction for blue-blazed Over the Top Trail, which heads left on a slightly longer and more strenuous alternative route that rejoins the main trail 0.5 mile ahead. The NET travels along a soft single-track path, slowly rises, and crosses an overgrown woods road. Carpets of hay-scented ferns fill the understory with a lush and delicate blanket of green. A brief rise then leads to the far end of Over the Top Trail (0.6/1,210) before the NET begins another steady descent, this time via several curving switchbacks.

The trail descends into a broad and peaceful vale, crosses an old woods road in a hemlock grove, and then eases as it turns north to quickly recross the woods road. Wind through shady hemlock forest, then cross a flowing stream (1.0/890). Top off your water supplies; this is the last quality water source from here to the cabin.

Next pass several semi-truck-sized boulders shaded by yellow birches. Nearby Hidden Pond soon peeks out from between the trees, but there is no established access to this shallow and marshy body of water. The surrounding terrain becomes rockier as you continue north among hemlock trees on a long, mostly level stretch.

The trail rises gently, climbs more noticeably, and rejoins a longer-existing section of trail. (Note the old yellow blazes beneath the newer white blazes.) Ascend steeply past more hemlocks, level briefly past some more large boulders, and then surmount a small rise, where the route curves to the left.

The steepest section yet rises on a traverse that briefly emerges into a more open ridge-top community of red and white oaks. The hike's first tantalizing views peek through the trees. The path soon returns among shady hemlocks on a long, level section; a double-blazed post in the trail indicates where the route makes a sharp turn right. The trail reaches an unposted junction with a blue-blazed trail, part of a small network of paths (Stratton Blue Trail Loop) that interlace around the summit of Stratton Mountain.

Continue straight on the NET to reach an open clearing by a power-line corridor, which offers an interesting rock structure that provides nice views to the west-northwest. The Connecticut River valley lies below you, while the more distant peaks of the northern Berkshires and southern Green Mountains line the horizon.

Continuing, the NET turns right at the clearing and joins a blue-blazed trail signed "East View." The route winds slowly uphill through more hemlocks, crosses an old woods road, and then emerges at the Richarson-Zlogar Cabin (2.9/1,230). Enjoy the fabulous view, which encompasses your continuing route east to the prominent hump of nearby Mount Grace (the fire lookout can be spotted on its summit), plus Mount Monadnock and the rugged terrain of the surrounding area. From the cabin, the NET descends the clear slopes below on a faint track, reenters dense hemlock woods, and reaches the power-line corridor at Alexander Hill Road trailhead (3.2/1,170). After emerging from the woods, follow the road to the left, then immediately turn right to relocate the trail.

The path rises briefly, passes a junction for blue-blazed Alexander Hill Trail on the left. Some beeches and red maples mix in as the route curves to the right and then starts to descend on the trip's faintest section of trail. Look for the blazes as you drop through a lush and more diverse forest and then cruise past an impressive 20-foot-high protruding rock face. Past this point, the trail

The Richardson-Zlogar Hikers Cabin looks east toward Mount Grace near the northern end of the New England National Scenic Trail.

becomes increasingly faint as it descends to a more substantial stream, which the trail follows to a winter snowmobile corridor (4.4/930).

The NET now turns right to follow this wide, fast-cruising pathway almost due east for the next 2.3 miles. The route passes a posted junction on the right, then drops briefly before traveling along a sandy stretch to cross Bass Road (5.0/950). Cruising fast through thick woods, cross a bridge over a marsh stream, and follow the route as it curves right off the primary straight-line corridor at a prominently signed and blazed fork. The trail winds around and slowly descends to a wet, ferny area, where a snowmobile route joins from the right. Past this point, the trail gets much rougher, curves left, and then bears right at an easily-missed fork—watch for the blazes.

Paved Northfield Road soon comes into view as the narrower trail curves to the right before crossing it at a set of trail mileage signs (6.7/900). Once on the other side, the narrower trail crosses a bridge over a melodious stream and quickly emerges at another snowmobile corridor.

Turn left onto the broad path, then quickly right to follow the NET as it returns to pleasant single-track. (Blue-blazed Around the Mountain Trail, which you'll intersect several more times, continues straight.) The NET rises and then turns left at another junction with a blue-blazed trail.

The route soon reencounters Around the Mountain Trail (7.4/1,020), where the NET turns left to begin a direct and steep ascent up the mountain. After peaking atop the forested and unmarked summit of Little Mount Grace

(7.7/1,225), the trail drops and then makes a gradual rise to emerge at the dirt access road that leads to the summit area (8.0/1,180).

For the final ascent, the NET first cuts left on a smaller woods road and follows along telephone and power lines past several large hemlock trees and up an increasingly grass-covered route. Pass a cell tower on the right shortly before an overgrown section of the trail leads you to the summit and fire tower (8.6/1,617), where a pair of picnic tables offers a convenient rest stop.

The lookout atop the 70-foot-high tower is locked and inaccessible, but you can still clamber up the staircase to enjoy impressive 360-degree views. To the west, Stratton Mountain and the clearing below the hikers' cabin are apparent. Beyond are the northern Berkshires and southern Green Mountains. To the northeast is Mount Monadnock. Beyond it and to the east-northeast is the long line of the Wapack Range (Trip 16), which stretches from the round hump of Mount Watatic to the south to the twin peaks of the Pack Monadnocks to the north. Farther east is the rounded hump of Wachusett Mountain. Portions of Quabbin Reservoir can be spotted to the south-southeast.

The trail continues on the far side of the summit clearing on a grassy road. In roughly 50 yards, the NET splits left away from the road, which leads down to Ohlson Field at the Mount Grace State Forest parking area on MA 78. The double-track path descends steeply past lush ferns and over some rock slabs to reach another fork in the trail. The NET bears left, descends more gradually, straightens out, and turns right away from the wider and more obvious path— watch for the blazes. It next passes unsigned Around the Mountain Trail again on the left just before encountering a pleasant brook.

The trail becomes more and more road-like as it slowly curves to the right, crosses the stream again, and reaches the Mount Grace shelter (10.1/740). From here, it's a short drop with one final stream crossing to reach the small parking area on MA 78 (10.4/570). Cross Around the Mountain Trail one last time at the end as it heads 1.4 miles south to the Ohlson Field parking area.

INFORMATION

New England National Scenic Trail, newenglandtrail.org; Mount Grace State Forest, 78 Warwick Road, Warwick, MA 01378, 978-544-3939, mass.gov/eea/agencies/dcr/massparks.

NEARBY

Food and amenities can be found nearby along MA 2 and 2A in Erving.

TRIP 8
THE TACONICS

Location: Appalachian Trail, northwestern Connecticut, southwestern Massachusetts
Difficulty: Challenging
Distance: 16.9 miles one-way
Total Elevation Gain/Loss: 4,600 feet/4,450 feet
Trip Length: 2–3 days
Recommended Maps: *Appalachian Trail Guide to Massachusetts-Connecticut, Maps 4 and 10* (Appalachian Trail Conservancy)
Highlights: Summits, ravines, waterfalls, vistas, old-growth forest.

The Appalachian Trail (AT) travels atop the ancient bedrock prow of the Taconic Range for nearly 17 miles without crossing a single road. Touring a broad swath of wildland in a far corner of New England, the hike visits the highest peak in Connecticut, the second-highest in Massachusetts, old-growth hemlock forest, stunted pitch pines, waterfalls, and nine different places to spend the night.

HIKE OVERVIEW

This point-to-point trip travels the AT from CT 41 in Salisbury, Connecticut, to its next road crossing at Jug End State Reservation in the town of Mount Washington, Massachusetts. The route ascends Lion's Head, passes over Bear Mountain (Connecticut's highest peak), drops into the old-growth haven of Sages Ravine, clambers atop the cliffs of Mount Race, climbs to the top of Mount Everett, then undulates north through a lightly traveled landscape to reach its terminus.

MA 41 runs parallel to the hike for most of its distance, down in the valley to the east a thousand feet below. Several trails access the AT from along the highway, providing options for shorter trips. Although it is possible to hike the route in either direction, the following description goes from south to north—the most common direction for travel. The area receives moderate use, and finding an available campsite is seldom a problem.

The Taconic Range began to form a half-billion years ago, when a tectonic collision mashed the sand and calcium-rich coral layers of an ancient seabed against North America. Over the ensuing eons, pressure transformed these jumbled layers into calcium-rich marble and erosion-resistant schist, and

THE TACONICS (NORTH)

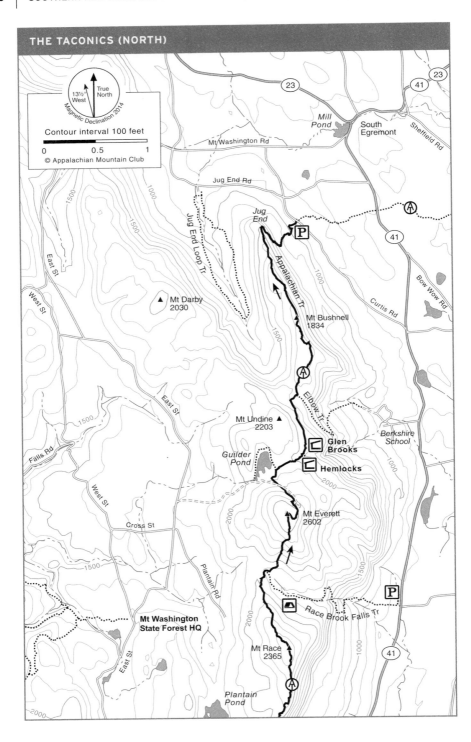

Magnetic Declination 2014
13½° West — True North

Contour interval 100 feet

0   0.5   1

© Appalachian Mountain Club

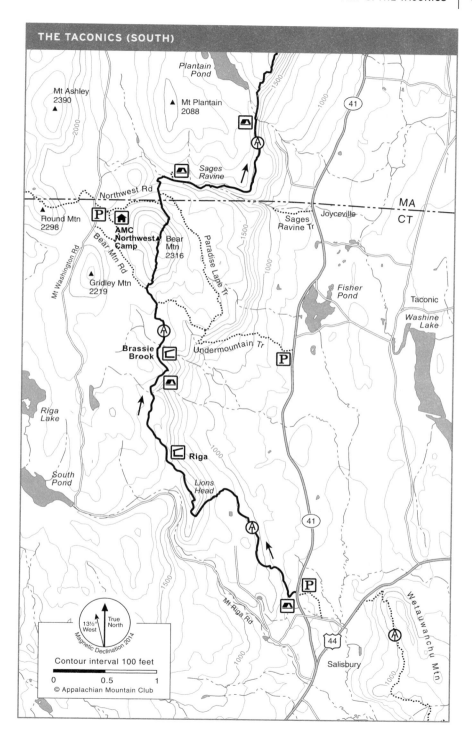

THE TACONICS (SOUTH)

the schist layer was thrust over the marble to form a hard cap in some locations. Over time, the exposed marble eroded away to form the flat valley of the Housatonic River; the erosion-resistant schist layer formed the hard backbone of today's Taconic Range. The calcium-rich soils produced by marble are rare in New England. This less acidic soil nurtures a variety of trees and plants uncommon elsewhere in the region. The area's ecological diversity is remarkable and includes an unusual pitch pine–bear oak forest along the ridgelines.

OVERNIGHT OPTIONS

There are nine designated overnight areas; four offer shelters and eight have tentsites. With a few exceptions (noted later), water is readily available from nearby streams. Campfires are permitted only at Race Brook Falls, Hemlocks Shelter, and Glen Brook Shelter. No camping is allowed outside designated areas.

Black bears are common in the area. As always, hang your food securely at night or use the bear boxes that have been installed at several overnight locations.

Plateau Campsite (0.2/830/41° 59.624′ N, 73° 25.705′ W) occupies a level clearing on steep slopes. Red oaks, beeches, and black birches shade the central area, and upslope, a small hemlock glade shelters a more secluded site. MA 41 traffic is audible, though the forest hides it from view. A trickling spring provides water; a pump may be necessary to collect it, depending on conditions. Because of the proximity of several private residences, there is a designated quiet period from 8 A.M. to 8 P.M.

Riga Shelter (3.4/1,620/42° 00.939′ N, 73° 27.120′ W) perches just below the ridgeline and offers a restricted overlook of the Housatonic River valley— the only overnight location to offer a view. Four adjacent tentsites and one large group site are located nearby. A nearby spring reliably provides water.

Ball Brook Campsite (4.0/1,700/42° 01.356′ N, 73° 27.296′ W) features two tentsites within earshot of rushing Ball Brook. Two large group sites cluster around a large split boulder beneath young hardwoods. A basic privy serves the sites, which offer 360-degree forest views. Obtain water from easily accessible Ball Brook.

Brassie Brook Shelter (4.6/1,730/42° 01.696′ N, 73° 27.204′ W) offers a large shelter and five tentsites—plus a bear box, group camping area, and privy—occupy the slopes 50 feet above musical Brassie Brook, a reliable water source. The surrounding woods support lush carpets of ferns and wildflowers.

Sages Ravine Campsite (6.8/1,550/42° 03.245′ N, 73° 27.171′ W) is located just over the state line in Massachusetts. It is spread along the slopes above rushing Sawmill Brook, in close proximity to old-growth hemlock forest.

Eight numbered sites and one group site are dispersed along a wide loop. Half the sites offer tent platforms. Sites 6, 7, and 8 offer the most seclusion. Water is readily available from the brook or from a nearby spring popular with frogs. Please use the metal bear boxes to store your food at night.

Laurel Ridge Campsite (8.7/1,710/42° 03.661′ N, 73° 26.310′ W) replaced Bear Rock Falls Campsite, which was located near its namesake falls but became severely impacted by overuse. This campsite provides three tent platforms, two bear boxes, and a privy dispersed on a steep and shady hillside among maples, oaks, and laurels. The sites are small but they are all nice and private. A nearby brook provides water.

Race Brook Falls Campsite (12.0/1,800/42° 05.412′ N, 73° 25.987′ W), located 0.4 mile off the AT on Race Brook Falls Trail, is a spread-out area shaded by a dense hemlock and beech forest. Three tent platforms and many adjacent sites are available, plus a privy and bear box. A small spring trickles by the campsite; Race Brook is also nearby and readily accessible. Campfires are permitted.

Hemlocks Shelter (13.4/1,950/42° 06.118′ N, 73° 25.961′ W), a spacious shelter and the newest along this hike, perches beneath its namesake trees. Water is readily available from an adjacent creek. Campfires are permitted. Tent camping is prohibited. A bear box and privy are also provided.

Glen Brook Shelter (13.5/1,940/42° 06.637′ N, 73° 25.647′ W) hides downslope and out-of-sight from the AT and offers good opportunities for seclusion. The surrounding understory is open, the site perches on the edge of steeper slopes, and several tent platforms and other good tentsites are available.

TO REACH THE TRAILHEADS

To Reach the Northern (Ending) Trailhead. Take MA 41 south from Great Barrington through South Egremont. Remain on MA 41 as MA 23 splits right, and then in 0.1 mile, bear right onto Mount Washington Road. In 0.8 mile, turn left onto Avenue 0-35 and proceed 0.5 mile to a three-way junction with Jug End Road. Proceed straight on the dirt road for 0.3 mile and look for the AT crossing. A pull-out (42° 8.674′ N, 73° 25.895′ W) on the right side of the road provides parking.

To Reach the Southern (Starting) Trailhead. Remain on MA 41 where Mount Washington Road splits right. Continue south, passing the Berkshire School on the right, and then 1.9 miles later the parking area for Race Brook Falls Trail on the right. The Undermountain Trail parking area—usually the most packed—is on the right 4.4 miles past the Race Brook Falls turn-off. Continue 2.5 miles past the Undermountain trailhead to reach your starting trailhead on the right. The small parking area (42° 0.067′ N, 73° 26.389′ W) is hidden and easy to miss—watch for the sign indicating a hikers crossing.

HIKE DESCRIPTION

Sugar maples and white pines shade the trailhead (0.0/710). Heading out, immediately pass an outhouse on the right and begin climbing, passing a large red oak on the right—note the flat, disk-shaped acorn caps littering the ground. Soon after, the spur trail to Plateau Campsite (0.2/830) splits left by another substantial red oak and a patch of cinnamon ferns.

The AT traverses upslope, steadily rising as it passes beneath a diverse forest of beeches, white oaks, hemlocks, and white ashes. Also common is invasive Japanese barberry, a thorny shrub proliferating in the understory. As the trail ascends the flanks of the Taconic Range, the route passes over marble bedrock. Marble produces calcium-rich soil, which is hospitable for sugar maples—many of which line the trail. Other species are found only in such calcareous soils. One of these is the delicate maidenhair fern, which can be spotted here—identify it by its lacy, finger-like fronds with black stems.

The trail becomes rockier and begins an undulating traverse. Mountain laurels soon appear, indicative of a change in bedrock—the plant thrives in the more acidic soils produced by the underlying schist. The trail crosses several small creeks and encounters low-lying blueberry bushes, another indicator of acidic soil. The broad hump of 1,738-foot Lion's Head appears through the trees to the west. Curving left, the trail steepens, switchbacks, and enters an increasingly thick forest of red oaks and striped maples. Soon you reach Lion's Head Trail on the left (2.5/1,480), which leads south to a nearby trailhead. Bear right to remain on the AT.

Abundant mountain laurels accompany you as the trail attains the ridgeline for the first time. Turning north, the trail resumes climbing and soon reaches a hemlock-shaded clearing where Lion's Head Bypass Trail splits left (2.6/1,690), rejoining the AT in 0.2 mile. The forested bypass skirts the summit to the west and is lined with numerous pink lady's slipper orchids in early summer, but unless the weather is horrible, remain on the AT and quickly clamber to the summit of Lion's Head (2.7/1,738/42° 0.429′ N, 73° 26.784′ W).

On the summit, an outcrop provides open views south and east. To the east, expansive vistas look across the hummocky terrain of the Housatonic River valley, with the Twin Lakes—Washining and Washinee—clearly visible. To the southeast, 1,461-foot Mount Prospect is located in the distance past a closer hilly complex and marks the AT's continuing southbound route. Views west encompass the unbroken forest of the Wachocastinook Creek watershed.

Look closely at the rock under your feet. Heavily metamorphosed—note the taffy-like banding caused by intense heat and pressure—it is pocked by numerous small, red garnets. This semi-precious stone forms as the surrounding rock partially melts and then recrystallizes in small pockets.

Descending north from the summit and past the second junction for Bypass Trail, reach an expansive vista north overlooking the ridgeline spine of your upcoming route. The rounded summit of 2,316-foot Bear Mountain is next; to its right is the long ridge of Mount Race. Between the two lies the deep gully of Sages Ravine. The prominent hump of Mount Greylock (Trip 10)—the highest point in Massachusetts—rises on the distant north-northeast horizon 45 miles away. Directly in line with Greylock is the distinctive profile of Monument Mountain near Great Barrington.

After dipping into a younger forest of sugar maples, paper birches, and red oaks, the trail rises to reach the spur to Riga Shelter (3.4/1,620). Continuing, pass through a fern-filled forest of laurels and hobblebushes, whose large dinner plate–sized leaves make them hard to miss. Next up are junctions for Ball Brook Group Campground (4.0/1,700), followed in short order by an easy rock-hop over Ball Brook and the main Ball Brook Campsite. Past the campsite, the mostly level trail winds past the fuzzy leaves of azalea, which flower in May, and more mountain laurels. Tantalizing views east peek regularly through the trees as you proceed to the junction for Brassie Brook Shelter (4.6/1,730).

Brassie Brook flows just beyond the junction, lined by yellow birches, red maples, ashes, and hemlocks. The trail rock-hops the stream's multiple channels and proceeds gently through young forest corridors of mountain laurel. Upon reaching Riga Trail (5.1/1,850), the AT abruptly widens to begin a heavily trafficked section. As the state's highest summit, Bear Mountain is one of Connecticut's most popular day-hiking destinations. Thousands walk the 5.6-mile summit loop from MA 41 on Undermountain and Paradise Lane trails.

The forest becomes younger as you continue, evidenced by small gray birch trees. A short-lived species, gray birch is shade-intolerant and quickly disappears from the forest once overtopped. Its white bark appears similar to the bark of paper birch, but it does not peel. The tree's distinctive triangular-shaped leaves make it easy to recognize.

After passing an unmarked spur on the left, the trail becomes rocky and starts rapidly ascending. The vegetation diminishes in height, and soon the route follows a thin ribbon of quartz-veined bedrock. The shrubby growth steadily shrinks, and a few boulders protrude from the hillside to offer scramble-accessible views south toward Lion's Head and the headwaters of Brassie Brook.

A massive rockpile greets you upon reaching the summit (6.0/2,316/42° 02.693′ N, 73° 27.265′ W), the highest mountaintop in Connecticut. (The state's highest *point* is found a few miles to the northwest on the flanks of Mount Frissell, whose summit is in Massachusetts.) The view east includes the boggy curves of Schenob Brook below and the Twin Lakes, just north of which is the state line. Peering north, the Taconic Range marches toward the horizon. Your journey next heads into Sages Ravine, which slices east-west in a deep cut below Bear Mountain, and then heads north over Mount Race and the rounded summit of Mount Everett.

Sandy glades of pitch pines surround the rocky summit as you proceed onward, soon dropping down the steepest section of the entire hike. The trail plummets more than 300 feet, and scrambling is required to navigate the large rock outcrops. The trail enters shady beech forest and then abruptly levels for a short distance. Carpets of hay-scented ferns fill the understory, and you soon resume the descent, crossing the unmarked state line and reaching the junction with Paradise Lane Trail (6.7/1,800).

The sounds of rushing Sawmill Brook infuse the forest as you drop into Sages Ravine. Hemlocks predominate as the trail finishes the descent to the crystalline stream and reaches the junction for Sages Ravine Campsite (6.8/1,550), located on the opposite side of the stream and accessible via a log bridge. Past the campsite, the trail travels adjacent to the rushing brook as it sluices downward. Look closely and you may spot brook trout in the stream's crystalline pools. A few holes are large enough for a refreshing dip.

A series of tumbling tributaries feed Sawmill Brook; one picturesque flow falls 8 feet directly into it. The canyon becomes increasingly gorge-like as the trail descends on wooden steps and soon rock-hops the brook. The ease or difficulty of fording the brook depends on the conditions. Past the crossing, the trail resumes climbing and quickly reenters a forest of beeches and oaks, punctuated by the appearance of young chestnut oaks. As the trail slowly curves north, it leaves the ravine behind on a steady traverse and reaches the junction for Laurel Ridge Campsite (8.7/1,710).

A short distance past Laurel Ridge, the sound of thundering Bear Rock Falls fills the forest. The former location of Bear Rock Falls Campsite is evident downslope to your right just before you cross Bear Rock Stream. A short distance below, the cascade pours 150 feet down in a sheet of foaming water. There is no good view of the cascades in their entirety; opt instead for the open views east from the rock ledge on the stream's northern edge.

Past Bear Rock Stream, the rocky trail begins climbing the long ridge of Mount Race. Grass grows in the less-traveled trail, and intermittent views peek through the trees to the right. After briefly topping out, the trail descends and then climbs to reach a dramatic open viewpoint. Here your route unfolds to the south, from the round dome of Bear Mountain to Lion's Head. Most remarkable are the sheer escarpments of the plateau's east edge, now visible soaring above MA 41 below.

The trail winds along the rocky edge of a cliff, offering continuous views east. Traveling over exposed bedrock, the trail also looks north to the distinctive profile of Mount Greylock and beyond to the distant mountains of southern Vermont. Head-high pitch pines appear, intermixed with extensive ground-hugging blueberry bushes. Ascend a gray quartz-streaked hunk of schist—it feels like scrambling up an arching whale's back—and pass a large rock cairn just before reaching the true summit of Mount Race (10.5/2,365/ 42° 04.936′ N, 73° 25.921′ W).

From the summit, the humping hulk of Mount Everett comes into view. (It is often described as the state's second highest mountain, though technically some of the sub-peaks on Mount Greylock are higher.) Vistas west also open up, and Alander Mountain and Mount Frissell dimple the terrain. Take time to also look beneath your feet. The striations in the rock running against the grain of the rock bands were left by the glaciers as they ground over and rounded off these peaks.

From the summit, the trail drops back into the trees, leaving pitch pines behind, and makes a mellow descent to the boggy saddle between Mounts Race and Everett. Entering a grove of stately hemlocks, the trail encounters trickling Race Brook and Race Brook Trail (11.6/1,920). To descend to Race Brook Falls Campsite, bear right and follow the triangular blue blazes through a hummocky hemlock forest for 0.4 mile (farther than the 0.2 mile indicated by the sign). From there, you can descend 750 feet to visit the trail's namesake series of falls. There are two cascades. The upper falls shoot through a narrow seam, splattering on a large boulder field. The lower falls pour down in a curtain of spray into a field of car-sized rocks.

Back on the AT, start your ascent of Mount Everett. The rocky trail becomes progressively steeper and soon begins following solid bedrock through a more stunted forest. The surrounding trees steadily shrink in stature and intermittent views begin looking south toward the peaks behind you. To the west, spot structures on the shore of nearby Plantain Pond. The trail moderates as it approaches the top, entering dense 10-foot-high woods before emerging on the shrubby summit (12.3/2,602/42° 06.118′ N, 73° 25.961′ W).

The concrete footings of an old fire tower pock the summit, cloaked with small mountain ashes and gray birches. Bear right to continue on the AT. Descending, the trail quickly reaches an open ledge with views east and north to Mount Greylock. Slabbing downward, the trail passes several more open views east and then curves north to cross a wide unmarked trail. From here, the rocky forest transforms into a world of black and yellow birches with a glowing understory of ferns. The AT crosses the old dirt service road to the summit, cuts left, and then descends to emerge at a grassy field and picnic area (13.0/2,100).

The Mount Everett Road was closed for many years, but recently reopened on a seasonal basis to provide access to the picnic area here, complete with barbecue pits, picnic tables, and a privy. From here, the AT bears right along a wide woods road and reaches Guilder Pond Trail on the left (13.1/2,080). Plastic blue triangles indicate the route of this side trip as it makes a 0.8-mile loop around the lake and passes some good swimming spots on the northeastern shore.

Back on the AT, you travel on a wide, level path beneath hemlocks and soon reach an east-flowing stream. Descending, the path reaches the junction for the Hemlocks Shelter at the bottom of a long staircase (13.4/1,950). The AT crosses the brook and immediately encounters the spur for Glen Brook Shelter on the right (13.5/1,940). Beyond this point, the trail feels considerably less traveled as it winds downhill through young forest and reaches the junction with Elbow Trail on the right (14.1/1,800), which descends east to reach a trailhead at the Berkshire School.

Continuing north, the AT passes through dense forest and past mountain laurels. After a brief climb, the trail winds along the rocky ledges of Mount Bushnell, which offer occasional views east and north. Zigzagging along a rocky spine, pass through a continuous pitch pine community, and reach a good vista south from the top of Mount Bushnell (14.6/1,834). To the west, radio towers atop Mount Darby can be spotted beyond the watershed of Fenton Brook. Mount Everett is visible to the south, and views northeast look toward the broad rise of East Mountain State Forest and the continuing route of the AT.

Sporadic views continue as you proceed along the ledgy trail. At the end of the ridge, the first view entirely north opens up. From here, the trail drops steeply, making one last rise to a rock outcrop. The trail switches back right and steadily traverses downward past chestnut oaks, fern-coated rocks, and more views. A few final switchbacks lead to a level area and an enormous boulder. The nice dirt trail then slowly descends past a large clearing to emerge on Jug End Road and the end of your journey (16.9/860).

INFORMATION

Mount Everett State Reservation, c/o RD, 3 East Street, Mount Washington, MA 01258, 413-528-0330, mass.gov/eea/agencies/dcr/massparks/region-west/mt-everett-state-reservation-generic.html.

NEARBY

Nearby Bash Bish Falls, the highest single-drop waterfall in Massachusetts, makes for a pleasant post-trip visit in one of the state's most scenic and remote areas. The falls drop nearly 60 feet over bedrock and the site is accessible via a short walk. To reach it from the northern trailhead, return to Mount Washington Road, turn left, and continue for 8.0 miles (road becomes East Street). Turn right onto Cross Road, then right onto West Street, and continue for 1.0 mile. Turn left onto Falls Road, and follow it 1.5 miles to the trailhead parking lot on the left.

AMC's Northwest Camp is also located just off route, just northwest of the Bear Mountain summit. Maintained by the Connecticut Chapter, the cabin's six bunks and nearby tent platform are available for use year-round with a reservation. Visit ct-amc.org/nwcamp for more information, including current rates and use policies.

TRIP 9
MONROE STATE FOREST

Location: Monroe, MA
Difficulty: Moderate
Distance: 2.0 miles round-trip
Total Elevation Gain/Loss: 300 feet/300 feet
Trip Length: 1–2 days
Recommended Map: *Monroe State Forest Map* (Massachusetts Department of Conservation and Recreation)
Highlight: Old-growth forest.

Dunbar Brook flows through some of the most isolated terrain in Massachusetts. Steep, boulder-pocked slopes rise above the stream as it drops into the deep gorge of the Deerfield River. Loggers could not penetrate the topography and today Monroe State Forest boasts some of the finest old-growth forest in southern New England.

HIKE OVERVIEW

The route journeys up Dunbar Brook Trail, winding along the slopes and waters of its namesake stream. The Dunbar Brook Shelter is located within a mile of the trailhead near the stream. Two other shelters—Ridge and Smith Hollow—can be found higher up on the forest slopes. The area is lightly used, and crowds tend to be minimal. Campfires are permitted. This hike is likely to pack in a bigger adventure than its distance might indicate. In general, Monroe State Forest receives little maintenance due to its light visitation; check in with the park for an update on current conditions before heading out.

Monroe State Forest's more than 4,000 acres and 9.0 miles of trails straddle an ecological divide between northern and southern New England. The resulting diversity is remarkable. Nearly every tree in New England is represented, from balsam fir, red spruce, yellow and paper birch, and striped maple—more common farther north and at higher elevations—to big-tooth aspen, black birch, white ash, and red oak, more frequent in southern regions and lower elevations. Hemlocks, beeches, and red and sugar maples complete the forest mosaic. These woods are a haven for wildlife, including moose and bear. But most remarkable of all is the 150 acres of old-growth forest.

In 2011, Hurricane Irene significantly damaged many of the established trails. The route to the Dunbar Brook Shelter is still passable, but prepare for

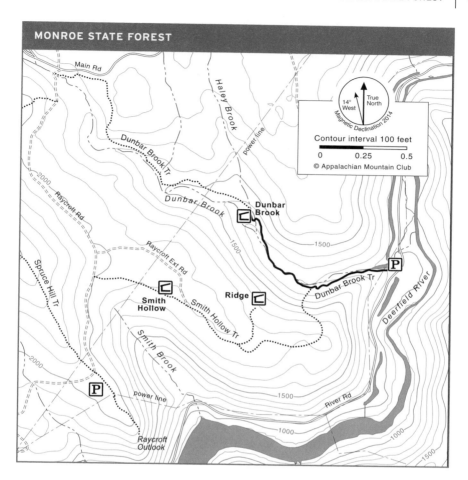

potentially rough conditions. There is no bridge across the brook; crossing may not be possible during periods of heavy rain and high water—and some route-finding may be required. Other sections of trail, including Smith Hollow Trail, have since been rerouted—a process that may still be ongoing.

OVERNIGHT OPTIONS

Camping is permitted only at Monroe's three designated shelters. All overnight sites are free and first-come, first-served; no registration is required.

Dunbar Brook Shelter (1.0/1,280/42° 42.456′ N, 72° 58.168′ W) is situated between Dunbar and Haley brooks in peaceful forest, washed by stereophonic stream sounds. An old cellar hole can be found nearby. Haley Brook is more accessible, but you can also reach bouldery Dunbar Brook via a steep slope. At least one pool is deep enough for a refreshing sit-and-soak.

Ridge Shelter (1,700/42° 41.982′ N, 72° 58.185′ W) perches up the valley slopes on what is now (post-Irene) a dead-end spur trail from Raycroft Extension Road. Small and dilapidated, the shelter is located in quiet hemlock forest next to a thin trickle of water. A fire ring is available.

Smith Hollow Shelter (1,750/42° 42.001′ N, 72° 58.797′ W) is located in the adjacent Smith Brook watershed, approximately 2 miles from the trailhead. The small, shaded facility is little-used. A seasonal water source sometimes runs near the shelter. Strongly consider bringing enough water with you, however, since no other nearby water source is available during dry periods. A fire ring and privy are also present.

TO REACH THE TRAILHEAD

Follow MA 2 to the Deerfield River crossing, 1.5 miles west of the MA 2/8A South junction. Head north on Zoar Road, which splits off MA 2 on the east side of the Deerfield River bridge and later turns into River Road. In 2.5 miles, turn left to remain on River Road at its junction with Rowe Road. After crossing under railroad tracks, continue 8.7 miles to the Dunbar Brook trailhead (42° 42.263′ N, 72° 57.154′ W), which abruptly appears on the left. Look for the Dunbar Brook Trail sign, posted by USGen New England.

HIKE DESCRIPTION

From the trailhead parking lot (0.0/1,050), begin up the dirt road on the left. After walking approximately 50 yards, bear right to follow the single-track trail. It enters shady forest and passes the scaly bark of a black cherry tree on the left. Marked by blue blazes and plastic skier signs, the narrow trail passes above the dammed waters of Dunbar Brook then enters a stately grove of large hemlock trees. The plate-sized leaves of hobblebush—ubiquitous farther north but unusual here in Massachusetts—appear in the understory.

Dunbar Brook soon comes alive below in rushing flow. The arcing branches of yellow birches frame the broad stream as it tumbles over boulders. A large ash soon appears, marking the edge of the old-growth stand. Keep an eye on the right for the deep, furrowed bark of two large big-toothed aspens, their brain-like bark a marked contrast to the smooth boles of younger trees.

The trail descends toward the creek, passing trillium, striped maples, and sarsaparillas in the understory, reaching unposted Smith Hollow Trail on the left (0.6/1,170). The blue blazes continue left and uphill on Smith Hollow Trail (see later), but stay right to remain near the creek.

At this point, the route may become indistinct. A bridge once crossed Dunbar Brook a short distance upstream from this point, but it was washed away

A hiker takes the Monroe State Forest challenge. (Photo courtesy of Kim Foley
MacKinnon)

in 2011 by Hurricane Irene. Before you cross, consider exploring the woods
upstream and upslope from this point. Some of the forest's most dramatic
trees grow on the boulder-pocked slopes, including huge sugar maples and
the state-champion white ash. Trees of all ages grow overhead throughout,
predominantly ashes, sugar maples, and beeches.

Cross the creek at a safe spot, and relocate Dunbar Brook Trail, which continues near the waterway for roughly the next 0.25 mile. Upstream, find the
journey's first white pine, an impressive specimen roughly 2.5 feet in diameter.
White pines are common today throughout New England, largely because of
their tendency to proliferate in abandoned fields. Shade-intolerant, they more
commonly grow in the sunny openings along streams and rivers found in set-
tings like these. Passing another enormous white pine, the trail ascends the
slopes beneath numerous paper birches. Approaching Haley Brook, bear left
at an unsigned fork to rock-hop across it (or potentially ford it, depending on
conditions). Just beyond is Dunbar Brook Shelter (1.0/1,280).

SIDE TRIP TO DUNBAR BROOK TRAIL

After setting up camp, tour some of the forest's other trails. Dunbar Brook Trail continues another 1.8 miles past the shelter to the forest's northern entrance at Raycroft Road. A round-trip from the shelter includes 700 feet of elevation gain and loss. En route, it passes more massive white pines near a power-line corridor, visits bulging boulders, and then emerges at unpaved Raycroft Road, where Dunbar Brook races through a series of small cascades below large rock slabs.

SIDE TRIP TO SMITH HOLLOW AND RIDGE SHELTERS

At the unposted junction with Smith Hollow Trail (0.6/1,170) follow the blue blazes uphill. The trail makes a broad, ascending S-curve, crossing a few small streams and traveling over rocks before reaching unpaved Raycroft Extension Road along a broad ridgeline.

Follow along the road and pass a smaller, unsigned woods road on the right, which leads to Ridge Shelter in a half-mile of easy walking. Remain on Raycroft Extension Road to continue to Smith Hollow Shelter, passing second-growth red oaks of considerable stature. Bear left 0.4 mile past the junction to Ridge Shelter—watch for the offset blue blazes—and proceed straight on a ski trail to an unmarked junction. Bear left for Smith Hollow Shelter, 0.3 mile from Raycroft Extension Road.

INFORMATION

Monroe State Forest, Tilda Hill Road, Monroe, MA 01350, 413-339-5504 (Mohawk State Forest), mass.gov/eea/agencies/dcr/massparks/region-west/monroe-state-forest-generic.html.

NEARBY

The eastern entrance to the Hoosac Tunnel is approximately 4 miles south of the trailhead near River Road and the big bend in the Deerfield River. This 4.75-mile tunnel cuts westward through the Hoosac Range to emerge in North Adams. At the time of its completion (1875), it was the second-longest tunnel in the world. Nearly 200 people died during its construction, earning it the moniker of "The Bloody Pit." Many consider it to be one of New England's most haunted sites.

TRIP 10
MOUNT GREYLOCK STATE RESERVATION

Location: Williamstown, MA
Difficulty: Challenging
Distance: 11.0 miles round-trip
Total Elevation Gain/Loss: 3,050 feet/3,050 feet
Trip Length: 1–2 days
Recommended Map: *AMC Massachusetts Trail Map; Map 1: Northern Berkshires* (AMC Books)
Highlight: The highest mountain in Massachusetts.

In the rolling hillscape of western Massachusetts, 3,491-foot Mount Greylock stands alone, an isolated massif carved by deep valleys and awash with diverse flora. A loop around the peak, from base to summit, offers an experience of the full range of the mountain, including mature forest, spattering waterfalls, and soaring vistas.

HIKE OVERVIEW

The hike makes a complete circuit of the mountain. From the mountain's west base, you enter a broad ravine known as the Hopper, which scoops deeply into the west flanks of the mountain. The journey travels along a burbling stream, climbs among massive red oaks, passes the 60-foot cascade of Money Brook Falls, and then reaches Wilbur Clearing Shelter near the summit ridge. Here you join the Appalachian Trail (AT) as it follows a wooded ridgeline over the developed summit, passing several side trails that plummet eastward to reach two additional overnight options: Bellows Pipe and Gould Brook shelters. The journey then returns to the Hopper and passes near Mount Greylock Hike-in Campground before descending to the trailhead through a magnificent forest of sugar maples and white ashes. Dogs are permitted, but must be leashed at trailheads, the summit, and in the hike-in campground.

OVERNIGHT OPTIONS

Camping is permitted only at designated shelters, the Mount Greylock Hike-in Campground, and in a dispersed camping area near the Hopper trailhead. The shelters and dispersed camping area are free, operate on a first-come, first-served basis, and all feature tentsites. Reservations are required for the hike-in campground from Memorial Day through Columbus Day weekend; a

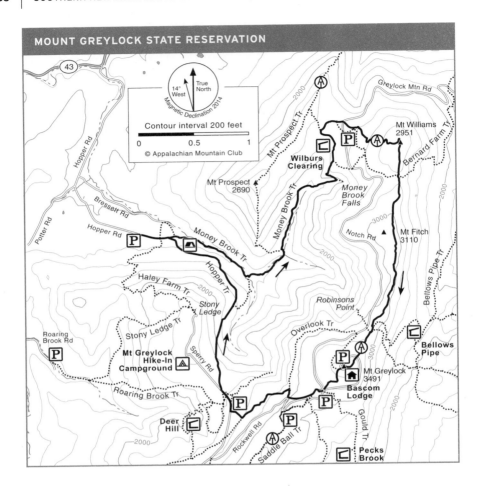

MOUNT GREYLOCK STATE RESERVATION

Contour interval 200 feet

0   0.5   1

© Appalachian Mountain Club

camping fee is also required. Campfires are permitted only at the designated fire rings in front of the shelters. The popularity of the sites varies markedly, based largely on their distance from the AT.

Hopper Brook Dispersed Camping Area (0.3/1,100/42° 39.292′ N, 73° 11.776′ W) is composed of several large, grassy fields, which provide excellent tenting close to Hopper Brook. The area allows for an evening arrival and an early start on the trail the next morning. The location is lightly used, sites are abundant, and no reservation or registration is required. Camping is limited to only one night. No campfires are permitted. A privy is available.

Wilbur Clearing Shelter (3.3/2,200/42° 40.088′ N, 73° 10.195′ W) is the first lean-to encountered on this hike. The surrounding forest is grand, with mature yellow birches and red oaks adjacent to the shelter, and large sugar maples interspersed throughout. Four tent platforms, plus several additional tentsites, provide camping space. Water is easily accessible from an adjacent brook, a bear box is available for overnight food storage (use it!), and a privy is nearby. Located only 0.2 mile from the AT, the shelter receives heavy use, especially during thru-hiker season in midsummer.

Bellows Pipe Shelter (7.4/2,250/42° 38.642′ N, 73° 09.121′ W). Located 7.4 miles from the trailhead along Bellows Pipe Trail at 2,250 feet, this shelter sits on Greylock's east side. Accessing the shelter requires leaving the AT and descending 1,000 feet in 1.1 mile, but its distance from the main hiking thoroughfare means that it's much less used. The basic structure sits in a pleasant maple-ash forest with an adjacent stream your water source. An ample number of level sites surround the area for camping. A night here adds 2.2 miles to the journey.

Pecks Brook Shelter (8.3/2,400/42° 37.484′N, 73° 09.907.284′ W) necessitates a 1.0-mile detour from Gould Trail 700 feet down the mountainside. Located near its namesake stream, which features a thin nearby waterfall, the shelter area features good tentsites in shady forest.

Mount Greylock Hike-in Campground (8.5/2,400/42° 37.950′ N, 73° 11.259′ W) is a developed camping area sitting high along the ridge that hems in the Hopper to the south. The nearest parking area is 1.3 miles away, which makes this a pleasant and tranquil camping experience. Fifteen tentsites (four-person maximum) and seven group sites (twelve-person maximum) are available for year-round use. Water is available from nearby Roaring Brook. Reservations are required from Memorial Day through Columbus Day weekend; a camping fee applies (reserveamerica.com).

TO REACH THE TRAILHEAD

Take MA 43 south from its junction with MA 2 in central Williamstown. In 2.4 miles, turn left onto Hopper Road at a distinctive rock bridge. Remain on Hopper Road as it forks left in 1.3 miles and becomes a moderately rough dirt road (still easily navigated by low-clearance vehicles). A parking area (42° 39.337′ N, 73° 12.284′ W) is located 0.8 mile farther at road's end across from a picturesque barn.

HIKE DESCRIPTION

From the kiosk at the head of the parking area (0.0/1,090), look for the wooded summit of 2,690-foot Mount Prospect rising over the barn; your route climbs below its east flanks. Heading out, Hopper Trail follows an old road through a farm gate and alongside open fields, passing a gnarled basswood tree on the right just before crossing through a second gate. Signs soon welcome you to the Hopper, and the trail follows a classic woods road flanked by stone walls and lined with sugar maples and black cherry trees. Continue straight as Haley Farm Trail splits right, followed quickly by Hopper Loop Trail on the left (0.1/1,130).

The level fields here are situated on old lake terraces. As the glaciers of the last Ice Age retreated northward roughly 10,000 years ago, a large body of water known as Bascom Lake briefly filled the valleys west and north of Greylock. Sediment deposited along its ancient shoreline created level terraces that today ring the slopes at roughly 1,100 feet. At the head of the last field, Hopper Trail (your return route) splits right (0.2/1,130). Continue straight on the blue-blazed Money Brook Tail.

The path leaves the terrace behind for steeper topography and descends to reach the Hopper Brook Dispersed Camping Area (0.3/1,100). Numerous woods roads crisscross the young forest here; the forest's age is indicative of its recent agricultural past. A grassy field on the left boasts an old snag-top sycamore tree near its edge, recognized by its distinctive mottled bark and large leaves. Pass two more camping fields (the second sports an outhouse), reenter shady forest, and descend to Hopper Brook.

The trail winds through young northern hardwood forest, running parallel to the creek as both a woods road and single-track path. The shallow brook offers a few waist- to chest-deep pools for a quick soak. After crossing Money Brook, a tributary of Hopper Brook, you reach Cutoff Trail to the Hike-in Campground and the Hopper Trail on the right (1.1/1,250). Remain on Money Brook Trail as it begins a steady climb, passing several nice hemlocks and rock-hopping two small creeks.

Watch for the first appearance of hobblebushes along this section, a low-lying shrub with dinner plate–sized leaves. Ubiquitous in northern New England, it is relatively uncommon in Massachusetts. The trail crosses Money Brook on a more challenging rock-hop, passes Mount Prospect Trail on the left (1.7/1,430), and then ascends above the stream course on a rising traverse.

At this point, your journey cuts through mature red oak forest. As a young tree, a red oak grows at roughly the same rate as other tree species. But most trees grow more slowly upon reaching heights of around 40 feet. Red oak trees, however, continues to grow vigorously, forming an umbrella-like canopy above the mature forest and sometimes attaining heights of 80 feet or more. Red oaks are readily identified by their leathery lobed spiny-tipped leaves, furrowed bark, and a distinctive reddish tinge that often appears in the cracks of the bark. Though common in southern New England, red oaks rarely occur in such mature stands, or predominate as dramatically as they do here.

The trail makes a brief but steep drop to cross a rushing tributary, heads up the increasingly narrow gorge, and encounters the spur to Money Brook Falls on the right (2.8/1,950). A signed, short 100-yard side trip leads to the falls.

Continuing, Money Brook Trail steadily traverses upward and then switchbacks right to briefly climb along a ridgeline. The gradient eases, passes a cutoff trail to nearby Notch Road on the right (3.2/2,190), and encounters the short spur to Wilbur Clearing Shelter (3.3/2,220).

Continuing, Money Brook Trail winds beneath stately red spruces, which rise overhead straight as arrows. These woods are one of the most southerly examples of spruce-fir forest in New England. Large snags on the forest floor indicate the forest's age and maturity. The route meets the AT (3.5/2,270); its white blazes head off in both directions.

The route turns right (south on the AT toward Georgia), but for one of the mountain's better views, you should drop your pack and briefly head left. This side trip quickly ascends 220 feet to the shoulder of Mount Prospect, where an open ledge looks north and west. To the west, the long ridge of the Taconics traces along the New York–Massachusetts border. North, the rolling rise of Vermont's Glastenbury Mountain (Trip 11) marks the horizon as the second peak visible north. The pastoral landscape of Williamstown lies below.

Back at the earlier junction, head north on the AT through young spruce forest. Cross paved Notch Road (3.6/2,330), and continue past a spur on the right that leads to a nearby day-use parking area. The AT now ascends Mount Williams, making several switchbacks before turning directly uphill to attain the summit (4.5/2,951/42° 40.098′ N, 73° 9.497′ W).

Continuing north, travel through a forest of twisted beeches and yellow birches that obscures all views. Descending to the saddle between Mount Williams and Mount Fitch, the trail encounters a four-way junction (4.7/2,780); right leads to Notch Road, and Bernard Farm Trail descends to the left to meet Notch Road.

Remain on the AT as it winds among thick and crusty yellow birches, stunted by the elements to heights no greater than 30 feet. After gently rising over Mount Fitch (5.5/3,110), you reach a restricted view east—the only vista on the AT between the summits of Williams and Greylock.

After traveling through a corridor of young spruces, you next reach Bellows Pipe Trail (6.3/3,080). To reach Bellows Pipe Shelter (7.4/2,250), turn left here and plummet 800 feet down Bellows Pipe Trail in 1.1 miles. The route follows a wide, curving ski trail, leveling out near the bottom as it passes nice hardwoods at the base of an overgrown field.

Continue on the AT, immediately passing adjoining Thunderbolt Ski Trail. Built in the early 1930s, Thunderbolt Ski Trail was once considered the most difficult ski run in the country and was the site of numerous races during the first half of the twentieth century. For a sense of its severe slopes, which have a maximum gradient of 35 degrees, follow Thunderbolt Trail a short distance to the top of its first major drop.

Past this junction, the AT quickly reaches a signed spur to Notch Road and Robinson's Point, a worthwhile 0.3-mile side trip. The trail drops 300 feet down a narrow path to reach a protruding boulder, which offers deep views into the northern section of the Hopper. The rounded summit of Mount Prospect is visible to the northwest.

Heading back south on the AT, a wide blackberry-lined trail corridor soon ascends to the developed summit area (6.8/3,480/42° 38.246′ N, 73° 09.967′ W). Take some time to wander around the maze of roads, paths, parking areas, and pavement that crown the peak. Rest inside the nearby Thunderbolt Cabin Warming Hut, built in 1934 by the Civilian Conservation Corps. Check out the myriad viewpoints in the area, many of which include signs identifying landmarks along the skyline. Climb up the War Memorial for a 360-degree view. Stop in at Bascom Lodge to warm up and buy some snacks.

Once you've had your fill of humanity, continue south on the AT, crossing the road once again and passing a humming building below the radio tower. After a steep, rocky drop through spruce-fir forest, the trail emerges at a three-way road intersection (7.3/3,200). Gould Trail splits left from the far side to descend to the Pecks Brook Shelter (8.3/2,400), but your continuing route on the AT crosses the intersection and bears right as it reenters the woods. Pass by a small pond and old pump house and reach Hopper Trail (7.5/3,150).

Bear right onto Hopper Trail, which continues to the trailhead. The forest quickly transitions back to yellow birches and beeches and passes Cheshire Harbor Trail on the left. Wide and rocky, Hopper Trail briefly parallels the road above, touches it momentarily, and then curves right to pass Overlook Trail on the right (7.7/2,900).

Traversing downward, the trail crosses several rivulets, passes Deer Hill Trail on the left (8.2/2,630), and then drops to reach unpaved Sperry Road (8.3/2,470). Turn right and follow Sperry Road 0.1 mile to March Cataract Trail on the right, which leads to its thin namesake falls in 0.8 mile. Just beyond on the right is the well-signed turn-off for Hopper Trail.

If you are spending the night at the hike-in campground—or just want to savor the excellent view from Stony Ledge at road's end—continue straight on Sperry Road to the camping area (8.5/2,400). Otherwise, follow Hopper Trail as it traverses downward and passes through magnificent forest. Calcium-rich outcrops have enriched the soils here, and humanity has barely disturbed the forest for more than a century. The result is a large, beautiful, and mature forest of sugar maples and white ashes, joined by impressive red oaks and occasional basswood trees.

Hopper Trail passes Cutoff Trail to Money Brook Trail on the right (9.4/1,600) and then curves to the west. The gradient eases and before long the forest abruptly diminishes in size and age. Invasive barberry plants line the trail corridor, which soon becomes a woods road and winds around a field to reach the junction with Money Brook Trail (10.8/1,130). Turn left and return to the trailhead (11.0/1,090).

INFORMATION

Mount Greylock State Reservation, P.O. Box 138, Lanesborough, MA 01237, 413-499-4262, mass.gov/dcr/parks/mtGreylock.

NEARBY

For something completely different, stop in North Adams to visit the Massachusetts Museum of Contemporary Art (MOCA), one of the country's largest and most renowned centers for contemporary visual and performing arts (413-662-2111, massmoca.org).

2
VERMONT

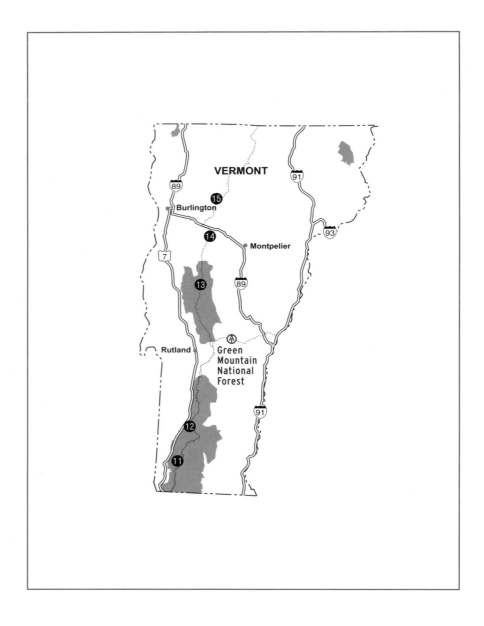

TRIP 11
GLASTENBURY MOUNTAIN WILDERNESS

Location: Woodford, VT; southern Green Mountain National Forest
Difficulty: Challenging
Distance: 22.7 miles round-trip
Total Elevation Gain/Loss: 4,700 feet/4,700 feet
Trip Length: 2 days
Recommended Map: *The Long Trail Guide* (Green Mountain Club)
Highlight: The most remote summit in the Green Mountains.

**Deep in the southern Green Mountains, 3,748-foot Glastenbury
Mountain rises above a vast sea of uninterrupted woodland. A fire
tower crowns the summit, offering 360-degree views over some of
Vermont's wildest terrain. Miles of easy-cruising solitude surround
it. But to reach the peak, you've got to earn it.**

HIKE OVERVIEW

The counter-clockwise loop along the southern ridges of Glastenbury Mountain is, in many ways, a tale of two very different trails. The first half follows
the Long Trail, a well-trod, popular path. Return via little-used West Ridge
Trail, a remote, quiet, and beautiful section that culminates with a remarkable view atop white-topped Bald Mountain. The summit and nearby Goddard Shelter are located at the hike's midpoint, neatly dividing the hike into
two days. A 1.7-mile road walk separates the starting and ending trailheads.
Campfires and dogs are permitted.

OVERNIGHT OPTIONS

Dispersed camping is permitted throughout this hike, and numerous potential
sites appear along the level terrain. Water is scarce, however—the hike travels
almost entirely along dry ridgelines. The only reliable sources are located near
the beginning of the hike (at the trailhead, Melville Nauheim Shelter, and Hell
Hollow Brook), and adjacent to Goddard Shelter.

Melville Nauheim Shelter (1.6/2,450/42° 53.271′ N, 73° 05.731′ W) is
surrounded by extensive blackberry bushes. The basic eight-person shelter
features four double sleeping platforms and a nice nearby tenting area. Fire
rings, a picnic table, and privy are available. Water is available nearby, though
a filter may be necessary to collect it from seasonally thin trickles.

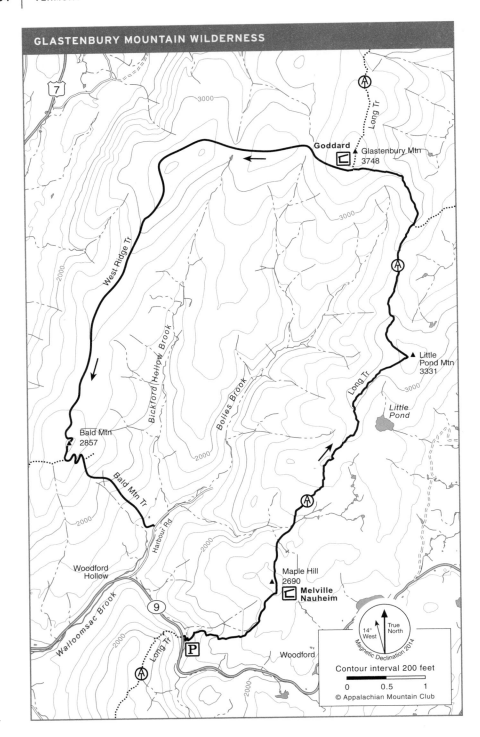

GLASTENBURY MOUNTAIN WILDERNESS

Goddard Shelter (10.1/3,560/42° 58.454′ N, 73° 04.329′ W), renovated by the Green Mountain Club in 2005, features a covered front porch, sleeps up to twelve, and perches in an open clearing that offers views south to distant Mount Greylock. An adjacent spring is reliable. Several tentsites are located along the Long Trail just north of the shelter.

TO REACH THE TRAILHEAD

These trailheads are less than two miles apart, offering the opportunity to either establish a shuttle or to walk the road between them.

To reach the Bear Wallow/Bald Mountain (ending) trailhead, follow VT 9 west past the Route 8/9 junction in Searsburg for 10 miles, then turn right onto unpaved Harbour Road. Proceed 0.7 mile to a large round, black water tank, located adjacent to a private residence. Park on the grass to the left of the driveway (42° 54.406′ N, 73° 07.394′ W). The posted trailhead is located about 50 yards up the driveway on the left.

To reach the starting trailhead, return to the intersection of Harbour Road and VT 9 and backtrack east 1.0 mile. The trailhead is located on the left; keep an eye out for the hiker sign (42° 53.116′ N, 73° 06.934′ W). Approaching from the west, the trailhead is located 5 miles from the Route 7/9 intersection in downtown Bennington.

HIKE DESCRIPTION

From the trailhead (0.0/1,400), head out on the Long Trail past a large information sign. Blackberry canes and thimbleberry vines line the trail, which passes a privy in front of a large aspen. The route briefly follows rocky City Stream and then crosses it on the William D. MacArthur footbridge. A few streamside tentsites can be found on the far side. Head upstream, hiking parallel to the creek beneath red maples, beeches, and striped maples.

The route turns uphill on a rocky path and ascends slabs and steps. The trail switchbacks twice and climbs through a young forest punctuated by sugar maples and a few older yellow birch trees—one striking specimen sprouts two enormous burls from its trunk. The trail switchbacks right, straightens, and passes two enormous boulders split in half. The diamond-patterned trunks of white ash join the forest mosaic as the trail traverses slowly upward. The route crosses two old woods roads and reaches a small stream and the spur to the Melville Nauheim Shelter (1.6/2,450), located a short distance uphill to the right.

From the intersection, the gradual ascent continues; a power-line corridor soon appears through the trees on your left, and after a short distance, the trail

The southern Green Mountains can be seen from the summit of Glastenbury Mountain. (Photo courtesy of Jennifer Lamphere Roberts)

crosses the open swath (1.9/2,610). The electric lines trace east toward 3,425-foot Haystack Mountain. The trail rises near the forested summit of Maple Hill and enters the Glastenbury Wilderness on a rocky descent. Mature yellow birches dot the forest. Drop past a trickling brook and make a level traverse to tumbling Hell Hollow Brook (3.2/2,350) and two small tentsites.

Cross the stream on a bridge, bear right, and slowly climb. The trail passes through sections of spruce-fir forest and travels across long stretches of bog bridging. The route attains the ridge, travels along the ridgeline, and reaches Porcupine Lookout, which offers a restricted view southeast (4.4/2,810). The distant Searsburg wind turbines are visible, smaller Hagar Hill is in the middle distance, and Haystack Mountain rises to the north. The campsite here doesn't have a water source.

The trail journeys along the ridge, passing numerous small campsites tucked in thick beech woods. The beech trees are heavily afflicted by the nectria fungus, which creates canker-like sores on their trunks, disrupts the tree's nutrient flow, weakens the trunk, and ultimately leads to the tree's demise.

Spruces, firs, and mountain ashes appear regularly above 3,000 feet. Pass some restricted views, including a glimpse of the rounded dome of Glastenbury Mountain and its prominent fire tower. As the route approaches the summit, it exits the Wilderness Area (8.7/2,900) and then curves left off the ridge to abruptly enter pure spruce-fir forest, one of the southernmost examples of this forest type in New England. After a steady, rising traverse, aided in places by nice rock steps, the trail levels and reaches a spring immediately before the Goddard Shelter (10.1/3,560).

Blue-blazed West Ridge Trail splits left from the far side of the shelter; the Long Trail continues uphill to the summit. Follow its white blazes up nice wooden steps past several campsites. A 50-foot tower crowns the summit of Glastenbury Mountain (10.4/3,748/42° 58.678′ N, 73° 04.292′ W), renovated in 2005 by the Green Mountain Club. Clamber up the metal staircase to the open-air lookout, but be prepared to linger—the view encompasses one of the largest contiguous swaths of wildland in Vermont.

First, look south over your approach route—the cradling arms of both the ascent ridge and returning West Ridge are visible. Spot the twin peak profile of Mount Greylock (Trip 10) in the distance; more of the Berkshire hills dimple the horizon beyond it.

Turn west to admire the rugged peaks of the Taconic Range, which parallel the Green Mountains. Just north of Glastenbury's West Ridge is West Mountain, separated from adjacent Grass Mountain by Dry Brook Hollow. Below Grass Mountain is the Batten Kill drainage; Red Mountain looms above the northern side of the watershed. Moving north, the deep cleft of Cook Hollow slices the west flank of 3,661-foot Mount Equinox—the highest peak in Vermont outside of the Green Mountains. (A keen eye can also spot the summit buildings.) Mount Aeolus and adjacent Owl's Head are the final Taconic peaks visible to the north. VT 7 separates the Taconics from the Green Mountains.

To the north, the Long Trail continues over hilly terrain toward Stratton Mountain, the prominent peak rising almost due north. The Lye Brook Wilderness (Trip 12) cascades down its flanks to the west. On the more distant northern horizon, Pico, Killington, and the south-facing ski trails of Bromley Mountain are all visible. To the northeast and east is Somerset Reservoir, the dammed headwaters of the Deerfield River. Haystack Mountain and the Searsburg wind turbines can be spotted southeast.

Wipe your chops clean after so much savory viewin' and return to the shelter (10.7/3,560). Head out on blue-blazed West Ridge Trail, which begins at the far (western) corner of the shelter. This lightly traveled path descends, reenters the Wilderness Area, and leaves spruce-fir forest to return among beech trees. The trail makes a long, level cruise, drops to cross an old woods road, and reaches a beaver pond in a boggy saddle (12.6/3,020).

The animals' effects are evidenced by the dead trees that protrude from the former pond area like drowned matchsticks. The trail skirts the shore to the north and, once beyond beaverland, crosses another woods road and curves around to the north side of the ridge. Old, scaly yellow birch punctuate this section, rising above thick blackberries and other dense undergrowth. Return to the ridge and steadily descend to a broad saddle. From here, the route slowly rises and falls over a highpoint along the ridge, passing several campsites (all lacking water sources) and a few restricted views west. Make a gradual ascent of Bald Mountain; a few switchbacks lead you to the summit (18.4/2,840/ 42° 55.339' N, 73° 08.623' W).

After so much continuous beech forest, the distinctive white rocks, scrubby evergreens, and prolific blueberries atop Bald Mountain are a refreshing change. The summit also offers the best views since Glastenbury Mountain, now visible to the north. To the south, look across southern Vermont to espy Mount Greylock and the northern Berkshires of Massachusetts. A large, open campsite with a fire ring is just north of the summit.

The trail descends 0.1 mile along the ridge and encounters Bald Mountain Trail, which heads right (southwest) down the mountain toward Bennington. Bear left to make the final journey to the trailhead. The trail immediately leaves the ridge, drops steeply via several switchbacks, and reaches the posted sign for Bear Wallow spring, a marginal water source located a short distance to your left.

The trail passes through thick spruce-fir stands sheltering an abundance of pink lady's slippers—blooming in late May and June—but the forest soon transitions back to hardwoods. After a steady and steep descent, cross a flowing creek in nice sugar maple forest, where the trail gradient eases. The trail turns sharply left and then follows a dirt road to emerge on Harbour Road (21.0/1,270). To return to your starting trailhead, turn right, walk downstream along the road for 0.7 mile to Route 9, turn left, and walk east for 1.0 mile along the highway (22.7/1,400).

INFORMATION
Green Mountain National Forest, Manchester Ranger District, 2538 Depot Street, Manchester, VT 05255, 802-362-2307, fs.usda.gov/greenmountain.

NEARBY
Downtown Bennington makes for a pleasant and scenic stop with excellent food and shopping opportunities. A short distance west of downtown, the striking 300-foot-high stone obelisk of Bennington Battle Monument also merits a visit. Constructed in the late nineteenth century, it commemorates the 1777 Battle of Bennington, a significant skirmish of the Revolutionary War.

TRIP 12
LYE BROOK WILDERNESS

Location: Manchester, VT; southern Green Mountain National Forest
Difficulty: Challenging
Distance: 14.8 miles round-trip
Total Elevation Gain/Loss: 2,500 feet/2,500 feet
Trip Length: 2 days
Recommended Map: *The Long Trail Guide* (Green Mountain Club)
Highlights: Streams, ponds, Prospect Rock, and the state's highest waterfall.

The 18,000-acre Lye Brook Wilderness perches atop a high-elevation plateau in the southern Green Mountains. Its west front drops steeply into the broad marble valley of Manchester. Century-old forest swathes the slopes, and lakes shimmer on the plateau. It is a classic Green Mountain destination and an outstanding hike in fall.

HIKE OVERVIEW

The hike loops through the west portion of the Wilderness. The journey first ascends Lye Brook Trail for 7.0 miles—past the state's highest waterfall Lye Brook Falls—to reach Bourn Pond and good camping options. The hike then heads north across flat terrain on Branch Pond Trail, reaching Douglas Shelter just before encountering the Long Trail. The route briefly follows the Long Trail to an open view from Prospect Rock and then follows a dirt road back down to pavement. A 1.4-mile road-walk returns you to the trailhead. Because this hike uses paths other than the Long Trail, it is much less traveled than other nearby areas. Some tricky stream crossings and several (very) boggy sections increase the hike's overall difficulty. Campfires are permitted.

OVERNIGHT OPTIONS

Dispersed camping is permitted throughout this hike. The terrain is often level, but the dense woods can make it difficult to find a good tentsite outside the three established overnight areas.

Bourn Pond Tenting Area (7.1/2,570/43° 06.202′ N, 73° 00.305′ W) features a large, open area for tenting, plus several nice sites along the pond's west and south shores; a privy is available. The South Bourn Pond Shelter appears on some older maps, but it burned down and no longer exists. Campfires are

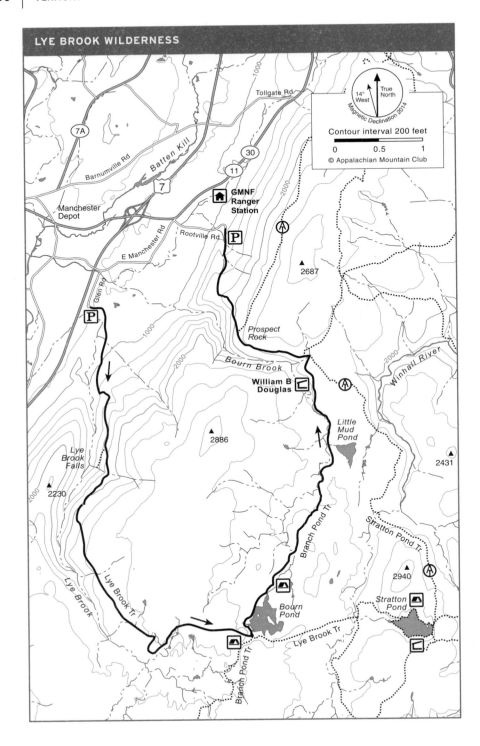

LYE BROOK WILDERNESS

Tollgate Rd

7A

30

11

7

Barnumville Rd

Batten Kill

Manchester
Depot

GMNF
Ranger
Station

E Manchester Rd

Rootville Rd

P

Glen Rd

2687

P

Prospect
Rock

Bourn Brook

William B
Douglas

Little
Mud
Pond

2886

2431

Lye
Brook
Falls

2230

Branch Pond Tr

Winhall River

Stratton Pond Tr

2940

Lye Brook Tr

Bourn
Pond

Stratton
Pond

Lye Brook Tr

Lye Brook

Branch Pond Tr

True
North

14°
West

Magnetic Declination 2014

Contour interval 200 feet

0   0.5   1

© Appalachian Mountain Club

permitted, and there is a large central fire ring for group gatherings. Water is available from the pond or a nearby stream.

North Bourn Tenting Area (7.6/2,560/43° 06.524′ N, 73° 00.211′ W) is located on Bourn Pond's northern shore. It features a large central area with a massive fire ring. Additional tentsites are scattered in the surrounding forest. Paths to the lake are few, though there's a nice overlook of the water at the main access point.

The William B. Douglas Shelter (10.5/2,230/43° 08.672′ N, 72° 59.451′ W) is located just before the junction of Branch Pond Trail with the Long Trail. Built in 1956, it was most recently renovated in 2005. A small spring reliably provides water; out-of-sight Bourn Brook also rushes audibly nearby. Young sugar maples shade the six-person shelter, which opens south for excellent midday sunshine. There are a few tenting areas in the nearby trees.

TO REACH THE TRAILHEAD

Take combined VT 11/30 east from Route 7 in Manchester for 2.0 miles to East Manchester Road. Turn right and follow East Manchester Road for 1.1 miles to Glen Road. Turn left, follow Glen Road about 100 feet, and then continue straight on the Lye Brook access road (signed), which dead-ends at the trailhead parking area (43° 09.541′ N, 73° 02.475′ W) in 0.4 mile.

HIKE DESCRIPTION

From the trailhead (0.0/800), strike out on posted Lye Brook Trail. The rocky double-track trail immediately reaches a five-way junction, where a brown arrow pointing left indicates the continuing route; a large red maple stands sentinel. Or, bear right here to access wide, tannin-soaked Lye Brook, which is shaded by the lacy branches of hemlocks. Access to the brook becomes difficult beyond this point.

The rocky route winds by black cherry trees—look for their dark, scaly bark—and levels out to begin its journey along a former railroad bed. Nearly all of the Lye Brook Wilderness was logged in the early twentieth century—most of this hike follows the old railroad beds used to extract timber.

Steep-cut banks hem-in the water below as the route parallels the brook and crosses into the Wilderness Area at a boundary sign (0.4/930). The trail rock-hops a flowing tributary, briefly becomes single-track as it makes a steep climb, and then returns to the railroad bed. The route makes a long, curving switchback left, and then gradually bears back right. Hemlocks, beeches, and red maples predominate in the surrounding hardwood forest, joined by occasional paper birches. The brook rushes below as the trail gently traverses across steep, boulder-pocked slopes and reaches the posted spur on the right for Lye Brook Falls (2.0/1,580/43° 08.245′ N, 73° 02.234′ W).

The side trip to the falls slowly descends a single-track path to emerge near the hissing base. On the nearby slopes, you can see a massive landslide caused by Hurricane Irene, which dropped as much as 7 inches of rain here over a two-day period in 2011. The multi-tiered Lye Brook Falls drops in a curtain of spray over sheer rock faces, a display of rushing droplets. The main upper fall is the tallest and most vertical; the waterfall in its entirety tumbles about 100 feet. Steep paths lead to multiple viewpoints—the best is located halfway up the falls.

Back on the main trail, continue steadily upward on the railroad bed, passing some large red maples. Roughly 0.3 mile past the falls junction, cross the stream that feeds it (2.3/1,850). The trail levels, crosses a few small brooks, and winds past tangles of hobblebushes. The trail soon resumes a steady ascent and then levels at 2,300 feet in a land of hobblebushes, paper birches, beeches, and endless red maples.

Next up is a stream crossing (3.5/2,470) that can be challenging in higher water. Once across, the rocky trail returns to single-track and makes a long, level cruise through damp hardwoods. In fall, it's a soft rainbow of color. The path becomes increasingly faint—watch closely for blazes—as you undulate along, crossing a small brook as you go. Then it abruptly enters spruce-fir forest.

Let the bog-hopping begin! The final section of Lye Brook Trail passes through an area that can be extremely swampy during wet periods. Slow, careful movement and delicate hops may be required to pass through without overtopping your boots. After the initial bog-hop, the trail crosses the marshy outflow of a nearby meadow and then curves around to cross the inflow as well. Pass a second meadow, bog-hop another section, and then briefly descend to the clearing for Bourn Pond Tenting Area and former site of the South Bourn Pond Shelter (7.1/2,570). A red maple is visibly charred, marking the location where the shelter burned down.

To continue, follow the signed directions to Branch Pond Trail, which bears right from the clearing and initially heads south before curving back at a flowing stream to head north on Branch Pond Trail. Cruising north, the trail follows a wide railroad bed before diverging on well-trod single-track, which curves around a boggy area and crosses two flowing brooks. Immediately past the second, on the right, is a lakeside campsite offering ready shore access and views across the water to Stratton Mountain and its summit fire tower. The lakeshore is generally sandy and muddy in spots, and swimming is a tempting possibility. A mix of evergreens and hardwoods ring the pond.

Continue onward. Another good campsite appears to your right, this one featuring marble rocks protruding from the shore. The wet trail passes a few more lake views before curving away from the water to reach the posted spur to the North Bourn Tenting Area (7.6/2,560) located a short distance away to the right.

Continuing, the easy-walking trail tours spruce-fir forest and encounters Bourn Brook, which drains the pond. Curve left onto the single-track and begin to parallel the out-of-sight stream. The railroad bed returns underfoot and slowly descends near the audible brook. Yellow and paper birch snags jut into the surrounding forest. Curve right off the railroad bed and gently drop to reach the brook. The stream crossing can vary from easy to exciting, depending on conditions, and you may wish for the bridge that used to be here, as evidenced by the small remaining footings.

Past the crossing, the route continues on a wide trail for a short distance, then makes a sharp turn left—watch for the double blaze—to descend through the woods on a narrow, rerouted section of trail. Return to the creek, now rockier and faster flowing; the rushing waters are now nearly river-like, with boulders protruding from a 10- to 20-foot-wide streambed. The route returns to the old railroad bed, which parallels the out-of-sight stream as it descends. Sugar maples slowly increase as you approach the William B. Douglas Shelter (10.5/2,230), located directly by the trail.

Past the shelter, continue on the railroad bed and immediately encounter the first quality puncheon of the hike—hooray! The trail now becomes more of an old road, lined with beeches and sugar maples. The going is easy over extensive puncheon, and you quickly reach the junction with the Long Trail/Appalachian Trail (AT) (11.1/2,310). This marks your departure from the Lye Brook Wilderness. Bear left onto the Long Trail to immediately cross a bridge over a small tributary. Turn left onto the opposite side to follow the route downstream; an arrow on a rusting machinery wheel indicates the way.

The wide trail soon begins journeying on an unpaved drivable road, which travels high above the rushing stream below. The easy-walking road steadily descends past sugar maples, beeches, black cherries, and red maples to reach a locked gate. White ashes have appeared as well—one to the left of the gate is marked with a blaze.

Soon thereafter, reach Prospect Rock (11.9/2,020), an open outcrop located to the left by an obvious clearing. From here, a grand view peers west and north. Below, Bourn Brook rushes out-of-sight through a deep ravine. Mount Equinox (3,672) and its neighboring peaks of the Taconic Range dominate the west horizon. Downtown Manchester is visible north, and the Valley of Vermont narrows as it recedes into the distance.

Just past Prospect Rock, the Long Trail/AT turns right off the road onto a narrower footpath, but remain on the road, which drops steeply. As you approach the bottom, the road begins a steep, quad-tensing drop next to a small stream on the right. Grayish-white marble boulders appear intermittently in the surrounding forest; they can be recognized by their lack of banding and tendency to fracture at right angles.

The road crosses the stream, the young forest becomes more lush, and hemlocks appear. Enter a small trailhead parking area (13.4/1,150), then curve sharply left to leave the woods and reach Rootville Road near a water tank and small grassy field.

To return to the trailhead, follow Rootville Road 0.6 mile down past several residences. Turn left onto Manchester Road, follow it 1.0 mile, and then turn left to return to the trailhead (14.8/800).

INFORMATION

Green Mountain National Forest, Manchester Ranger District, 2538 Depot Street, Manchester, VT 05255, 802-362-2307, fs.usda.gov/greenmountain.

NEARBY

For an exceptional view—which includes the forested landscape of Lye Brook Wilderness—drive to the top of 3,848-foot Mount Equinox via 5.2-mile Skyline Drive, a toll road that heads west from VT 7A south of Manchester Center. For more information, call 802-362-1114 or go to equinoxmountain.com.

TRIP 13
BREADLOAF WILDERNESS

Location: Lincoln, VT; northern Green Mountain National Forest
Difficulty: Challenging
Distance: 12.4 miles round-trip
Total Elevation Gain/Loss: 3,500 feet/3,500 feet
Trip Length: 1–2 days
Recommended Map: *The Long Trail Guide* (Green Mountain Club)
Highlight: Forested heart of the Green Mountains.

The Breadloaf Wilderness's 25,000 acres include 27 miles of the Long Trail and a chain of rugged 3,000-foot peaks. Views are precious in this forested region, but the streams, forests, trails, and shelters are a microcosm of the Green Mountains. Plus you'll likely enjoy long stretches of solitude; not many hikers travel these trails.

HIKE OVERVIEW

The hike uses Cooley Glen, Long, and Emily Proctor trails to loop clockwise around the headwaters of New Haven River near the center of the Wilderness Area. Along the way, visit melodious streams, climb over the Presidential summits of Mounts Cleveland (3,482), Roosevelt (3,550), and Wilson (3,790), and enjoy a few excellent views southeast. Dogs are permitted.

OVERNIGHT OPTIONS

The hike passes two shelters, each of which has adjoining tentsites. Dispersed camping is permitted throughout the hike, though finding a level location to pitch a tent is difficult at best. Campfires are permitted.

Cooley Glen Shelter (3.2/3,100/44° 02.989′ N, 72° 54.844′ W), a basic shelter surrounded by spruce-fir woods, is dark and has not been well treated by recent visitors. Several tentsites are nearby and offer a more pleasant overnight experience. A large fire ring sits in front of the shelter. Water is available at Cooley Spring, 100 feet down Cooley Glen Trail.

Emily Proctor Shelter (8.9/3,560/44° 00.086′ N, 72° 55.928′ W), similar to Cooley Glen, is tucked within spruce-fir forest and provides space for six people and a fire ring. A melodious stream flows adjacent to the site. Dispersed campsites nestle in nearby mossy areas and there are also two tent platforms located uphill on a surprisingly long spur trail.

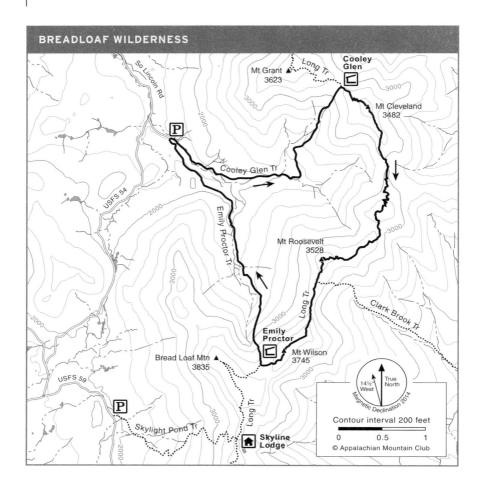

TO REACH THE TRAILHEAD

Follow VT 116 1.3 miles north of Bristol Village, and turn right onto Lincoln Road immediately after crossing the New Haven River. Proceed for 4.5 miles on Lincoln Road, which becomes West River Road, then River Road in the village of Lincoln, and then East River Road past town. Immediately after crossing the New Haven River, turn right onto unposted USFS 54/South Lincoln Road. Stay on the main road as you pass Ripton Road on the right, and then reach Grimes Road, where a large USFS sign directs you to stay left to reach Cooley Glen Trail, Emily Proctor Trail, and Breadloaf Wilderness via USFS 54. Continue 2.4 miles past this junction on USFS 54/South Lincoln Road, turn left onto unsigned USFS 201, and continue 0.4 mile to reach the trailhead and small parking area (44° 02.452′ N, 72° 57.191′ W).

HIKE DESCRIPTION

A sign by the trailhead (0.0/1,610) indicates Cooley Glen Trail leading off to the left; Emily Proctor Trail—your return route—comes in from the right. Head out on blue-blazed Cooley Glen Trail, which immediately narrows to single-track and parallels the New Haven River on the left. Over the next 3.0 miles, the route passes among hardwoods typical of New England's middle elevations (1,000 to 3,000 feet). Beeches and yellow birches are common, joined occasionally by sugar maples, black cherries, and balsam firs. The dinner-plate leaves of hobblebush fill the understory along with the distinctive lined bark of striped maples.

Past the trailhead sign, the trail skirts a gate and then turns right on a recently rerouted section that climbs over a small ridge before returning to the riverside. The bouldery streambed is readily accessible and offers numerous spots to relax. The path reaches a bridge over the river and a trail registry (0.4/1,710). From here, the route crosses the bridge, passes the posted Wilderness boundary, and winds near the river on a slow climb; some tantalizing swimming holes offer the opportunity for a quick soak along this section. After crossing several small streams, the trail travels on a small island between a stream and the main river and reaches the confluence of two equal-sized tributaries (1.4/2,020).

The trail rock-hops the north branch and follows the south fork to the right. The gradient increases and briefly parallels the creek before curving back left up a more sustained rise. Before the trail levels out, it passes limited views north toward Mount Grant. The route contours back into the corridor of the stream's north branch and leads past numerous large and mature yellow birches, including one monster specimen whose ponderous girth extends 30 feet off the ground before diminishing.

The trail steadily climbs, crosses the stream twice, and then passes a final trickle that marks the stream's headwaters—Cooley Spring. Here, the forest abruptly transitions to spruce-fir. Just ahead in the saddle is the white-blazed Long Trail (3.2/3,110).

Cooley Glen Shelter is located about 50 yards to the north, but your continuing journey heads south. It has been easy cruising up to this point, but the route abruptly transforms into a rocky trail challenge more typical of New England hiking, ascending steep rocks and a series of switchbacks to the wooded summit of Mount Cleveland (3.7/3,482).

The trail descends more easily down the other side and reaches a saddle (4.4/2,980). The route steepens and makes several long looping switchbacks to attain the summit of Peak 3348, also known as Little Hans Peak (5.4/3,348).

Down the far side, descend steadily via switchbacks that offer glimpses through the trees of the ridge ahead. The first and only water along the ridge is a dribbling rivulet in the next saddle.

A steep, traversing rise leads up the east flanks of the ridge, then crosses over to the west side. Occasional views look north. At one point, Mount Abraham becomes briefly visible to the north, located just north of Lincoln Gap and framed by Mounts Grant (left) and Cleveland (right). The path momentarily levels, then heads up over rock slabs and a ribbon of exposed bedrock to reach the trip's most dramatic view (6.8/3,550).

Perched just below the summit of Mount Roosevelt, enjoy unrestricted vistas south and southeast. To the south is Mount Wilson, the final peak of your ridge traverse. To the southeast, VT 100 runs through its creased valley, backed by the long, rounded spine of the Braintree Mountains and their highpoint, 2,750-foot Mount Cushman; beyond is the more distant hump of Mount Ascutney. On the horizon are the ski mountains of Pico (right) and Killington (left).

The trail drops steeply, passing signed Clark Brook Trail on the left (7.2/3,390). The path undulates through another saddle and begins a steady rise to the summit of Mount Wilson (8.0/3,790). A few glimpses west reveal the southern end of Lake Champlain. Near the summit, a spur trail leads left to another excellent view, similar to that of Roosevelt.

The trail drops toward the Emily Proctor Shelter, passing a spur to the tenting area shortly before reaching the lean-to (8.9/3,560). Emily Proctor Trail, your return route, joins here. Follow it away from the shelter and begin a steep, rocky drop, which tapers slowly to a mellow traverse.

The forest transitions from spruce-fir forest. Yellow birches appear first, followed by beeches and striped and sugar maples. The trail crosses several small brooks and becomes increasingly gentle, curving left along an old, level roadbed. This road likely provided access for selective logging activity. Note how more valuable sugar maples and conifers disappear near the road, leaving behind yellow birches and beeches.

The route parallels the creek below and descends to cross it above a confluence and a delightful swimming hole (10.2/2,020). The trail makes a level traverse, descending occasionally on nice rock staircases. The creek below curves away to the right, red maples appear in increasing abundance, and the occasional glimpse north reveals Mount Grant looming overhead. The trail becomes increasingly road-like and soon steadily descends to cross the posted Wilderness boundary. Near the end, pass a beautiful field of hay-scented ferns, bowing softly as they wish you farewell (12.4/1,610).

INFORMATION

Green Mountain National Forest, Middlebury Ranger District, 1007 Route 7, Middlebury, VT 05753, 802-388-4362, fs.usda.gov/greenmountain.

NEARBY

Bristol offers several good restaurants and cafes for a pre- or post-hike stop. For a post-hike dip, consider visiting the potholes along the lower New Haven River, which you can find where VT 116/17 crosses the river north of Bristol. They are beautiful, popular, and a little perilous—be careful!

TRIP 14
CAMEL'S HUMP STATE PARK

Location: Duxbury, VT
Difficulty: Challenging
Distance: 7.0 miles round-trip
Total Elevation Gain/Loss: 2,700 feet/2,700 feet
Trip Length: 1–2 days
Recommended Maps: *The Long Trail Guide* (Green Mountain Club), *Northern Vermont Hiking Trails* (Map Adventures)
Highlight: The highest never-developed peak in Vermont.

A hump of solid stone composes the 4,083-foot summit, tufted with a small patch of alpine tundra. Expansive views sweep across the state. A 20,000-acre protected landscape surrounds it. No structure has ever stood upon the summit, making it Vermont's highest undeveloped peak. It's a popular destination, but the scenery and views merit the crowds.

HIKE OVERVIEW

The hike ascends on Monroe and Dean trails, passing the Hump Brook Tenting Area midway up the mountain and the Montclair Glen Lodge on the ridgeline. Follow the Long Trail north, clamber over the rocky summit, and descend. Though it could be a day hike, spending the night makes this trip a more leisurely adventure and provides the opportunity to reach the summit before day-hikers arrive en masse. Dogs are permitted but must be leashed above treeline and at designated shelters and camping areas.

OVERNIGHT OPTIONS

Green Mountain Club caretakers collect an overnight per-person fee at both designated sites. Dispersed camping is permitted below 2,500 feet throughout the park, but must be at least 200 feet (75 adult paces) away from the any trail or water source; good sites are hard to find on the steep slopes.

Hump Brook Tenting Area (1.6/2,400/44° 18.575′ N, 72° 52.323′ W) spreads out beneath lush hardwoods and offers eight tent platforms on a first-come, first-served basis. The higher the site number, the quieter the spot. Sites 1 to 3 sit close to the entrance and each other, but have the only permitted fire ring.

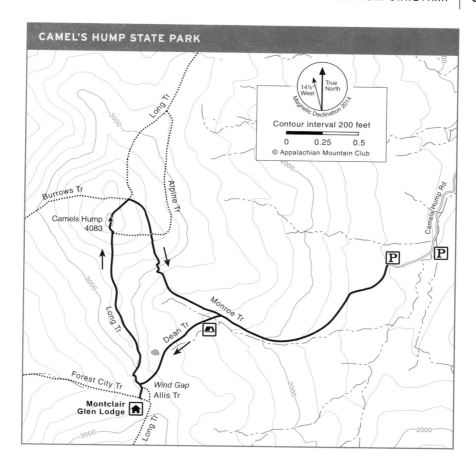

CAMEL'S HUMP STATE PARK

True North

14½° West

Magnetic Declination 2014

Contour interval 200 feet

0   0.25   0.5

© Appalachian Mountain Club

Long Tr

Alpine Tr

Burrows Tr

Camels Hump
4083

Long Tr

Monroe Tr

Dean Tr

Camels Hump Rd

P   P

Forest City Tr

Wind Gap
Allis Tr

Montclair
Glen Lodge

(Fires are prohibited at other sites.) Hump Brook provides water and soothing lullabies. A bear line is available for hanging food.

Montclair Glen Lodge (2.5/2,770/44° 18.064′ N, 72° 52.981′ W), built in 1948, is a small cabin with tables and bunks for a maximum of twelve hikers. A nearby brook provides reliable water. The shelter is busy during the July and August thru-hiking season, but otherwise often has space. There are also a few campsites nearby. No fires allowed.

TO REACH THE TRAILHEAD

Take VT 100 south from I-89 (Exit 10), and proceed 0.7 mile to Winooski Street, the first right after the railroad bridge. Turn right onto Winooski Street, proceed 0.3 mile to River Road, turn right, and follow River Road for 3.9 miles. Turn left onto Camel's Hump Road, which reaches Scrabble Hill Road in 2.2 miles, where a green sign indicates the remaining distance to the trailhead.

Rocky trails and exceptional views punctuate the upper reaches of Camel's Hump. (Photo courtesy of Jennifer Lamphere Roberts)

Continue straight on Camel's Hump Road for another 0.9 mile to reach the winter parking area on the left and a brown Camel's Hump summit trails sign. A short 0.3 mile after that, reach the lower parking lot on the left. An upper parking area (44° 18.974′ N, 72° 50.990′ W) is 0.1 mile farther up the road, though be aware that it is gated and locked from dusk until dawn and that the road to it can be extremely rough depending on the season.

HIKE DESCRIPTION

From the upper lot (0.0/1,520), head out on Monroe Trail. Hardwoods—red maples and paper, gray, and yellow birches—fill the surrounding forest. Pass a short spur trail on the left that leads to a plaque honoring the victims of a 1944 airplane crash, when a U.S. Army B-24J bomber hit the mountainside. (Visit remaining debris later in the hike.) The wide, blue-blazed trail reaches an information sign, then continues past a privy on the right.

Sugar maples and beeches appear as the trail crosses a dry gully on a small bridge. Stone walls line the woods and expose the area's agricultural past. Balsam firs and big-tooth aspens join the forest mosaic as the trail steepens and passes a stand of large, healthy beeches unaffected by the nectria fungus—compare their smooth bark with the cankered skin of afflicted trees. The trail gently rises, crossing several rivulets and climbing to Dean Trail (1.3/2,350).

Bear left onto narrower and less-traveled Dean Trail. Cross Hump Brook on a bridge. Savor the crystalline sounds of the rushing stream. The posted spur for Hump Brook Camping Area is ahead on the left (1.6/2,360). Past the campground, hobblebushes and hardwoods transition to spruce-fir forest of mountain ashes, blueberry, and bunchberry. The trail crosses a small brook and levels out to contour into Wind Gap. Here, a shallow tarn opens north toward the south face of Camel's Hump, a lofty lump lording over the forest. The trail navigates some boggy and slippery sections, passes a wet meadow, and reaches Allis Trail and Long Trail (2.3/2,870).

Turn left to Montclair Glen Lodge, located 0.2 mile south on the Long Trail, which passes below a 60- to 80-foot cliff base and then drops roughly to Forest City Trail and the lodge just beyond. (Alternatively, follow Allis Trail for 0.3 mile to emerge just south of the lodge after passing a memorial bench with views south to nearby Mount Ethan Allen.)

Back on the Long Trail, heading north from Dean Trail junction (2.3/2,870), the route begins its summit journey. A sign warns of the challenges you'd face if you attempted this in winter.

The trail steepens, climbs rock steps, and offers occasional views south through the trees toward Mount Ethan Allen. After a switchback right, the route heads directly up the mountain but soon eases, reaching an outcrop with full views to the east (2.7/3,140). The prominent ridgeline of the Worcester Range fills the east view; several Green Mountain ridges are visible to the south. The trail levels briefly, heads toward a rocky cliff, and scrambles over large boulders with more nice vistas. Catch a glimpse west after cutting through a cleft in the rock. Lake Champlain and the Adirondacks fill the horizon.

The summit's bald pate looms north as the trail reenters trees and descends past a trickling and inconsistent water source. The path slices though spruce-fir woods to reach the final ascent. The summit peeks out ahead. Dogwoods, cherries, hazels, and mountain ashes line the trail. Bank left and pass a good view to the southwest, then head straight up to Alpine Trail (3.6/3,820), which can be used to bypass the summit during bad weather.

The remains of the crashed bomber also await a few hundred feet away. To check it out, head right down Alpine Trail, which steeply descends, switchbacks right, and then traverses along the slopes. Views south of Mount Ethan Allen appear shortly before you encounter a 20-foot-long section of wing. The old wheel well and landing gear are easily recognized.

Back on the Long Trail, the summit and cliffs loom ahead. Views to the south unveil themselves at the base of the crags. The trail banks left around the cliff base, reenters diminutive fir forest, and then cuts back right to attain the summit (3.8/4,083/44° 19.173′ N, 72° 53.179′ W) and its 360-degree view.

To the north, 4,393-foot Mount Mansfield's bald hump (Trip 15)—the state's highest peak—rises above I-89 and the Winooski River valley. Below to the east, the Camel Brook watershed drains north into the Winooski. To the south are the Mad River Glen Ski Area and Sugarbush Resort. On a clear day, look to Killington and Ascutney in the southern Greens and as far east as Franconia Ridge and Mount Washington in the Whites. Lake Champlain, Burlington, and the Adirondacks line the west horizon. Do not walk on the vegetation here. The surrounding alpine tundra is extremely rare in Vermont, and wayward boots can easily damage it. Caretakers watch the summit throughout the summer and fall to help protect the fragile ecosystem.

The Long Trail heads north from the summit and reenters the forest. The trail traverses downward, at one point dropping steeply over damp rock slabs. Views north continue intermittently along Bamforth Ridge toward the bald knobs and more distant Mansfield. The four-way junction with Burrows and Monroe trails (4.1/3,810) is in Camel's Hump Hut Clearing.

Bear right on Monroe Trail to return to the trailhead. The slick path is often muddy in spots. Paper birches reappear on your descent toward Alpine Trail, which crosses your route on its way back to the Long Trail (4.5/3,330). Remain on Monroe Trail, cruising down a constant grade over rocky terrain. The route crosses a creek, briefly follows it downstream, and then banks left to recross it. Increasing numbers of paper birches and hobblebushes indicate the transition back to hardwood forest.

The stream course winds into a beech forest and generally heads left. Black cherries and yellow birches join in abundance and sugar maples speckle the woods as the trail gently returns to Dean Trail (5.7/2,350). Bear left to remain on Monroe Trail, and retrace your steps to the trailhead (7.0/1,520).

INFORMATION

Vermont Department of Forests, Parks, and Recreation, Essex District Office, 802-879-6565, vtstateparks.com; Green Mountain Club, 4711 Waterbury-Stowe Road, Waterbury Center, VT 05677, 802-244-7037, greenmountainclub.org.

NEARBY

Downtown Waterbury and Waterbury Center offer an abundance of good eating, beer, and ice cream.

TRIP 15
MOUNT MANSFIELD

Location: Underhill, VT; Mount Mansfield State Forest
Difficulty: Challenging
Distance: 10.6 miles round-trip, plus as many as 3 miles of extreme bonus adventure
Total Elevation Gain/Loss: 3,800 feet/3,800 feet
Trip Length: 1–3 days
Recommended Maps: *The Long Trail Guide* (Green Mountain Club), *Northern Vermont Hiking Trail* (Map Adventures)
Highlights: The tallest mountain in Vermont, gnarly trails.

Mount Mansfield's long alpine spine resembles a human face. He looks upward; the top of his head points south. His features are named promontories—the Forehead, the Nose, the Adam's Apple—but the Chin juts highest and at 4,393 feet is the tallest point in Vermont. The Long Trail walks across this craggy visage, providing expansive views of the landscape. A series of wild trails run parallel to the ridgeline, offering thrilling explorations through the weathered furrows of Mansfield's face.

HIKE OVERVIEW

This loop around Mansfield's alpine ridgelines heads east from Underhill State Park. The journey ascends the open bedrock of Maple Ridge, traverses the mountain's 1.9-mile ridgeline on the Long Trail, and then returns to the trailhead via view-laden Sunset Ridge. Side trips explore fantastic caves, fissures, and giant rocks along the way. Crowds atop the Chin and Forehead are usually heavy, but diminish rapidly away from the main routes.

The journey can be completed as a long day hike, but spending a night (or two) at one of the mountain's three overnight sites allows for more extensive exploration and enjoyment. Note that the mountain's trails are closed during Mud Season (generally April through Memorial Day) to prevent erosion. Dogs are allowed, but they must be leashed above treeline to protect the sensitive alpine environment.

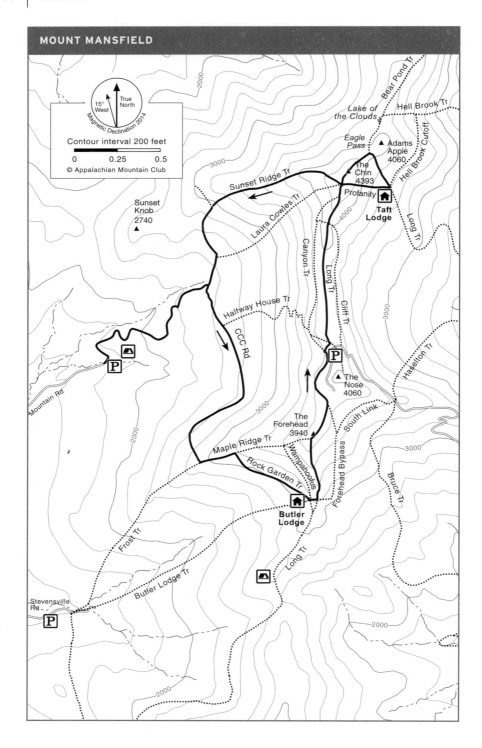

MOUNT MANSFIELD

OVERNIGHT OPTIONS

Overnight use is restricted to three designated sites. The Green Mountain Club (GMC) maintains two lodges on either end of Mansfield's long ridge, and a designated camping area is located south of the Forehead. A nice drive-in campground is available at the trailhead in Underhill State Park, though there is a minimum two-night stay.

Twin Brooks Tenting Area (4.8/2,300/44° 30.205′ N, 72° 49.047′ W) lounges in a pleasant hardwood forest. Located 1.3 miles south of Butler Lodge, it requires a moderate detour off the main route. It is a tent-only area and receives much less use than the two lodges. Several platforms are scattered about, each nicely private with a fire ring. A large group camping area is also available. The closest water source is 0.25 mile away in either direction on the Long Trail.

Butler Lodge (3.5/3,040/44° 30.931′ N, 72° 49.212′ W) perches less than a mile south of the Forehead. The enclosed cabin overlooks a rolling hillscape toward the south end of Lake Champlain. A reliable water source trickles nearby. The lodge sleeps a maximum of fourteen people and is available on a first-come, first-served basis. A caretaker onsite collects an overnight per-person fee during the summer and fall.

Taft Lodge (7.0/3,650/44° 32.614′ N, 72° 48.555′ W) is located almost directly below the Chin. Built in 1920 (and renovated several times since), it tucks against steep, forested slopes and is the largest overnight facility on the Long Trail. As many as 24 people can squeeze onto two large platforms; space is available on a first-come, first-served basis. A small deck by the front door offers views east. Water is 50 feet away in a nearby brook. A caretaker is in residence during summer and fall and collects an overnight per-person fee.

TO REACH THE TRAILHEAD

From the east, take Exit 11 off I-89, and go west on US 2 a very short distance to the stop light at VT 117/River Road. Turn right onto VT 117, then immediately right again onto Governor Peck Highway. After 2.3 miles, turn left onto Brown's Trace Road, and follow it 5.3 miles through Jericho Center to its end at VT 15. Turn right onto VT 15, and proceed 0.5 mile to River Road on the right, posted for Underhill State Park. Turn right and follow River Road 2.7 miles to Underhill Center, where the road becomes Pleasant Valley Road. In another 1.0 mile, turn right onto unpaved (but easily passable) Mountain Road, which heads upward for 2.7 miles to reach the lower parking area (44° 31.768′ N, 72° 50.514′ W) and park entrance. There is a nominal per-person entrance fee.

From Burlington and points west, take Exit 15 off I-89 and follow Route 15 east for 12.3 miles to the junction with River Road. Proceed as described in the previous paragraph.

HIKE DESCRIPTION

The hike begins on Eagle Cut Trail, which leaves from the upper parking area by a blue-blazed post (0.0/1,870). The single-track trail starts out among hardwoods—beeches, white ashes, and yellow and paper birches—and quickly crosses the paved road to the group camping area. Interrupted ferns and jack-in-the-pulpit plants punctuate the understory. The route crosses the road again, widens, and then recrosses it at a tantalizing view of Maple Ridge (your route up) to the southeast. Spruces appear in the mix and Eagle Cut Trail next turns left to travel directly along the CCC Road (0.6/2,150).

Pass a spur trail to the nearby youth group camping area as the CCC Road ascends to reach a large signboard (1.0/2,360), where Sunset Ridge and Laura Cowles trails join from the left. Here the CCC Road makes a hard right turn and heads south along the base of the mountain, cruising gently past Halfway House Trail on the left (1.2/2,440) and then slowly rising past several rivulets.

There is a sense of increasing elevation, and soon you reach a bench with a restricted view northwest (1.8/2,680). Lake Champlain is visible; the Adirondacks rise beyond in the distance. Just past the viewpoint, a two-tiered mini-waterfall marks the road's highpoint. Start a gentle descent and reach Maple Ridge and Teardrop Ski trails (2.2/2,530).

Turn left onto Maple Ridge Trail, which immediately narrows to a single-track and starts ascending steeply over roots and rocks. The surrounding forest quickly transitions to spruce-fir forest. Yellow *Clintonia*, hobblebushes, and bunchberry plants appear underfoot; mountain ashes rise overhead. The trail clambers up rock slabs and reaches a sunny outcrop surrounded by diminutive spruces. Just past this point, you reach an open ledge with 180-degree views west.

Looking south, the prominent massif of Camel's Hump (Trip 14) is readily spotted; the lumpy terrain of the Green Mountains trails away behind it. To the north, the long spine of Mount Mansfield terminates at the Chin, where Sunset Ridge joins from the west.

Continuing, you next reach Frost Trail joining from the right (2.5/2,910). You now begin the ascent along Maple Ridge's open terrain, which provides endless views in all directions. Nearby to the southeast rises 3,371-foot Dewey Mountain. Nebraska Notch sits below it, followed next by Bolton Mountain and then Camel's Hump on the skyline beyond. The Worcester Range serrates the east sky.

Continuing up the rocky ridge, pass a cleft on the right against a hulking boulder. From here, the trail alternately slabs over open rocks and passes through stands of stunted trees. Watch for the presence of cones on these small but ancient specimens. Next up is Rock Garden Trail, which joins from the right (2.9/3,120).

Bear right onto Rock Garden Trail to head toward Butler Lodge. Narrow Rock Garden Trail descends into a sheltered forest of paper birches and mountain ashes and immediately becomes more challenging. You'll need to scramble as the route winds by small cliffs, passes through a 3-foot-high squeezer cave (you can also climb over it), visits a 20-foot-high megalith, and then squishes through a narrow crack of stone. You're not done yet! Scramble past small crevasses and through a crack barely 1-foot wide, where you'll need to remove your pack to fit. Pass a few breaks in the trees and reach Wampahoofus Trail (3.5/3,080). Bear right to head toward Butler Lodge, following Wampahoofus Trail as it slabs out into a clearing with southerly views and glimpses of the cliffs below the Forehead. Butler Lodge (3.5/3,040) is just ahead.

SIDE TRIP TO TWIN BROOKS TENTING AREA

To head to Twin Brooks Tenting Area—located 1.3 miles south—bear right on the Long Trail rather than continuing left along the route. The trail runs mostly level, then begins a slow descent. The forest transitions back to hardwoods. Spruces diminish and quickly disappear, replaced by sugar maples, beeches, striped maples, and yellow birches. The Long Trail levels out briefly by a flowing creek—fill up here if staying at Twin Brooks since this is the last water source—and then crosses a ski trail to resume its downward course. The path levels again and moseys along to reach the spur for Twin Brooks Tenting Area (4.8/2,300).

From the shelter, head past the lodge to Wallace Cutoff Trail, located opposite the privy path. Follow the single-track trail as it climbs up a small ladder and stone staircase to reach the Long Trail (3.6/2,880).

To continue your traverse across Mansfield, head north on the Long Trail from the Wallace Cutoff junction (3.6/2,880). The trail travels over bog bridging and then a giant pile of rocks, moss, and tree debris. The route steepens. Cliffs loom overhead. Walk along their base to pass through the Needle's Eye, a passageway between two boulders. On the opposite side, Forehead Bypass Trail comes in from the right (3.9/3,210), a bad-weather alternative if summit conditions are too gnarly. (It rejoins the Long Trail in 1.2 miles, just before the Nose.)

Remain on the Long Trail as it switchbacks left and starts ascending the cliffs along a particularly hair-raising section of trail. The route follows a series of five ladders to negotiate near-vertical terrain, winding by nerve-wracking gullies and crevasses that would severely punish a misstep. The forest shrinks around you and dead snags increase; intermittent views look south toward Dewey Mountain. You can also spot the roof of Butler Lodge below.

After the final ladder, the trail makes a steady but less wild ascent to reach Maple Ridge Trail (4.6/3,880). Continue north on the Long Trail, ascending slightly to pass near the summit of the Forehead. Enjoy the views before reentering the trees. Abundant trillium, yellow *Clintonia*, and bracken ferns fill the understory as the trail cruises along a level, easygoing section through spruce-fir woods. Forehead Bypass Trail rejoins from the right (4.9/3,880), and you emerge on an unpaved service road.

Antennas, fences, and small buildings pimple Mansfield's Nose, located above you to the right. Turn left on the service road and quickly pass Lakeview Trail on the left. This 0.8-mile loop travels along the slopes, but is not really recommended. Past the rocky cliffs of the Nose, reach the Summit Station and Mount Mansfield Visitor Center (5.2/3,850). Inside are some interesting displays about the history of the summit ridge and the ecology of the mountain.

Views look north along the ridgeline to the Chin; the Adam's Apple is just beyond. The Long Trail continues on the opposite side of the Summit Station, reenters the trees, and then quickly crosses the road to leave the cankered proboscis behind. The trail soon emerges on open slabs with views west and reaches Halfway House Trail (5.4/3,900). Remain on the Long Trail as it traverses more rock slabs and passes the final tower. It's a good area for checking out the alpine tundra, but please stay on the trail while you look for ground-hugging plants like bilberry, Labrador tea, mountain sandwort, and creeping snowberry.

Pass Amherst Trail (5.5/3,930) by two large boulders. The Long Trail now alternately travels over solid rock and wooden walkways that protect the fragile tundra. Views are excellent. Pass a short spur trail on the left that leads to Canyon North Trail (5.7/3,960). Undulate toward the Chin, and reach the junction with Cliff and Subway trails (5.9/4,080). A recommended and very adventurous side trip starts from here (see later). A quick and easy excursion left down Subway Trail provides a taste of it.

Climbing north, ride the Long Trail along a rock-ribbon highway and quickly pass the upper junction for Subway Trail. Exposed rock intersperses

Hikers approach the summit of Mount Mansfield, Vermont's highest point. (Photo courtesy of Jennifer Lamphere Roberts)

with pockets of fir trees, sheltering Canada mayflowers, bracken ferns, and bunchberry plants in their sheltered crevices. Next up is the four-way junction with Sunset Ridge and Profanity trails (6.2/4,270). Remain on the Long Trail, soon passing a sign for the West Chin Natural Area. Note that off-trail hiking is prohibited to protect the alpine vegetation. You climb upward, reach the Chin, and stand atop the highest point in Vermont (6.4/4,393/44° 32.637′ N, 72° 48.858′ W).

Open views look north for the first time. You can see your next stop ahead, the Adam's Apple and adjacent Lake of the Clouds. The deep cleft of Smugglers' Notch lies beyond. Beyond the notch are Madonna Peak and the Smugglers' Notch Ski Area, then Sterling Mountain, and the Butternut and Caraway mountains. On clear days, the Cold Hollow mountains peek out beyond Sterling. Views to the south look over the now familiar features of Mansfield's long face.

The continuing hike now drops to the Adam's Apple and Taft Lodge below it before returning to the Chin for the journey home. (You can skip this 1.1-mile segment and return directly to the trailhead from the summit via Sunset Ridge Trail; see later.) Continuing north on the Long Trail, drop steeply into

Eagle Pass—a few sections require scrambling—and reach the saddle between the Chin and Adam's Apple. Here you meet the junction with the Hell Brook and Hope trails (6.6/4,050).

A short 0.4-mile side-loop circuits over Adam's Apple and past Lake of the Clouds. To check it out, head left on narrow and occasionally boggy Hell Brook Trail to reach Adam's Apple Trail. Lake of the Clouds is just out-of-sight to your left; the Chin protrudes sharply above you. Turn right up Adam's Apple Trail, which immediately makes a staircase-like climb to emerge on the open summit. Hop on the apple. A spur leads to a view north into Smugglers' Notch.

Back at Eagle Pass, follow the Long Trail north as it descends through a fir corridor. The sloping rock underfoot is treacherous when wet; a small creek flows on or near the path. The trail levels, enters much taller forest, and reaches Profanity Trail on the right (6.9/3,690). The spur to Taft Lodge (44° 32.614' N, 72° 48.555' W) is just ahead.

From the lodge, your journey home begins. Return to Profanity Trail and follow it up the mountainside. The path crosses several rivulets, including the lodge's water source (keep it clean), and soon ascends a flowing creek. Pass a brief view west, and then traverse down to reach the Long Trail and Sunset Ridge Trail junction (7.4/4,270).

Descend Sunset Ridge Trail, passing an endless parade of vistas and soon intersecting Laura Cowles Trail on the left (7.5/4,230). The route next traverses right, dropping and entering a taller fir forest with some shelter from the elements. Past it, the trail climbs briefly to the ridgeline and the continuation of drool-worthy views.

The route makes a mellow descent, remaining largely in the open with continuous views. Numerous cairns guide you along the way. Eventually the open rock slabs peter out and the trail enters a taller forest. It cuts left to offer one final view as it winds past blasted trees. The gradient increases and soon scrambling is required. The forest greens with wood ferns in a lush understory. A series of stone staircases lead you downward. Pass mega-boulders with a passageway around them. Spruces and firs diminish. The trail switchbacks right and traverses briefly to reach the spur to Cantilever Rock (8.9/2,920).

Cantilever Rock is worth a visit. The 0.1-mile spur climbs briefly to reach a seamless mass of solid rock. Wedged within it is a huge finger of stone suspended horizontally from the cliff face. The walls drip with water, paper birches enhance the scene, and you can spot a view of Camel's Hump from surrounding boulders.

SIDE TRIP: CLIFFS AND CANYONS LOOP

This 2.6-mile loop tours both sides of the mountain's upper slopes and runs parallel to the ridgeline. It includes some of the craziest sections of trail you'll find in New England, which is saying something. Only the fit and adventurous should attempt this strenuous excursion, and they should be prepared for the unexpected as these trails are not well maintained. Total elevation gain/loss is 1,100/1,100. Expect it to take 2 to 3 hours.

Consider stashing your large overnight pack somewhere safe before you head out—you won't fit through some places with it on. From the four-way junction with the Long, Cliff, and Subway trails (0.0/4,080), strike out east down Cliff Trail. The path descends steeply below a prominent cliff; notice Cave of the Winds, a large fissure. A path leads to its mouth, where you can peer inside at wedged boulders and snow, which lingers into the summer. Light filters through the back of the drip-dripping tunnel.

Scrambling down steep boulder fields, the trail runs along the cliff base and starts to curve south. The Nose appears overhead. Reach the junction for the nearby Gondola (0.3/3,760), located 0.1 mile away to the left. A sign here warns you that the Cliff Trail is extremely difficult and is NOT RECOMMENDED for small children or inexperienced hikers. Only experienced hikers should continue on Cliff Trail as it runs below vertical outcrops and soon enters a long dark gash in the mountainside, a 3-foot gap between the cliff face and a two-story boulder. Basic climbing skills are required to descend into this dark pit of dripping walls and then clamber over a large chockstone near the bottom.

Once on the other side, the route descends over more boulders, passes an unsigned spur trail to the Gondola, and then passes close to a ski run. The trail makes a long traverse before it drops and climbs several times. Ladders aid you in spots; the last, tallest one marks your final climb to Amherst Trail (1.1/3,820). Turn left to quickly reach the toll road.

Go right onto the paved road, crossing the Long Trail and immediately reaching Canyon Trail opposite a concrete bunker (1.2/3,850). Follow Canyon Trail down the side of the mountain. You drop over loose rocks and pass open views west. The trail then goes through a crack in the rocks and enters the Canyon, a narrow cleft between the mountain and an enormous section of cracked stone. It's narrow and progress can be difficult with a pack on. Make a spelunking scramble through a tiny passageway, emerging to reach the junction with Halfway House Trail (1.8/3,700).

The trail now becomes Canyon North Trail. After a slow, rising traverse, squeeze through another slot and reach a spur junction leading down from the Long Trail. Now the continuing route is called the Canyon North Extension (2.1/3,800).

Climbing, the trail leads past an open, 180-degree view west and then heads through another tight cave passage. A rising traverse through a boulder maze reaches a junction by another large cave passage, marked with a blue Y blaze. The Long Trail is only a short distance to your right, but instead continue straight into the deepest chasm yet. A ladder aids in the descent, a gift from a 1989 Eagle Scout project. Once you're through, the trail winds upward past giant boulders and great views. It then banks right and quickly rejoins the Long Trail (2.5/4,100). Turn right to quickly return to the earlier junction with Cliff and Canyon trails (2.6/4,080).

Back on Sunset Ridge Trail, continue your steady descent into hardwood forest. The trail crosses a small brook on a plank bridge, then recrosses it and slowly descends past extensive birch trees. After crossing another stream—the biggest yet—the path makes a level traverse, hops across another creek, and reaches Laura Cowles Trail on the left (9.5/2,380). Remain on Sunset Ridge Trail and pass over two more streams to return to the CCC Road (9.6/2,350). Turn right and retrace your earlier route to the trailhead (10.6/1,870).

INFORMATION

Underhill State Park, 352 Mountain Road, Underhill, VT 05490, 802-899-3022, vtstateparks.com; Green Mountain Club, 4711 Waterbury-Stowe Road, Waterbury Center, VT 05677, greenmountainclub.org, 802-244-7037.

NEARBY

For grub, goodies, and a classic small-town experience, stop by the general store in Jericho Center on your way to or from Underhill State Park. For a great, scenic drive before you head home, follow Route 108 through Smugglers' Notch to experience dramatic scenery from the other end of the Mansfield spectrum—the cliffs at the bottom.

3

NEW HAMPSHIRE

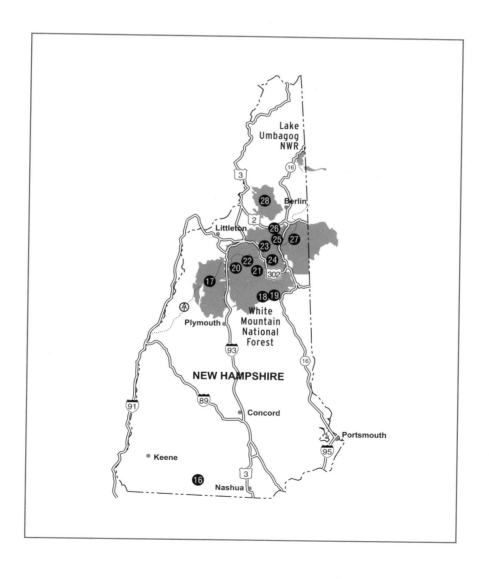

TRIP 16
WAPACK TRAIL

Location: Wapack Range, southern New Hampshire
Difficulty: Moderate
Distance: 21.4 miles one-way
Total Elevation Gain/Loss: 5,100 feet/5,030 feet
Trip Length: 2 days
Recommended Map: *Wapack Trail Map* (Friends of the Wapack)
Highlight: Ridgeline backpacking less than 50 miles from Boston.

The Wapack Range rises above the dimpled landscape of southeast New Hampshire, one of the closest backpacking options to the Boston area. Wapack Trail runs the length of the range and earns its name from the starting and ending points (Mount WAtatic and PACK Monadnock). Its open peaks are loaded with blueberries and view-rich stretches. The trail between the popular summit hikes sees relatively few visitors and makes an excellent early- or late-season foray.

HIKE OVERVIEW

This point-to-point hike journeys from Mount Watatic in north-central Massachusetts to the trail's terminus at Pack Monadnock in southern New Hampshire. The route connects a series of linear ridges, dipping between them as it goes, and is most commonly done south to north, as described here. The trail encounters intermittent wilderness as well as dirt and paved roads. The trip's only overnight options are located 8.0 miles from the trailhead, dividing the journey into south and north segments of 8 and 13 miles, respectively. Dogs are generally permitted, though the trail passes through a variety of public and private lands, each with its own rules about dogs. Be courteous and respectful, and conservatively leash your dog anytime it seems necessary.

When it opened in 1923, Wapack Trail became the first interstate hiking route in the Northeast. Today it is maintained by the nonprofit Friends of the Wapack.

OVERNIGHT OPTIONS

The overnight options are located near the hike's midpoint at Windblown Cross-country Ski Area, which maintains two shelters for backpacker use.

There is an $8 fee per person with a $25 minimum charge. Advance reservations are required and can be made by calling 603-878-2869. Send the non-refundable $25 deposit to Windblown, 1180 Turnpike Road, New Ipswich, NH 03071. It is not necessary to check in when you arrive; pay your balance by leaving a check in the mailbox located by the Windblown sign on NH 124A.

Mountain Top Shelter (7.9/1,800/42° 45.948′ N, 71° 54.792′ W) perches in a spruce-ringed clearing near the top of a ski run and can sleep up to six hikers. Views scatter about the area, including glimpses of nearby Kidder Mountain, the rolling hills to the northwest, a profile of Mount Monadnock, and the Boston skyline. Amenities include a fire ring and privy. No water is available nearby. To access the closest source, hike east halfway down Barrett Mountain to where a wide ski trail crosses over a stream on a small bridge; note that it can run dry late in the season.

Valley View Shelter (8.2/1,450/42° 46.075′ N, 71° 54.136′ W) nestles in the middle of the cross-country ski area and is accessed via a short 0.3-mile detour off Wapack Trail. It features a large deck, a fire ring, wood pile, and outhouse. A stream flows right by the shelter. Red oaks and yellow birches shade the forested dale. Good tentsites can be found along adjacent ski paths.

TO REACH THE TRAILHEADS

To Reach the Northern (Ending) Trailhead. Head to the town of Peterborough, New Hampshire, and proceed east on Sand Hill Road, located 1.1 miles north of the downtown bridge on NH 202/123. In 2.9 miles, Sand Hill Road passes East Mountain Road to the right. Continue straight on Sand Hill Road through two successive dogleg turns (left, then right). The road is now Old Mountain Road. Proceed straight, passing Brantwood Road on the left. The trailhead parking lot (42° 54.075′ N, 71° 52.081′ W) is 0.25 miles beyond on the south (right) side of the road.

To Reach the Southern (Starting) Trailhead. Follow Route 119 west 1.4 miles past the Route 119/101 junction in Ashburnham, Massachusetts. The large trailhead parking area is located on the north side of the road; look for the Midstate Trail signs. Approaching on Route 119 from the east, the trailhead (42° 41.777′ N, 71° 54.268′ W) is located 1.8 miles past the state line.

HIKE DESCRIPTION

Throughout the hike, abundant yellow triangle blazes mark the route of Wapack Trail. A sign at the trailhead (0.0/1,250) indicates upcoming distances. Cross the gate and head down the wide dirt road, immediately passing a pond with signs of past beaver activity. Hemlocks, red maples, yellow birches,

WAPACK TRAIL (NORTH)

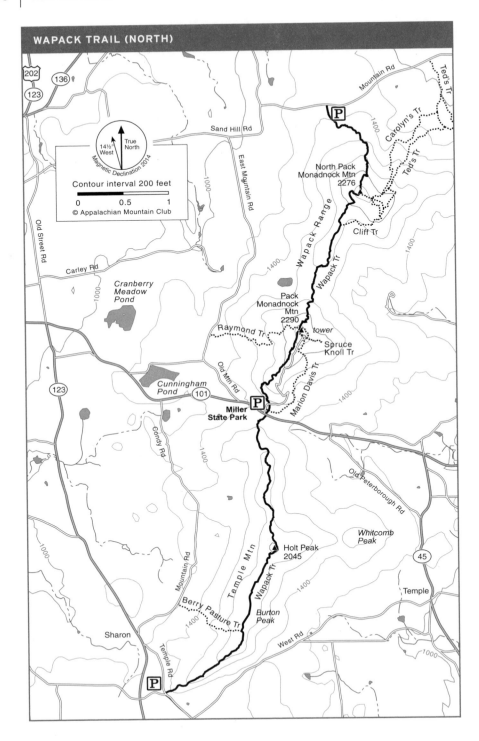

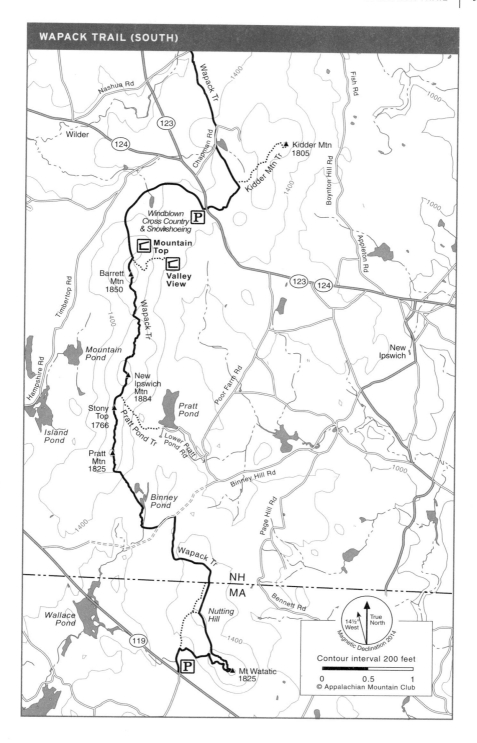

WAPACK TRAIL (SOUTH)

Nashua Rd

Wilder

123

124

Wapack Tr

Chapman Rd

1400

Fish Rd

1000

Kidder Mtn
1805

Kidder Mtn Tr

1400

Boynton Hill Rd

1000

P

Windblown
Cross Country
& Snowshoeing

Mountain
Top

Valley
View

Barrett
Mtn
1850

123   124

Appleton Rd

New
Ipswich

Timbertop Rd

Wapack Tr

1400

Mountain
Pond

New
Ipswich
Mtn
1884

Pratt
Pond

Poor Farm Rd

Hampshire Rd

Stony
Top
1766

Pratt Pond Tr

Lower Pratt
Pond Rd

Island
Pond

Pratt
Mtn
1825

Binney Hill Rd

1000

Binney
Pond

Page Hill Rd

1400

Wapack Tr

NH
MA

Bennett Rd

True
North

14½°
West

Magnetic Declination 2014

Wallace
Pond

Nutting
Hill

1400

119

Contour interval 200 feet

P

Mt Watatic
1825

0   0.5   1

© Appalachian Mountain Club

and red oaks shade the rocky road as it climbs slightly to a posted junction (0.2/1,270). Turn right to follow Wapack/Midstate Trail.

Now single-track, the path crosses a bubbling stream and winds between a cloven boulder to reach the base of Mount Watatic's slopes near ashes and peeling hop hornbeams. The route rises through hemlocks, soon curving left to make a steeper ascent of the boulder-pocked hillside. Spot black birches and some old gnarly beeches as you climb. Reaching the base of solid rock slabs, the trail heads directly up to the top of the outcrop, where views look south over the rolling Massachusetts landscape.

From here, the trail curves right and runs level along a stone wall. The spiny needles of red spruce trees join the forest mix. Intermittent views pass by as you follow bedrock and then reach a ledge with more views to the south; nearby Wachusett Mountain bulges as the centerpiece. The trail curves back to the left and resumes its climb. It bends right again, leveling out shortly before reaching a section rife with illicit, off-trail switchbacks. It's easy to lose the trail here; take care to follow the marked trail. From here, a brief climb leads to the open summit (1.2/1,832/42° 41.810′ N, 71° 53.547′ W).

Enjoy the 360-degree view. To the east is the Boston skyline, and to the south the hump of Wachusett Mountain. The nearby ridges and peaks of the Wapack Range run north—your continuing route. Look for the summit tower atop Pack Monadnock. Watatic's lower south summit is visible nearby, readily accessible by well-used paths and worth the side trip.

Near the summit marker, a granite monument proclaims the mountain saved. In 2002, developers purchased land at the summit to install a cell phone tower. The dedicated work of local conservation groups led instead to its protection as parkland.

Continuing north from the summit, Wapack Trail briefly follows the road constructed to service the never-built cell tower. The route quickly splits left, descends past hemlocks and along stone walls, then widens and parallels a wall. The trail reaches a saddle, narrows, and climbs atop Nutting Hill (1.9/1,610). Past the peak, the trail widens and quickly reaches the junction with the Midstate Trail on the left. Bear right to remain on Wapack Trail and cross the state line at a gap in a stone wall (2.4/1,540), where Wapack Trail signs are posted.

As you enter New Hampshire, pass through an open, recently logged area. After the clear-cut, the trail reenters the woods on a double-track road. The trail next forks at unpaved Binney Hill Road (3.5/1,380). Bear left and then turn right on a smaller woods road—watch for the double-blaze and sign indicating this turn-off.

Now rising, the trail encounters the swampy outflow from Binney Pond, enters tiny Binney Pond State Forest, and curves right to wind along the boggy shore, more marsh than pond. Find a posted spring at the far end of the pond, the last quality water source for the next 4.0 miles. From here, the trail rises steeply past large sugar maples and oaks on a rocky hillside. Look also for red trillium, jack-in-the-pulpits, and red elderberries—indicators of an enriched soil environment. Climb steadily, and look back toward Binney Pond and Watatic; a posted overlook at the top offers the best vista.

The trail crests atop Pratt Mountain (5.0/1,817/42° 43.975′ N, 71° 55.154′ W), where open ledges look north and west toward your upcoming route, a ridgeline topped by New Ipswich Mountain, visible ahead. The continuing trail reaches a clearing revealing views of nearby Mount Monadnock in full profile. Stony Top marks the end of this ridge section (5.5/1,770), where an open slab offers unobstructed views west toward Mountain Pond and Monadnock beyond.

The trail descends, returning to forest and reaching the saddle below New Ipswich Mountain. Water often trickles in the depression. Orange-blazed Pratt Pond Trail joins from the right. Climbing up New Ipswich, pass stonewalls en route to a small boulder at the viewless summit (6.1/1,884/42° 44.721′ N, 71° 54.979′ W). Continuing, the broad dome of approaching Barrett Mountain appears at times; the Pack Monadnocks are visible in the distance. The trail reaches the saddle below Barrett Mountain, where flowing water can be found (6.9/1,600).

The rocky route now climbs past the red mottled leaves of trout lilies. The gradient eases in a spruce grove and winds over the viewless summit (7.5/1,830). The level duff-covered path heads through stands of dense spruce and soon reaches the boundary of the Windblown Cross-country Ski Area (7.8/1,820). Bright yellow signs indicate the East Side Drop on your right; posted Wapack Trail turns right just beyond. If you're heading to either shelter, go straight on the wide ridge-top trail.

In approximately 25 yards, a side trail on the right leads downhill to the Valley View Shelter through an opening in a stone wall. Go through the stone wall, and turn left onto the wide ski trail that heads north and then right at the sign that says Valley View Renters. Cross two more ski trails on the way down the east side of Barrett Mountain. At the bottom, turn right (south) onto a ski trail (Valley Trail); Valley View Shelter is on a knoll 50 yards to the left.

To reach the Mountain Top Shelter, proceed straight on the ridge-top trail for 100 yards to find both the shelter and expansive views.

To continue north, follow the bright yellow Wapack Trail sign, and begin a steady descent around the perimeter of the ski area. As the drop begins, pass a side trail to the right to the Mountain Top and Valley View shelters. The trail descends, then levels, crosses a power-line corridor, and passes cross-country ski trails on the right and private residences on the left. After recrossing below the power lines, emerge by the Windblown Base Lodge and lower parking area shortly before NH 123/124 (9.1/1,450).

Turn right, follow the pavement a short distance, and turn left onto Old Rindge Road, located across from Wapack Road. A trail sign, blazes, and a small parking area mark the spot. The single-track trail winds below a private residence and edges along a large field. Curving right, briefly climb to reenter the woods, cruise through young forest, and reach a woods road. Turn left to quickly reach a power-line corridor (9.7/1,550). The posted side trip to Kidder Mountain starts here.

SIDE TRIP TO KIDDER MOUNTAIN

Kidder Mountain (1,805) is crowned with an abundant amount of blueberries and open views east and south. A side trip to its summit requires a 1.8-mile round-trip hike with 350 feet of elevation gain and loss. Lowbush blueberries flourish around the ledgy summit area, ripening in early to midsummer. The route initially follows the often muddy power-line mud road, then cuts off it to the left and rises. After climbing through hemlock groves, enter a recently harvested area and rise over rocky outcrops. Stone walls and cairns line the final section to the top.

From the Kidder Mountain Trail junction, Wapack Trail follows a gentle woods road and reaches unpaved Wildcat Hill Road (10.1/1,440), where you turn right. Wildcat Hill Road forks right to become a private driveway (10.4/1,430), but continue straight on a less-used woods road closed to motorized vehicles.

The route slowly descends on the overgrown road parallel to a small brook, the last water source for the next 6.0 miles. The route skirts around a beaver pond and then crosses posted Todd Road. Follow a nice wide path between stone walls, running next to land owned by the Monadnock Conservancy on the right. To avoid wet sections, the trail occasionally parallels the road on single-track—watch for blazes.

The route rejoins the road, crosses a brook, and then quickly encounters paved Temple and Nashua roads (11.3/1,250). The route continues straight there, following Temple Road for the longest paved section of the journey. You pass numerous homes on your way to the junction of Greenleaf and Temple roads (11.7/1,300); a small parking area sits across from the continuing trail.

The double-track trail heads straight up from here to the 2.2-mile stretch known as the Cabot Skyline. A sign and map explain that Thomas D. Cabot donated a trail easement across these lands. Ascend past an abandoned house on the right, and the trail narrows, becomes rockier, and begins to run parallel to a stone wall. Reach the posted spur to the Roger Myrick Overlook (12.1/1,700).

Pass another posted overlook with a similar view; then the rocky trail makes its final rise to the ridgeline. Now slowly rising, the path passes stunted oaks, beeches, paper birches, red maples, and an abundant number of cairns. The trail drops briefly through a spruce grove, resumes climbing, parallels a stone wall, and then curves left away from it to reach Berry Pasture Trail on the left (13.0/1,970). Crest posted Burton Peak (13.1/2,020) and then resume alongside the earlier stone wall, soon crossing it.

The trail continues, passes another outlook to the northeast, then comes upon a nice rock with views of Monadnock. The stone wall curves away again, then reappears in the saddle below Holt Peak (13.9/1,940). The route bottoms out and climbs steeply past ledgy outcrops to reach the viewless summit (14.2/2,045), accessible by a short spur.

Pack Monadnock peeks through the trees north as you descend on the widening trail, which becomes steadily more road-like and soon reaches the first unobstructed view to Pack Monadnock. Bottoming out in stands of juniper, the trail quickly returns to single-track.

From here, the trail rises briefly past smaller cairns, then resumes its descent and drops into a spruce-filled saddle. Slowly rising among conifers, the trail reaches a fork—bear left (watch for blazes). Cruise around a cell tower and building, then reach an access road offering full views of Pack Monadnock and NH 101 below. The route follows the service road down and soon bears left at a double blaze (15.5/1,770) to immediately pass the top of a defunct ski lift. Welcome to Temple Mountain Ski Area, which shuttered operations in 2001 and is now a state of New Hampshire-owned recreation area.

The route descends steadily via the service road and reenters the woods straight ahead near the bottom of the service road (where the road bears sharply right) to soon reach NH 101 (16.0/1,470). (If you miss the trail, follow the service road a short distance to the large Temple Mountain Recreation Area parking lot, then cross NH 101 to rejoin the trail at Miller State Park.)

Cross the highway to the large Miller State Park parking area, where the Wapack and Marion Davis trails strike out from the lot. Blue-blazed Marion

Davis Trail heads straight and to the right, but your continuing route on Wapack Trail leads left. Quickly cross the summit access road near the base of rock cliffs and slabs. The trail now ascends steeply over blocky talus, with views of Mount Monadnock and the Temple Mountain Ski Area behind you.

Climb through a rock maze, then traverse left through a more forested section before turning steeply uphill again over more loose rock and talus. The trail continues over bedrock, eases above the cliffs, and drops into a small gully with trickling water—the first source in 6.0 miles.

The trail slowly ascends through spruce forest, crosses a stone wall, and steadily rises toward the summit loop (17.3/2,220) and its painted red circles. Wapack Trail curves right to join it, follows a wide gravel path, and quickly reaches the often-crowded summit complex (17.4/2,280/42° 51.749′ N, 71° 52.734′ W), which includes a parking area, fire lookout tower (closed, though you can climb the stairs for a view), picnic tables, air-quality station, and an old stone shelter constructed by the Civilian Conservation Corps.

The view from the tower stairs is excellent. The city of Manchester dots the landscape to the northeast; the three hills of Pawtuckaway State Park are visible beyond. To the north is the undeveloped summit of North Pack Monadnock—your final peak. Mount Monadnock stands out in profile to the west-northwest, and the mountains of Vermont are visible along the northwestern horizon. Looking south, the whole line of the Wapack Range traces your route to this point.

Continuing north, Wapack Trail initially follows a gravel path past picnic tables and more views and in 0.2 mile reaches Raymond Trail on the left. Wapack Trail then travels along a stretch of solid rock and begins to descend. Cross trickling water and reach a spur to Joanne Bass Bross Outlook, which offers another view northeast.

The path drops steadily and makes a few switchbacks. Reach a saddle (17.9/1,730), and shortly afterward cross into The Nature Conservancy's Joanne Bass Bross Preserve. Shortly thereafter, enter Wapack National Wildlife Refuge, marked by a sign and map. The trail undulates through dense spruce stands, rising steadily to top out by a cairn, then drops on a root-laced trail to quickly encounter Cliff Trail entering from the right (19.1/1,860). An indication of the junction is painted on the rocks.

The rocky trail runs level past conifers, encounters a stone wall, then climbs steeply and briefly parallels the wall before curving left to start a rising traverse toward the summit cairn of North Pack Monadnock (19.8/2,276/42° 53.138′ N, 71° 51.959′ W). Bare rock slabs here provide vistas west and northwest, which include the prominent mass of Mount Kearsarge. If you look closely at the slabs, you'll notice grooves and polished rock along a northwest-southeast line—evidence of the ice sheet that smothered this summit during the last Ice Age.

The trail turns left at the cairn, passes a second summit knob, and then descends directly over solid rock through spruce forest. After a few switchbacks, it resumes a steep descent before leveling out. White pines and birches reappear, and you encounter more open slabs. A gentle, winding descent leads past numerous views north and extensive juniper trees before a final steep drop returns you to a mellow traverse that crosses several small trickles. You then curve right by the most substantial brook yet, descend parallel to it, and then cross it shortly before reaching a trail-junction sign indicating trailhead parking to the left and Old Mountain Road (and hike's end) straight ahead (21.4/1,320).

INFORMATION

Friends of the Wapack, P.O. Box 115, West Peterborough, NH 03468, wapack. org, info@wapack.org.

NEARBY

The picturesque Peterborough and Jaffrey offer a variety of eating establishments and other amenities and provide opportunities for a pleasant visit to two classically New England towns.

TRIP 17
MOUNT MOOSILAUKE

Location: Southern White Mountain National Forest
Difficulty: Challenging
Distance: 3.0 miles round-trip to Beaver Brook Shelter, 7.6 miles round-trip to summit
Total Elevation Gain/Loss: 1,800 feet/1,800 feet to shelter; 3,100 feet/3,100 feet to summit
Trip Length: 1–2 days
Recommended Map: *AMC White Mountains Trail Map, Map 4: Moosilauke–Kinsman* (AMC Books)
Highlight: Riveting brookside ascent to an alpine summit.

Mount Moosilauke is the westernmost massif of the White Mountains. Isolated from adjoining peaks, hemmed by deep valleys, this 4,802-foot peak offers 360-degree panoramas from an open summit of alpine tundra. Beaver Brook scores the mountain's east flank, tumbling down continuous cascades and providing the most direct route to the summit. The Appalachian Trail (AT) ascends alongside it, climbing the mountain with the aid of 140 wooden steps and more than a dozen metal railings riveted into the rock.

HIKE OVERVIEW

This fun overnighter or exciting day hike follows Beaver Brook Trail for its entire length. The first half is very steep—climbing 1,700 feet in 1.2 miles—and travels over wet rock slabs. The knee-compressing descent is challenging, especially in wet conditions—this is not a good rainy-day excursion. Beaver Brook Trail is part of the AT and consequently receives heavy thru-hiker use in July and early August. Come midweek if possible, to avoid crowds, or spend the night at Beaver Brook Shelter and climb to the summit early.

Mount Moosilauke boasts more history than perhaps any peak in the Whites, save Mount Washington. In 1860, the first summit building was constructed. During the winter of 1869 to 1870, Joseph Huntington and Amos Clough spent two months sheltered inside and were the first to measure above-treeline winter weather conditions in the Whites, including winds in excess of 100 miles per hour, a record at the time.

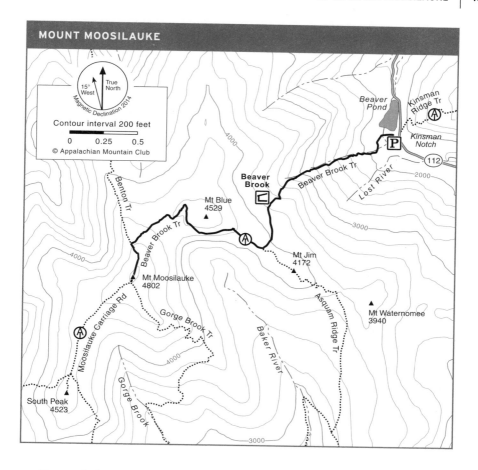

MOUNT MOOSILAUKE

15° West | True North

Magnetic Declination 2014

Contour interval 200 feet

0   0.25   0.5

© Appalachian Mountain Club

Beaver Pond

Kinsman Ridge Tr

Kinsman Notch

P

112

Lost River

Beaver Brook Tr

2000

Beaver Brook

3000

Benton Tr

Beaver Brook Tr

Mt Blue
4529

Mt Jim
4172

4000

Mt Moosilauke
4802

Moosilauke Carriage Rd

Gorge Brook Tr

Baker River

Asquam Ridge Tr

Mt Waternomee
3940

4000

Gorge Brook

South Peak
4523

3000

Turn-of-the-century logging operations clear-cut nearly the entire mountain; the little old-growth that remained was demolished by the 1938 hurricane. Following passage of the Weeks Act in 1911, the federal government began purchasing land for the White Mountain National Forest and acquired 7,000 acres on Mount Moosilauke in 1914. In 1920, the Summit House proprietors donated their land holdings to Dartmouth College, including Moosilauke's summit and a broad swatch of land in Jobildunk Ravine. Dartmouth has acquired additional parcels since and today owns 4,500 acres on the mountain. The Dartmouth Outing Club (DOC)—the oldest outdoor club in the nation—maintains trails, posts a summit caretaker during the busy summer months to protect the alpine vegetation, and operates the Ravine Lodge at the base of the mountain.

Most people agree that the name of the mountain comes from the original Algonquin designation—translated it means "bald place"—but pronunciation is a different matter. Whether it's pronounced *Moose-a-lock-ee* or *Moose-a-lock* depends on whom you talk to; it's surprising how many people have an opinion.

OVERNIGHT OPTION

Besides the following shelter, dispersed camping is permitted 200 feet or more away from the trail, but there is essentially no flat ground along this trail. Camping is prohibited within 0.25 mile of NH 112.

Beaver Brook Shelter (1.5/3,650/44° 1.981' N, 71° 48.684' W) features a northeast view that stretches as far as Mount Washington. Three shady tent-sites are located near the shelter. A small creek dribbles nearby. Campfires are permitted only in the shelter fire ring.

TO REACH THE TRAILHEAD

Take I-93 to Exit 32 in Lincoln. Head west on NH 112 for 6.5 miles. The large trailhead parking lot (44° 02.417' N, 71° 47.572' W) is on the left. A WMNF parking permit is required.

HIKE DESCRIPTION

Rocky cliffs loom above the parking lot. The Beaver Brook watershed can be seen draining the mountain's flank. A sign warns of the approaching challenge: "Sections of this trail are steep and challenging. Know your limitations and heed them." The white-blazed trail begins at the back of the lot (0.0/1,870). Shrubby pin cherries are on the right; mountain maples, beeches, and paper birches on the left.

The trail immediately bears left at a signed trailhead junction by NH 112 and enters thicker forest. Yellow birches and hobblebushes highlight the woods. Rock-hop across a brook, and head toward another stream crossing—this one on a solid wooden bridge. After crossing another stream on a bridge, the trail starts its direct ascent (0.3/1,890).

Here a sign fashioned by the DOC warns: "This trail is extremely tough. If you lack experience, please use another trail. Take special care at the cascades to avoid tragic results." As the route climbs, the sound of rushing water infuses the air, and the trail reaches its first waterfall view. Brookside boulders sit below a series of cascades that curtain the rock with spray.

From here, the trail climbs a veritable staircase of rock and wood steps. Rungs drilled into the rock provide handholds. On the right, Beaver Brook flows parallel to the trail, sliding down smooth rock faces. The beautiful cascades go on and on.

The trail ascends sections impossible to climb without the aid of the wooden steps. The gradient finally eases from its ladder-like angle and passes an overgrown logging road in thick spruce-fir forest. Though less steep, the trail remains very rocky as it curves away from Beaver Brook and banks left up a small tributary gurgling over mossy stones. A steady climb through boulder fields leads to the short spur trail for Beaver Brook Shelter (1.5/3,650).

The summit beckons. From the shelter junction, the trail rises to Asquam-Ridge Trail on the left (1.9/3,970). Turn right to remain on Beaver Brook Trail, which runs level and then slowly ascends over increasingly bouldery terrain. Views open up to the south, peering over the deep valley and steep headwall cliffs of Jobildunk Ravine. A glacial cirque, Jobildunk Ravine is reportedly named for three nineteenth-century loggers—Joe, Bill, and Duncan—who worked in the area.

The trail traverses rock slabs then skirts the 4,529-foot summit of Mount Blue. Views west appear for the first time. The path drops briefly and then rises to meet Benton Trail (3.4/4,580). Bear left on Benton Trail and enter the alpine zone. The fragile, lawn-like terrain of this alpine tundra is tempting to walk on, but stay on the trail as you climb the last hundred feet of elevation to the summit (3.8/4,802/44° 1.398′ N, 71° 49.889′ W).

The stone foundation of the old Summit House (1860–1943) sits almost directly atop the peak, providing windbreaks for hikers. Soak in the 360-degree view. Mount Washington, 31 miles away to the northeast, peeks over the long spine of Franconia Ridge (Trip 20); Mount Lafayette's mile-high, pyramidal summit caps the north ridge. The Sandwich Range (Trips 18 and 19) fills the southeastern horizon, and the shimmering waters of Lake Winnipesaukee can be spotted 35 miles away. To the west, the distant Green Mountains dimple the horizon—Mount Mansfield (Trip 15) is almost due northwest and the prominent knob of Camel's Hump (Trip 14) a few degrees south of that. After all the fun, return the way you came.

INFORMATION

White Mountain National Forest, Pemigewasset Ranger District, 71 White Mountain Drive, Campton, NH 03223, 603-536-6100, fs.usda.gov/white-mountain; Dartmouth Outing Club, 113 Robinson Hall, Hanover, NH 03755, 603-626-2429, dartmouth.edu/~doc, thedoc@dartmouth.edu.

NEARBY

North Woodstock and Lincoln both provide places to eat, refuel, and purchase any last-minute supplies.

TRIP 18
SANDWICH RANGE WILDERNESS–
WESTERN LOOP

Location: Southern White Mountain National Forest
Difficulty: Strenuous
Distance: 13.6 miles round-trip
Total Elevation Gain/Loss: 4,750 feet/4,750 feet
Trip Length: 2 days
Recommended Map: *AMC White Mountains Trail Map, Map 3: Crawford Notch–Sandwich Range* (AMC Books)
Highlights: Sweeping summits, easy access, minimal crowds.

For more than 25 miles, no road crosses the Sandwich Range's rugged spine on the southern front of the White Mountains. Lofty summits, including six 4,000-footers, pierce the sky. The 36,000-acre Sandwich Range Wilderness protects the wild heart of these mountains. Near its center, Mounts Whiteface and Passaconaway and exciting ridgeline trails encircle a deep valley known as the Bowl.

HIKE OVERVIEW

The clockwise loop around the Bowl ascends 4,020-foot Mount Whiteface via the view-rich Blueberry Ledge Trail before circling to the base of Mount Passaconaway. On the loop's return leg, the route passes massive Square Ledge and then follows a burbling brook along Kelley Trail back to the trailhead, offering more highlights than other myriad routes back. Water is scarce for long sections. Dogs and campfires are allowed.

OVERNIGHT OPTIONS

Three former shelter sites offer good tenting opportunities. Dispersed camping is also permitted, but finding a site is difficult in the steep terrain.

The first two lofty sites are located near the summit of Mount Whiteface, with dramatic views only a few strides away, but there is no reliable water for several miles in either direction. Obtain water near the trailhead or bring it with you from the get-go. Limited space and fragile conditions of the summit environment also make these less desirable options. If you do stay here, take special care to minimize your impact and leave no trace.

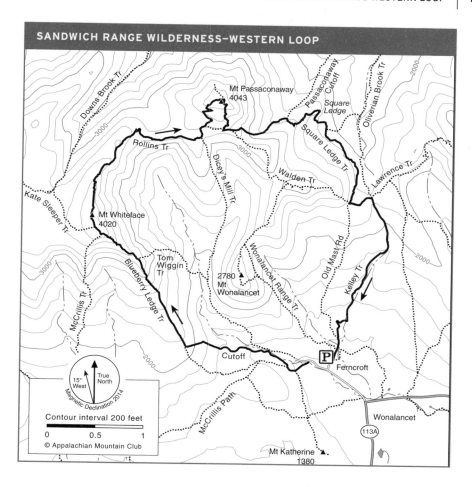

SANDWICH RANGE WILDERNESS—WESTERN LOOP

Camp Heermance (3.8/3,900/43° 56.198′ N, 71° 24.463′ W) was once perched 3.8 miles from the trailhead. Now an open clearing is tucked away in the trees by a large boulder. Tentsites are ample.

Camp Shehadi (4.0/3,890/43° 56.095′ N, 71° 24.459′ W) once occupied a clearing at the junction of the Rollins and Kate Sleeper trails. The small site is ringed by mountain ashes, paper birches, firs, and spruces, and offers space for only a small group.

Camp Rich (6.6/3,500/43° 57.071′ N, 71° 23.075′ W), the most recommended site, is located near the midpoint of the hike, close to the Passaconaway summit loop trail. The former shelter site features substantial clearing situated by a briskly flowing stream. Numerous tentsites can be found in a large clearing, along with several others in the trees. A privy is available, located up a signed, steep spur to the right of the main clearing.

TO REACH THE TRAILHEAD

Take NH 113 north from NH 25 (the turn-off is located 3.6 miles west of the NH 25/16 junction). In 0.4 mile, turn left to remain on NH 113 and proceed 2.4 miles to reach the junction with NH 113A. Continue straight (north) on NH 113A, following it for 6.5 miles as it heads northwest and then west through the small community of Wonalancet. Turn right onto unpaved Ferncroft Road, located next to the white church, and proceed 0.5 mile to a turn-off on the right for the designated parking area (43° 54.744' N, 71° 21.489' W). All of the property around you is private—please respect the landowners and park only in this designated area.

HIKE DESCRIPTION

An information kiosk at the trailhead marks the start of your journey (0.0/1,170). To reach the Blueberry Ledge Trail, follow the signs back down the parking lot road. Enjoy the idyllic view of a nearby farmhouse, Mount Whiteface (left), and the symmetrical dome Mount Wonalancet (right). The surroundings here are private property. Your passage is granted through the owners' generosity. Please remain on established paths; the trail is clearly marked to distinguish driveways from footpaths. Wait to obtain water until you reach Blueberry Ledge Cutoff Trail and its river access a short distance ahead.

Turn right onto Ferncroft Road, parallel the Wonalancet River a short distance, and then turn left to cross it on Squirrel Bridge Road (0.3/1,200). Follow the smaller road past several private residences, watching for the trail signs that indicate your route. After passing a final home on the left (#32), your backcountry journey begins.

The forest encroaches around the single-track path. Pass the signed junction for Pasture Path on the left (0.5/1,210) and then reach Blueberry Ledge Cutoff Trail (0.6/1,250) on the right. This slightly rougher but more scenic alternative rejoins Blueberry Ledge Trail in 1.4 mile. The path immediately leads down to the river by the National Forest boundary and then traces along the banks on a narrow path. Moisture-loving white ashes and hemlocks shade the forest. Granite boulders litter the streambed. Pass a signed spur on the right to Dicey's Mill Trail on the far side of the river, then continue on Cutoff Trail as it turns away from the water and quickly rises above it. The trail climbs to the signed Wilderness boundary (1.5/1,550). Ascend past granite boulders to the ridgeline and Blueberry Ledge Trail (2.0/2,140).

Turn right to head up the mountain on Blueberry Ledge Trail. Established in 1899, it is one of the oldest actively used trails in the Whites. The rocky route rises steadily, offering occasional views toward Mount Wonalancet. The surrounding woods gradually transition to spruce-fir, and the trail steepens markedly. It ascends a veritable rock staircase past tantalizing views and then briefly levels. The summit of Mount Whiteface looms ahead just before Tom Wiggin Trail on the right (3.2/3,220).

Blueberry Ledge Trail briefly eases as it approaches the base of the summit dome. Begin the final ascent, the most challenging section yet. At 3,500 feet, the trail emerges atop the first of many open ledges with exceptional views. Open vistas look southwest to the prominent massif of Sandwich Dome and, at the southern edge of the range, the distinctive pyramid of Mount Israel.

The trail ascends a very steep slab that may be difficult to negotiate in wet or icy conditions. Holes in the rock used to support steps, but they are no longer present. Scramble up for a mouth-watering view.

Outstanding views look east. The Bowl Natural Research Area fills the valley below. The ravine's west slopes harbor old-growth red spruce forest, one of the largest stands in the state. The stature of these untouched trees is apparent even from here. Mount Passaconaway looms over the Bowl. In the eastern distance are Mount Paugus and Mount Chocorua's rocky summit profile (Trip 19).

The route navigates a jumbled fortress of rocks, scrambling up slabs and small gullies. Ledge after ledge offer views. Most outlooks peer east, but a few look west toward the mountain flanks. Giant rock slabs paste against the mountainside and help give the mountain its name.

The trail crests the summit ridge, reenters the forest, and reaches a spur on the right to the former site of Camp Heermance (3.8/3,900), dismantled in 2002. Just beyond McCrillis Path enters from the left near open granite knobs (3.9/3,920). Far-reaching views south greet you here. Old names are carved into the rock underfoot, including one from 1896; spot the grooves of glacial striations, a signature of the mile-high sheet of ice that smothered all of New Hampshire during the last Ice Age.

Just past this viewpoint is the former site of Camp Shehadi. Built in 1912, it was removed in late 2001. Past the shelter site, the trail descends to a small saddle where views west and northwest reveal Mount Osceola, right, and Mount Tecumseh, left. Kate Sleeper Trail joins from the left (4.0/3,890), marking the end of Blueberry Ledge Trail. Continue straight on Rollins Trail, which rises to the viewless summit of Whiteface (4.2/4,020/43° 56.197′ N, 71° 24.463′).

The trail drops and then steepens again; look for the summit of Mount Washington, which rises north above the distant peaks of the Pemigewasset Wilderness. Pass a spur to another open panorama to the east, and then encounter a view northwest toward the peaks of the nearby Tripyramid massif.

The route now becomes mostly forested and descends steadily over rocky terrain. The trail levels, passes paper birches and hobblebushes, and ends at Dicey's Mill Trail on the right (6.4/3,250). Bear left onto Dicey's Mill Trail, which climbs past a seeping, unreliable spring and then crosses a flowing brook—the first reliable water source in 6.0 miles. Encounter East Loop Trail (6.6/3,420) and turn left to stay on Dicey's Mill Trail to immediately reach the site of former Camp Rich. It fell into disrepair and collapsed in 2000.

To ascend Passaconaway—a strenuous climb that rewards with a panoramic view north—continue up Dicey's Mill Trail. (Alternatively, skip the summit and follow East Loop for 0.2 mile to Walden Trail.) Dicey's Mill Trail ascends switchbacks and rocky terrain, passing an open view northwest just before the summit. The multi-peaked Tripyramids appear once again; Waterville Valley Ski Area can be spotted beyond. The wooded summit (7.5/4,043/43° 57.282′ N, 71°22.849′ W) offers no views, but don't despair. A short distance past the summit, a posted path on the left drops 200 feet on an occasionally boggy path to a small outcrop with an exceptional view north.

The mountain slopes fall away into the Swift River valley, traced by the Kancamagus Highway. Looking west, North Tripyramid and the Fool Killer loom nearby. Past them and to the right is trailless Mount Kancamagus. In the northwest distance are Kinsman and Franconia ridges, the latter topped by Mount Lafayette (Trip 21). The bump of Mount Garfield is visible east of Lafayette. Almost due north, look for the bulging massifs of Mounts Carrigain and South Hancock. The distinctive cleft of Carrigain Notch is to the right of Carrigain (Trip 20); Vose Spur and Mount Lowell stand sentinel over the notch to the west and east, respectively. On a clear day, Mount Washington is visible to the north-northwest; to its right are the even more distant peaks of the Carter Range. Return to the summit and continue onto Walden Trail; another excellent view immediately follows. This one looks east over the entire east Sandwich Range. Below, the rocky knob of Square Ledge protrudes from the slopes. The trail then plummets down a steep bouldery route to reach the east end of East Loop Trail (8.1/3,410).

Turn left to remain on Walden Trail, which drops steeply via rock and log stairs to Square Ledge Trail (8.2/3,320). Bear left and follow Square Ledge Trail's long descent from spruce-fir forest into hardwoods. Loose and gritty in spots, the trail parallels an audible but inaccessible stream below. Next reach the base of a large open rock slide—a quick scramble reveals a view of Mount Passaconaway looming overheard and Mount Washington in the distance.

Red and sugar maples appear alongside abundant paper birches and the trail soon curves right, away from the stream valley. Climb briefly to Passaconaway Cutoff Trail on the left (8.9/2,550), where a 4-foot-high boulder appears to be supported by a single paper birch, an amusing illusion. Continue on Square Ledge Trail, rising momentarily to views of nearby Mount Paugus and more distant Mount Chocorua. From here, the trail once again descends, passing through jumbled terrain marked by large spruces and yellow birches. The path becomes indistinct in spots—watch for blazes.

The base of Square Ledge (9.5/2,400) abruptly emerges. The route winds along its side, but you can scramble atop this massive stone with some creative gymnastics; a thin path leads to its north end and a view of Mount Passaconaway, Carrigain Notch, and points south. Square Ledge Trail continues past its namesake stone and reaches a viewpoint looking down the Oliverian Brook valley; ample tentsites are available, but there is no nearby water source.

From here, the trail turns sharply right and drops into a gully between sheer rock faces. Giant chunks have calved off in places but remain stuck in position overhead, waiting to tumble. The route becomes very indistinct— watch closely for blazes—as it remains close to the cliff face. After descending more than 200 feet, the trail enters a thick forest of beeches, sugar maples, and yellow birches. Brief glimpses behind reveal the rocky visage of Square Ledge. The path then levels, crosses a stream, and encounters Square Ledge Branch Trail on the left (9.9/2,090).

Continue straight on Square Ledge Trail, passing through an area rich with pink lady's slippers. A single orchid sprouts from their large, grooved, twin basal leaves in spring and early summer. The narrow trail rolls gently through dense vegetation and reaches the four-way junction with Walden, Old Mast Road, Lawrence, and Square Ledge trails (11.0/2,320). Turn left onto Lawrence Trail, gently dipping to reach another four-way junction (11.3/2,220) with Oliverian Brook, Lawrence, and Kelley trails.

The saddle here marks the lowest point along the Sandwich Range divide. Bear right onto Kelley Trail to return to the trailhead. The narrow path descends a wide gully and parallels a small trickling creek. The rocky trail steepens and descends rock stairs. As a stream disappears underground, begin traveling atop the moss-coated boulders of the dry streambed.

Hemlocks grow in increasing numbers as the creek reemerges from beneath the rocks. Continue to follow the stream, crossing it twice. The trail stays level as the stream abruptly flows downward out-of-sight. Make a gentle descent to rejoin the creek by a cascade. The ravine broadens here and fills with a pleasantly mature forest of ashes, sugar maples, and beeches.

The trail meets a grassy road (13.0/1,320)—bear right, perhaps stopping to enjoy abundant blackberries if your timing is right. In 0.1 mile, the trail splits

A hiker enjoys the view before summiting Mount Passaconaway. (Photo courtesy of Victoria Sandbrook Flynn)

left and leaves the road—watch for the sign—to descend to Old Mast Road (13.3/1,260). Continue straight on Kelley Trail, and follow it through thick hemlock forest, passing Wonalancet Range Trail on the right immediately before the parking area (13.6/1,170).

INFORMATION
White Mountain National Forest, Pemigewasset Ranger District, 71 White Mountain Drive, Campton, NH 03223, 603-536-6100, fs.usda.gov/white-mountain; Wonalancet Out Door Club, HCR 64, Box 248, Wonalancet, NH 03897, wodc.org.

NEARBY
The Big Pines Natural Area in Hemenway State Forest on NH 113A protects a stand of large white pines, including one of the biggest in New England. A short loop path accesses the area from NH 113A; look for the sign and trailhead 2.8 miles north of the 113/113A junction in Tamworth.

TRIP 19
SANDWICH RANGE WILDERNESS–
EASTERN LOOP

Location: Southern White Mountain National Forest
Difficulty: Challenging
Distance: 12.7 miles round-trip
Total Elevation Gain/Loss: 4,800 feet/4,800 feet
Trip Length: 2 days
Recommended Map: *AMC White Mountains Trail Map, Map 3: Crawford Notch–Sandwich Range* (AMC Books)
Highlights: Rocky peaks, quiet streams, remote mountains, challenging trails.

Tucked deep within a seldom-trod portion of the Sandwich Range Wilderness, hemmed between the massifs of Mounts Passaconaway and Chocorua, Mount Paugus's cliffy visage looms over a hidden watershed. Whitin Brook flows through a valley protected from all humanity, a small wilderness within a Wilderness. To the east, the distinctive summit of Mount Chocorua stands sentinel, a pyramid of granite with unrestricted views in all directions.

HIKE OVERVIEW

This loop hike highlights the eastern Sandwich Range, first through the little-visited region around 3,198-foot Mount Paugus, where solitude, scenery, and some very faint and challenging trails await. The route then enters the Mount Chocorua Scenic Area to ascend the area's namesake peak to enjoy the outstanding view from the open summit.

OVERNIGHT OPTIONS

Dispersed camping is permitted throughout the Sandwich Range Wilderness Area. There are several areas with good camping potential in the Mount Paugus/Whitin Brook area, including the summit of Mount Paugus, near Whitin Brook, and on the west side of Bolles Trail.

Dispersed camping is *not* permitted on and around Mount Chocorua within the designated Mount Chocorua Scenic Area, which starts on the east side of Bolles Trail and encompasses most of the mountain. Overnight stays

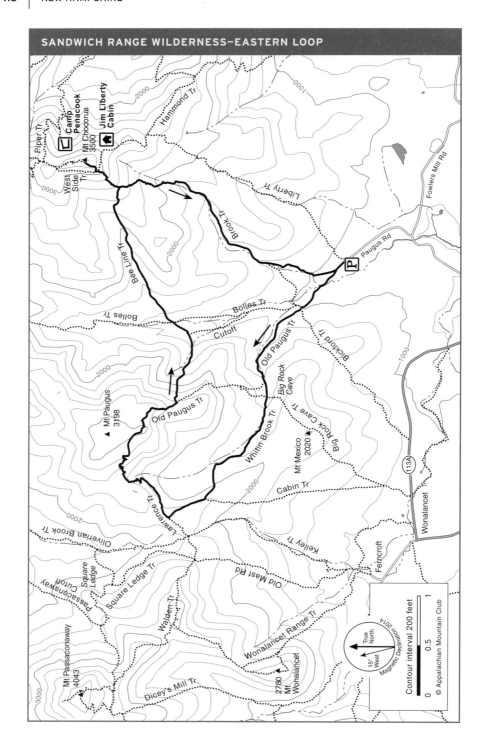

SANDWICH RANGE WILDERNESS–EASTERN LOOP

within the scenic area are limited to two designated sites: Jim Liberty Cabin and Camp Penacook.

Jim Liberty Cabin (9.3/3,100/43° 57.067′ N, 71° 16.269′ W) perches just below the summit of Chocorua at the former site of the Peak House Hotel (1892), which was blown off the mountain by high winds in 1915. Massive chains run over the roof of today's cabin, constructed by the U.S. Forest Service in 1932. The cabin is free and provides first-come, first-served space for roughly ten people. A small, unreliable water source is located 130 feet downhill. A clearing in front of the cabin provides views of the lower summit cliffs. Camping and fires are prohibited.

Camp Penacook (10.9/2,700/43° 57.449′ N, 71° 16.160′ W) sits on the east flanks of Mount Chocorua, a strenuous 3.4-mile round-trip detour with more than a thousand feet of elevation gain and loss. The basic shelter offers a few restricted views of the adjacent mountain slopes; Chocorua's summit palpably looms nearby. A fire pit is available and several tentsites can be found in the immediate vicinity. Water is available from a stream below the shelter and can be accessed from the spur trail to the shelter.

TO REACH THE TRAILHEAD

Follow NH 16 to NH 113 and head west on NH 113 for 2.9 miles to Route 113A/Chinook Trail. Turn right onto NH 113A, proceed for 3.3 miles, and then turn right onto Fowlers Mill Road. Drive 1.3 miles—the road changes from pavement to dirt—and then turn left onto unpaved Paugus Road at the sign for Liberty and Brook trails. In about a mile you reach the trailhead parking lot (43° 55.024′ N, 71° 17.602′ W) at road's end, which offers space for up to roughly 15 vehicles.

HIKE DESCRIPTION

After parking, walk past Liberty trailhead and around the gate at the head of the forest road. Amble down the road through open forest to the posted intersection with Bolles and Brook trails (0.2/930). Bear left to remain on Bolles Trail, which leads to a large campsite by flowing Paugus Brook. Rock-hop the creek, and enjoy a level streamside ramble through young hemlock forest with good camping possibilities.

Next, Old Paugus Trail enters on the left (0.7/1,010). Bear left to follow it toward Whitin Brook. Immediately pass Bickford Trail, which splits off to the left; Old Paugus Trail then quickly enters the Sandwich Range Wilderness and passes through a stately hemlock grove. Nearby Whitin Brook hisses as the surrounding terrain steepens. Weave along the creek then cross it (1.3/1,200).

Pass a gigantic boulder on the left as the trail rises to reach Whitin Brook Trail (1.6/1,410). Continue straight on Whitin Brook Trail, which climbs briefly to Big Rock Cave Trail on the left (1.8/1,520).

You can visit Big Rock Cave, located 0.1 mile and 200 feet up on Big Rock Cave Trail. Sprouting from the smooth hillside are boulders so enormous, they should be called "collosaliths." This jumbled fortress harbors several inviting caves, crevices, and cliffs—an explorer's delight. To reach it, turn left onto Big Rock Cave Trail, cross Whitin Brook (a rock-hop or ford, depending on conditions), and ascend to the collosaliths.

Back on the main route, continue on Whitin Brook Trail as it parallels its namesake stream, climbs briefly, and then crosses the brook. The path follows a tributary, crossing it twice before curving away through a wind-damaged forest of beeches, sugar and red maples, and yellow birches. Blowdowns are common in the area, though good camping locations can still be found. Mount Paugus peeks through the trees to the right, then the trail curves left to climb steeply through dense conifer forest to Cabin Trail (3.1/2,200).

Turn right and follow Cabin Trail on a root-laced traverse that offers great views of the rocky scars on Mount Paugus. The trail then reaches Lawrence Trail (3.6/2,340). Bear right and descend on Lawrence Trail past views of approaching Mount Paugus, and drop steeply into a beech forest. The gradient eases and the trail bottoms out (3.8/2,140) before ascending via recently constructed switchbacks interspersed with short, undulating sections. This new section of trail replaced what used to be one of the gnarliest paths in the entire Sandwich Range.

After a steady climb, the trail contours upward around the upper slopes of Mount Paugus and crosses several small headwater streams of Whitin Brook (4.4/2,400). Watch for Mounts Passaconaway, Whiteface, and Wonalancet rising behind you through the trees as you travel over roots, rocks, and occasional steps. The gradient finally eases near the summit plateau of Mount Paugus, crossing a few boggy spots and a flowing stream. After a final climb through dense forest, the trail emerges in a clearing atop a large, granite slab (5.1/3,080).

The actual summit is 0.3 mile to the north, but this location offers the best views. Vistas west and southwest take in Squam Lake, Passaconaway, Whiteface, and Sandwich Dome (left of Whiteface). Ragged Mountain and Mount Kearsarge rise in the distance, almost directly in line with Squam Lake. This point also marks the end of Lawrence Trail and the start of Old Paugus Trail, which continues from the other side of the clearing. The next 0.7 mile of trail is the faintest and most difficult of the entire hike to follow.

Follow Old Paugus Trail and make a sharp right turn to the immediate right of a view of Chocorua. Travel along a faint path down the side of a ledge, making a steep scrambling descent over slick rocks and cross a creek. After rising briefly, the trail curves right by an unmarked trail. This turn is easily missed—be watchful!

Dropping over more slick slabs, the trail passes an open ledge with good views south and then cuts right to make yet another scrambling plummet. Proceed carefully to remain on the mostly unblazed route. Mount Chocorua appears through the trees as the trail makes a final descending traverse to reach the posted junction with Bee Line Trail (5.8/2,450).

Bear left on Bee Line Trail, and begin a sharp descent. The steep path is generally rock-free and more forgiving than previous sections, though heavily overgrown and clogged with blowdowns in several spots. The trail eventually curves right, winds past some car-sized boulders, and parallels a hemlock-shaded creek. The trail crosses the rushing stream, cruises through a marshy area, and reaches Bee Line Cutoff Trail on the right (6.7/1,300).

Go left to remain on Bee Line Trail, which winds through the woods and surmounts a small ridge before dropping to Paugus Brook. Rock-hop the creek to reach a riverside campsite and Bolles Trail (6.9/1,300), which marks the boundary between the Wilderness Area and Mount Chocorua Scenic Area.

Remain on Bee Line Trail and climb on a narrow and rockier path through paper birch forest, flirting with a small creek as you go. The gradient steadily increases, and the trail becomes gnarlier. A few rock steps aid your ascent. The trail crosses the creek, climbs briefly, and then returns to the stream to recross it. The route curves away to the right, rises, and reaches Brook Trail (8.6/2,550).

Bear left onto Brook Trail—your later return route enters from the right—and begin ascending rock slabs. Scrambling is necessary in places. Views west start to appear, and you soon reach the open slabs of the summit cone (8.8/2,930). Now the scrambling really begins. Granite outcrops abound as you clamber to Liberty Trail (9.0/3,120). The rounded summit dome rises above you, a solid mass of granite exfoliating in sheets. To reach the top, continue uphill on Brook Trail. For Jim Liberty Cabin, bear right and follow Liberty Trail for 0.3 mile, traversing 200 feet downhill over rock slabs to reach the trailside structure.

Heading for the summit on Brook Trail, you immediately reach West Side Trail on the left, which curves below the summit to the west. Continue straight on Brook Trail, climbing up an open ledge and then passing through a stand of dwarf spruce. Piper Trail joins from the left shortly before the summit

(9.1/3,420). Following the yellow blazes, proceed directly up the rock slabs to the summit. Soon you stand upon the small plateau that crowns Mount Chocorua (9.2/3,500/43° 57.262′ N, 71° 16.392′ W).

The view sweeps 360 degrees across the landscape. Look west to trace your previous route over Mount Paugus, with Mounts Whiteface and Passaconaway beyond (Trip 18). The Kancamagus Highway cuts through the Swift River valley to the north. Mount Washington and the Southern Presidential Range (Trip 23) rise in the northern distance; the Carter Range (Trip 27) rises beyond to the right. Identify the peaks of the Pemigewasset Wilderness to the northwest. On the far northwestern horizon are the Franconia Ridge and the west edge of the Pemigewasset Wilderness (Trip 21). Looking south, the largest visible body of water is Ossipee Lake; Silver Lake shimmers north of it. Return to the earlier junction with the Piper and Brook trails (9.3/3,420).

SIDE TRIP TO CAMP PENACOOK

To reach Camp Penacook, follow Piper Trail north as it traverses along open ledges with endless views. Yellow blazes mark the initially mellow route, which reenters the trees and passes West Side Trail in 0.5 mile. Remain on Piper Trail, descending to Champney Falls Trail at 0.7 mile. Turn right to remain on Piper Trail, and begin a rapid drop down a bouldery ridge. Enjoy views of the summit face and cliffs as you descend; then the route curves right off the ridge and down occasional rock staircases. At 1.5 miles, reach the posted spur to the shelter, which heads right and ascends 200 feet in 0.2 mile to the shelter.

To return to the trailhead, make the short drop to the junction with Liberty Trail (9.4/3,120). At this point you have two return options. Brook Trail, as described here, provides a slightly shorter, more direct, and more exciting route downward with far fewer hikers, though it is steep and challenging in places; several sections descend directly down rock slabs that can be dangerously slippery in wet conditions. Liberty Trail is a much safer, less challenging option in wet conditions, but is 0.3 mile longer and offers far less solitude.

To head down Brook Trail, return to the Bee Line–Brook Trail junction (9.8/2,550), and bear left to remain on Brook Trail as it descends into thick spruce forest. Pass over giant slabs with views south before dropping back into hardwood forest. The rocky, lightly used path steadily descends through lush woods and then levels. Rushing Claybank Creek becomes audible, and the

The open summit ledges of Mount Paugus offer remote views of the central Sandwich Range Wilderness. (Photo courtesy of Philip Werner)

trail soon crosses it (10.3/1,880). The route parallels the creek, which weaves in and out of sight, and leaves the Mount Chocorua Scenic Area. The gradient mellows and crosses several rivulets in more gentle terrain—camping is possible along this section. The trail runs level and then turns away from the water to cruise through dense hemlock forest to Bickford Trail on the right (11.9/1,140). Continue straight on Brook Trail, which becomes a gravel road shortly before its junction with Bolles Trail (12.7/950), and reach the trailhead.

INFORMATION

White Mountain National Forest, Pemigewasset Ranger District, 71 White Mountain Drive, Campton, NH 03223, 603-536-6100, fs.usda.gov/white-mountain; Wonalancet Out Door Club, HCR 64, Box 248, Wonalancet, NH 03897, wodc.org.

NEARBY

The Big Pines Natural Area in Hemenway State Forest on NH 113A protects a stand of large white pines, including one of the biggest in New England. A short loop path accesses the area from NH 113A; look for the sign and trailhead 2.8 miles north of the 113/113A junction in Tamworth.

TRIP 20
PEMIGEWASSET WILDERNESS–
MOUNT CARRIGAIN LOOP

Location: White Mountain National Forest
Difficulty: Strenuous
Distance: 13.5 miles round-trip
Total Elevation Gain/Loss: 4,200 feet/4,200 feet
Trip Length: 2 days
Recommended Map: *AMC White Mountains Trail Map, Map 2: Franconia–Pemigewasset* (AMC Books)
Highlights: Little-visited Carrigain Notch, a wild ascent on Desolation Trail, and one of the best views in the White Mountains atop 4,700-foot Mount Carrigain.

Mount Carrigain stands sentinel on the eastern edge of the Pemige-wasset Wilderness, a landmark summit with superlative views over the entire Wilderness from a summit lookout platform. The deep cleft of Carrigain Notch cuts the landscape below it to the east and provides entry into the Wilderness Area and the backside of the mountain, which is climbed via a thrilling, heart-pumping scramble up Desolation Trail.

HIKE OVERVIEW
From Sawyer River Road near the southeastern border of the Pemigewasset Wilderness, the route loops counter-clockwise around and then over the summit of Mount Carrigain. The first half of the hike follows Carrigain Notch Trail, a lightly used route that connects with even-steeper Desolation Trail at the northern base of Mount Carrigain. From there, the hike summits via Desolation Trail before returning to the trailhead on rocky and more popular Signal Ridge Trail.

OVERNIGHT OPTIONS
Dispersed camping is permitted throughout most of this hike, though sites are hard to come by in the steep and rocky terrain. Some potential camping areas can be found near the midpoint of the hike along a flat section just prior to reaching Desolation Trail, but the best area is along Carrigain Notch Trail just below its junction with Desolation Trail, 6.6 miles from the trailhead. Here

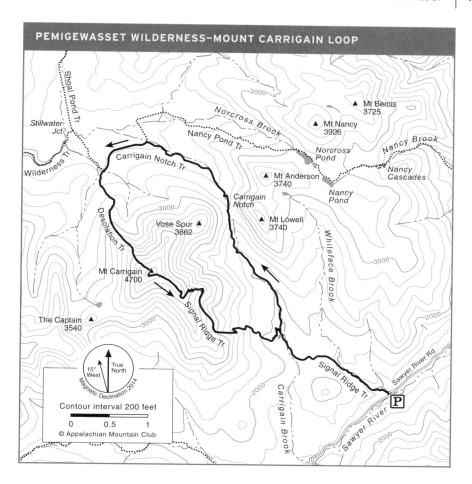

PEMIGEWASSET WILDERNESS–MOUNT CARRIGAIN LOOP

rushing Carrigain Brook races downhill over granite slabs and boulders and several good campsites can be found nearby.

A Forest Protection Area has also been established around Mount Carrigain summit. Though several very nice and obviously used campsites have been established right near the top, no overnight use is permitted within 0.25 mile of the summit. The lack of a nearby water source would make an overnight stay a challenge in any case.

TO REACH THE TRAILHEAD

Follow NH 302 east of the Highland Center in Crawford Notch for 10.7 miles to Sawyer River Road on the right. Approaching from the west, the turn-off is 3.0 miles past Bartlett. Follow unpaved (but easily passable) Sawyer River Road for 2.2 miles to the large parking area (44° 04.188′ N, 71° 23.054′ W) on the left.

HIKE DESCRIPTION

The trailhead was recently relocated directly across from the parking lot entrance (0.0/1,380) from its former spot by the large information sign just down the road. Nearby Whiteface Brook rushes crystal-clear over boulders and beneath shady mountain ashes and hemlocks.

Strike out on yellow-blazed Signal Ridge Trail. This trail was recently moved into the woods and away from Whiteface Brook. The soft, squishy, and sometimes muddy ground underfoot is evidence of the trail's newness.

Common species of the northern forest accompany you—hobblebushes, yellow and paper birches, red maples, hemlock, and spruces—as you gently climb through dense woods near the audible and occasionally visible brook below. The trail soon rejoins its original route (the change in trail character is apparent) and begins running parallel to the stream, with several good access points to the water.

The gradient steepens past pleasant rushing cataracts, then switchbacks left to follow another new section of trail. The path briefly climbs, makes a quick switchback right, and parallels the brook farther up the slopes before it once again rejoins its old route. Some nice rock staircases soon lead away from the stream and into a flat area, where the trail cruises among healthy yellow birches and diseased beech cankered by the nectria fungus. The trail crosses a woods road, gently descends, and runs parallel to nearby Carrigain Brook.

Pass an old trail junction—where Signal Ridge Trail used to cross the brook—and proceed a short distance ahead to reach the designated crossing. Getting across usually involves an exciting rock-hop, but it can be more challenging (and potentially dangerous) during periods of heavy rains and high water. Once on the other side, the flat and mellow trail continues over some new puncheon to reach posted Carrigain Notch Trail (1.7/1900).

You'll return from the left on Signal Ridge Trail, but for now continue straight ahead on less-traveled Carrigain Notch Trail. The initially level path proceeds through pleasant broadleaf forest punctuated by white ashes and sugar maples and parallels diminishing Carrigain Brook. The single-track path crosses a tributary, then several more small trills and trickles as it makes a gentle and slow rise.

The trail abruptly becomes much rockier, crosses the stream, and ascends more steeply. The terrain underfoot becomes increasingly rough through woods that steadily transition to spruce-fir forest punctuated by trillium and extensive numbers of hobblebushes. The trail thins and narrows, views start to peek out to the right of the steep flanks of Mount Lowell, then the route noticeably steepens up rock slabs and along a rocky gully.

Signal Ridge descends from the summit of Mount Carrigain.

Roots and rocks crisscross the path as it continues steadily upward, levels briefly, then resumes its ascent to crest the notch and cross into the posted Pemigewasset Wilderness (4.0/2,630). Enjoy some of the best glimpses yet of the cliffs and steep slopes of adjacent Mount Lowell, including some unusual and distinctive red rockslides.

The single-track now descends over occasional granite boulders and through dense spruce-fir forest. Cross a few clear-flowing streams that mark the upper headwaters of Notch Brook, which soon begins to flow alongside (and sometimes directly in) the trail. After crossing some old puncheon, the path curves left and begins a long, mostly level traverse through more open forest. Roots lace the duff-covered trail as it proceeds through unchanging scenery, crossing several small trickles as it makes a slow descent. Notch Brook becomes increasingly audible once again, the trail returns alongside it, and you then encounter a potentially confusing section.

A small creek flows directly in the trail, sometimes covering it entirely and necessitating some careful footwork and route-finding. After a short distance, however, emerge at the posted Nancy Pond Trail (5.8/2,160), which joins from the right.

Continue left on Carrigain Notch Trail, which cruises fast and level along an old railroad bed. Paper birches and a few red maples mix in with the surrounding conifers. The trail crosses a few small streams then reaches Desolation Trail (6.6/2,230). To explore rushing water, rocks, and potential campsites, bear right here and head a short distance downstream. Otherwise, bear left onto Desolation Trail. After crossing Carrigain Branch (your last reliable water for the next 3.5 miles), walk along some rotten puncheon, and climb up Mount Carrigain.

The easy-to-follow trail is in good shape and steadily ascends over dirt and roots through a pleasant forest. The trail briefly traverses to the right, curves straight uphill, and then makes a rising traverse to the left. Distant mountains peek through the trees, and there's a feeling of growing elevation. The trail traverses up a steep slope to the left and becomes rockier around 3,200 feet. By 3,500 feet, you're ascending the first section of rock and talus. Then the trail heads directly uphill on a radical talus staircase that requires hand-over-hand scrambling. You soon reach the trail's best view thus far, encompassing the Webster Cliffs above Crawford Notch, the Presidentials beyond, and much of the eastern Pemigewasset Wilderness.

Past this point, the trail becomes somewhat less vertical. As you near the top, the trail traverses left and levels. Bank right and complete the final climb to the summit lookout tower (8.5/4,700/44° 05.612′ N, 71° 26.810′ W).

The view from the Carrigain lookout is one of the best in New England. First admire the eastern Pemigewasset Wilderness (Trip 22), from the Hancocks to your west, to the Bonds to your north, to the Appalachian Trail traversing Zealand and down Zeacliff, including a great view of U-shaped Zealand Valley. Owl's Head and all of Franconia Ridge are to the west. To the east is a grand view of the Presidentials and the Dry River watershed that drains its southern tier. In the eastern distance are the Carter Range and more distant Baldface Range that hem in the Wild River watershed (Trip 27). The whole Sandwich Range fills the southern vista; you can make out Ossipee Lake to the right of pyramidal Mount Chocorua. The rocky spine of Signal Ridge is to the south and drops down into the Sawyer River drainage toward Hancock Notch.

Several established campsites are just below the summit, including a large clearing with a fire ring; remember, however, that camping is no longer permitted within 0.25 of the summit. Head down Signal Ridge Trail, immediately descending a rock staircase into mature spruce-fir forest. The rocky trail switchbacks left before resuming its descent. Another slow, traversing descent deposits you on open Signal Ridge, which offers views—your last!—into Carrigain Notch below, including the scarred flanks of Mount Lowell on its far side.

Rise briefly along the ridge to its highpoint (9.0/4,500), and then resume a sharp descent. A minefield of rocks fills the trail for the remainder of the descent. The trail switchbacks right, makes a slow descending curve back left, levels out, and then drops more gradually. After another switchback right, the sinuous trail curves back and forth and then at about 4,000 feet takes a more direct line down. Paper birch reappears. Several small switchbacks lead down the ridge, and the path curves right onto a mile-long traverse that passes a series of flowing springs—the first significant water since Carrigain Branch.

The trail makes a long, steady drop, encounters another spring, and then steepens further. The trail cuts left, switchbacks right, and continues on a rocky traverse. By 2,500 feet, beeches and yellow birches appear. The trail switchbacks left by a nice yellow birch. By the time the route switchbacks right again the transition to northern hardwood forest is complete.

As you approach the bottom, the gradient eases, and the route curves to the left on a recently relocated section of trail. Cross a small brook on a large puncheon bridge, and rise slightly before beginning the final descent via a pair of switchbacks. One last curve to the right deposits you at Carrigain Notch Trail (11.8/1,900). Turn right and retrace your steps to the trailhead (13.5/1,380).

INFORMATION

White Mountain National Forest, Saco Ranger District, 33 Kancamagus Highway, Conway, NH 03818, 603-447-5448, fs.usda.gov/whitemountain.

NEARBY

AMC's Highland Center in Crawford Notch offers an array of information and amenities, including educational displays; a small retail store that stocks books, maps, and other backcountry essentials; and a dining room that offers a buffet breakfast, a la carte lunch, and a sit-down, family-style dinner. For more information, call 603-278-4453 or go to outdoors.org.

TRIP 21
PEMIGEWASSET WILDERNESS–
WESTERN LOOP

Location: White Mountain National Forest
Difficulty: Challenging
Distance: 25.2 miles round-trip
Total Elevation Gain/Loss: 6,800 feet/6,800 feet
Trip Length: 2–3 days
Recommended Map: *AMC White Mountains Trail Map, Map 4: Moosilauke–Kinsman* (AMC Books)
Highlights: Easy cruising, a remote waterfall, five 4,000-footers, a long alpine ridgeline.

The Pemigewasset Wilderness protects the watershed of the East Branch of the Pemigewasset River. Ringed by lofty peaks, including sixteen taller than 4,000 feet, it is New England's largest Wilderness Area, with 45,000 acres of protected backcountry. In many ways, it is also one of the friendliest. Many trails follow old railroad beds—wide, easy-cruising pathways—deep into the backcountry. The well-traveled and rugged Appalachian Trail (AT) runs along the mountain spine.

HIKE OVERVIEW

Follow easy-cruising Lincoln Woods and Franconia Brook trails. Pass the sculpted granite slabs of Franconia Falls en route to 13 Falls Tentsite and its accompanying cascade. Ascend lofty Garfield Ridge and head south on the AT, pass Garfield Ridge Campsite as it summits Mount Garfield. Traverse the length of Franconia Ridge, including 3.0 miles above treeline, and tag the summits of Mounts Lafayette, Lincoln, Liberty, and Flume. A long, mellow descent on Osseo Trail returns you to the trailhead.

This hike visits some of New England's most heavily used backcountry trails. This section of the AT—especially Franconia Ridge—is a hiking highway where you may see literally hundreds of people. Avoid weekends if possible. Dogs are allowed.

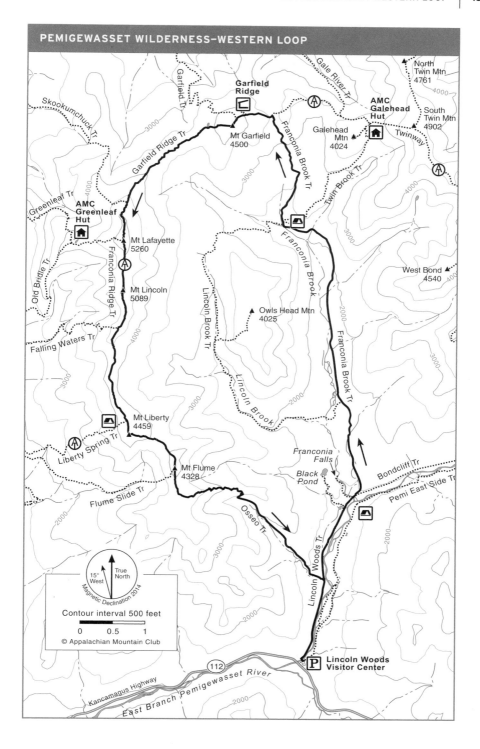

PEMIGEWASSET WILDERNESS—WESTERN LOOP

OVERNIGHT OPTIONS

Dispersed camping is permitted throughout most of the Pemigewasset Wilderness, though there are a number of restrictions in busier areas (see later). The hike visits three designated camping areas. Resident caretakers collect a per-person overnight fee from Memorial Day weekend through Columbus Day. The funds are used to maintain these heavily used sites.

Camping is prohibited:
- within 0.25 mile of the East Branch of the Pemigewasset River from the trailhead to Franconia Brook (a distance of 0.6 miles),
- at the former Franconia Brook Campsite near Franconia Falls,
- within 0.25 mile of all designated campsites and huts and within 200 feet of Black Pond, the AT, Liberty Spring Trail,
- and within 200 feet of the section of trail from Franconia Brook from its junction with the East Branch of the Pemigewasset River to the second island above Franconia Brook Falls.

13 Falls Tentsite (8.1/2,250/44° 09.922′ N, 71° 35.590′ W) hides out in spruce-fir forest near the headwaters of Franconia Brook. Nine tent pads are available, most on boulder terraces resembling rocky nests. The site is named for both the beautiful falls that wash the sites with sound and Camp 13, a former logging camp from the late nineteenth century. The falls—and a swimming hole at its base—are accessible. Bear boxes are provided by the entrance at the designated cooking area. Because it sits away from the AT, 13 Falls receives fewer visitors than the other overnight options on this hike, though it is still busy in July and August.

Garfield Ridge Campsite (10.8/4,000/44° 11.506′ N, 71° 36.401′ W) perches on the upper flanks of Mount Garfield. Seven tent platforms and a 12-person shelter are available. The shelter was custom built by an artisan log-home builder in 2011. Facing east, it catches good morning sunlight from the entrance. Enjoy far-reaching views to the northeast and east; South Twin Mountain, Mount Guyot, Mount Bond, West Bond, Bondcliff, and Galehead Hut are all visible. Due to heavy use, expect to share the shelter or a tent platform with others during July and August. The water source is located on the spur trail to the site, and food storage is available.

Liberty Spring Tentsite (18.5/3,800/44° 06.901′ N, 71° 28.539′ W) is located 18.5 miles from the trailhead on Liberty Spring Trail, 300 feet below Franconia Ridge. Ten numbered tent platforms are dotted within thick spruce-fir woods. Several are relatively private, especially sites 8, 9, and 10. This heavily used location fills most summer nights; expect to share tent platforms with other parties. Water is available from the site's namesake spring, and a bear box is available.

Galehead Hut (10.8/3,780/44° 11.285′ N, 71° 34.139′ W) and *Greenleaf Hut* (15.8/4,220/44° 09.689′ N, 71° 29.582′ W) offer alternatives to sleeping out-side. Each requires a small detour off the route, but can be blissful experiences in bad weather. Learn more about these overnight options at outdoors.org/lodging or call 603-466-2727 for reservations and information. No camping is allowed near the huts.

TO REACH THE TRAILHEAD

Follow I-93 to NH 112 in Lincoln (the Kancamagus Highway) and head east for 5.2 miles. The Lincoln Woods Trailhead is signed on the left and fea-tures a huge parking area (44° 03.917′ N, 71° 35.093′ W) and visitor center (open Tuesday to Sunday from 9 A.M. to 3:30 P.M.). A WMNF parking permit is required.

HIKE DESCRIPTION

From the parking lot (0.0/1,140), check trail and weather conditions at the visitor center. Heading out on the Lincoln Woods Trail, immediately cross a large suspension bridge over the Pemigewasset River, flowing broadly over thousands of round boulders. Information signs on the opposite side tell the region's history. Twenty-four logging camps and 50 miles of railroad track once laced this portion of the White Mountains—a striking contrast to the area's Wilderness status today.

Past the signs is one of the old railroad beds—your route for the next 8.0 miles—and a large mileage sign. Bear right to head out on wide, easy-cruising Lincoln Woods Trail; look for old railroad ties underfoot. The route parallels the river, roughly 20 feet above it. The river is often out-of-sight and usually difficult to access—a scramble down steep embankments is necessary in most spots. (Note that portions of Lincoln Woods Trail from the trailhead to Osseo Trail were damaged by high water during Hurricane Irene in 2011. The Forest Service did significant trail work in the fall of 2013 to improve the pathway.)

The flanks of Mount Hitchcock are visible east across the river. The sur-rounding forest is a young and diverse hardwood mosaic of black cherries, beeches, yellow and paper birches, hemlocks, sugar and red maples, red pines, and white ashes. The trail makes an almost imperceptible rise to Osseo Trail on the left (1.4/1,270)—your return route—located in a paper birch grove by a flowing brook.

The trail narrows to double-track, passes a good river access point, and then widens and travels closer to the river. Views upstream reveal the lower slopes of the Bonds. Cross Birch Island Brook on a plank bridge and cruise away from the river to Black Pond Trail on the left (2.6/1,360). Franconia Brook tenting area used to be located here, but overuse led to its closure; camping is now prohibited here.

Franconia Brook and the trail to Franconia Falls adjoin the route on the left (2.8/1,370). For a highly recommended 0.4-mile side trip, follow Franconia Falls Trail, briefly ascending before dropping down to the falls. An enormous chunk of granite bedrock has been worn smooth by sluicing water, leaving extensive swaths of rock ideal for lounging. Back on Lincoln Woods Trail, continue over a wooden bridge atop old railroad trestles and reach the signed Wilderness boundary. Just past it, Bondcliff Trail enters from the right, and Franconia Brook Trail splits left (2.9/1,430).

Bear left onto Franconia Brook Trail, which narrows and quickly rises before leveling out and returning to double-track. Cross and then recross a brook as the route becomes increasingly single-track. Root-laced and muddy in spots, the trail curves around, recrosses the brook, and then climbs up the opposite bank to regain the railroad bed. Now cruising level, reach Lincoln Brook Trail on the left (4.6/1,730).

Continue straight, following level, single-track Franconia Brook Trail with views of the lower flanks of nearby Owl's Head. The route continues over a beaver dam, a 50-foot-long structure that requires some delicate footwork. The trail crosses Hellgate Brook (5.5/1,770) and briefly touches Franconia Brook; this section can get wet during heavy rains. The woods slowly transition to spruce-fir forest, brush lines the trail in spots, and you reach Redrock Brook (6.5/1,890). Beyond it, the route has a perceptible upward gradient for the first time and crosses slopes far above Franconia Brook. Large, big-tooth aspens proliferate around you.

The trail slowly rises, crosses a rocky streambed, and makes a level traverse to Twin Brook (7.6/2,090). Crossing the brook, the trail curves northwest and reaches the end of the railroad line by rushing, sheeting 13 Falls. The large and deep swimming hole at its base can be accessed with some scrambling. The trail turns uphill, abruptly becomes a steeper and rockier route, and quickly meets Lincoln Brook Trail returning from the left (8.1/2,200). Water sluices over rock slabs here, and there are more views of Owl's Head. Just beyond is the spur to 13 Falls Tentsite.

Immediately past the campground, the trail reaches the intersection of Twin Brook and Franconia Brook trails. Twin Brook Trail continues right, rising 1,500 feet in 2.7 miles to reach AMC's Galehead Hut. Continue straight on rocky, root-chocked, wet Franconia Brook Trail as it heads upward toward

**Hikers gather on the porch of AMC's Galehead Hut. (Photo by Lori Duff,
© Appalachian Mountain Club)**

Garfield Ridge; Mount Garfield peeks out above. A much-diminished Franconia Brook, audible but seldom seen, runs parallel below.

The trail levels briefly, the brook rises to meet it, and the water becomes accessible in spots. Paper birches and hobblebushes proliferate. Cross over a small brook—which floods in heavy rains—and some puncheon. The path gradually rises with an occasional steep section over rock slabs, and ascends directly up a rocky creek bed—the trickiest portion of trail yet. As you approach the ridge, cross the posted Wilderness boundary and enter a chaotic stand of spongy spruce-fir forest. Hop through a boggy area over some bog bridging to reach the junction with the AT (10.3/3,430).

Bear left on the white-blazed AT, which has been ground down to bedrock by millions of boot steps. From here on out, the hike is much rockier. The trail climbs steeply, quickly ascends a rock face, drops, levels briefly, and crosses a small stream flowing north. Brief glimpses of Garfield ahead help motivate you. Surmount another vertical rock staircase, and enjoy a restricted view southeast. Water flows down the rock face, the source for the approaching Garfield Ridge Campsite. The spur to the camping area soon splits right (10.8/3,900), immediately crossing the water source before climbing up the rocky slopes. Fill up your water bottles—this is the last quality source for the next 8.0 miles.

Continuing, the AT ascends a steady staircase of stone and rock steps. The gradient eases just before Garfield Trail, which enters from the right (11.0/4,250). Remain on the AT as it ascends the summit via a short spur trail on the left (11.2/4,500/44° 11.343' N, 71° 36.580' W). Old tower footings crown the peak, the remains of a fire lookout tower that operated here between 1940 and 1948. The views south are outstanding. The whole Franconia Ridge lies out in front of you. From north to south, the peaks are Mounts Lafayette, Lincoln, Liberty, and Flume. The bulging massif of Owl's Head is below you, and the Sandwich Range (Trips 18 and 19) serrates the horizon—the broad pyramid of Passaconaway is to the left, Tripyramid and Osceola right. Past the summit, the AT plummets 200 feet down a rocky staircase, then levels and descends more gradually. Make a radical rock scramble down and resume a steady rocky descent. Watch for diminutive Garfield Pond on the right as you descend. Eventually the trail reaches a saddle and a thin ephemeral trickle of water. The trail crosses some puncheon, climbs again, and then undulates to the base of Franconia Ridge. The trail rises steadily, passing the dead snags of a fir wave. The route steepens and continues upward at a constant grade. The trail switchbacks left, travels along a strip of solid bedrock, and then emerges above treeline at 4,500 feet.

This is the alpine zone. Grassy tufts of Bigelow's sedge wave in the wind. Far-reaching views are everywhere. Cairns and painted blazes indicate the route, which soon passes Skookumchuck Trail on the left (13.9/4,690). The well-marked trail crests at 5,000 feet and for the first time you peer west into Franconia Notch and south along the ridge to the summit of Mount Lafayette. Greenleaf Trail runs from Greenleaf Hut up the west summit ridge and is often lined with easily spotted hikers. Savor this next quiet section of the AT—it will soon be much busier. A final climb leads you to the summit and accompanying hiker mania (14.7/5,260/44° 09.770' N, 71° 38.702' W).

The peak is crowned by the vestiges of the former Summit House. Greenleaf Hut perches 1,060 feet and 1.1 miles below via Greenleaf Trail. Enjoy views south toward Mounts Lincoln, Liberty (just visible), and Flume (the prominent pyramid). Marvel at the hiker super-highway ahead of you. Legions of day-hikers often line the ridge for 1.7 miles to Falling Waters Trail.

Continue south on the AT toward the saddle between Lincoln and Lafayette, passing views west into the steep drainage of Walker Brook. Climbing again, top out on a false summit—Greenleaf Hut perches on the mountain's shoulder behind you—then head to Mount Lincoln's true highpoint (15.7/5,089/ 44° 08.923' N, 71° 38.660' W). Pause once again to savor the far-reaching views.

Descend to Little Haystack (16.4/4,780), where the hiking masses branch down Falling Waters Trail to the right. Remain on the AT and the ridge, reentering the trees. The duff-covered trail leads to another open view west before plummeting toward the broad saddle below Mount Liberty. The path levels out and then slowly rises to Liberty Spring Trail joining from the right (18.2/4,290). To reach Liberty Spring Tentsite—and the first good water source since the Garfield Ridge Campsite—turn right and descend 300 feet for 0.3 mile.

The AT continues south down Liberty Spring Trail, but remain on the blue-blazed Franconia Ridge Trail. A quick rise leads to the open summit of Mount Liberty (18.5/4,459/44° 06.948′ N, 71° 38.167′ W). More nice views look to the east, with Owl's Head and the entire Pemigewasset Wilderness unfolding beneath you. Dropping off the summit, scramble over some steep boulders and quickly lose elevation, passing views of Mount Flume. The trail bottoms out in a rocky saddle and steadily climbs along a wider footpath to the summit (19.6/4,328/44° 06.524′ N, 71° 37.691′ W).

The mountaintop is rocky and open, but does not offer 360-degree wide views like previous peaks. Instead, it looks west into the deep bowl of Flume Brook, where you can trace the transition between the dark greens of boreal forest and the lighter greens of hardwoods farther down. From the summit, drop steeply past a few more ledgy outcrops to Flume Slide and Osseo trails (19.7/4,230). This marks the end of Franconia Ridge Trail. Head down pleasant and easy-to-travel Osseo Trail. Though narrow and less trod than previous paths, the duff-covered path has few rocks. Occasional yellow blazes line the route.

The gentle trail initially runs level, then descends and curves left. There is a palpable sense that you are approaching the edge of a steep drop, and you do, descending wooden staircases with the occasional view east toward Bondcliff. Equally nice rock steps interrupt the wooden staircases at times, and you soon pass a posted viewpoint on the left (20.6/3,540) looking northeast past Owl's Head toward the Twins, Mount Guyot, and Mount Bond. The wooden steps continue down, ending at a series of tight switchbacks. Paper birches increase and a cliff face peeks out ahead as the trail traverses toward an audible creek. The trail then curves left and heads downhill.

At 2,500 feet, the trail curves. The creek appears below for the first time; some potential camping areas can be spotted nearby. Big-tooth aspens and red maples add further diversity to the woods as you next traverse a steep slope of hemlocks. The trail now descends more rapidly, widening to double-track and slowly approaching the stream. Near the bottom, quickly drop and hike parallel to the brook, cruising across level terrain. Sounds from the nearby

Pemigewasset River fill the air just before you reach the Lincoln Woods Trail (23.8/1,270). Turn right and head back to the trailhead (25.2/1,140).

INFORMATION
Lincoln Woods Visitor Center, Kancamagus Highway, Lincoln, NH 03251, 603-630-5190, fs.usda.gov/whitemountain, open Tuesday to Sunday from 9 A.M. to 3:30 A.M.

NEARBY
Lincoln provides places to eat, refuel, and purchase any last-minute supplies. The Kancamagus Highway—one of New England's most scenic drives—continues east from the Lincoln Woods trailhead for another 29 miles to Conway. The highway is popular for its fall foliage, and six Forest Service campgrounds are available along its length, including two—Hancock and Big Rock campgrounds—close to the Lincoln Woods trailhead.

TRIP 22
PEMIGEWASSET WILDERNESS– EASTERN LOOP

Location: White Mountain National Forest
Difficulty: Challenging
Distance: 31.4 miles round-trip
Total Elevation Gain/Loss: 4,500 feet/4,500 feet
Trip Length: 2–4 days
Recommended Map: *AMC White Mountains Trail Map, Map 2: Franconia–Pemigewasset* (AMC Books)
Highlights: Four 4,000-footers, Thoreau Falls, and a total White Mountain backcountry experience.

Soaring open summits, rushing waterways, and long easy-cruising sections of trail—this is the total Pemigewasset experience. The hike circles through the eastern half of the Pemigewasset Wilderness, lounges by the rushing Pemigewasset River, scales the remote Bonds, visits roaring Thoreau Falls, and then cruises through moose-rich lowlands to return to the trailhead.

HIKE OVERVIEW

From the Lincoln Woods trailhead on NH 112 (the Kancamagus Highway), cruise quickly along Lincoln Woods and Bondcliff trails before climbing steeply to the striking open summits of the Bonds (Bondcliff, Mount Bond, and West Bond). The route next passes Guyot Campsite and joins the Appalachian Trail (AT) on its way north to Zealand Falls Hut, at which point the journey returns via remote, much less traveled, and often faint Shoal Pond and Wilderness trails. The final section is along the wide, flat, and fast-hiking Pemi East Side Trail.

The hike can be completed in two long days, with a potential overnight near the midpoint at Zealand Falls Hut. A better option is a three-day outing, with overnights at Guyot Campsite and along Shoal Pond Trail. Note that black bear encounters have increased in this area in recent years. Properly hang or secure your food at night; bear canisters are available at the Lincoln Woods Visitor Center on a first-come, first-served basis.

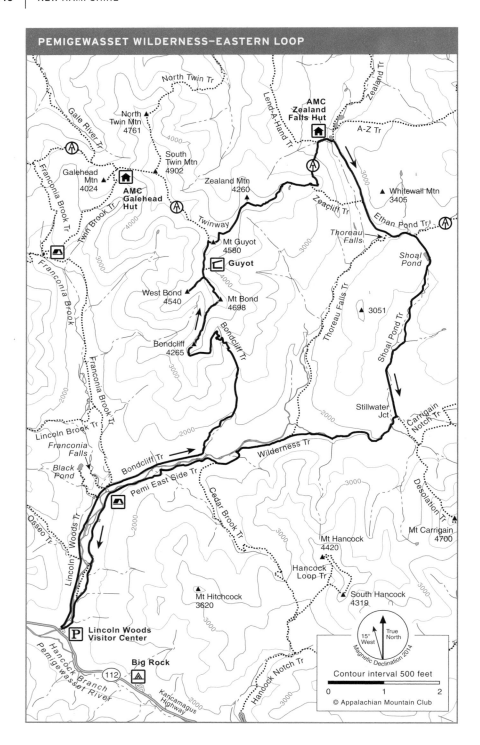

PEMIGEWASSET WILDERNESS–EASTERN LOOP

OVERNIGHT OPTIONS

Dispersed camping is permitted throughout the Pemigewasset Wilderness, though a number of restrictions are in place in areas of heavy use (see later). The only designated overnight camping area is Guyot Campsite; the other recommendations that follow identify clearly established tentsites. Numerous other options await the intrepid camper elsewhere on the route. Campfires are permitted.

Camping is prohibited:

• within 0.25 mile of the East Branch of the Pemigewasset River from the trailhead to Franconia Brook (a distance of 2.6 miles),
• at the former Franconia Brook Campsite near Franconia Falls,
• within 200 feet of Black Pond and Franconia Brook from its junction with the East Branch of the Pemigewasset River to the second island above Franconia Brook Falls,
• south of Bondcliff Trail but allowed on the north side more than 200 feet from the trail corridor,
• and at Thoreau Falls, within 200 feet of the East Branch of the Pemigewasset River from the Wilderness boundary to its crossing with Thoreau Falls Trail.

Bondcliff Trail between Franconia Brook Trail and Black Brook: Potential camping areas can be found on the left (north) side of the trail beginning about a mile beyond Franconia Brook Trail; options increase near Black Brook. Note that camping is not permitted at the site of the old Camp 16 logging camp, located just past the old junction for a now-closed section of Wilderness Trail where Bondcliff Trail turns left.

Guyot Campsite (12.0/4,100/44° 09.682′ N, 71° 32.100′ W) perches on the slopes below Mount Bond. It offers campsites and a cabin-like shelter with space for roughly a dozen hikers. Six tent platforms—two are double-size—nestle in dense spruce-fir forest. A few overflow sites are located on the ridge. Views are limited, though you can spot Mount Willey to the east from the shelter deck. A caretaker staffs the location from June through mid-October and collects an overnight fee. Guyot is the primary overnight option in a popular area, and it's usually a pretty crowded scene. A nearby brook reliably provides water.

Zealand Falls Hut (15.7/2,650/44° 11.742′ N, 71° 29.661′ W) offers an alternative to sleeping outside. Learn more about this overnight option at outdoors.org/lodging or call 603-466-2727 for reservations and information. No camping is allowed near the hut, though an established tenting area is located nearby along Ethan Pond Trail, just past the limits of the 0.25-mile Forest Protection Area boundary.

Shoal Pond (18.8/2,540/44° 09.838′ N, 71° 27.352′ W) has a few decent campsites a short distance from the lakeshore and near a small brook. There are also several sites tucked among the dense evergreens along the 3.5-mile stretch of Shoal Pond Trail south of the pond.

Wilderness Trail from Shoal Pond Trail to Cedar Brook Trail: Camping options are limited until you near Cedar Brook Trail and the site of the former bridge crossing the Pemigewasset River; at least one established campsite can be found where Wilderness Trail curves markedly to the south.

Franconia Brook Tentsite (28.7/1,400/44° 06.109′ N, 71° 33.893′ W) is located 2.0 miles from the end of the hike along Pemi East Side Trail, close to the rushing Pemigewasset River. It offers nearly twenty campsites, a privy, fire pits, and a bear box. A caretaker is on site in season to collect the required overnight fee.

TO REACH THE TRAILHEAD

Follow I-93 to NH 112 in Lincoln (the Kancamagus Highway) and head east for 5.2 miles. The Lincoln Woods Trailhead is signed on the left and features a huge parking area (44° 03.917′ N, 71° 35.093′ W) and visitor center (open Tuesday to Sunday from 9 A.M. to 3:30 P.M.). A WMNF parking permit is required.

HIKE DESCRIPTION

From the parking lot (0.0/1,140), check trail and weather conditions at the visitor center. Heading out on the Lincoln Woods Trail, immediately cross a large suspension bridge over the Pemigewasset River, flowing broadly over thousands of round boulders. Information signs on the opposite side tell the region's history. Twenty-four logging camps and 50 miles of railroad track once laced this portion of the White Mountains—a striking contrast to the area's Wilderness status today.

Past the signs is one of the old railroad beds—your route for the next 8.0 miles—and a large mileage sign. Bear right to head out on wide, easy-cruising Lincoln Woods Trail; look for old railroad ties underfoot. The route parallels the river, roughly 20 feet above it. The river is often out-of-sight and usually difficult to access—a scramble down steep embankments is necessary in most spots. (Note that portions of Lincoln Woods Trail from the trailhead to Osseo Trail were damaged by high water during Hurricane Irene in 2011. The Forest Service did significant trail work in the fall of 2013 to improve the pathway.)

The flanks of Mount Hitchcock are visible east across the river as you continue north. The surrounding forest is a young and diverse hardwood mosaic of black cherries, beeches, yellow and paper birches, hemlocks, sugar and red maples, red pines, and white ashes. The trail makes an almost imperceptible rise to Osseo Trail on the left (1.4/1,270)—your return route—located in a paper birch grove by a flowing brook.

The trail narrows to double-track, passes a good river access point, and then widens and travels closer to the river. Views upstream reveal the lower slopes of the Bonds. Cross Birch Island Brook on a plank bridge and cruise away from the river to Black Pond Trail on the left (2.6/1,360). Franconia Brook tenting area used to be located here, but overuse led to its closure; camping is now prohibited here.

Franconia Brook and the trail to Franconia Falls adjoin the route on the left (2.8/1,370). For a highly recommended 0.4-mile side trip, follow Franconia Falls Trail, briefly ascending before dropping down to the falls. An enormous chunk of granite bedrock has been worn smooth by sluicing water, leaving extensive swaths of rock ideal for lounging. Back on Lincoln Woods Trail, continue over a wooden bridge atop old railroad trestles and reach the signed Wilderness boundary. Just past it, Bondcliff Trail enters from the right, and Franconia Brook Trail splits left (2.9/1,430).

Bear right on Bondcliff Trail, and continue cruising along another old railroad bed. The trail rises almost imperceptibly beneath a mix of hardwoods, some towering overhead, and encounters a few wet patches of trail. The East Branch of the Pemigewasset River rushes below, but reaching it would require a steep downhill scramble of 25 to 50 feet.

About a mile past the Franconia Brook Trail junction, rock-hop over a small, unnamed brook. The trail widens, and camping opportunities increase as the terrain flattens out. Approaching Black Brook, Bondcliff Trail turns left and moves uphill (4.9/1,600). (For some brief exploration, continue straight ahead to venture onto a portion of Wilderness Trail, which is no longer maintained. As a reward for your curiosity, you'll encounter a 20-to-30-foot section of old railroad track lying to the side. Farther ahead are the remnants of railroad trestles and stone columns, parts of a former bridge; the bridge is not safe for foot traffic.)

Head up blue-blazed Bondcliff Trail, quickly crossing a small brook. The trail briefly touches Black Brook and passes an old campsite on the left (no overnight use permitted). Pass another old site on the right as the single-track trail rises among dense hardwoods. Cross another small creek as you steadily climb.

Contouring level along the slopes, the path parallels the audible but invisible Black Brook. Wet and boggy in spots, the trail descends to the rushing stream by another no-camping site on the far shore. The rocky route runs up along Black Brook, and the woods start to transition back to spruce-fir. Step over a few more streams and then cross Black Brook. The gradient steepens and leads upward at a consistent angle—good for maintaining a steady, cruising climb. The trail recrosses the brook and drops briefly before resuming the ascent parallel to a small tributary. A rock staircase aids your efforts.

The trail levels out again, contours back toward Black Brook, and crosses it once more. Twisted paper birches dot the slopes, framing the bouldery watercourse. The trail charges higher, steady and steep, crossing two brooks before curving right and easing upward. It then curves back left and begins the final, long traverse, passing several small springs. The trail curves right again, makes its final ascent, and enters the alpine zone, immediately encountering a large outcrop that requires hand-over-hand scrambling. On top is your first unobstructed view of the western Pemigewasset Wilderness.

In the southeast, the Pemigewasset River drains toward the Kancamagus Highway. Scar Ridge rises on the opposite side. To the west, Franconia Ridge (Trip 21), topped by Mount Lafayette, towers over the humped massif of Owl's Head.

The trees diminish immediately past this point, and you quickly top out on Bondcliff (9.1/4,265/44° 08.431′ N, 71° 32.433′ W). A jumbled wall of stone that boasts an exceptional view, the mountain draws its name from the blocky vertical cliffs below the summit. The whole eastern half of the Pemigewasset Wilderness rolls out before you. To the south, Mount Carrigain and the Hancocks bulge upward. Look for evidence of old logging roads on Mount Hancock; Cedar Brook's broad drainage is visible to its west. East of Carrigain, in order, are the red-orange slopes of Mount Lowell, the round hump of Mount Anderson, and Mount Nancy. Shoal Pond Brook—your return route—flows down the second stream valley to the east. In the southern distance are Osceola and distinctive Greeley Notch. Scar Ridge and the slopes of Loon Mountain Ski Area are visible to the southwest, and due west is the hulking hump of Owl's Head. Franconia Ridge rises behind it, crenulated by Mounts Lafayette, Lincoln, Liberty, and Flume from north to south. Below to the northeast is the deep gully of Redrock Brook.

From here, the rocky trail traces visibly up Mount Bond ahead and travels along the open ridge and past alpine vegetation. Distinctive clumps of diapensia dot the ground in dense rounded mats. The path drops briefly, resumes climbing up Mount Bond, enters chest-high krummholz, and in short order reaches the open summit and its 360-degree views (10.3/4,698/44° 09.171′ N, 71° 31.877′ W).

The view here penetrates farther to the northeast. The bare cliffs of White-wall Mountain above Zealand Notch are visible. Mount Washington and the Presidential Range are almost directly in line with the cliffs. To the north-northwest is the bald peak of South Twin, but your continuing route heads north over Mount Guyot and Zealand Mountain. Farther east, Mount Field and the deep scalloped slopes of Mount Willey hide Crawford Notch from view. Ethan Pond shimmers below Mount Willey.

Past the summit, return to the trees, hopping along rocks and bog bridging. Intermittent glimpses northwest reveal Mount Garfield. The trail steepens, offering open views of South Twin Mountain, Lafayette, and Guyot, among other peaks. A spur on the left leads to West Bond (10.8/4,470).

SIDE TRIP TO WEST BOND

To bag this 4,000-footer (1.0 mile round-trip with 350 feet of elevation gain), turn left onto West Bond Spur and follow the rocky, single-track path through dense spruce-fir woods. The path drops, then steadily rises and encounters a bouldery section before the rocky summit knob (44° 09.283′ N, 71° 32.619′ W) and another excellent view of the western Pemigewasset Wilderness.

Back on Bondcliff Trail, turn left, drop steeply, and enter the Forest Protection Area that surrounds Guyot Campsite. Several overflow campsites appear by the trail before it reaches the spur for the camping area (11.0/4,340).

Continuing onward, head toward Mount Guyot. The trail climbs slowly, leaves the Forest Protection Area, and levels briefly before descending a short distance. Mount Guyot's broad, bald summit dome appears ahead. Climb steadily uphill into the alpine zone, where the path navigates a minor boulder field and then busts out atop the open summit plateau. Dropping from the summit area, pass briefly among head-high trees and traverse a slope to reach the Twinway and the AT (11.6/4,510).

Turn right on the Twinway, joining the white-blazed AT, and climb briefly to reach Guyot's actual summit (44° 10.089′ N, 71° 32.043′ W). The trail quickly reenters head-high trees and leaves the alpine zone. It's a steep and rocky drop—the rockiest yet—and on some sections you feel like you're hopping down a talus field. The trail moderates and becomes less rocky, though now rooty and boggy, and soon resumes a steady drop. The rounded hump of

Zealand Mountain appears ahead shortly before you bottom out in a saddle (12.7/4,020).

Resume climbing, this time over large rocks and stone stairs. Pass a small spring shortly before the trail crests (12.9/4,220), where a short spur leads to the actual (viewless) summit of Zealand Mountain (44° 10.798′ N, 71° 31.279′ W) .

The trail now steadily descends, passing through a fir wave marked by numerous bleached snags. A long, gradual downhill leads over forgiving terrain. The trail levels, follows ribbons of bedrock, then briefly rises to reach a coarse-grained granite boulder with large crystals of rectangular white feldspar. Ethan Pond is visible from here, as is Shoal Pond for the first time. Carrigain Notch frames Mount Chocorua to the southeast (Trip 20). Look eastward to spot Mount Washington, Mount Jefferson, and beyond to Mount Hale in the Carter Range (Trip 27).

The route plummets over solid rock, a ladder, and some steep staircase-like drops. It mellows shortly before reaching a spur on the right to swampy—and tent-unfriendly—Zealand Pond (14.1/3,760). Continuing, the trail momentarily rises, cruises along, and breaks out at a good view of Mount Willard to the east and the Presidentials beyond. The junction for Zeacliff Trail is just ahead (14.5/3,740).

ZEACLIFF TRAIL SHORTCUT

The described route continues straight, but at this point you have the option to instead descend steep Zeacliff Trail, which shortens the trip by 1.6 miles but skips the pleasant layover at Zealand Falls Hut.

To take this shorter option, turn right and head down narrow Zeacliff Trail, which immediately crosses back into the Pemigewasset Wilderness. Paper birches increase as you descend sharply past boulder outcrops and views of Mount Carrigain. After negotiating a challenging drop over solid granite slabs, the trail contours left and passes some bulging stones. The plummet soon resumes. A staircase of roots and rocks soon leads you down the middle of a small, flowing creek.

From the junction with Zeacliff Trail, the route bends left, curves right, and offers a tempting view of the prominent cliffs of Whitewall Mountain. Looming above Zealand Notch, the cliff was laid bare by the large-scale wildfires that followed extensive logging in the early twentieth century. The trail next enters a serene grove of paper birches, where the going gets easier. Blackberry canes, bracken fern, and trillium punctuate a dense understory of hobblebush—a beautiful flowering scene in late May and early June.

The trail briefly traverses a flat section before resuming a plummeting trajectory downward toward the banks of Whitewall Brook. Rock-hop the burbling stream to a pleasant camping area on the opposite bank. The trail climbs a boulder field to emerge in a swath of talus, created during construction of the old railroad bed above you. Follow the blazes to the former railroad route, today Ethan Pond Trail, and turn right.

To proceed to Zealand Falls Hut, continue straight on the Twinway from the Zeacliff Trail junction. In 0.2 mile, reach the posted spur to the top of Zeacliff—one of the White Mountains' classic views. Looking across the eastern Pemigewasset Wilderness, the vista encompasses Whitewall Brook, Whitewall Mountain, the Willey Range, and Shoal Pond, among many other landmarks.

The spur trail loops you back to the Twinway, which descends with the aid of stone steps. Wet sections and a few small water crossings ensue as you lose elevation. The trail crosses cascading Whitewall Brook on some rock ledges shortly before crossing Lend-A-Hand Trail (15.6/2,700). Some of Zealand Falls Hut's external systems, including a water pump, appear along the trail, indicating that the hut (15.7/2,640) is just ahead. Its wide, wooden steps and two porches offer a welcome place to rest your legs and look out at Zealand Notch and Mount Carrigain. A short side trail to the right leads out to Whitewall Brook, where water flows over wide, smooth rocks and ledges.

Departing the hut, a short descent on stone steps leads to a side trail on the right, which quickly brings you to the hut's namesake Zealand Falls. A small pool and sun-soaking rocks provide an opportunity to relax at this picturesque spot.

Continuing, the trail rock-hops briefly and crosses a few bog bridges to reach a large boulder and Ethan Pond Trail. Turn right to follow fast-walking Ethan Pond Trail south, soon passing a much-used camping area that marks the 0.25-mile Forest Protection Area boundary from the hut.

Ethan Pond Trail runs on a gentle uphill grade. Easy stretches periodically intermingle with rockier sections and several small water crossings. Almost all the common constituents of the northern hardwood forest appear along this section: hobblebushes, red maples, mountain ashes, yellow *Clintonia*, red spruces, firs, yellow and paper birches, sugar maples, false Solomon's-seal, wake robins, hazels, wild blueberries, and quaking aspens. Zealand Falls Hut is visible up the valley behind you as the trail cruises alongside massive talus fields and passes Zeacliff Trail on the right (17.0/2,450).

The cliffs of Whitewall Mountain tower overhead; giant boulders look like they could fall at any moment. Increasingly dense spruce-fir forest surrounds the trail before it reaches a brook dotted with the large veined leaves of false hellebore and then rises slightly to reach Thoreau Falls Trail on the right (17.8/2,450).

SIDE TRIP TO THOREAU FALLS

This short detour is well worth it. Located only a few minutes' walk down Thoreau Falls Trail, this zigzagging cascade roars over polished slabs, dropping 70 feet in sheets of foaming white. A head-deep swimming hole fills a pool at the base of the falls but reaching it requires careful scrambling. Continuing Thoreau Falls Trail provides no water access.

Continue on wide Ethan Pond Trail, hiking closer to the increasingly audible North Fork of the East Branch of the Pemigewasset River. The trail narrows to single-track and runs along the waterway before crossing it on a wooden footbridge. The path parallels the stream on the opposite side and passes at least one established tentsite; the area has good potential for camping, with abundant level ground and a relatively open forest. The trail next encounters Shoal Pond Trail on the right (18.3/2,520)—watch for the double-white blazes to indicate its approach.

Turn right on Shoal Pond Trail and leave the AT behind. The blue-blazed trail immediately thins. Moose frequent the area; look for fresh tracks in the mud. The level path next reaches shallow Shoal Pond (19.0/2,580). The pond's one established campsite is located midway down the pond on the left side of the trail, just past a small creek. A nicer site can be found on the rise adjacent to the obvious trailside site. The pond can be accessed in several spots, but the shore is generally boggy with few good spots for lounging. Spring peepers and fish are abundant; moose are in the vicinity. Fishing is catch-and-release; only single barbless hooks are allowed.

Past the pond, Shoal Pond Trail parallels the tannin-brown outlet stream, soon crosses it, and then leaves it behind. The path travels over old puncheon and then widens as it returns to a railroad bed. Puncheon increases as you proceed through dense forest, at one point following a flowing streambed. The trail descends slightly and recrosses Shoal Pond Brook (19.9/2,400), now a rocky stream. Your journey now tours long stretches of puncheon, narrow and very overgrown sections, boggy bits that require rock-hopping, and occasional dry spots. You cross a rocky tributary and then return to Shoal Pond Brook, which requires a trickier rock-hop to cross (20.7/2,260). The trail turns downstream to the left (not up and out) and becomes thinner, brushier, and more difficult to follow. After a narrow traverse above the water, the trail then descends a rock staircase to return near the stream. The route returns to the railroad bed and passes a few small campsites on the left, one near a swimming hole and rock sluice.

The route now sticks to the railroad bed, traveling at times along a raised berm. After a long, level stretch, pass some metal debris near a small field—another former logging camp. The trail next cuts right, dropping off the berm to return to the brook. Pass some potential camping areas and rock-hop across the stream (21.7/2,190). Once across, the trail quickly regains the berm; fire up your boilers for a long stretch of chugging down a straight and flat thoroughfare, and reach Anderson Brook, where there is another established campsite (22.3/2,080). The trail turns left along the shin-deep brook and then crosses it by old railroad bridge footings. Rock-hopping is not an option—you'll need to ford it. A trail junction is on the far side. It is posted for Carrigain Notch Trail on the left and Shoal Pond Trail behind you, but you bear right instead on unsigned Wilderness Trail.

Turn right onto Wilderness Trail, pass through a conifer thicket, and soon the trail emerges on the banks of Carrigain Brook, where a small stone cairn marks where to cross. The trail continues on the far side directly across from the cairn. Yellow blazes intermittently mark the trail, which remains relatively flat, with occasional undulations and wet and rocky sections. The river is never far; the water audibly cascades its way past boulders and over numerous rocks, though accessing it is generally challenging.

Pass an old iron range on the right of the trail just before reaching an open meadow, the location of Camp 18, a former logging site. Shortly thereafter, the trail heads left and up a small incline with a few stone steps. (Continuing straight leads you to an established nearby campsite.)

The route continues its gentle meander along the river, with several small water crossings. At times, the path narrows and roots and rocks become more apparent. Occasional wet patches greet you as you travel beneath maples (striped, red, and sugar), firs, and birches. Ferns dot the trail's edges. The trail eventually moves farther away from the river, providing a newfound silence punctuated by the occasional bird call. Ditches run parallel to the trail throughout this section, which help minimize erosion by diverting water off the main path.

Zealand Valley cuts a deep cleft in the northeast section of the Pemigewasset Wilderness. (Photo © Jerry and Marcy Monkman)

Wilderness Trail reaches a junction with Thoreau Falls Trail on the right (24.9/1,780). Continue straight ahead to remain on Wilderness Trail and resume cruising. A few twists and turns among larger boulders and rocks punctuate the hike, along with several small water crossings. The trail levels off, and camping begins to become a possibility.

The trail then encounters the junction with Cedar Brook Trail (25.8/1,650), which enters from the left and joins Wilderness Trail for the next 0.5 mile. A right turn here leads to the site of the former bridge crossing over the river, which was removed in 2009. Cables and other bridge debris remain behind.

To continue, turn left onto Wilderness/Cedar Brook Trail to ascend on an old railroad bed, crossing two small brooks along the way and encountering two deep washouts that cut across the trail; the trail detours left to avoid them. Wooden railroad ties also appear in the trail, guiding your steps to the junction with Pemi East Side Trail (26.4/1,720).

Bear right onto Pemi East Side Trail, which gradually descends alongside dense thickets of hobblebush and beneath tall white pines before returning by the river at a white granite boulder. The trail now curves to the left and widens on its way toward its crossing of Cedar Brook, which requires an ankle- to knee-high ford, depending on conditions. (It may be deeper during high water periods.)

The route never ventures far from the river, which becomes accessible at times. The trail emerges briefly on rock slabs offering a gorgeous view of the river just before a sign indicating approaching Franconia Brook Campsite. Immediately before reaching the campsite, pass a locked gate across the trail and then cruise through the camping area (28.7/1,400).

You are now on the easiest of trails: a narrow gravel and dirt road that parallels the river on the right. Continue on the road all the way back to the trailhead, or, for a more scenic walk, veer off to the right when you reach Pine Island Trail (30.1/1,280), which rejoins Pemi East Side Trail in 0.8 mile. Completely reestablished after the 2011 devastation of Hurricane Irene, this tranquil yellow-blazed path offers soft footing beneath its namesake trees. It then passes through a mix of pines, birches, sugar maples, oaks, and hemlocks. Wide and easy to follow, the final section travels close to the river, where the damage inflicted by Hurricane Irene is clearly apparent. On the far side, you may be able to spot Lincoln Woods Trail, on which you began your journey.

Gently swinging to the right, and slightly uphill, Pine Island Trail then rejoins Pemi East Side Trail (30.9/1,200), which returns you to Lincoln Woods Visitor Center (31.4/1,140).

INFORMATION

Lincoln Woods Visitor Center, Kancamagus Highway, Lincoln, NH 03251, 603-630-5190, fs.usda.gov/whitemountain, open Tuesday to Sunday from 9 A.M. to 3:30 P.M.

NEARBY

Lincoln provides places to eat, refuel, and purchase any last-minute supplies. The Kancamagus Highway—one of New England's most scenic drives—continues east from the Lincoln Woods trailhead for another 29 miles to the town of Conway. Outstanding fall foliage is a highlight in season, and six Forest Service campgrounds are available along its length, including two—Hancock and Big Rock campgrounds—close to the Lincoln Woods trailhead.

TRIP 23
THE SOUTHERN PRESIDENTIALS

Location: White Mountain National Forest
Difficulty: Strenuous
Distance: 17.3 miles round-trip
Total Elevation Gain/Loss: 5,950 feet/5,950 feet
Trip Length: 2–3 days
Recommended Map: *AMC White Mountains Trail Map, Map 1: Presidential Range* (AMC Books)
Highlights: Alpine peaks, continuous views, and four 4,000-footers, including the summit of Mount Washington.

The Southern Presidential Range leads from Crawford Notch north to the highest point in New England, the 6,288-foot Mount Washington. The bare summits of Mounts Eisenhower and Monroe—and the long alpine ridge that connects them—offer superlative views of the area, including the mighty Rockpile itself, which crowns New England's highest mountain range in all its hulking glory.

HIKE OVERVIEW

This strenuous out-and-back hike follows the historic Crawford Path from Crawford Notch to Mount Washington. After climbing steeply and relentlessly to attain the mountain ridge by Mizpah Spring Hut and Nauman Tentsite, it heads northeast to follow the Appalachian Trail (AT) on a steady ridgeline climb to Lakes of the Clouds Hut, which nestles nearly a mile high in an alpine saddle below Mount Washington's summit cone. After tagging Mount Washington's summit, it's a long, rocky return back to Crawford Notch.

OVERNIGHT OPTIONS

Camping is prohibited above treeline,. Book huts as far in advance as possible, especially for weekend stays (603-466-2727, outdoors.org/lodging).

Mizpah Spring Hut (2.6/3,777/44° 13.160′ N, 71° 22.173′ W) is tucked within dense woods. *Nauman Tentsite,* a more affordable option, is located adjacent to Mizpah Spring Hut and provides seven tent platforms within a thick spruce-fir forest. An AMC caretaker is in residence between Memorial Day and Labor Day, plus most fall weekends, and collects an overnight per-person fee. As one of the few designated camping areas in the Presidentials, it receives

THE SOUTHERN PRESIDENTIALS

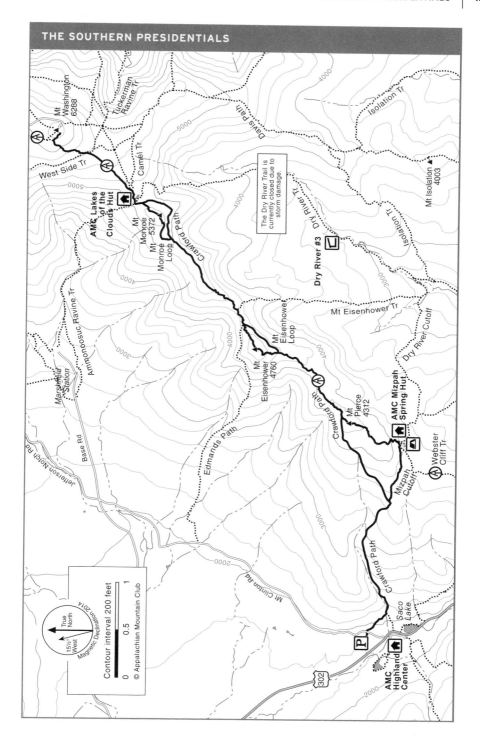

The Dry River Trail is currently closed due to storm damage.

Contour interval 200 feet

© Appalachian Mountain Club

0   0.5   1

steady use. Both the hut and tentsite are good options if you are interested in starting the trip later in the day, making this a three-day adventure, with the second night at Lakes of the Clouds Hut, or using this as an overnight base camp for the out-and-back to Mount Washington.

Lakes of the Clouds Hut (7.3/5,012/44° 15.525′ N, 71° 19.136′ W) perches a mile high near the midpoint of the hike and is located in a dramatic alpine setting with incredible dining room views. This hut is extremely popular in the system and full most weekends.

TO REACH THE TRAILHEAD

Take NH 302 0.1 mile north of the Highland Center in Crawford Notch, turn north onto Mount Clinton Road, and proceed 0.1 mile to the large parking area on the left (44° 13.399′ N, 71° 24.693′ W).

HIKE DESCRIPTION

From the trailhead on Crawford Connector (0.0/1,900), quickly cross Mount Clinton Road, and gradually ascend to Crawford Path (0.4/2,100). Turn left on Crawford Path and climb to reach a posted spur trail on the left to Gibbs Falls, a narrow cascade that drops 30 feet down a rocky runnel (0.6/2,280). The well-graded trail continues relentlessly upward, running parallel to mostly out-of-sight Gibbs Brook, and passes among increasing numbers of paper and yellow birches to reach Mizpah Cutoff on the right (1.9/3,530).

SIDE TRIP TO MIZPAH SPRING HUT AND NAUMAN TENTSITE

Making the side trip to Mizpah Spring Hut and Nauman Tentsite adds 0.3 mile to the overall trip, but it provides a pleasant place to rest (or spend the night) before striking out for the higher elevations. Follow Mizpah Cutoff to reach the hut in 0.7 mile. From the junction, the trail steadily ascends via extensive cobblestones and rock and log steps, then runs level along a rocky path through dense woods to emerge at Webster Cliff Trail. Turn left and proceed approximately 200 feet to the hut and nearby tentsites.

To continue, follow Webster Cliff Trail (part of the AT) north for the next 0.8 mile. Past the hut, climb via several switchbacks through more thick woods. Ascend steeply and directly up a rocky corridor, switchback right, and rise over rocky slabs. The trail undulates past a pair of open areas—one with views north to Mount Washington, the other south to the Sandwich

Range—and ascends via more slabs in wooded terrain. A spur leads to another view shortly before emerging below the forested summit of Mount Pierce. The site offers the first full view of the Presidentials. Look north down the spine of the mountains to trace nearly the entire route to Mount Washington. Pass over the summit and quickly reach Crawford Path. Turn right and continue as described below.

To skip Mizpah, remain on Crawford Path, which ascends steadily at moderate grades through increasing numbers of spruces and firs; most of the primary constituents of this forest type are readily spotted, including mountain ashes, yellow *Clintonia*, and bunchberry bushes. The continuing trail crosses several rivulets on its way to meet Webster Cliff Trail, which joins from the right (3.1/4,300). Tag the forested summit of 4,312-foot Mount Pierce (44° 13.614′ N, 71° 21.926′ W) by following Webster Cliff Trail a short distance south.

Continuing north on Crawford Path—now part of the white-blazed AT from this point to Mount Washington—slowly descend, enjoying views north to Mount Washington and its nearest summits, Mount Jefferson (north of Washington) and Mount Monroe (south of Washington). Traverse a wet and boggy section over rotten puncheon, and cross a small creek. This is the last reliable water source until Lakes of the Clouds Hut, 4.0 miles ahead.

The route passes through corridors of 8-foot high trees with occasional boggy bits. Mount Eisenhower, your next summit, is visible at times and entices you onward. Increasingly open and slabby terrain steadily brings you closer to treeline as Mount Eisenhower Loop connects on the left (4.3/4,440).

In inclement weather or tired-leg conditions, remain on Crawford Path to traverse through head-high forest around the south flanks of Mount Eisenhower. In all other conditions, ascend Eisenhower for the view. Mount Eisenhower Loop climbs steeply, cuts right at a switchback, and then traverses upward to reach the summit (4.7/4,760/44° 14.445′ N, 71° 21.020′ W), marked by a giant pile of rocks and a 15-foot-diameter stone ring.

This is the first tremendous 360-degree mega-view of the hike. Enjoy it! Past the summit, the trail drops gradually over the rounded summit dome, then makes a steep and rocky descent with occasional switchbacks to reach the four-way junction (5.1/4,450) with Edmands Path (left) and Crawford Path. The puddle of Red Pond is nearby to the right.

Continue north on Crawford Path, briefly descending and making a quick switchback left to reach the col below Mount Eisenhower. A short rise then

The long ridge of the Presidentials stretches south from Mount Eisenhower. (Photo © Jerry and Marcy Monkman)

brings you to Mount Eisenhower Trail (5.4/4,490), which climbs out of the Dry River valley to the right. Crawford Path proceeds upward over rock slabs, leaving the route's final section of head-high (and view-obscuring) trees before emerging on a mostly level section that leads toward Mount Franklin (6.3/5,001), a small promontory accessed via a short spur trail on the right. The views are once again excellent.

As the trail continues onward, the endless views now make watching your footing difficult in the rough terrain. Rocks border the trail, both to highlight the path and discourage off-trail wanderings in the fragile alpine vegetation. Mount Washington peeks out ahead of you through a gap above nearby Mount Monroe, next on the route. Stunted spruces and firs appear intermittently in the tundra-scape as you reach Mount Monroe Loop on the left (6.5/5,070).

The view from Mount Monroe is arguably the best of the entire hike and well worth the effort, though in poor weather you can also continue around the summit on Crawford Path, which saves 0.1 mile and a few hundred feet of climbing. Follow steep, rocky Mount Monroe Loop around some large boulders on its way toward the summit. The trail appears at one point to almost reconnect with Crawford Path below, but it bears left to clamber over a small rise and reach the view-tacular summit (6.9/5,372/44° 15.301' N, 71° 19.280' W).

North are Mounts Washington, Jefferson, Adams, and Madison, marching in that order to the horizon in all their rockpile glory. To the east and south, stare down the entire Dry River drainage. The prominent pyramid of Chocorua appears farther south; the Sandwich Range runs to its west (Trips 18 and 19). Lake Winnipesaukee peeks out to Chocorua's right; the even-more distant Belknap Range can be spotted above the lake's south shore. Down below to the west are the Mount Washington Hotel and Bretton Woods Ski Area. The spine of Franconia Ridge lies out in the western distance (Trip 21), and the peaks of Vermont's Green Mountains dot the horizon.

Head down the far side of Monroe, first on a mostly direct descent over solid bedrock, and then with the help of rock stairs, to return to Crawford Path. Turn left (north) to encounter Ammonoosuc Ravine Trail (left) and Dry River Trail (right). Lakes of the Clouds Hut is immediately beyond (7.3/5,012); snacks, views, water, and a bowl of soup await you inside.

The final portion of the journey ascends Mount Washington. Follow Crawford Path north past the hut, bearing left at the junction with Crossover and Camel trails (7.4/5,120). Ascending moderately to the northwest over rocky terrain, the trail rises to reach Davis Path on the right (8.0/5,600), followed immediately by Westside Trail to the left. Commence the final climb, through jumbled boulders and naked geology. Just before the summit, Crawford Path hits Gulfside Trail and turns right for the final stretch. Keep heading straight (north) once you hit pavement. Pass the Glen House and reach the Tip-Top House and Sherman Adams Summit Building. The true summit is at the top of the rockpile to your left. (8.8/6,288/44° 16.240' N, 71° 18.220' W). Return to Crawford Notch the way you came (16.9/1,900); skipping the summit of Mount Eisenhower saves you 0.3 mile.

INFORMATION

White Mountain National Forest, Saco Ranger District, 33 Kancamagus Highway, Conway, NH 03818, 603-447-5448, fs.usda.gov/whitemountain; Pinkham Notch Visitor Center, 603-466-2725, open daily 6:30 A.M. to 10 P.M. from May to October.

NEARBY

AMC's Highland Center offers an array of information and amenities, including educational displays; a retail store that stocks books, maps, and other backcountry essentials; overnight rooms; and a dining room that offers a buffet breakfast, a la carte lunch, and a sit-down, family-style dinner. For more information, call 603-466-2725 or go to outdoors.org/lodging.

TRIP 24
MONTALBAN RIDGE

Location: White Mountain National Forest
Difficulty: Strenuous
Distance: 17.7 miles one-way
Total Elevation Gain/Loss: 7,100 feet/6,100 feet
Trip Length: 2 days
Recommended Map: *AMC White Mountains Trail Map, Map 1: Presidential Range* (AMC Books)
Highlight: The least-traveled ridge in the Presidential Range.

Montalban Ridge runs due south from Mount Washington for 15 miles. The Davis Path traverses its spine, one of the longest and most remote sections of trail in the Whites—remarkable given its location in the heavily trod Presidential Range. Crowds gravitate to the alpine peaks of the Southern Presidentials (Trip 23), which run parallel to the west, but Montalban Ridge boasts three exceptional summits of its own, offering 360-degree views of jagged mountainous horizons.

HIKE OVERVIEW

The point-to-point journey treks from the Davis Path trailhead on Route 302 to the Glen Boulder trailhead on Route 16. As of 2013, the trail was faint and challenging to navigate in several sections; careful route-finding may be necessary.

Davis Path ascends nearly 2,000 feet in the first 2.0 miles to reach open ledges and remarkable views from the summit of Mount Crawford. From there, cruise along a forested ridgeline, punctuated by Stairs Mountain, a ledgy promontory with another quality viewpoint. Visit more excellent views atop Mounts Davis and Isolation and then ascend into the alpine zone to reach Boott Spur on Mount Washington's southeastern flank. The route's final leg descends Glen Boulder Trail to NH 16, passing the trail's impressive namesake stone en route.

Traffic is light on Davis Path, though hikers become more common north of Mount Isolation, the only 4,000-footer on the ridge and a popular peakbaggers' destination. Water is scarce, with only a few sources along the ridge. Dogs are allowed.

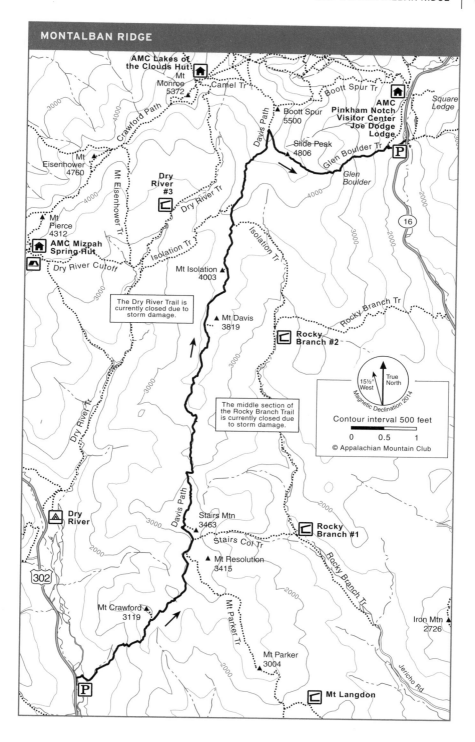

MONTALBAN RIDGE

AMC Lakes of
the Clouds Hut

Mt
Monroe
5372

Camel Tr

Boott Spur Tr

Square
Ledge

Crawford Path

3000

4000

Davis Path

Boott Spur
5500

AMC
Pinkham Notch
Visitor Center
Joe Dodge
Lodge

Slide Peak
4806

Glen Boulder Tr

Glen
Boulder

P

16

Mt
Eisenhower
4760

Dry
River
#3

Dry River Tr

4000

3000

4000

2000

Mt Eisenhower Tr

Mt
Pierce
4312

AMC Mizpah
Spring Hut

Dry River Cutoff

Isolation Tr

Mt Isolation
4003

Isolation Tr

The Dry River Trail is
currently closed due to
storm damage.

▲ Mt Davis
3819

3000

Rocky Branch Tr

Rocky
Branch #2

3000

2000

The middle section of
the Rocky Branch Trail
is currently closed due
to storm damage.

15½°
West

True
North

Magnetic Declination 2014

Contour interval 500 feet

0   0.5   1

© Appalachian Mountain Club

Dry River Tr

3000

Dry
River

302

2000

Davis Path

3000

2000

Stairs Mtn
3463

Stairs Col Tr

Rocky
Branch #1

Rocky Branch Tr

▲ Mt Resolution
3415

2000

Mt Crawford ▲
3119

Mt Parker Tr

2000

Iron Mtn ▲
2726

Jericho Rd

Mt Parker
3004

P

Mt Langdon

LONGER VARIATIONS

From Boott Spur, connect with routes over the Northern and Southern Presidentials for longer trips with sustained alpine scenery. Consult Trip 23 to return south via the Southern Presidentials and end at Crawford Notch. Review Trip 25 for a description of the route over the Northern Presidentials, which ends at Pinkham Notch on NH 16. These variations add many miles and at least one extra day.

OVERNIGHT OPTIONS

The Forest Service has established designated campsites along Davis Ridge, each indicated by a small sign. Dispersed camping is permitted, but finding a site in the thick and uneven woods is difficult. The former site of Resolution Shelter is located near a reliable spring, but camping is no longer allowed within 0.25 miles of the site. None of the other campsites have water nearby—you'll need to pack in whatever you need for the night.

Designated campsites spread along the ridge and are highlighted in bold in the following text. They are generally small and not suitable for larger groups. Three sites are located within a few miles of the former shelter site. The first perches high on Stairs Mountain; the second and third ensconce themselves in saddles a few miles farther. For a longer first day (12.2 miles) consider using two sites near the end of the ridge, located in the trees just before the trail emerges in the alpine zone on Boott Spur. For late starters, there is also a site located 0.8 mile from the trailhead.

TO REACH THE TRAILHEAD

To Reach the Ending Trailhead. Head to the Glen Boulder Trailhead (44° 14.758′ N, 71° 15.200′ W) on NH 16, located a mile south of Pinkham Notch Visitor Center. A WMNF parking pass is required. You can also park at Pinkham Notch Visitor Center, though this will lengthen your trip by 0.6 mile.

To Reach the Starting Trailhead. From the Willey House Site in Crawford Notch State Park follow NH 302 south for 5.6 miles, or just over 6 miles north from Bartlett. The large paved trailhead lot (44° 07.123′ N, 71° 21.224′ W) is visible from the highway. A WMNF parking pass is required.

HIKE DESCRIPTION

From the parking lot (0.0/990), follow Crawford Valley Way. The dirt road quickly leads to Bemis Bridge over the Saco River. Once on the other side, the double-track trail passes a private residence on the right and then forks right, respecting the private property to the left. Leaving the road, the now-narrower path crosses a swampy stream on a small bridge. The Davis Path was once a bridle path to the summit of Washington in the mid-nineteenth century, but it fell into disuse around 1853. AMC rehabilitated it as a footpath in 1910.

Look for common members of the northern hardwood forest: white ashes, red oaks, yellow birches, hobblebushes, striped maples, paper birches, and beeches. Cross into the national forest near an information sign, and start a slow, steady climb, traversing along a small brook shaded by hemlocks. The boundary of the Presidential Range–Dry River Wilderness is posted by a nice rock staircase. The hike's first **designated campsite** is not far beyond (0.8/1,250), accessed via a short spur. From here, the trail relentlessly climbs up the mountain flanks. The route becomes rockier, spruce increases, and limited views behind indicate the rising elevation.

Views through the trees become more common, and Mount Willey appears beyond Frankenstein Cliffs to the northwest. The vegetation transitions to spruce-fir forest, marked by the appearance of bunchberry plants underfoot and mountain ashes overhead. The trail levels out briefly as it attains the ridge and then climbs for the final push to Mount Crawford. Views to the south open up, revealing the Sandwich Range (Trips 18 and 19) beyond the closer Moat Mountains.

A short distance farther are open ledges and, to the south, the hike's first outstanding view. To the southwest are the Attitash Ski Area and Moat Mountains; the tallest peak in the range is North Moat Mountain. Pointy Mount Chocorua peeks out behind Bear Mountain to the southeast. The two peaks west of Bear Mountain are Bartlett Haystack and Tremont. Below Tremont, trailing to the southwest, is the deep cleft of the Sawyer River valley. Mount Carrigain (Trip 20) looms above it.

Continue on the rocky trail, and enjoy more views south and west. The first glimpse northeast appears shortly before the spur to the summit of Mount Crawford (2.2/2,900). The continuing trail banks right to reenter the forest, but head left up the rock slabs on an indistinct pathway. Open ledges loaded with blueberries lead to the summit and savory views north (2.5/3,119/ 44° 08.185′ N, 71° 19.946′ W).

The view encompasses the entire Dry River drainage, extending north to the summit cone of Mount Washington and hemmed to the northwest by the Southern Presidential peaks (Trip 23). Look north along Montalban Ridge to the flat summit of Mount Resolution and the adjacent ledges and cliffs of Stairs Mountain. To the northwest, Mount Willey looms above the deep gash of Crawford Notch. In the western distance, discern the ridge of Mount Bond and Bondcliff in the Pemigewasset Wilderness (Trip 22). On a good day, you can spot Mount Lafayette on Franconia Ridge (Trip 21), 16 miles away.

Back on the Davis Path (2.8/2,900), reenter the woods on a mostly level path. Views behind of Mount Crawford punctuate this stretch, as do a handful of larch trees on your right. North America's only deciduous conifer, larches feature small needle clusters and an overall lacy appearance. The trail reaches Mount Parker Trail (right) and the spur to the former site of the Resolution Shelter (left; 4.3/3,060). A steep 140-foot drop on the spur leads to one of the few reliable water sources found on the ridge; fill up here.

The Davis Path encounters Stairs Col Trail on the right (4.6/3,060), makes a steep climb, and then levels. Becoming rockier, the path ascends directly and passes a sign for views south to Mount Crawford and beyond. The route returns to the ridgeline, where it encounters a spur on the right for Stairs Mountain (5.0/3,430). A worthwhile 0.2-mile side trip takes you to the ledges and **designated campsite** atop Stairs Mountain. A nice, flat tentsite in the trees provides ready access to outstanding views southwest.

Davis Path drops slowly and gently through spruce-fir forest. The trail steepens before bottoming out in a boggy saddle and crossing an intermittent spring near a large beech tree. The route ascends the opposite bank, away from the stream, and becomes more overgrown; do not follow the path downstream that has developed in this potentially confusing spot. On the way back up, the trail passes another **designated campsite** (6.0/2,970) tucked into the woods on the right.

The route now becomes rough and uneven, and passes a few unreliable water sources. The trail steadily rises past rock-and-spruce formations, then levels out in a boggy section and passes an unremarkable **designated campsite** (7.3/3,480). There are two small sites, one near the trail in a rocky clearing, the other 50 yards back in a low-lying spot.

Your at-times boggy traverse continues, passing through a few clearings of dead firs with views toward the Southern Presidentials. Marginal wood ferns are common along the trail's edge. Reach Mount Davis Spur Trail on the right (9.1/3,610).

Bear right and make the trip to the summit. The steep and bouldery climb requires hand-over-hand scrambling as the path clambers over steep rock slabs. The surrounding terrain is steep until the top (9.3/3,819/44° 12.230' N, 71° 18.653' W), where there are many flat rocks for soaking in the views.

You're close to the center of the Whites. Mountains and ridges lance the sky in all directions. To the north, the alpine horseshoe of Mount Monroe, Mount

A hiker looks north from Stairs Mountain.

Washington, and Boott Spur arcs around the upper Dry River valley. The Southern Presidentials—Mounts Franklin, Eisenhower, and Pierce—line the opposite ridge. To the south is the entire Sandwich Range, from the distinctive pyramid of Mount Chocorua in the east, west to Tripyramid's summit. To the southwest, Mounts Carrigain and Hancock mark the southeast boundary of the Pemigewasset Wilderness. To the southeast is the Rocky Branch drainage. To the east is Doublehead Mountain. To the northeast are the Carter Range and the peaks of the Wild River watershed.

Back on the Davis Path (9.5/3,610), descend to a small brook in the saddle between Mounts Davis and Isolation. Loaf-sized boulders dot the trail as it resumes climbing and curves around the east flanks of Isolation. Reach the unposted spur to the summit on the left (10.7/3,910).

To summit Mount Isolation (44° 12.886′ N, 71° 18.561′ W), follow the spur up to open slabs with great views north of Mount Washington and Oakes Gulf. Good views west look toward the ridges of the Pemigewasset Wilderness—you can make out Zeacliff, the Bonds, and Mount Lafayette.

From its intersection with the spur, Davis Path descends the northern slope of Mount Isolation and traverses the ridgeline. Pass the first junction with Isolation Trail on the right (11.6/3,850) and the second junction for Isolation Trail on the left (11.9/4,150). Now begins an almost continuous rise into the alpine zone.

The trail briefly crests in a young forest of firs and snags and comes to a clearing. A **designated campsite** is by the side of the trail (12.2/4,280). Onward, the trail quickly arrives at a viewpoint looking toward Boott Spur ahead. After a slight drop, ascend and reach the final **designated campsite** on the right (12.3/4,330), located in a secluded grassy clearing.

Bid the trees farewell. They thin and shrink as the trail climbs the rocky route. Views open to the Southern Presidentials. The steady, sustained climb is never radically steep, making this stretch most enjoyable as you ascend into the alpine zone around 4,700 feet. Cairns guide the way in more open terrain. Views sweep from southeast to southwest and include the long line of Montalban Ridge behind you. The bald summits of Mounts Isolation and Davis are visible. Continuing, leave the Presidential Range–Dry River Wilderness and reach Glen Boulder Trail on the right (13.5/5,170). You can see your route ahead as it crosses Slide Peak.

Head out on the 0.5-mile out-and-back trip to Boott Spur's summit. Follow Davis Path as it curves to the right of a rocky hump and soon rewards with views of knobby Boott Spur ahead. At times, the trail climbs parallel to a rocky outcrop on the left. Mount Washington reemerges from behind the ridge. Upper Huntington Ravine comes into view to the north. From here, the trail drops to Boott Spur Trail (14.0/5,420). The actual summit (44° 15.148′ N, 71° 17.644′ W) is accessible with some minor scrambling—walk on durable rock surfaces to avoid damaging the fragile alpine plants.

The views from the summit are the equal of any on the hike. The deep valley of NH 16 lies below. The ski runs trace down the Wildcat peaks on the opposite side. Looking south, trace your entire journey along the ridge. The Sandwich Range punctures the southern horizon.

From here, connect with the Southern Presidentials (Trip 23) by following the Davis Path and then Camel Trail to reach Lakes of the Clouds Hut. To connect with the Northern Presidentials (Trip 25), remain on the Davis Path for 1.4 miles, turn right onto Crawford Path, and follow it over the summit of Washington to Gulfside Trail.

Return to the Glen Boulder–Davis Path junction (14.5/5,170) and head down Glen Boulder Trail, quickly entering scrubby waist-high fir trees before returning to open terrain with views southeast. The trail bottoms out and then rises slightly to reach the summit of Slide Peak (15.1/4,806).

Enjoy your last look at the Boott Spur summit and ridges, the Southern Presidentials, and Montalban Ridge. Enter forest on a gradual descent. Emerge from the trees for a vista (15.7/4,410) looking toward upper Huntington Ravine, Mount Washington, and the nearby Gulf of Slides, now on the far side of an unnamed ridgeline to your north. To the north is Pinkham Notch and the distant smokestacks of Berlin, located beyond the rocky outcrops of small Pine Mountain.

The trail descends over loose talus, provides clear views, and encounters the trail's namesake boulder (16.1/3,730). The dump truck–sized rock perches precariously on the ridgeline, delicately placed here by the receding glaciers of the last Ice Age. The trail curves left below the boulder, briefly reenters the trees, and then emerges into the open for some final views.

Begin a steep scrambling descent in the trees, aided at times by rock steps. Rushing water becomes audible; red maples, raspberries, and cinnamon ferns appear as you approach and cross the stream (16.7/2,850). The trail gradient eases, yellow birches join the forest mix, and the path crosses Avalanche Brook Ski Trail (16.9/2,640).

The trail banks left away from the stream and the forest continues its transition to hardwoods—look for sugar maples, beeches, and hazels. After a gradual descent, the trail makes one final steep drop, crosses a small brook flowing over little ledges, and reaches the Direttissima on the left (17.3/2,370). Remain on Glen Boulder Trail for the final descent to the trailhead parking lot (17.7/2,010). Alternatively, follow the Direttissima, a level trail that runs parallel above Route 16 on rocky slopes, left for 1.0 mile to reach Pinkham Notch.

INFORMATION

White Mountain National Forest, Saco Ranger District, 33 Kancamagus Highway, Conway, NH 03818, 603-447-5448, fs.usda.gov/whitemountain; Pinkham Notch Visitor Center, 603-466-2725, open daily 6:30 A.M. to 10 P.M. from May to October.

NEARBY

AMC's Pinkham Notch Visitor Center offers an array of information and amenities, including educational displays; a retail store that stocks books, maps, and other backcountry essentials; and a dining room that offers a buffet breakfast, a la carte lunch, and a sit-down, family-style dinner. Overnight accommodations are available at the adjacent Joe Dodge Lodge. For more information, call 603-466-2725 or go to outdoors.org.

TRIP 25
GREAT GULF WILDERNESS

Location: White Mountain National Forest
Difficulty: Epic
Distance: 19.3 miles round-trip
Total Elevation Gain/Loss: 7,250 feet/7,250 feet
Trip Length: 3 days
Recommended Map: *AMC White Mountains Trail Map, Map 1: Presidential Range* (AMC Books)
Highlight: A yawning chasm, an alpine ridge, and one of New England's most challenging big-mountain adventures.

The Great Gulf carves deep into the mountains, guarded thousands of feet overhead by the peaks of the Northern Presidentials. Born here, the Peabody River tears down a steep and boulder-strewn watershed. At the head of the ravine, tiny Spaulding Lake glistens in an amphitheater of cliffs.

HIKE OVERVIEW

Tour the powerful Peabody River and pass a series of designated campsites on Great Gulf Trail. After ascending the Great Gulf's formidable headwall—rising 1,700 feet in less than a mile—travel along the open ridgeline of the Northern Presidentials, passing over the summits of four 5,000-footers: Mounts Clay, Jefferson, Adams, and Madison. Descend north off the ridge to your choice of tentsites or cabins, or remain on the ridge and stay at AMC's Madison Spring Hut. After tagging Madison, the adventure concludes with a long, rocky descent on Osgood Trail.

Traffic is light in the Great Gulf, especially higher up near the headwall, but the crowds increase markedly on the ridge—expect to see dozens, if not hundreds, of people. Be aware that above-treeline, weather can get very nasty very quickly. Be prepared! Escape routes back into the Great Gulf—Sphinx, Six Husbands, and Madison Gulf trails—are very challenging. Dogs are allowed but not recommended, given the challenges of this hike.

OVERNIGHT OPTIONS

The Forest Service has established a series of designated campsites in the Great Gulf. Dispersed camping outside of designated sites is permitted, but you must

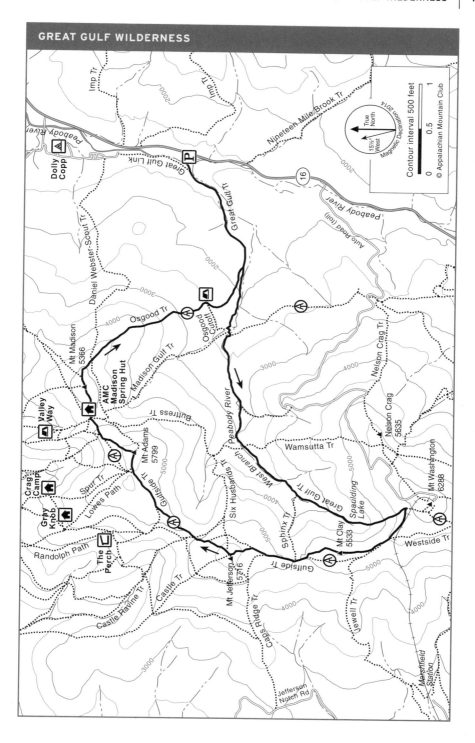

GREAT GULF WILDERNESS

Contour interval 500 feet

© Appalachian Mountain Club

Magnetic Declination 2014

True North

15½° West

Imp Tr

Imp Tr

Nineteen Mile Brook Tr

Peabody River

Dolly Copp

Great Gulf Link

Great Gulf Tr

16

Auto Road (toll)

Peabody River

Daniel Webster-Scout Tr

Osgood Tr

Osgood Cutoff

Nelson Crag Tr

Mt Madison 5366

AMC Madison Spring Hut

Madison Gulf Tr

Peabody River

Nelson Crag 5635

Valley Way

Buttress Tr

Mt Adams 5799

Wamsutta Tr

Mt Washington 6288

Crag Camp

Spur Tr

Gulfside Tr

Lowe's Path

West Branch

Six Husbands Tr

Great Gulf Tr

Spaulding Lake

Gray Knob

Sphinx Tr

Mt Clay 5533

Westside Tr

Randolph Path

The Perch

Gulfside Tr

Mt Jefferson 5716

Castle Tr

Castle Ravine Tr

Caps Ridge Tr

Jewell Tr

Marshfield Station

Jefferson Notch Rd

be more than 200 feet from any trails—a difficult proposition in this rugged and overgrown terrain. No camping is permitted in the upper Gulf above the junctions of Sphinx and Great Gulf trails. Campfires are prohibited.

Overnight options are limited once you attain the Presidential Ridge. No camping is permitted above treeline, and most overnight locations require descending off the ridge for the night, climbing back up the following morning. They are also extremely popular. Try to complete this section on a weekday or after August, when Appalachian Trail (AT) thru-hiking traffic tapers.

The Bluff (2.6/2,280/44° 18.289′ N, 71° 15.658′ W), the closest designated campsite to the trailhead, offers space for several tents. At least one smaller site is tucked in the surrounding trees. The site boasts an excellent view of the lower Great Gulf. Water is located 0.1 mile away in Parapet Brook. A bear box is available for storing your food at night.

Campsite #2 (2.8/2,250/44° 18.267′ N, 71° 15.706′ W) sits atop a small bluff sandwiched between Parapet Brook and the Peabody River and has two good tentsites. There are no views, but the river is a scramble away. A bear box is available.

Clam Rock Campsite (3.1/2,380/44° 18.333′ N, 71° 16.003′ W) is situated close to the river by its large namesake rock. The site has room for several tents. Besides being close to the river, it is also near swimming holes. Overhanging Clam Rock offers some shelter in rainy conditions, though water drips down the face. A bear box is available.

Campsites #4 and #5 (5.0/3,350/44° 17.993′ N, 71° 17.569′ W) are the farthest designated sites, located close to each other on opposite sides of the trail. Site #4 is in a grassy, level clearing with good exposure to the sun and stars. Trees shelter site #5, 100 feet farther down the trail. A number of other small sites have been established in the area. An adjacent brook provides water.

The Perch (12.6/4,300/44° 19.446′ N, 71° 18.713′ W) provides the first camping option from the ridgeline and is located in the upper reaches of Cascade Ravine. A small, vintage shelter and four tent platforms are available. J. Rayner Edmands built the first structure here in 1892. The current cave-like incarnation from 1948 has a limited view north to the peaks of the Kilkenny. There are no views from the tentsites, though the uppermost platform offers glimpses north. The Gray Knob caretaker will visit to collect a per-person fee. Water is available from adjacent Cascade Brook. Campfires are prohibited.

Crag Camp (13.5/4,300/44° 20.092′ N, 71° 18.131′ W) and *Gray Knob* (13.5/4,300/44° 19.957′ N, 71° 18.577′ W) are self-service cabins maintained by the Randolph Mountain Club (RMC). Crag Camp (capacity 20) perches on the lip of King Ravine and provides a view into the abyss. Gray Knob (capacity 15) is located a short distance away in the trees and lacks views, though a full panorama north is locted nearby. Both are situated on the northern slopes of Mount Adams, 1.2 miles and 1,200 feet below the ridgeline route. They are both first-come, first-served facilities and cost $20 per night ($15 for RMC members). Both are open year-round.

Madison Spring Hut (13.6/4,810/44° 19.665′ N, 71° 16.991′ W) nestles in the saddle between Mounts Madison and Adams. It is the lowest-effort option—you don't have to drop off the ridge for the night—but it's also the most expensive. Weekends are typically booked well in advance. Call 603-466-2727 or visit outdoors.org/lodging/huts for reservations and more information.

Valley Way Tentsite (14.3/4,100/44° 20.050′ N, 71° 17.197′ W) is free and quickly accessible from the ridge, 700 feet and 0.7 mile below Madison Spring Hut. Located on Valley Way, it offers two tent pads, a pair of fire rings, and a privy. It also receives heavy use; its limited space can make for a crowded camping experience. Water is available by Valley Way Trail. Good views from the upper area look out at the alpine flanks of Mount Madison.

Osgood Tentsite (16.7/2,500/44° 18.520′ N, 71° 15.300′ W) is one final possibility, though it's not well positioned for this hike. Located on Osgood Trail, it's very far from the Great Gulf campsites and less than 3.0 miles from hike's end. The site is located along the AT, which means it receives regular use, especially during thru-hiker season (July to August).

TO REACH THE TRAILHEAD

Follow NH 16 to Great Gulf trailhead (44° 18.679′ N, 71° 13.222′ W), located 4.2 miles north of Pinkham Notch and 3.4 miles past Wildcat Ski Area. The turn-off is on the left. A WMNF parking pass is required; privies are available.

HIKE DESCRIPTION

Head to the kiosk at the end of the parking area (0.0/1,380). Great Gulf Trail starts on a paved path, briefly travels along the Peabody River, and then curves left to cross the wide, shallow waterway on a substantial wooden suspension bridge. Notice the tall shade-intolerant white pines just downriver. The open river corridor provides them with plenty of sunlight.

On the opposite bank, the wide trail travels through mature hardwood forest punctuated by water-loving hemlock trees and some large red spruces. Great Gulf Trail passes Great Gulf Link Trail on the right (0.3/1,400) and continues past a series of ski trail junctions, crossing several small creeks as it rises slowly. Substantial white pines and abundant sugar maples line the trail as it parallels the nearby Peabody River, which is audible but difficult to access. Pass Hayes Copp Loop Ski Trail (1.6/1,750), cross into the Great Gulf Wilderness, and reach Osgood Trail entering from the right (1.8/1,830)—your return route. A short distance farther is Boulder Falls, accessible by a short spur, where cascades funnel between three colossal rocks.

The trail climbs steeply and parallels the river far below. Tiny bunchberry plants line the root-laced trail, yellow birches become increasingly common, and mountain ashes appears—all signs of the transition to spruce-fir forest.

The trail briefly rejoins the river then makes a steep climb over rock steps to reach the Bluff campsite (2.6/2,280) and its delicious view. Looking up the Gulf, the pyramidal hulk of Mount Adams (5,799) looms to the right, and Mount Jefferson (5,716) can be spotted farther in the distance to the left. The steep ridge falling into the Gulf from Jefferson's summit is known as Jefferson's Knee. The deep and trailless Jefferson Ravine lies between the two peaks. To the west, the Great Gulf curves out-of-sight behind Mount Washington's Chandler Ridge. Spot the Mount Washington Auto Road snaking around the summit-like prow of the Horn.

The trail quickly reaches Osgood Cutoff (2.7/2,230), part of the AT. Bear left as Great Gulf Trail drops down and crosses strong-flowing Parapet Brook, a difficult crossing in high water. On the opposite bank, encounter Madison Gulf Trail on the right (2.8/2,250) and a spur to Campsite #2 on the left.

From here, Great Gulf Trail descends to the river and crosses it on a substantial bridge. The route winds along the river and meets Clam Rock (3.1/2,380), an overhanging 12-foot-high boulder. The canyon palpably narrows. The river gradient becomes much steeper. Pulsing rapids intermix with swimming holes as the trail crosses Chandler Brook and reaches Chandler Brook Trail (3.9/2,760), which splits left to ascend steeply to the Horn.

Steadily ascend past brief views of looming Jefferson's Knee and reach the four-way junction with Wamsutta and Six Husbands trails (4.5/3,100). Continue straight on Great Gulf Trail as it passes through young, dense forest then through an area of newly regenerating trees beneath bleaching snags—indications of a fir wave.

The trail maintains its steady grade, alternately climbing above and then winding alongside the river, which now starts to noticeably diminish in size. Pleasant pools and sluicing cascades are abundant. The route passes Campsites #4 and #5 (5.0/3,350), briefly levels, and then rock-hops the river (5.4/3,560), a potentially hazardous maneuver at high water. Mount Clay heaves into view as the route continues up-canyon. Cross Sphinx Brook, and reach the junction with Sphinx Trail (5.6/3,580).

Bear left to remain on Great Gulf Trail as it recrosses the Peabody River and encounters a sign reminding you that there is no camping beyond this point. Next is Weetamoo Falls (5.8/3,660), a sluicing 20-foot cascade with an emerald pool at its base. Past the falls begins a steep and rocky ascent that continuously flirts with the river corridor, passing impressive boulders and spews of foaming water. Reach tiny Spaulding Lake by its outlet (6.5/4,230), where the mighty face of the Great Gulf headwall comes into view.

For the area's best view, scramble atop the prominent rock at the head of the pond. Stare down the gullet of the Great Gulf as it plummets past Spaulding Lake. The Northern Presidentials' profiles are punctuated by the bulwarks of Mounts Adams and Madison. The headwall sweeps around behind you in an arc of bulging rock and alpine gullies.

Past Spaulding Lake, the trail follows a small, flowing streambed. Trees rapidly diminish in stature, and the trail passes a sign that welcomes you to the alpine zone (6.7/4,330). Now the vertical ascent begins. Views down the Gulf quickly become continuous. The trail closely follows the flowing stream for most of the ascent, often traveling directly in it, curving slightly left as it climbs. The path follows the most obvious route. Faint yellow-orange blazes and small cairns help keep you on track.

The stream disappears under the rocks as you crest 4,900 feet and enter a wide talus field. The blazes cease at this point, and the route becomes indistinct in spots as it continues its ascent near the audible stream burbling underground. Next, enter a zone of loose rock, where caution is advised. *Do not bear to the right at this point—it leads to the sheer cliffs below Mount Clay.* If the footing is treacherous, instead angle slightly left to find more secure terrain, though near the top of the headwall you will need to curve back and to the right to emerge at the top of the trail. At 5,400 feet, more distant peaks appear over the Northern Presidentials, the trail becomes more defined, and you leave the trickling headwaters of the Peabody River. Hug solid rock on the edge of the talus field and ascend a narrow gully to surmount the headwall.

As the trail crests the lip, the sense of untrammeled wilderness is abruptly shattered by the appearance of the nearby Sherman Adams Building atop Mount Washington's summit and the Cog Railway tracks, which run past here a mere 75 yards away. Immediately reach Gulfside Trail (7.5/5,940), part of the AT. Bear right to follow Gulfside Trail north. (If you are interested in summiting busy Mount Washington, bear left onto Gulfside Trail and follow it 0.4 mile to the summit marker.)

Gulfside Trail initially runs alongside the Cog tracks and features substantial cairns placed roughly 50 feet apart to aid navigation in low-visibility conditions. The trail wanders to the edge of the Great Gulf, affording deep glimpses into the bowl and of Spaulding Lake far below. The views of Mounts Jefferson, Adams, and Madison are excellent. Passing Westside Trail on the left (8.1/5,500), Gulfside Trail descends to Clay Col. Here, Mount Clay Loop splits right (8.2/5,390). Bear right onto Mount Clay Loop to continue the view-packed journey. (Continue left onto Gulfside Trail for an easier and slightly shorter route that skirts the peak to the west.)

Mount Clay Loop rolls along the peak's long ridge, affording good views of the upper Great Gulf headwall, your earlier route. The Southern Presidentials appear, lined up past AMC's Lakes of the Clouds Hut. The trail crosses a grassy meadow, attains the summit (8.9/5,533/44° 17.164' N, 71° 18.945' W), and then makes a much rockier and steeper descent. Careful footwork is required on the drop to Gulfside Trail (9.4/5,100).

Greenough Spring—a reliable water source—is 0.2 mile south on Gulfside Trail, located in scrubby chest-high trees (44° 17.351' N, 71° 19.076' W). Continuing north, Gulfside Trail descends to Sphinx Col and Sphinx Trail (9.5/4,960), which drops back into the Great Gulf. Nearby, large rocks along the upper portion of Sphinx Trail offer shelter from west winds. One outcrop is said to resemble the trail's Egyptian namesake. A reliable spring is located in a small boulder field a short distance farther down Sphinx Trail (44° 17.602' N, 71° 18.934' W).

Gulfside Trail resumes climbing. Mount Jefferson appears to the north, and views southwest encompass Mount Eisenhower's rounded summit and the deep cleft of Crawford Notch. Huge cairns mark the route ascending past Cornice Trail on the left (10.0/5,360). The terrain becomes rougher as the trail meanders through the open Monticello Lawn to Mount Jefferson Loop on the left (10.1/5,380).

Gulfside Trail curves around Mount Jefferson to the east, but bear left and head for the summit on Mount Jefferson Loop. Scramble over loose rocks, including a glistening pocket of white quartzite, to the summit (10.4/5,716/44° 18.255' N, 71° 18.994' W). Views southeast reveal a profile of the Great Gulf headwall that look considerably steeper than it is. To the north is the rocky pyramid of Mount Adams. Mount Jefferson Loop descends from the summit on a more mellow route. After a short section of talus-hopping, pass through a krummholz corridor and rejoin the super-cairns of Gulfside Trail (10.8/5,220).

Continue north on Gulfside Trail as it drops past prominent Dingmaul Rock. The outcrop looks into the wild and trailless Jefferson Ravine, hemmed to the south by the distinctive ridge of Jefferson's Knee. After a steep and rocky descent through krummholz, the trail reaches Edmands Col and the four-way junction with Edmands Col Cutoff and Castle Ravine Trail (11.0/4,940). Gulf-side Spring (44° 18.599′ N, 71° 18.735′ W), a good flowing water source, is a short distance down the Cutoff. Spaulding Spring (44° 18.704′ N, 71° 18.772′ W), a less reliable source, is located roughly 25 yards down Cornice Trail from Castle Ravine Trail and Randolph Path. Look to your left for a small rock, painted red, on top of a collection of other small boulders, marking the location of the spring.

Continuing, remain on Gulfside Trail as it climbs to the ridgeline. This section is fully exposed to the elements. Even some of the boulders look wind-swept. Look northwest into the deep glacial cirque of Castle Ravine, bordered to the west by Castellated Ridge. The linear arête sweeps down the west edge of the ravine, punctuated by several gendarmes known as the Castles.

The trail levels out and passes Israel Ridge Trail on the left (11.7/5,250). To head to the Perch, descend Israel Ridge Trail for 0.8 mile, and then turn right onto Perch Path to reach the shelter and campsites.

Gulfside Trail continues north past small Storm Lake, a pool that can be seen after periods of wet weather. The route banks right through sheltered krummholz below the flanks of Mount Sam Adams, which is a satellite summit of Mount Adams, and passes thin Peabody Spring (44° 19.045′ N, 71° 18.158′ W), where you can fill up your water bottle. The best source is at the base of the largest trailside boulder. The trail slowly climbs, becoming loose and rubbly. A continuation of Israel Ridge Path splits right just before the mountainous cairn that marks Thunderstorm junction (12.3/5,490).

Five trails converge on this point. Great Gully Trail heads north down the headwall of King Ravine. Lowe's Path also leads north, down the ridge toward Gray Knob and Crag Camp. (For Gray Knob, remain on Lowe's Path for 1.2 miles and 1,000 feet of elevation loss. For Crag Camp, follow Lowe's Path a short distance, and then bear right onto Spur Trail, which leads to the cabin in 1.1 miles.)

The rockpile of Mount Adams looms overhead. The ascent to the summit is all rubble. To reach the peak, follow the final section of Lowe's Path upward. (To skip the summit, continue on Gulfside Trail as it curves northeast around the base of Mount Adams, providing decent footing and good shelter from southerly winds.)

Small cairns mark the route as it scrambles over large piles of rocks. From the top of the peak (12.6/5,799/44° 19.234′ N, 71° 17.492′ W), savor your first good views north. Mount Madison rises at the end of the ridge, with tiny Star Lake nestling at its base. Osgood Trail follows the alpine ridge on the far side of Mount Madison. The Mahoosucs (Trip 30) march off in the distance in line with Madison. The smokestacks of Berlin are visible in the valley below. The rolling mountains of the Pilot Range (Trip 28) appear due north. Good views south stare into the Great Gulf, and the Carter Range, including the cleft of Carter Notch, can be spotted southeast.

Descend from the summit on Air Line, which rubble-hops northeast and looks into King Ravine. A keen eye will discern Crag Camp perched on the chasm's west ridge. Rejoining Gulfside Trail (13.2/5,230), bear right and head toward Madison Spring Hut, which quickly appears below. The trail descends a series of nice rock stairs to reach the hut and saddle (13.6/4,810).

Madison Spring Hut sits on the edge of treeline, surrounded by stands of head-high trees. Even if you're not staying, stop in to refill your water bottles and warm up. To access the Valley Way Tentsite, bear left and descend 0.7 mile and 700 feet on Valley Way Trail.

The continuing route heads over Mount Madison on Osgood Trail, which is very exposed to the elements. (If conditions are bad, you can also return to Great Gulf Trail from Madison Spring Hut via Madison Gulf Trail. An adventure in itself, the 2.6-mile trail starts out by dropping 1,000 feet in less than a mile—good scrambling skills are required—before steadily descending to reach Great Gulf Trail by Parapet Brook.)

Osgood Trail strikes out from Madison Spring Hut and immediately rises again above treeline. A well-trod and rocky route leads upward to the summit (14.1/5,366/44° 19.729′ N, 71° 16.593′ W), where Watson Path joins from the north. Enjoy your last summit view, which encompasses the route of almost your entire journey. The final leg traces southeast along the long bare ridge before you.

It's all downhill from here. Osgood Trail traverses down an exposed, boulder-strewn ridge and clambers over more than half a dozen rocky mounds capped with large cairns. White blazes appear sporadically, but the trail can be difficult to discern between the cairns; careful footwork and navigation are often required. After dropping off the summit of Mount Madison, first pass Howker Ridge Trail on the left (14.4/5,100) and then reach the four-way junction with Parapet and Daniel Webster-Scout trails (14.7/4,830). Remain on Osgood Trail, following the ridge over a series of steps, with more forgiving sections interspersed between steep drops. Views look straight up the Great Gulf to the crown of Mount Washington.

The trail finally reaches the trees, curves right, and then directly descends through forest that shows clear storm damage; many blowdowns and newly created clearings are apparent. Extensive recent trail work, including the maintenance and addition of numerous stone steps and water bars, eases the journey to Osgood Cutoff on the right (16.7/2,500), where a spur leads left to the Osgood Tentsite. Follow the final section of Osgood Trail to Great Gulf Trail (17.5/1,830), turn left, and retrace your earlier steps to the trailhead (19.3/1,380).

INFORMATION

White Mountain National Forest, Saco Ranger District, 33 Kancamagus Highway, Conway, NH 03818, 603-447-5448, fs.usda.gov/main/whitemountain/home; Pinkham Notch Visitor Center, 603-466-2725, open daily 6:30 A.M. to 10 P.M. from May to October.

NEARBY

AMC's Pinkham Notch Visitor Center offers an array of information and amenities, including educational displays; a retail store that stocks books, maps, and other backcountry essentials; and a dining room that offers a buffet breakfast, a la carte lunch, and a sit-down, family-style dinner. Overnight accommodations are available at the adjacent Joe Dodge Lodge. For more information, call 603-466-2725 or go to outdoors.org.

TRIP 26
KING RAVINE

Location: Northern Presidential Range, White Mountain National Forest
Difficulty: Strenuous
Distance: 10.2 miles round-trip
Total Elevation Gain/Loss: 4,900 feet/4,900 feet
Trip Length: 2 days
Recommended Map: *AMC White Mountains Trail Map, Map 1: Presidential Range* (AMC Books)
Highlights: Ravines, cliffs, ridgelines, alpine scenery, and the second-highest summit in New England.

Trails lace the flanks of Mount Adams, a peak lined with rocky ridges and gouged by deep valleys. King Ravine cuts deepest, a giant bowl scooped from the mountainside. The densest collection of trails in New England explores the surrounding area. This hike unravels the knot of possibility and guides you along the most dramatic combination of trails.

HIKE OVERVIEW

The hike loops around King Ravine, winding along Snyder Brook, passing the Valley Way Tentsite, and then surmounting Durand Ridge to ascend dramatic Air Line above the King Ravine headwall. The route climbs to the top of 5,799-foot Mount Adams and then descends along the west edge of King Ravine to Crag Camp and Gray Knob, public cabins maintained by the Randolph Mountain Club (RMC). Descend brook-lined Amphibrach Trail.

The area is popular, but the multitude of trails means that beyond the main arteries, you will likely have sections to yourself. Limited overnight options can make for crowded experiences, however, especially on weekends. Water is abundant. Dogs are permitted.

OVERNIGHT OPTIONS

All tentsites, shelters, and cabins on the route are first-come, first-served; AMC's Madison Spring Hut usually requires reservations (see later). Dispersed camping is permitted in areas below treeline—you must be 200 feet from any trail and 0.25 mile from designated shelters and campsites—but

KING RAVINE

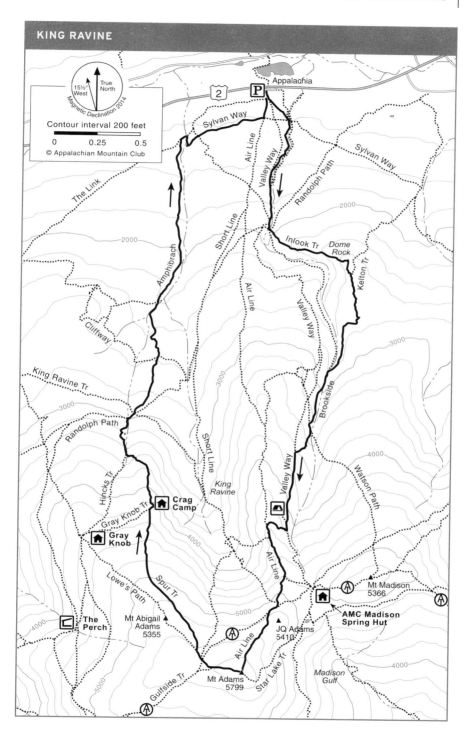

Appalachia

2

True North

15½° West

Magnetic Declination 2014

Contour interval 200 feet

0   0.25   0.5

© Appalachian Mountain Club

Sylvan Way

Air Line

Valley Way

Randolph Path

Sylvan Way

The Link

2000

2000

Short Line

Inlook Tr

Dome Rock

Kelton Tr

Amphibrach

Air Line

Valley Way

3000

Cliffway

King Ravine Tr

3000

Brookside

4000

Randolph Path

3000

Short Line

King Ravine

Valley Way

Watson Path

Hincks Tr

Gray Knob Tr

Crag Camp

4000

Gray Knob

4000

Valley Way

Air Line

Lowe's Path

Spur Tr

Mt Madison 5366

AMC Madison Spring Hut

The Perch

4000

Mt Abigail Adams 5355

5000

Air Line

JQ Adams 5410

Madison Gulf

4000

Gulfside Tr

Mt Adams 5799

Star Lake Tr

5000

usable sites are nearly impossible to find in the steep, rugged, and densely forested terrain. Camping is prohibited above treeline. The weather may dictate where you choose to spend the night—take advantage of good weather for the above-treeline portion of the hike.

Valley Way Tentsite (3.4/4,100/44° 20.050′ N, 71° 17.197′ W) offers two large tent pads, fire rings, and a privy. It is a good option if 1) you are starting late in the day or 2) the weather higher up is disagreeable and you want to wait for better conditions the following day. The site's heavy use and limited space can make for a crowded camping experience. Water is available a short distance from camp by Valley Way Trail. Good views from the upper area look out at the alpine flanks of Mount Madison.

Crag Camp (6.5/4,250/44° 20.092′ N, 71° 18.131′ W) perches on the lip of King Ravine's west headwall. The deck and inside common area offer impressive views of the ravine. The first-come, first-served RMC cabin has bunk space for twenty, split between two bunkrooms of eight and one of four. The building is unheated and floor vents connect directly with the outside; a pipe organ (!) is available for use as well. A year-round caretaker collects $20 per person per night ($15 for RMC members). Open year-round.

Gray Knob (7.0/4,370/44° 19.957′ N, 71° 18.577′ W) shelters in the woods 0.5 mile from Crag Camp and is an excellent overflow option if Crag Camp is full. The two-story cabin feels cozier than Crag Camp, with a large upstairs area for sleeping and a common area replete with books, and booth-style tables. No views are available from the cabin itself, but excellent vistas east are less than 0.1 mile away at the Quay. It also costs $20 per person. The cabin is open year-round. An RMC caretaker fires up the cabin's woodstove only during periods of extreme winter cold.

The Perch (6.7/4,300/44° 19.446′ N, 71° 18.713′ W) sits in the upper reaches of Cascade Ravine. A small, vintage shelter and four tent platforms are available. J. Rayner Edmands built the first structure here in 1892. The current cave-like incarnation from 1948 has a limited view north to the peaks of the Kilkenny. There are no views from the tentsites, though the uppermost platform offers glimpses north. The Gray Knob caretaker will visit to collect the per-person fee. Water is available from adjacent Cascade Brook. Campfires are prohibited.

Madison Spring Hut (4.4/4,810/44° 19.665′ N, 71° 16.991′ W) nestles in the saddle between Mounts Madison and Adams. Accessing it requires a short 0.2-mile detour, but it provides a (pricier) overnight option, as well as the opportunity to fill up water bottles or stop in for an inexpensive hot drink. Weekends are typically booked well in advance. Call 603-466-2727 or visit outdoors.org/lodging/huts for reservations and more information.

TO REACH THE TRAILHEAD

Follow US 2 to the Appalachia Trailhead, located in the town of Randolph, approximately a mile west of Dolly Copp/Pinkham B Road. The large parking area (44° 22.290′ N, 71° 17.324′ W) is adjacent to the highway and has space for many cars, but it is often full on busy days.

HIKE DESCRIPTION

From the trailhead (0.0/1,310), head past the Appalachia trailhead sign. Young beeches and red maples shade the trail as it immediately crosses the Presidential Range Rail Trail. Bear left on the Valley Way, immediately cross a powerline corridor, and turn left onto Maple Walk.

The path runs through a stand of sugar maples, joined by beeches, yellow birches, and other hardwoods. The route slowly rises to Snyder Brook and Gordon Falls (0.2/1,410), a sliding curtain of water over bedrock. Turn right to follow the yellow-blazed Fallsway.

The Fallsway parallels the brook upward and winds below mature hemlocks, some greater than 2 feet in diameter. Pass Lower Salroc Falls, a 10-foot bouldery cascade that drops into a deep swimming hole. Just above is 15-foot-high Upper Salroc Falls, another smooth sheet of water. The Fallsway then rejoins Valley Way (0.6/1,630).

Bear left to head uphill on blue-blazed Valley Way. Follow Tama Fall Loop on the left (0.7/1,650), which quickly rejoins Valley Way past its staircase slab falls; there's a swimming hole just above the cascade. Back on Valley Way, steadily climb and pass Beechwood Trail on the left to The Brookside, also on the left (0.8/1,950).

Bear left onto The Brookside to Snyder Brook. A massive house-sized boulder guards the opposite bank. Rock-hop the stream to the triple junction if The Brookside, Randolph Path, and Inlook Trail. Go straight on yellow-blazed Inlook Trail, which narrows and steepens as it ascends a rocky staircase. Firs, spruces, and big-tooth aspens appear, as do blueberry bushes underfoot. The trail becomes less rocky, the surrounding forest thicker and younger. Mountain ashes and bunchberry plants join the spruce-fir community as the trail levels out and comes to an open slab with good views north up the Snyder Brook drainage (1.1/2,360). Lower Durand Ridge is visible on the southwestern horizon. The Randolph valley runs off to the west.

Past the viewpoint, the trail clambers over open rocks and ledges with intermittent views of Madison Col at the head of the Snyder Brook watershed. The views become more frequent as the trail levels, bears left, and attains Dome Rock (1.4/2,662). The view catches glimpses to the northeast of the Mahoosucs, including the distinctive cleft of Mahoosuc Notch (Trip 30). The town of Randolph is visible below. To the north is the Crescent Range; Mount Crescent is due north. The Carter Range is visible to the east.

Continuing, the trail curves south to a similar view at the Upper Inlook—though this looks primarily to the northeast—where Kelton Trail joins from the right (1.5/2,730).

Bear right onto Kelton Trail for a long, level stretch through dense spruce-fir forest. Cross a flowing creek where a massive yellow birch stands sentinel. The trail remains level and crosses the slopes. The valley bottom and its rushing creek waters slowly rise up to meet you. The trail returns to Snyder Brook, rock-hops across, and rejoins The Brookside (2.3/2,730).

Bear left and follow The Brookside up the valley, climbing more steeply up rock steps, to Salmacis Falls (2.4/2,830), another cascading bedrock sheet. Past the falls, the trail follows the brook, here almost nothing but sluicing whitewater. Ascend steadily to Watson Path (2.8/3,260).

Bear left onto Watson Path toward Mount Madison, quickly passing signed but nondescript Bruin Rock. Shortly afterward, reach Lower Bruin Trail (2.9/3,340). Here, Watson Path crosses the creek to the left and ascends Mount Madison; instead turn right up Lower Bruin Trail. Make your first hand-over-hand scramble then follow Lower Bruin Trail as it makes a steep, direct, and root-laced climb to reach Valley Way (3.1/3,580).

Turn left and continue upward on Valley Way, a rocky affair with a few glimpses of Mount Madison through the trees to the left. Climb steadily to the signed spur for the Valley Way Tentsite (3.4/4,100); a reliable spring is located a short distance from here, toward the camping area.

Past the spur, the Valley Way encounters another stream and then reaches Upper Bruin Trail (3.6/4,150). Turn right up a direct, narrow, and rocky climb on Upper Bruin Trail. The route curves right, goes back left, and reaches a sign indicating that you are entering the alpine zone. A few feet past the sign, emerge onto open Durand Ridge and reach Air Line (3.8/4,410).

The gaping maw of King Ravine opens before you. A jumbled pile of boulders sits at the base of its headwall. Across the ravine, almost due west, Crag Camp perches on the edge of this great divide. Good views also extend north; the Pilot Range rises behind and above the Crescent Range. Turn left and as-

Snow still covered the trail along King Ravine on this particular day in April. (Photo © Jerry and Marcy Monkman)

cend Air Line, soon passing Chemin des Dames (3.9/4,500), which plummets into the ravine on the right.

The route travels on Knife Edge, a relatively narrow (though not precarious) open ridgeline. Impressive outcrops, balanced slabs, and good scenery deserve a slow pace. The trail next reaches Air Line Cutoff on the left (4.2/4,770), reaching Madison Spring Hut—now visible in the col to your left—in 0.2 mile. Looking north, identify the peaks of the Pilot Range (Trip 28). Mount Cabot is to the left; the Horn is the prominent peak to the right.

The final ascent of Durand Ridge leads above Madison Col and passes King Ravine Trail on the right (4.4/5,130), which drops into the ravine through a prominent cleft in the headwall. Immediately reach Gulfside Trail, here part of the Appalachian Trail (AT), and turn right. Slowly ascend below the summits of Mount Adams and its smaller, closer satellite, Mount John Quincy Adams. Though rocky, the trail is well traveled and marked by regular cairns. Air Line quickly splits left (4.5/5,160).

Bear left on Air Line and head toward the summit of Mount Adams. (To skip the summit, remain on Gulfside Trail to curve around the mountain's flanks and reach Thunderstorm Junction in 0.6 mile.) The trail up Mount Adams's loose rocks and boulders would not be navigable without blazes; watch your footing carefully on this scrambling ascent. Bag the second-highest peak in New England (5.1/5,799/44° 19.235′ N, 71° 17.495′ W) and enjoy one of its best views.

Mount Madison rises at the end of the ridge, with tiny Star Lake nestling at its base. The Mahoosucs (Trip 30) march off in the distance in line with Mount Madison. The rolling mountains of the Pilot Range (Trip 28) appear due north. Southern views stare into the Great Gulf, and the Carter Range, including the cleft of Carter Notch, can be spotted to the southeast.

Descend equally rugged Lowe's Path down Mount Adams's west side to the giant mega-cairn of Thunderstorm Junction (5.4/5,490), where five trails converge. The jumbled slopes of Mount Adams are visible overhead to the east, and the lower mass of Mount Sam Adams hulks to the east. Take a moment here to walk a short distance farther on Gulfside Trail to stare south across the Great Gulf (Trip 25) to Mount Washington. The Northern Presidential peaks are apparent in their entirety. Mount Jefferson is closest, the prominent ridge of Jefferson's Knee plunging into the Gulf. To the left of Mount Washington's summit, the Auto Road snakes its way up the mountain.

Back at Thunderstorm Junction, follow Lowe's Path for less than 0.1 mile, then bear right onto Spur Trail. (To head straight to Gray Knob, remain on Lowe's Path, descending directly to the cabin in 1.2 miles. To head straight to the Perch, continue south on Gulfside Trail for 0.5 mile, and then turn right on Israel Ridge Path to head down 0.8 mile to Perch Path, near the shelter.) Spur Trail slowly descends below and parallel to the rocky sub-peak of Abigail Adams, offering views of your earlier route. Knife Edge stands out in profile. Mount Madison rises beyond.

The trail passes below the promontory of Abigail Adams and becomes rockier and more challenging. Crag Camp is visible ahead, a thousand feet below, and the trail starts a more direct descent. Continuing, enjoy the striking views of pyramidal Mount Madison. Reenter forest, drop down a wide corridor, and leave the alpine zone behind (6.1/4,750).

Pass a spur on the right to Knight's Castle (6.3/4,590). This side trip leads to a ledgy outcrop with excellent views into King Ravine and toward Mounts Madison, John Quincy Adams, and Adams. From here, the steep rocky descent continues to Gray Knob Trail (6.5/4,250). Turn right to immediately reach Crag Camp.

SIDE TRIP TO GRAY KNOB

To reach Gray Knob from Crag Camp, follow Gray Knob Trail west for 0.5 mile through dense spruce-fir forest. The trail passes the spring and water source for Crag Camp, rises briefly, then descends to reach a signed spur to another nearby spring. From here, the rocky route runs mostly level. Cross a water source beneath the rocks, pass another spring, and reach the cabin.

To visit the Quay, an open ledge with views west of Mount Jefferson's ridge-lined slopes, continue on Gray Knob Trail a short distance past the cabin. Immediately below you to the west is the deep scoop of Cascade Ravine (the Perch shelters in its upper reaches). On its far side, Israel Ridge divides it from Castle Ravine to the west. Castellated Ridge is the next ridgeline west. It boasts some distinctive rock outcrops, especially along its upper lengths. Farthest away is the Ridge of the Caps, easily identified by the gendarmes along its prow. To the north, you also have views of the Pilot Range and the valley of US 2.

SIDE TRIP TO THE PERCH

If you're looking for more solitude than can be found at the cabins (or if they're both full), consider heading over to the Perch. From Gray Knob (0.0/4,370), it's 1.4 miles round-trip, with an elevation gain/loss of 600/600. Continue past the Quay on Gray Knob Trail, crossing Lowe's Path and breaking out into chest-high trees with good views. A rising traverse with continuous vistas allows you to look deep into the heart of rushing Cascade Ravine. Next reach Perch Path entering from the right (0.3/4,550). Bear right to follow it. Perch Path descends along a narrow, lightly used trail, passes several rivulets, and then crosses the upper reaches of Cascade Brook to the Perch on the opposite side (0.7/4,300).

Back at Crag Camp (6.5/4,250), continue down Spur Trail. (Those staying at Gray Knob can follow Hincks Trail 0.7 mile down to reach Spur Trail.) This forested path begins as a steep and rocky drop along the ridgeline and soon passes a sign on the right for Lower Crag (6.6/4,210), your last opportunity to peer into King Ravine. The trail continues its plummet down a wooden staircase, then moderates and curves left to head down into the gully of Spur Brook. Drop steeply to upper Spur Brook, rock-hop across it, and reach Hincks Trail on the opposite side (7.1/3,440).

Continue down Spur Trail. The route remains in the gully but curves away from the stream, passing a posted spur on the right for Chandler Falls

(7.2/3,180). A nice rest stop for the knees, the 30-foot falls hiss over bedrock and split into a triangular fan at the base.

Past the falls, hobblebushes appear as the woods transition to hardwoods. The trail briefly mellows, steepens, descends some stairs, and returns alongside the stream to reach Randolph Path (7.4/2,960). Go right on Randolph Path, rock-hopping the brook and passing large paper birches to reach a five-way junction with King Ravine Trail, Randolph Path, and Amphibrach Trail (7.5/2,930).

Follow Amphibrach Trail's gentle descent along a leafier trail. Yellow birches appear as the forest transition continues. Cross Cliffway Trail (7.9/2,500), remaining on the Amphibrach as it continues its mellow descent. Red and sugar maples soon appear, joined shortly by abundant number of beeches. Return to the banks of Spur Brook by some pleasant cascades, and then rock-hop across it to Monaway Trail on the left (8.3/2,220). Here, a short spur leads right to the Cold Spur Ledges, a solid rock outcrop near the confluence of Spur Brook and an unnamed tributary, which combine to form Cold Brook.

Continue down easy-cruising Amphibrach Trail, parallel to nearby Cold Brook. Shortly before Amphibrach Trail reaches Link Trail (9.4/1,450), it passes pulsing Cold Brook Falls. The largest falls of the hike, the cascade rushes through a narrow rock gorge and can be approached from either side of the brook. At Link Trail junction, turn right and cross over Memorial Bridge, held in place by stone foundations.

To return to the trailhead, follow signs to the Link. The trail runs through an active sugar maple operation; tubing runs to and fro between the trees to collect the sap for maple syrup, and numerous paths crisscross the area. Watch for trail signs, which lead you to the Link + Amphibrach trail. The single-track trail parallels the highway above the rail-trail and power lines. Turn left once you reach Air Line Trail (10.1/1,330) to immediately cross the rail-trail and power lines and return to the trailhead (10.2/1,310).

INFORMATION

White Mountain National Forest, Androscoggin Ranger District, 300 Glen Road, Gorham, NH 03581, 603-466-2713, fs.usda.gov/whitemountain; Pinkham Notch Visitor Center, 603-466-2725, open daily 6:30 A.M. to 10 P.M. from May to October.

NEARBY

Gorham is a short drive from the trailhead on US 2 and offers a variety of pre- or post-hike food and drinking options.

TRIP 27
WILD RIVER WILDERNESS

Location: White Mountain National Forest
Difficulty: Challenging
Distance: 25.3 miles round-trip
Total Elevation Gain/Loss: 6,100 feet/6,100 feet
Trip Length: 2–3 days
Recommended Map: *AMC White Mountains Trail Map, Map 5: Carter Range–Evans Notch* (AMC Books)
Highlights: Streams, rivers, and mountains in New Hampshire's newest Wilderness Area.

This Wilderness protects a broad watershed in the eastern White Mountain National Forest. Hemmed by the Carter and Baldface ranges, it is the second largest roadless area in New England and is much less traveled than most other areas in the Whites. Forest cloaks much of the wilderness, sheltering abundant wildlife and crystalline waterways. Great stands of paper birches dot the woods. View-rich mountains rise above it all.

HIKE OVERVIEW

This journey loops around the Wild River Wilderness, first ascending on the Appalachian Trail (AT) along the spine of the Carter Range before dropping back into the Wild River valley to return along the river. The hike begins along Moriah Brook, a small stream loaded with idyllic swimming holes, and then reaches Imp Campsite atop the Carter–Moriah Range. From here, a long ridgeline traverse on the AT leads over five 4,000-foot peaks en route to Carter Notch Hut. The route then descends into the remote headwaters of the Wild River and returns to the trailhead alongside the river on Wild River Trail.

Like much of the White Mountains, the Wild River area was intensively logged in the late nineteenth and early twentieth centuries. Railroad lines snaked up the valley to haul out timber. The entire drainage was felled. Vast amounts of woody debris littered the denuded terrain, which burned in 1903 in a massive conflagration that charred most of the watershed. Today, the Wild River valley is a study of nature's resiliency, a testament to what a century of regeneration can bring.

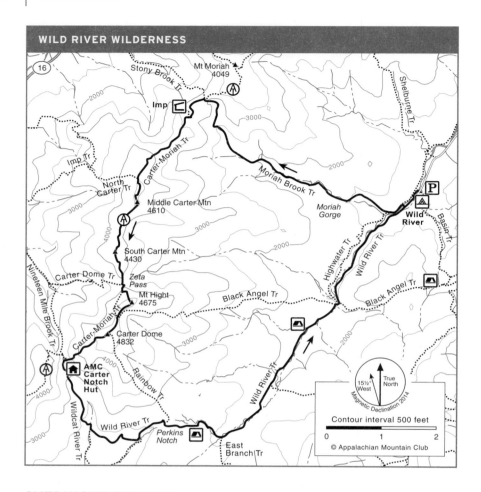

OVERNIGHT OPTIONS

Dispersed camping is permitted throughout the Wilderness Area. Good campsites are scarce along the ridgelines and mountain slopes, but numerous options can be found early in the hike along Moriah Brook Trail, at the former Perkins Notch Shelter site, and later along the Wild River. The Wild River Campground is a good option for an evening arrival at the trailhead.

Imp Campsite (6.5/3,200/44° 19.750′ N, 71° 09.031′ W) is located just below Carter–Moriah Trail—part of the AT. The forested site features a cabin-like shelter and five tent platforms. A bench offers a limited view northwest, but the best sunset is viewed from the ledges on Carter–Moriah Trail above the site. An adjacent runnel provides water; a bear box is on site. The site receives moderate use. Visit midweek or arrive early on the weekends to snag a good spot. A caretaker is in residence from mid-June to the second week of September and collects a per-person fee.

Carter Notch Hut (13.8/3,288/44° 15.556′ N, 71° 11.724′ W) is situated below the rocky cliffs of Wildcat Mountain and Carter Dome. Front-porch views look out at the Ramparts, a debris field of massive talus. A giant stove, fully equipped kitchen, and running potable water make it a pleasant layover. Two bunkhouses divided into smaller bunkrooms sleep 40 guests. Carter Notch Hut is self-service (and more affordable) for most of the year, full-service in June through mid-September. Call 603-466-2727 or visit outdoors.org/lodging/huts for reservations and more information. Several heavily used campsites are located at the junction of Nineteen Mile Brook and Wildcat Ridge trails, 0.3 mile from the hut (no water). Find another site in a clearing of young spruce-fir along Wildcat River Trail, a 0.3-mile, 130-foot drop past the second bunkhouse.

Perkins Notch Tentsite (18.3/2,600/44° 14.562′ N, 71° 08.748′ W) no longer hosts a shelter, but camping is still possible. This remote site, more than 5 miles from a trailhead, is located near the headwaters of the Wild River and adjacent to a large boggy area known as No Ketchum Pond. Carter Dome is partly visible from the former shelter site, though the edge of the pond/swamp offers better views of the mountain and the rocky prow of Mount Hight. Tentsites are scattered in the area, including one large group campsite. The site lacks a good water source, though a trickle runs by near the former shelter site—you'll likely need a filter. Water also flows near the bog outlet on Wild River Trail; good camping potential can be found downstream from this point.

Spruce Brook Tentsite (21.8/1,650/44° 16.123′ N, 71° 06.353′ W) offers pleasant riverside camping along Wild River Trail, 3.5 miles downriver from Perkins Notch. The spot gets good afternoon sun and offers several established tentsites. The nearby river murmurs pleasantly; soak in waist-deep pools in both the river and adjacent Spruce Brook. The old shelter at this site has been removed.

TO REACH THE TRAILHEAD

Follow US 2 east from the 113/2 junction for 3.1 miles, and turn right onto unpaved, but easily navigable, Wild River Road. The road ends at the campground entrance in 5.7 miles. A hiker parking area (44° 18.328′ N, 71° 03.839′ W) is located on the left.

HIKE DESCRIPTION

From the parking lot (0.0/1,170), cross the entrance road and follow Wild River Trail. The path descends over a small brook to the wide and rocky Wild River. The route turns upstream, parallels the river past hobblebushes, spruces, and red and striped maples, and reaches an old logging road above the campground; turn right to remain on Wild River Trail.

After some easy cruising, the trail intersects posted Moriah Brook Trail on the right (0.3/1,180). Two substantial trees—a red oak and a yellow birch—stand sentinel at the junction. Turn right on wide Moriah Brook Trail down to the broad river and across a nice suspension bridge. Two trails diverge on the opposite side, then rejoin and reach Highwater Trail (0.4/1,220). Bear left onto the yellow-blazed trail, winding past some exceptional hemlocks. Pass through a birch glade then reach the junction where Moriah Brook and Highwater trails divide (0.7/1,270).

Turn right to follow blue-blazed Moriah Brook Trail on an old railroad bed. Paper birches and sugar maples line the trail curving up and away from Moriah Brook, out-of-sight below. The path curves back left, and a rushing roar fills the woods. As the stream comes into view, glimpses of deep swimming holes and giant boulders tantalize.

The trail reaches Moriah Brook by a mini gorge (1.7/1,540). The waterworn faces of giant boulders stare back. A good swimming hole—the first of many—invites you in. Cross the brook on a precarious rock-hop, potentially dangerous in high water. The trail resumes a gentle climb, joined by moisture-loving white ashes. Watch the surrounding granite rocks for xenoliths, pieces of overlying rock that were not fully melted by the liquid magma that rose up and surrounded it.

The path briefly leaves the stream, returns to it, and winds through a grove of substantial paper and yellow birches, interspersed with large aspens nearly 2 feet in diameter. The mellow trail crosses a small tributary and climbs past big-leaf and quaking aspens.

Recross Moriah Brook in a clearing (3.1/1,770), and resume the ascent. The stream rushes over extensive outcrops of solid bedrock and plunges into several ideal swimming holes. Reaching the confluence of two equally sized streams (3.5/1,940), the trail follows the branch to the left. Pass the reach of the railroad bed. The trail becomes thinner and root-crossed.

The swimming hole parade continues along the increasingly steep terrain. The forest transitions to spruce-fir forest. Beeches and hemlocks disappear. Maples become less common. Blueberries line the trail, thriving in the acidic soil of the boreal woods. Approach Moriah Brook's upper headwaters, which branches into numerous small tributaries; several pass underfoot.

The climb steepens through thick stands of paper birches. Boulders increase, the route becomes rockier, and you pass a collection of giant stones. The creek has seemingly split one giant boulder into two. Others are as large as school buses.

The trail continues to parallel the brook, becoming boggy in spots. The Moriah Cliffs peek out ahead and above. Reach another confluence of small streams. From here, the trail climbs up the rocks by the creek on the right. The Moriah Cliffs now loom overhead as you ascend a difficult section. The path briefly levels, winds through alder bog, and then markedly steepens again for the final rise to Carter–Moriah Trail, part of the AT (5.8/3,110).

Bear left to head south on the white-blazed AT. The AT quickly crosses bog bridging and immediately reaches Stony Brook Trail on the right. Scattered glimpses look west and northwest toward the Kilkenny Range (Trip 28). Rocky and rough, the AT gradually rises, undulates along, and then climbs a steep rock staircase. Cross a flowing water source and continue steeply up, following a ribbon of rock through surrounding moss.

A sign announces the Forest Protection Area that surrounds Imp Campsite. Shortly thereafter, reach an open view northwest. The twin summits of the Percy Peaks are evident, as are the mountains of the Pilot Range. The Androscoggin River drainage defines the ridge-lined landscape.

The trail opens out on rock slabs with dramatic views to the rumpled terrain of the northernmost portion of New Hampshire. Gorham winds along the Androscoggin River as it curves north to Berlin. To the northwest is the small massif of Pine Mountain; the Crescent Range rises beyond it, cut by a deep and obvious gash. Beyond are the peaks of the Kilkenny; Mount Cabot is just past the gash. Nearby to the south, along the ridgeline from closest to farthest, are Imp Mountain, North Carter, and then South Carter.

The rocky trail drops toward a small saddle and reaches the spur for Imp Campsite (6.5/3,360), located 0.2 mile down the hillside. Water is available from a small creek on the campground trail.

Continuing onward, the AT climbs over bedrock and traverses sloped, often wet, slabs. The trailless summit of Imp Mountain passes on the right. The footing is challenging, but the trail levels out and travels over a long section of bog bridges by flowing water.

Views of North Carter Mountain appear. The mountain looks steep, and indeed it is—the path gains 800 feet in the next 0.6 mile. The trail reaches a steep, rocky rise, climbing 100 feet to reach some puncheon. Resume the severely steep climb, clambering over slabs as you go. The route crosses flowing water, and then resumes its climb. Views peer back into the Wild River drainage. Spot your approach route along the Moriah Brook watershed, below the cliffs of Mount Moriah. On the northern horizon rise the Mahoosucs (Trip 30).

The route requires hand-over-hand scrambling as it rises above 4,000 feet and provides increasingly expansive views north. The entire Mahoosuc Range is now apparent, including its highest, most distant peak, 4,170-foot Old Speck. The cleft of Grafton Notch (Trip 31) is to its right. The radical steep scrambles continue. The trail becomes walkable then eases to a gradual rise. The first views appear of the upper Wild River watershed and your continuing route.

The broad gap at the head of the Wild River valley is Perkins Notch. Mount Hight rises west of the notch, at the south end of the Carter Range. To the west (left) of Perkins Notch are the trailless peaks of Sable and Chandler mountains. The high round knob of North Baldface is apparent a few miles farther north.

The summit of North Carter is clear (8.1/4,530/44° 18.712′ N, 71° 09.891′ W). A short distance farther are a boulder and your first views of Mount Washington and the Northern Presidentials. The deep gouge of the Great Gulf (Trip 25) pierces the range. Mounts Clay, Jefferson, Adams, and Madison march north from Washington.

The mellow trail follows the ridge to North Carter Trail on the right (8.4/4,470). Continue straight and remain on the AT as it winds through a short, wind-blasted forest. Increasingly good views appear of the Presidential Range, from Boott Spur to Mount Madison at the northern end of the range. Views south also open up, encompassing Carter Dome ahead and Wildcat Ski Area to the southwest. Crest the wooded summit of Middle Carter (9.0/4,610/44° 18.171′ N, 71° 10.060′ W).

From here, the trail drops slowly, passing a view of the route over South Carter, Mount Hight, and Carter Dome. After a long, easy section, begin the heart-pumping ascent of South Carter. The trail briefly levels, resumes its steady ascent, and then curves right to the wooded and viewless summit (10.3/4,430/44° 17.379′ N, 71° 10.586′ W).

Past the summit, the trail drops steeply, then quickly moderates for an easier descent into Zeta Pass, where Carter Dome Trail joins from the right (11.1/3,900). Find two small trickles of water here. The AT reaches a fork (11.3/4,080). Carter Dome Trail goes right, bypassing the summit of Mount Hight. It could save you a few hundred feet of climbing and 0.4 mile of effort, but you'd miss the view! Go left instead to ascend Mount Hight. A short distance from the top, enter the alpine zone and scramble over boulders to the clear summit plateau. Continue just past the clearing to the true summit (11.7/4,675/44° 16.533′ N, 71° 10.216′ W).

Look east over the entire Wild River watershed. The prominent bald knobs of North and South Baldface are apparent. Below is a tremendous bowl of paper birches, filling the Spruce Brook watershed. The Wild River is visible in the large, marshy area near its headwaters. To the north, you can see Mount Moriah; farther down the ridge are the bald knobs of Shelburne Moriah Mountain. The Mahoosucs rise in the distance beyond it. To the south, identify the pointy summit of Mount Chocorua (Trip 19) beyond the Moat Mountains. To the west are the Presidentials, including all of Montalban Ridge (Trip 24).

Leaving the summit, gradually descend and undulate along to Carter Dome Trail on the right and immediately afterward Black Angel Trail on the left (12.1/4,570). Continue on the AT on a steady, upward cruise to Carter Dome's summit (12.5/4,832/44° 16.027′ N, 71° 10.748′ W). The remains and foundation of an old lookout tower dot the large clearing. A look north reveals your entire route thus far. Rainbow Trail splits left here, providing a more direct route down to Perkins Notch (1.5 miles) through extensive paper birch stands. (This variation saves 2.2 miles of hiking, but skips impressive Carter Notch.)

Remaining on the AT, drop steadily over a rocky path. The trail traverses left and soon the first glimpses into the approaching cleft of Carter Notch appear. Wildcat A looms on the far side, rising a thousand feet. The route drops significantly. Below 4,000 feet, the trail curves right and takes a direct line downward.

A view looks into the notch; spot Carter Notch Hut by two small ponds. The steep trail switchbacks left and follows large rock steps on a plummeting descent. The trail curves right and briefly eases before resuming its stair-aided descent. The grade eases near the bottom and an increasing amount of paper birches and hobblebushes appear alongside.

Reach the shore of a small, idyllic pond and encounter Nineteen Mile Brook Trail on the right by the pond's outflow. Bear left to remain on the AT, passing a second small pond that reflects the cliffs of Carter Dome. The hut is just ahead (13.8/3,288).

Take a leisurely break and consider exploring the Ramparts, the talus field that fills much of the notch. A network of unmarked paths explores the boulders, best accessed by the posted spur just past the second bunkhouse. Once you're in the boulders, scramble as far as you care to go. Icy caves and views await.

The continuing route leaves the AT (and crowds) behind as it journeys toward the Wild River headwaters. Follow Wildcat River Trail past the second bunkhouse to a steady drop through the Wildcat River watershed, which ultimately feeds the Saco River to the southwest. Paper birches increase. Red maples, yellow birches, and sugar maples appear below 3,000 feet. The trail crosses a small brook and leaves the spruce-fir forest behind.

The trail follows an old road bed, briefly parallels a small inaccessible stream, then traverses away to the left.

Rock-hop across the Wildcat River, here still a stream. Red maple becomes increasingly common before reaching Wild River Trail (15.7/2,390). Bear left onto Wild River Trail, making a level traverse over occasional rocks and boggy bits. Sugar maples line the trail. The route crosses a small tributary to Bog Brook, rises briefly, and then curves left to Bog Brook Trail (16.8/2,420).

Bear left to stay on Wild River Trail as it winds through a long stretch of young hardwoods. Spruces and firs reappear in boggier areas, joined by red maples and blueberries. Climb briefly, traverse the slopes just above Perkins Notch, and crest the height-of-land. The trail bends right and reaches Rainbow Trail on the left (17.5/2,580).

Remain on Wild River Trail, which crosses a flowing water source—fill up here if you are staying at Perkins Notch. After a short climb along a wet trail, make a brief drop, enter the Wild River watershed, and reach the former site of Perkins Notch Shelter (18.3/2,600).

To continue, follow Wild River Trail, which leaves to the left of the shelter. Quickly pass another spur down to the bog's edge and then hear the flowing headwaters. The trail banks left, crosses the young Wild River, and drops gently to parallel the now-rushing stream. This section offers good camping potential.

The route continues through a hardwood forest dotted with occasional spruces and firs, and then recrosses the now-rockier stream. East Branch Trail joins from the right on the opposite bank (19.0/2,400). Remain on Wild River Trail as it drops, parallels the stream, passes another streamside campsite, and then hops across boggy areas and a few rock staircases. The often-wet path winds through thick, young spruce-fir forest, returns among hardwoods, and then descends to reach the Eagle Link on the right (20.5/2,050).

Continue straight on Wild River Trail. Now thin, rocky, and root-crossed, the trail winds through hardwood forest and makes a steady descent near the river, which is audible but not readily accessible. The route steepens as it drops into and crosses the Red Brook drainage (20.9/1,860), briefly running alongside the stream as it courses over bedrock and boulders. Several nice pools can be found at the confluence with the Wild River.

Hurricane Irene significantly impacted Wild River Trail in 2011. High water washed out several sections beyond this point; you will encounter multiple reroutes and small detours downriver.

Keep your eyes peeled for relics of the logging era. Large metal spikes jut from the bedrock as the trail eases and starts cruising along an old railroad bed. Pass several nice campsites, and soon begin to parallel the river, occasionally detouring washouts and undercut banks. The trail becomes increasingly wide. Approach Spruce Brook, rock-hop across it, and immediately reach Spruce Brook Tentsite (21.8/1,650).

Past the tentsite, the trail winds along the river, and hemlocks begin to reappear. The going is easy along this section, which soon leads past Black Angel Trail on the left (22.5/1,540). A short distance beyond it, Highwater Trail splits left at the site of the old Spider Bridge. Wild River Trail crosses at a wide, shallow spot; you can usually rock-hop across. (If the river is running dangerously high, follow Highwater Trail instead. This slightly longer route climbs slopes and traverses several hundred feet above the river to Moriah Brook Trail in 2.9 miles.)

Once on the opposite side, continue downstream on Wild River Trail, quickly passing the old bridge footings. The route cruises alongside the deepening river and becomes a gravel road. From here on out, the hiking is easy and almost entirely level. The trail curves right, passes through a raspberry-laden meadow, and reaches the earlier Moriah Brook Trail junction (25.0/1,180). From here, either follow the single-track trail you started on, or remain on the road to emerge in the campground (25.3/1,170).

INFORMATION

White Mountain National Forest, Androscoggin Ranger District, 300 Glen Road, Gorham, NH 03581, 603-466-2713, fs.usda.gov/whitemountain; Pinkham Notch Visitor Center, 603-466-2725, open daily 6:30 A.M. to 10 P.M. from May to October.

NEARBY

Several scenic and lesser traveled WMNF campgrounds—Cold River, Basin, and Hastings—are in the Evans Notch area. They provide excellent base camping opportunities for exploring the area, including the wonderful swimming hole at the upper end of the Bickford Slides (see Trip 29). For supplies and grub, ample amenities are available in Gorham, New Hampshire, and Fryeburg, Maine.

TRIP 28
THE KILKENNY

Location: Northern White Mountain National Forest
Difficulty: Moderate
Distance: 16.1 miles round-trip
Total Elevation Gain/Loss: 4,600 feet/4,600 feet
Trip Length: 2 days
Recommended Map: *AMC White Mountains Trail Map, Map 6: North Country–Mahoosuc* (AMC Books)
Highlight: The wild and empty northern White Mountains.

A mountain range in miniature, the Pilot Range rises above the Great North Woods of northern New Hampshire. Known as the Kilkenny, the surrounding region is set apart from the rest of White Mountain National Forest and is a landscape of roaming moose, bald summits, looming ledges, and few people.

HIKE OVERVIEW

The hike loops counter-clockwise up and along the highest points of the Pilot Range's spine. Along the way are some of the region's best highlights, including open cliff-top views from Rogers Ledge, reflections in Unknown Pond, a 360-degree vista from the summit of the Horn, and a small cabin atop Mount Cabot, one of New Hampshire's 4,000-footers. This hike is a good option on busy summer weekends and holidays, when other areas in the Whites may be overrun, and in late September, when the forest here blushes with peak color—earlier than anywhere else in the Whites. Dogs are allowed.

OVERNIGHT OPTIONS

The hike travels past two designated tentsites, Rogers Ledge and Unknown Pond, as well as a small and dilapidated cabin atop Mount Cabot. Dispersed camping is permitted throughout the hike but good sites are hard to find in the densely forested terrain. Campfires are permitted.

Rogers Ledge Tentsite (3.8/2,450/44° 32.715′ N, 71° 21.849′ W) is surrounded by a forest of paper and yellow birches. A few level tentsites are scattered about. Water is available from a nearby brook, a short distance north on Kilkenny Ridge Trail. A privy and fire ring complete the amenities. The site

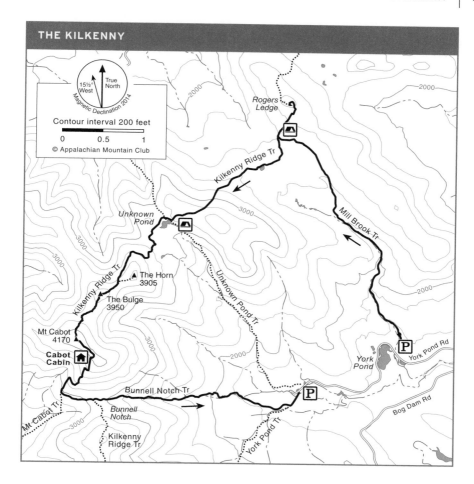

THE KILKENNY

makes a convenient base for a sunset visit to Rogers Ledge, 0.6 mile north on Kilkenny Ridge Trail.

Unknown Pond Tentsite (7.1/3,190/44° 31.689′ N, 71° 23.429′ W) shelters several established sites by its namesake lake. The uppermost offers glimpses through the trees toward the Northern Presidentials. Water is obtained from the pond. (A filter is useful for removing the inevitable floaters.) This is the most popular overnight location in the area and one of the few spots in the region that may attract a crowd. A privy is available. A variety of heavily used sites are scattered near the pond as well—not the most environmentally friendly options.

Cabot Cabin (8.7/4,080/44° 30.192′ N, 71° 24.619′ W) perches just below the summit of Mount Cabot. The small, run-down structure once accompa-nied an adjacent fire tower (built 1924, abandoned 1946, and dynamited by the Forest Service in 1965). The tiny, green-shingled building offers four small bunks free of charge on a first-come, first-served basis. Water is obtained from a small spring 200 feet down the mountainside—head toward the summit to find the posted spur. Good views from the cabin's small deck look west toward the distant Green Mountains. A privy and small fire ring are available.

TO REACH THE TRAILHEAD

Follow NH 110 north from Berlin for 7.3 miles and turn left on York Pond Road. In 1.6 miles, reach Bog Dam Road on the left. Continue straight on paved York Pond Road for another 3.2 miles to reach a gate and a small parking area on the left by the entrance to the Berlin Fish Hatchery. The trailhead is a short distance farther up the road, but leave your vehicle here (44° 30.128′ N, 71° 19.885′ W). The hatchery is open 8:30 A.M. to 4 P.M. and the gate may be locked after closing time.

HIKE DESCRIPTION

From the parking area (0.0/1,480), walk down the road toward the hatchery. Big-toothed aspens line the road, joined by red and striped maples. Pass the covered Foster's Raceways and a sign detailing the trout life cycle. At a fork in the road, a trail sign points right, toward Mill Brook Trail. As you approach the trailhead on a paved road, pass the Fire Warden headquarters and raceways full of hundreds of squirming fish. A circular pool holds some particularly large specimens.

The trail begins to the left of the Fire Warden building (0.2/1,530) on an old dirt road, briefly following Cold Brook before curving around a water supply to the right. The route turns sharply left onto a single-track path. Passing beneath spruce trees, the obvious trail soon bears slightly to the left. Rejoining Cold Brook, the hike is now accompanied by an understory of blueberry, hobblebush, and bunchberry plants.

The gentle trail slowly climbs along the gurgling creek. In spots, grass grows directly in the trail, which slowly becomes rockier as the creek valley narrows. The path soon traverses along the adjacent slopes, at times rising a short distance above the stream.

The trail, which can be quite muddy in some areas, returns along the placid stream, then once again climbs the slopes. Watch for pink lady's slippers as the forest becomes increasingly dominated by spruces and paper birches. The trail then levels, curves away from the creek, and crosses a trickling tributary. The route now runs roughly parallel to this small watercourse, climbing slowly and steadily, and then levels out to roll gently past abundant paper birches and hobblebushes. The trail drops through a dense young forest to reach a three-way junction with Kilkenny Ridge Trail (3.8/2,400). Turn right onto Kilkenny Ridge Trail to immediately reach the Rogers Ledge Tentsite and the start of the highly recommended side trip to Rogers Ledge, 1.2 miles round-trip with 550 feet of elevation change.

SIDE TRIP TO ROGERS LEDGE

Head north on Kilkenny Ridge Trail, winding past bracken ferns, paper birches, and sugar and red maples. The route is intermittently indicated by yellow blazes, and soon a view appears of Rogers Ledge and its naked rock face. The route steadily climbs, curves right past a large boulder, and then ascends a series of rock steps to reach a flat clearing atop Rogers Ledge (4.4/3,000). Open slabs along the cliff's edge are readily accessible. The panorama overlooks a mix of hardwoods and conifers, in fall a painted mosaic of foliage. To the west, the rolling summits of the northern Pilot Range are capped by 3,730-foot Hutchins Mountain. Return the way you came.

From the junction with Mill Brook Trail (5.0/2,400), head south on Kilkenny Ridge Trail to immediately cross the flowing headwaters of Mill Brook. The trail passes over roots and rocks beneath spruce and fir trees and passes tiny Kilback Pond, a shallow and boggy beaver pond. A few small rocks along the shore provide options for a moment of relaxation. Just past the pond, look northeast for a view of Rogers Ledge.

The path crosses the pond outlet and climbs, soon offering better views of Rogers Ledge. The trail levels and slowly rises through groves of paper birches, spruces, and firs. Wood ferns proliferate in the understory. The trail crests (6.7/3,320) and then makes a gentle descent, widening as it approaches Unknown Pond Trail and adjacent Unknown Pond Tentsite (7.1/3,190). Savor views across the water toward the Horn's distinctive summit.

Continue on Kilkenny Ridge Trail, which soon begins undulating away from the pond. Drop briefly to cross a rivulet, and then begin a rising traverse up the Horn's west flanks. The rocky trail attains the saddle between the Bulge and the Horn (8.2/3,680), where an unsigned spur heads left toward the summit of the Horn (8.5/3,930/44° 31.067′ N, 71° 24.026′ W).

The Horn offers the hike's best views. Follow the spur trail to the open summit knob, scrambling up some large boulders to reach the top. The view encompasses all of northern New Hampshire. To the south is the rounded

The Horn offers exceptional views of western Maine and the northern White Mountains. (Photo courtesy of Dan Eisner)

dome of nearby Mount Cabot; farther away and to its left are the northern flanks of the Presidential Range. The prominent bowl of King Ravine gouges deeply into the slopes below Mount Adams (Trip 26), and Mounts Jefferson and Washington and the rounded hump of Mount Eisenhower trail away to the south. To the southeast, the Carter Range and prominent cleft of Carter Notch are apparent (Trip 27). Northeast, the rugged Mahoosucs straddle the Maine–New Hampshire border (Trip 30).

Continuing from the saddle (8.8/3,680), the path makes a direct ascent to the viewless summit of the Bulge (9.0/3,950), situated in a forest of snags. The trail narrows as it descends the opposite side to reach an easy-cruising section. As the trail ascends its final climb toward the summit of Mount Cabot, the surrounding slopes become lumpy moss gardens of boulders and fir trees. The trail gradient eases as it approaches the summit ((9.9/4,170/44° 30.364′ N, 71° 24.867′ W), which is marked by a sign and a pile of rocks.

Views in the area look south toward more near peaks, including the adjacent summits of Mounts Waumbek (left) and Starr King (right) and beyond to the Presidential Range. Descending from the summit, pass a posted spur to a nearby spring, and then make a momentary rise to reach a clearing on the lower summit with views east. Pass Bunnell Rock on the left—another good viewpoint—shortly before reaching Cabot Cabin (8.7/4,080).

From the cabin, the trail drops steadily over sharp basketball-size rocks. A series of switchbacks leads to a more direct descent over rocky terrain, including some large slabs. As the trail descends, watch for a spur that leads to an open rock ledge with more views south. Soon paper birches and hobblebushes reappear in the spruce-fir mosaic. The trail then traverses east to reach Cabot Trail on the right (11.3/2,970).

Bear left to remain on Kilkenny Ridge Trail as it curves past sugar maples, blackberries, and raspberries to Bunnell Notch and Bunnell Notch Trail (11.6/3,030). Turn left to head down yellow-blazed Bunnell Notch Trail and return to the trailhead. The path is initially level, but soon descends above a small gully. A creek flows audibly below, and the forest transitions back to hardwoods. Beeches appear first, followed by paper birches and striped and sugar maples. Abundant springs flow from the adjacent hillside, creating numerous boggy sections, many bridged by rock steps. The gradient steepens, the trail narrows, and soon the route leads you alongside the pretty stream as it cascades over mossy stones.

The route eventually eases and runs level through a lush forest of sugar maples and yellow birches. Rise above the creek and pass through a dense stand of saplings—the first signs of recent logging activity in the area. Soon the trail widens, descends slowly past more stick forest, and then banks right to encounter a logging road. The continuing route bears right (don't continue uphill to the left) and returns to single-track, winding along an old road overgrown with raspberries and blackberries.

The trail returns to the creek (13.1/1,770), rock-hops its crystalline waters, and then crosses a gully to pass through a clearing. Beyond the clearing, the single-track trail winds along a grassy road and reaches another logging road. Look up the road to spot pyramidal Terrace Mountain.

The trail rambles through older forest and reaches York Pond Trail on the right (13.8/1,700). Glance up York Pond Trail to spot Mount Weeks. Continue left onto the road—now York Pond Trail—crossing the creek on a footbridge and reaching a metal gate (14.0/1,660). Just beyond is the dirt hatchery road by a small parking area and the 2.1-mile road walk to the trailhead (16.1/1,480). Look behind for views of the Horn, Bulge, and Mount Cabot.

INFORMATION

White Mountain National Forest, Androscoggin Ranger District, 300 Glen Road, Gorham, NH 03581, 603-466-2713, fs.usda.gov/whitemountain.

NEARBY

Grab supplies and a bite to eat in Berlin or Gorham along US 2.

4

MAINE

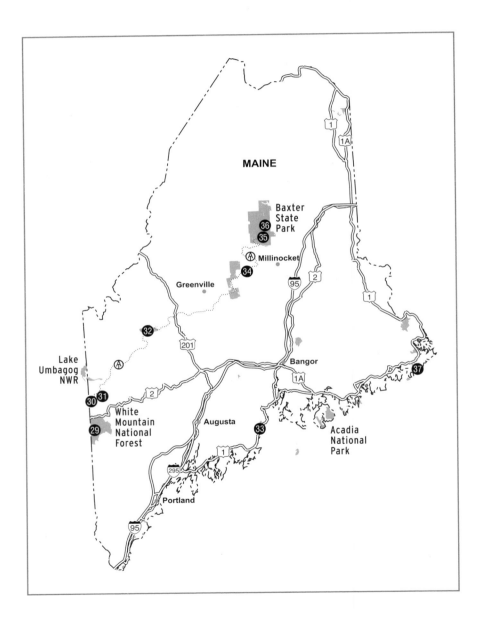

MAINE

1
1A

Baxter
State
Park
36
35

Millinocket
34

95 2

Greenville

1

32

201

Bangor

Lake
Umbagog
NWR

1A

30 31

2

White
Mountain
National
Forest
29

Augusta

33

37

Acadia
National
Park

1

295

Portland

95

TRIP 29
CARIBOU-SPECKLED MOUNTAIN WILDERNESS

Location: White Mountain National Forest
Difficulty: Moderate
Distance: 8.6 miles round-trip
Total Elevation Gain/Loss: 2,500 feet/2,500 feet
Trip Length: 1–2 days
Recommended Map: *AMC White Mountains Trail Map, Map 6: North Country–Mahoosuc* (AMC Books)
Highlight: Maine's quiet and scenic White Mountains.

Speckled Mountain hides in the eastern Whites. Secluded east of the Baldface Range, over the Maine state line, and invisible from elsewhere in the Whites, it offers a quiet ledge-walking escape with good views. Speckled Mountain is part of the 12,000-acre Caribou–Speckled Mountain Wilderness, designated in 1984.

HIKE OVERVIEW

This short loop uses Bickford Brook and Blueberry Ridge trails to ascend 2,906-foot Speckled Mountain. After passing a series of small cascades—the Bickford Slides—the route sticks to the mountain ridges, which offer several exceptional views. Most of the trip is dry and without water—the slides are your only reliable source. The hike is described counter-clockwise here, but it can easily be done in the opposite direction. Opt for Blueberry Ridge Trail (and its views) on the day with better visibility.

The Brickett Place awaits you at the trailhead, undoubtedly the quietest visitor center in the White Mountains. Built in the early nineteenth century, the unusual brick building has had a diverse life: it has been a farmhouse, a Civilian Conservation Corps regional headquarters, a Boy Scout facility, and even an AMC hut. Today, it's a sleepy wayside that opens only sporadically during hiking season.

OVERNIGHT OPTIONS

Dispersed camping is permitted throughout the Caribou–Speckled Mountain Wilderness, though good campsites are hard to find on the wooded slopes of this hike. Small bivy sites and the occasional tentsite scatter along a few ledges

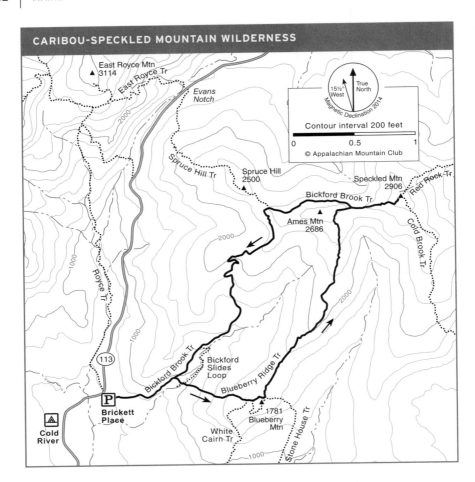

CARIBOU-SPECKLED MOUNTAIN WILDERNESS

Contour interval 200 feet

Magnetic Declination 2014

15½° West   True North

0   0.5   1

© Appalachian Mountain Club

on Blueberry Ridge Trail. Bedrock exposures on the summit also provide several options.

TO REACH THE TRAILHEAD

Take NH 113 north from Fryeburg for 20 miles. The trailhead (44° 16.026′ N, 71° 0.246′ W) is on the right and signed for the Brickett Place, 0.3 mile past the Basin Recreation Area turn-off and immediately across the Maine state line. A WMNF parking pass or daily permit from the trailhead fee station is required to leave your vehicle here.

HIKE DESCRIPTION

From the trailhead parking lot (0.0/640), head out on single-track Bickford Brook Trail. Immediately pass through woods of paper birches, beeches, white ashes, and sugar and striped maples—common members of the northern hardwood forest. Red oaks appear in the mix as the trail quickly rises. The gradient soon eases, and the trail reaches an old woods road (0.3/860), where the route bears right on a wider path. Snags punctuate the boulder slopes. The trail crests, the creek below becomes audible, and you cross the wilderness boundary. After a brief rise, reach Blueberry Ridge Trail (0.7/1,010).

Bear right onto yellow-blazed Blueberry Ridge Trail, and head toward the brook by descending the single-track path (0.8/940), where signs indicate the nearby presence of Upper and Lower Bickford Slides.

SIDE TRIP TO BICKFORD SLIDES

Head downstream to reach the Lower Slides, where the creek sluices through a smooth foot-wide channel before sheeting over a two-tiered waterfall and into a sliver of head-deep water. The riparian corridor is lush, cool, and full of hemlocks. The slides past this point, spilling over exposed bedrock, but access becomes increasingly challenging as you continue downstream.

To visit the Upper Slides—and a nice swimming hole—head upstream to immediately cross the brook, and follow Slide Trail along the right (east) bank. Pass some stately yellow birches and sugar maples, and cross a few small streams. The trail then switchbacks twice to climb above a spilling ramp of water that drops into an emerald pool. From here, the trail climbs steeply and runs parallel to the creek, which sluices through deep and inaccessible grooves in the bedrock. The route drops to cross the creek and then cuts left up the opposite slope to reach the unposted junction with Bickford Brook Trail, 0.5 mile from Blueberry Ridge Trail. (Coming down Bickford Brook Trail, look on a yellow birch for the prominent yellow blaze that marks the junction.)

Back on Blueberry Ridge Trail (0.8/940), rock-hop the stream and bear right at the junction with Upper Slides Trail. The rocky trail climbs steeply, quickly gaining elevation. Occasional glimpses through the trees reveal the adjacent Rattlesnake Brook drainage to the east. The trail's namesake blueberry bushes make an appearance as you climb and encounter open slabs (1.1/1,330). Views look north to East and West Royce mountains. The bare ridgeline continues to an open clearing with views west. North and South Baldface mountains rise on the far side of the Cold River They are connected by a long ridge that extends north to Mount Meader, above The Basin and its cliffs, and ends at West and East Royce mountains on the far side of Evans Notch. Peeking over the Baldface Range are the more distant summits of the Carter Range (Trip 27).

The route continues upward on a granite highway interspersed with patches of vegetation. Small white pines, spruces, and firs grow from green clumps. The trail levels and reenters spruce-fir forest, where blueberry bushes, pin cherries, bunchberries, and Indian cucumbers are common in the understory. Numerous pink lady's slippers bloom here in June.

The trail soon returns to open ledges where sun-exposed blueberry bushes produce abundant fruit. Red pines cling to the sparse granite slabs. You next reach White Cairn Trail on the right (1.4/1,730). Continue straight on Blueberry Ridge Trail, and quickly reach the junction for the outlook—an old sign marks it.

The worthwhile side trip to the outlook follows a 0.5-mile loop to open views south from atop the Blueberry Mountain cliffs. From this vantage point, you can look down at Shell Pond, with Harndon Hill just beyond it and Deer Hill behind it to the right. East of Shell Pond are the twin bumps of Palmer and Adams mountains. South Baldface is visible to the southwest. Complete the loop by following small cairns and the occasional blaze to Blueberry Ridge Trail.

Back at Blueberry Ridge Trail, you can see the low ridge rising above you to the north—this is along your continuing route. The summit of Speckled Mountain rises to the right. Continue across the open slabs to reach Stone House Trail (1.6/1,770), remaining on Blueberry Ridge Trail as it makes a gentle drop to the base of the upcoming ridge.

The route soon begins traveling through the forest along a ribbon of solid rock. Pass abundant blueberry bushes, and quickly reach another open ledge with views west; Mount Chocorua (Trip 19) can be spotted to the southwest. The open slabs continue, many with bivy potential but few with flat tentsites. The trail encounters a small alpine bog populated with larches and laurels, which are able to survive in the highly acidic soil. The steady ascent continues. Views west now reach as far as Mount Washington, which peeks out just to the right of Mount Hight in the southern Carter Range.

A series of giant rock steps lead to a level clearing near the summit of Ames Mountain (3.7/2,660). The trail curves right and briefly descends to reach Bickford Brook Trail (3.8/2,620). Your return route heads left, but definitely visit the top of Speckled Mountain before heading back (1.0 mile round-trip, 300 feet of elevation gain). To tag the summit, turn right on double-track Bickford Brook Trail, which cruises along a duff-covered path, winds through

The view from atop Speckled Mountain spans a full 360 degrees. (Photo courtesy of Wendy Almeida)

a clearing full of blackberries and elderberries, and then attains the summit (4.3/2,906/44° 17.456′ N, 70° 57.300′W).

The footings from a long-gone fire tower crown the summit. Open views look north for the first time, revealing the long line of the Mahoosucs (Trip 30) marching toward the horizon; Goose Eye Mountain is the prominent peak at the northern end of the range. To the west, Mounts Washington, Adams, and Madison peer over the Carter Range. To the northwest, Mount Moriah rises behind West and East Royce mountains. Due north, and much closer, Caribou Mountain rises beyond Haystack Notch and the cliffs of Haystack Mountain. To the east is Red Rock Mountain, near the edge of the Wilderness Area.

Back at the earlier junction with Blueberry Ridge Trail (4.8/2,620), head west on Bickford Brook Trail. The route follows an old woods road and easily descends through nice spruce-fir forest. A few gnarly, century-old yellow birches punctuate the scenery. The trail makes a long level traverse, then resumes its descent and passes Spruce Hill Trail on the right (5.5/2,410).

The trail steadily drops and returns to northern hardwood forest. As you descend below 2,000 feet, a pair of broad switchbacks leads you toward a small stream. The trail switchbacks down several more times and then crosses the creek. The path then becomes more road-like as it descends into woods of beeches and maples.

The trail mellows around 1,500 feet, and you can hear Bickford Brook rushing out-of-sight below. Pass the junction for Upper Slides Trail, (7.5/1,300) and then return to the earlier junction with Blueberry Ridge Trail (7.9/1,010). Follow Bickford Brook Trail back to the trailhead (8.6/640).

INFORMATION

White Mountain National Forest, Saco Ranger District Office, 33 Kancamagus Highway, Conway, NH 03818, 603-447-5448, fs.usda.gov/main/whitemountain/home.

NEARBY

Several scenic and lesser traveled WMNF campgrounds—Cold River, Basin, and Hastings—can be found in the Evans Notch area and provide excellent base camping opportunities for exploring the area, including this hike. For supplies and grub, ample amenities are available in Conway, New Hampshire, and Fryeburg, Maine.

TRIP 30
MAHOOSUC NOTCH

Location: Mahoosuc Range, the Appalachian Trail
Difficulty: Strenuous
Distance: 15.1 miles one-way
Total Elevation Gain/Loss: 6,200 feet/6,200 feet
Trip Length: 2–3 days
Recommended Maps: *AMC White Mountains Trail Map, Map 6: North Country–Mahoosuc* (AMC Books), *AMC Mahoosucs Map & Guide* (AMC Books)
Highlights: Rugged mountains, alpine bogs, summit views, the Hardest Mile on the AT

The Mahoosuc Range straddles the Maine–New Hampshire border northeast of the White Mountains. Even by New England standards, these mountains are remarkable for their ruggedness. Mahoosuc Notch slices through the heart of the range, a deep cleft filled with enormous boulders and traversed by the Appalachian Trail (AT). It is one of the most challenging sections of trail in New England and readily earns its moniker as the AT's Hardest Mile.

HIKE OVERVIEW

This hike can be done either as an overnight trip or as a leisurely three-day excursion that provides time to relax and savor the scenery. The trip begins and ends at trailheads located 4.8 miles apart on unpaved Success Pond Road.

Speck Pond Trail climbs from Success Pond Road through active logging areas to reach Speck Pond and the ridgeline. The route travels south on the AT and the ridgeline for 9.5 miles. Past Speck Pond, the hike quickly descends into adventure. It scrambles through Mahoosuc Notch and then rises steeply back to the ridgeline for five very long miles south of Speck Pond to Full Goose Campsite. From here, the route continues on the AT for another 4.4 miles, passing open views atop Goose Eye Mountain and Mount Carlo before reaching Carlo Col Campsite. An easy descent down Carlo Col Trail returns you to Success Pond Road.

Only a narrow corridor of land is protected within the mountain range, including the AT corridor in New Hampshire and a slightly broader swath of state land in Maine. The remaining area is unprotected, owned largely by log-

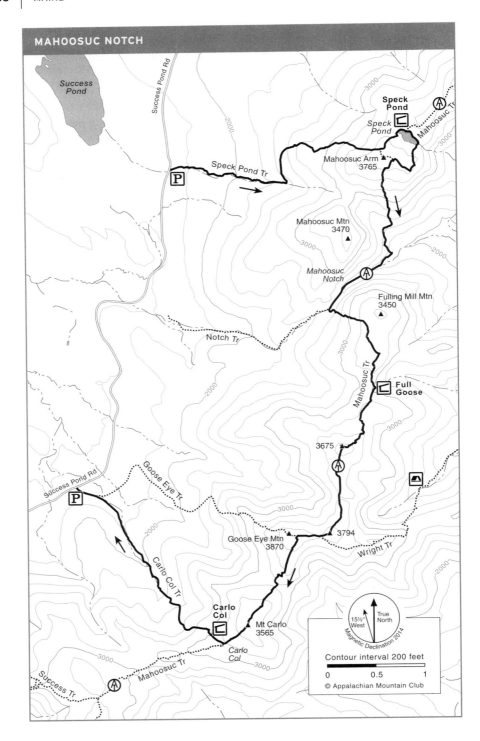

MAHOOSUC NOTCH

Success Pond

Success Pond Rd

Speck Pond Tr

P

Speck
Pond

Speck
Pond

Mahoosuc Tr

Mahoosuc Arm
3765

Mahoosuc Mtn
3470

Mahoosuc
Notch

Fulling Mill Mtn
3450

Notch Tr

Mahoosuc Tr

Full
Goose

3675

Goose Eye Tr

P

Success Pond Rd

3794

Goose Eye Mtn
3870

Wright Tr

Carlo Col Tr

Carlo
Col

Mt Carlo
3565

Carlo
Col

Success Tr

Mahoosuc Tr

15½°
West

True
North

Magnetic Declination 2014

Contour interval 200 feet

0   0.5   1

© Appalachian Mountain Club

ging companies. Clear-cuts and other intensive logging practices are common sights in the area.

OVERNIGHT OPTIONS

Stick to the three established camping areas located along this hike. The approach trail crosses private land, and the ridgeline is not a good place to camp. Bear boxes are provided at all three locations to store your food at night. Use them.

Speck Pond Campsite (3.6/3,400/44° 33.893′ N, 70° 58.373′ W) is near the shore of its namesake pond. A shelter sleeps eight to ten comfortably, and there are six tent platforms, three doubles and three singles. From Memorial Day through late September, and on weekends in October, a caretaker is on hand to collect an overnight per-person fee. Though the site receives moderate use compared to many locations in the Whites, it is still busy in July, August, and on most weekends. A seasonal spring provides water, or you can obtain it from Speck Pond.

Full Goose Campsite (8.2/3,000/44° 31.524′ N, 70° 58.915′ W), sitting in dense spruce-fir forest, has a shelter and four tent platforms. Water is available from a spring a short distance down the mountainside; a thin seasonal stream also flows nearby.

Carlo Col Campsite and Shelter (12.7/3,000/44° 29.337′ N, 71° 0.993′ W), 2.4 miles from hike's end, features an enclosed cabin-like shelter. Four tent platforms complete the nicely maintained site.

TO REACH THE TRAILHEADS

To Reach the Ending Trailhead. Take NH 16 north toward Berlin. Turn east off NH 16 to cross the Androscoggin River on the Cleveland Bridge, located 4.5 miles north of the east US 2/NH 16 junction in Gorham. Turn left onto Unity Street, and proceed through a stoplight. The road then curves right, crosses the railroad tracks, and becomes Hutchins Road. Follow Hutchins Road 1.2 miles past the stoplight to reach unpaved Success Pond Road on the right.

Success Pond Road is the main artery for logging operations in the region and is usually dusty, muddy, or heavily washboarded. It is passable, albeit slowly, in a low-clearance vehicle. Be watchful for high-speed logging trucks, and always give them the right-of-way. From the start of Success Pond Road at Hutchins Street, proceed 8.0 miles to the turn-off for Carlo Col Trail and parking area (44° 30.641′ N, 71° 02.602′ W)—your ending trailhead—on the right.

To Reach the Starting Trailhead. From the Carlo Col parking area, continue another 4.8 miles on Success Pond Road to reach the start of Speck Pond Trail on the right. There is a small parking area (44° 33.566′ N, 71° 01.377′ W) adjacent to the road on the left. Be watchful—trail signs are small and difficult to spot.

HIKE DESCRIPTION

From the roadside parking area (0.0/1,750), cross to the posted Speck Pond Trail trailhead. A few young denizens of the forest can be identified at the trailhead: balsam firs to your left, yellow birches on your right, and big-tooth aspens overhead. The single-track trail initially runs parallel to trickling Sucker Brook and passes through young northern hardwood forest. Paper birches and red, striped, and sugar maples are all present. Cross a small tributary, leave the brook, and begin hiking parallel to the audible stream below.

The trail slowly rises, returns along the boulder-strewn brook, and cruises past extensive pink lady's slippers, which bloom in May and June, on the forest floor. Steadily climb through a shady riparian corridor, and pass a nice spa-sized soaking pool in the brook. The route steepens markedly and switchbacks left. Mature yellow birches line the rocky and root-laced path as it traverses up the slopes. Other trees are young and small, an indication of past logging efforts that selectively removed the most valuable trees but left less precious species like birch behind.

Evidence of recent logging activity begins to encroach, and the first of several old skid roads crosses the trail corridor. The broad linear cuts run straight up the mountain slopes and provide access for harvesting equipment. The trail briefly disappears where it crosses such cuts, but is easily spotted on the opposite side.

The trail climbs more steeply and eventually bears right to take a more direct line upslope, using several nice rock staircases en route. The gradient briefly eases as the trail passes through stands of paper birches and the surrounding woods transition to spruce-fir forest. The route then resumes a long, rising traverse and slowly gains altitude. The gradient increases markedly as the trail passes 3,000 feet and becomes progressively steeper near the top, where a log staircase and some scrambling are necessary to proceed. Top out just below the summit of Mahoosuc Arm and reach May Cutoff (3.1/3,710), which bears right to reach the AT in 0.3 mile. Follow it to skip Speck Pond and shave 1.1 miles off your hike.

Otherwise, remain on Speck Pond Trail as it drops steeply. Old Speck Mountain looms ahead. Speck Pond shimmers in the basin below. A rocky descent deposits you at the lakeshore. Speck Pond Campsite is just ahead (3.6/3,400). From here, you can make the side trip up Old Speck Mountain, Maine's fourth-highest peak. To tag the summit (44° 34.275′ N, 70° 57.218′ W) —and its unparalleled views of the surrounding landscape—follow the AT north for 1.4 miles, gaining 770 feet of elevation.

The hike continues south from Speck Pond on the AT, wrapping around the east shore, where there is a view of Mahoosuc Arm across the water. The trail crosses the pond outlet and then climbs steeply via rocks, slabs, and rock staircases, passing a restricted view of Old Speck Mountain en route. After topping out, the route travels over some bog bridging and then undulates along the top of Mahoosuc Arm. Views look southeast into the Androscoggin River valley and northeast to the peaks beyond Grafton Notch.

The trail then reaches an open viewpoint looking south toward the deep cleft of Mahoosuc Notch, shadowed beyond by Fulling Mill Mountain, North Peak, and Goose Eye Mountain—summits on your continuing route. Sunday River, the namesake for the nearby ski resort, drains the slopes below you to the east. To the north, you can make out the fire tower atop Old Speck.

Continuing south, the trail reaches May Cutoff on the right (4.5/3,680); follow it a short distance to reach the summit of Mahoosuc Arm (44° 33.646′ N, 70° 58.684′ W) and views southwest. Heading south, the AT starts the descent into Mahoosuc Notch, visible ahead. The trail passes a rock slab offering unobstructed views into the notch, then plummets over solid rock. Conditions are slick in spots, and scrambling is often required to safely navigate the drop. The trail descends several hundred feet and then eases somewhat. Though still steep, most of the rock slab sliding is now behind you.

Giant boulders begin to appear as you approach Mahoosuc Notch, and the trail descends. The notch comes into view, as do the flanks of Mahoosuc Mountain to the north. Leveling out, the trail bears right among increasing numbers of yellow and paper birches and encounters a brook. Water emerges from mossy boulders, sluices over rock slabs, and fills a few 2-feet-deep small pools that are nice for a refreshing soak.

The rocky path resumes its descent, winding past mature spruces and yellow birches. The trail passes a large sugar maple and curves right to reach the foot of Mahoosuc Notch (5.6/2,150). Mats of polypody ferns crown boulders. Multitudes of ferns, mountain maples, and false Solomon's seal fill the understory. Fulling Mill Mountain looms above you to the south.

The first boulder field and the Hardest Mile begin next. The moss-covered rocks come in all sizes, from microwave- to semitruck-size. The trail drops through a crevice and squeezes through a small cave. It reaches a highpoint and then cuts underneath a large boulder. It passes through a crack so narrow that you must remove your pack, feeding it behind you.

The stream flows directly underneath you, occasionally audible but always invisible underneath the boulders. The rock-hopping gymnastics continue. Sheer rock cliffs rise above you to the left. The trail passes under another giant boulder. The section concludes with a final scramble through a dark cave crevice. Misty smoke emerges from nearby cracks as hidden ice slowly melts away.

The trail rises steeply beneath overhanging cliffs along a boulder-free route. Surmount a few more boulders, and continue along to reach the height-of-land and Notch Trail (6.7/2,460).

Turn left to remain on the AT, which immediately climbs. Slabs, rock staircases, and a pair of log ladders lead straight up the flanks of Fulling Mill Mountain. After gaining more than 500 feet of elevation, the route bends right and the gradient eases. The trail now gradually rises, makes a level traverse, and then resumes its gentle climb to enter the unique alpine bogs of the Mahoosuc Range.

The trail travels along puncheon through a low-lying alpine garden of blueberries, leather leaves, Labrador teas, cranberries, and sheep laurels. Keep an eye out for small larch trees, deciduous conifers able to tolerate the extremely acidic soils. Bag the rocky summit of South Peak (7.7/3,395/44° 31.826′ N, 70° 58.793′ W), where vistas sweep north once again toward Old Speck. North Peak is nearby to the south. Goose Eye peeks over its shoulder. To the west is the Pilot Range (Trip 28); Mount Cabot is its highest peak. The Presidential Range rises to the southwest; Mounts Washington (Trip 23) and Madison (Trip 26) are visible.

The AT descends from here, passes a few restricted views west, and then begins a steeper drop. The descent is steady but at first not radically steep. But the gradient increases as the trail descends stone stairs and crosses a creek. A wooden ladder on the opposite shore immediately brings you to Full Goose Campsite (8.2/3,000).

Continuing south, the AT descends more wooden steps, runs briefly level, and then climbs a bouldery slab. The level traverse resumes, offering glimpses northwest through the trees toward Success Pond. The trail bears right and slowly climbs through an interesting forest that diminishes in size to near-pygmy stature. Then encounter an open slab with more views north and east.

The views continue as you steadily rise along the blueberry-dotted ridge. The trail then reenters the trees, levels briefly, and resumes a more direct ascent. North views from the lower summit of North Peak look first to South

Peak, then Mahoosuc Notch, Mahoosuc Mountain, and the long ridge that leads to Old Speck Mountain. Looking south you can see the bald hump of Goose Eye Mountain—your final ridge-top destination.

Continuing south, the AT immediately reaches the true summit of North Peak (9.2/3,675/44° 30.977′ N, 70° 59.301′ W), where views west reveal the Pilot Range. The Presidential Range juts to the southwest. Looking north, you can see the mountains of northern New Hampshire, including the distinctive twin humps of the Percy Peaks.

From the summit, briefly drop among trees before entering another open alpine bog. The trail slowly descends, bottoming out in a narrow gulch before rising to another mostly bald plateau. A final brief drop deposits you at Wright Trail (10.2/3,480), which heads off to the left down the range's little-visited east flanks.

Remain on the AT as it begins a real-life version of chutes and ladders. Dozens of wooden ladders and stairs traverse up and along the slopes. The amount of trail work that went into this section is staggering. Eventually reach the summit of Goose Eye Mountain's East Peak (10.4/3,790). Goose Eye itself looms just ahead, with Mount Carlo beyond. Views north encompass the long ridgeline of the Mahoosucs.

Continuing south, the AT makes a steep but quick drop to reach Wright Trail South Fork on the left (10.5/3,640). From here, a steady climb leads through the trees to an open view. Goose Eye Trail joins from the right (10.8/3,840).

To tag the summit of Goose Eye Mountain (44° 30.156′ N, 70° 59.926′ W), follow Goose Eye Trail less than 0.1 mile to more great views. Looking north, the cleft of Mahoosuc Notch and all the peaks leading up to it are visible. Moving your gaze south along the ridge, Mount Carlo is next up, followed by the bald peak of Mount Success in New Hampshire. (Note that you can return to Success Pond Road via 3.2-mile Goose Eye Trail. This variation reduces the overall hike by a mile, but it is steeper and rougher than the easy-cruising exit via Carlo Col Trail.)

Proceeding south on the AT, the route makes a steep ladder-aided drop, then levels out and heads gently down to the last alpine bald. Leave it all behind, and steadily wind down through thick spruce-fir forest, bottoming out in the saddle between Goose Eye Mountain and Mount Carlo (11.6/3,180).

The trail climbs steadily through the trees, tops out on the summit plateau, and then continues to reach Mount Carlo's actual summit, indicated by a marker (12.2/3,565/44° 29.352′ N, 71° 0.494′ W). Limited views reach north to Goose Eye Mountain and Wright Peak and south to Success Mountain. The route then descends through spruce-fir forest and reaches Carlo Col Trail on the right (12.4/3,190).

Bear right on Carlo Col Trail to descend off the ridge. The rocky path drops slowly at first, but soon steepens as it follows a boulder stream course downward. Passing below 3,000 feet, cross a thin stream, rise up the opposite bank, and reach Carlo Col Shelter (12.7/3,000).

Past the shelter, the trail continues down the watercourse over slippery rocks. Yellow birches appear as the trail leaves the streambed, bears left, and then returns to the creek and crosses it. This point marks the state line between Maine and New Hampshire. The path descends steadily to the right, accompanied by an increasing number of paper and yellow birches, and reaches the main branch of the creek (13.3/2,350). Cross and enter an increasingly lush forest that transitions steadily to hardwoods. Soon it's almost all ferns, sugar maples, and yellow and paper birches.

The long, gradual descent reaches an easy-cruising rock-free section that soon enters thicker, younger forest. The creek reappears by the trail and bigtooth aspens flutter overhead. After an easy rock-hop over the stream, the trail follows an old woods road surrounded by encroaching vegetation. The trail next enters a clearing and rambles past prolific blackberry and raspberry bushes, which offer nice end-of-the-hike refreshment in late summer. Emerge in the Carlo Col parking area, where Goose Eye Trail joins from the right (15.1/1,680). Shuttle back around, or drop your pack and walk the 4.8 miles back along Success Pond Road to retrieve your car.

INFORMATION
Grafton Notch State Park, 1941 Bear River Road, Newry, ME 04261, 207-824-2912, 207-674-6080 (off-season), maine.gov/graftonnotch.

NEARBY
You can grab supplies and a bite to eat in Berlin, but the options are better and more varied in Gorham along US 2.

TRIP 31
GRAFTON LOOP TRAIL

Location: Mahoosuc Range, western Maine
Difficulty: Strenuous
Distance: Full loop: 38.2 miles round-trip; western section: 17.1 miles
one-way; eastern section: 21.1 miles one-way
Total Elevation Gain/Loss: Full loop: 10,500 feet/10,500 feet; eastern
section: 6,300 feet/5,500 feet; western section: 4,200 feet/5,000 feet
Trip Length: 3-5 days
Recommended Map: *AMC Maine Mountain Trail Map 6: Mahoosuc
Range* (AMC Books)
Highlights: Exploring the mountainous terrain of western Maine on
one of New England's newest trails.

**The full Grafton Loop features about 30 miles of new trail around
Grafton Notch, along with an 8-mile section of the Appalachian
Trail (AT) between Old Speck Mountain and Baldpate Mountain.
The hike connects a series of scenic peaks and other natural features,
and explores some of Maine's most rugged and scenic backcountry.**

HIKE OVERVIEW

The hike loops around Grafton Notch and is roughly bisected by ME 26,
which creates two access points: a southern trailhead in Newry and a northern trailhead in Grafton Notch State Park. The resulting eastern and western
sections of the trail can be combined for a full loop, or done independently as
point-to-point hikes.

This route starts at the southern trailhead and completes the full loop
in a counter-clockwise direction. The first, eastern half of the hike is more
scenic and challenging than the latter half, and consists of 21.1 miles that
traverse four mountain peaks, visit several excellent viewpoints, and stop at
five designated camping areas. The second, western section provides access to
three designated campsites and an excellent view from Sunday River Whitecap
(though views from the rest of this section are limited). Grades along this section are mostly easy to moderate with a few short, steep pitches.

This major new trail was constructed over a six-year period by AMC and
other members of the Grafton Loop Trail Coalition. It was completed and
opened to the public in 2007.

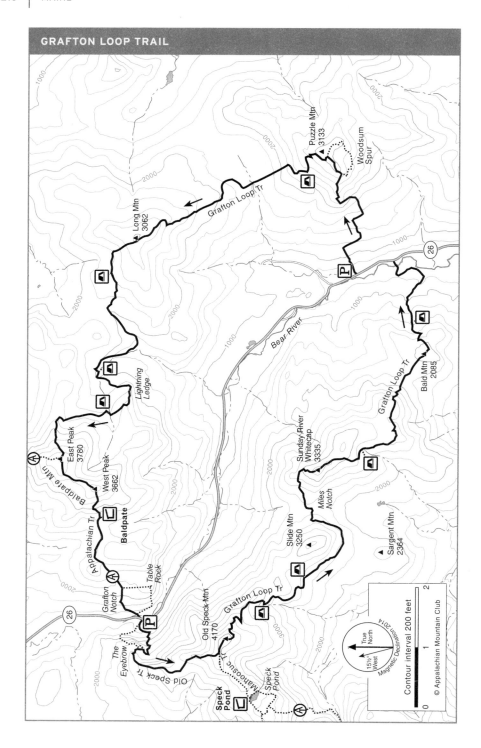

GRAFTON LOOP TRAIL

Contour interval 200 feet

© Appalachian Mountain Club

True North

Magnetic Declination 2014

15½° West

OVERNIGHT OPTIONS

Overnight use is only permitted at the route's eight designated campsites, each of which features a reliable water source nearby. Campfires are prohibited. Nearby Speck Pond Campsite provides an additional option.

Stewart Campsite (4.9/2,500) is located on the flanks of Puzzle Mountain, the site offers raised-earth tent pads and an outhouse.

Town Corner Campsite (10.4/2,420) perches on Long Mountain.

Lane Campsite (13.2/1,960) sits on the upper slopes of a wooded valley.

East Baldpate Campsite (15.0/2,450) is located in a broad stream valley.

Baldpate Lean-to (19.1/2,650) receives more use than other overnight locations on this hike, given its location on the Appalachian Trail (AT).

Speck Pond Campsite (25.7/3,400) is on the AT 1.1 miles off of Grafton Loop Trail. It features a shelter and six tent platforms. A caretaker collects an overnight fee from Memorial Day through late September, and on weekends in October.

Bull Run Campsite (26.8/2,900) is 5.7 miles from the northern trailhead. Amenities include two wooden tent platforms, a composting outhouse, and bear boxes (use them).

Slide Mountain Campsite (27.8/2,600) features tent platforms, an outhouse, and bear boxes.

Sargent Brook Campsite (32.2/2,600) is 6.0 miles from the southern trailhead; platforms, outhouse, and bear boxes are included here as well.

TO REACH THE TRAILHEADS

Parking for the southern trailhead (44° 32.319′ N, 70° 49.766′ W) is located on the east side of ME 26, 4.9 miles north of its junction with US 2 in Newry and just north of Eddy Road. (Note that the western section begins 0.6 miles south of the trailhead parking area and requires a short road-walk to access it.)

The northern trailhead (44° 35.392′ N, 70° 56.805′ W) is located 11.5 miles north of US 2, on ME 26 in the Grafton Notch parking area, where the AT crosses ME 26.

HIKE DESCRIPTION

Eastern Section

From the southern trailhead, Grafton Loop Trail begins at a blue-blazed post (0.0/720). Leaving the parking lot, the trail heads through a young forest, crosses a small brook, and then an overgrown logging road. It switchbacks several times on a gradual incline, passing through an area of young spruce and white birch before entering an area thick with downed balsam fir. The trail is clearly marked with blue blazes and cairns. Avoid turning left onto smaller unmarked paths. At about 2 miles, turn left and begin a steep climb. At about 2.4 miles, the trail crosses over several exposed granite boulders and ledges offering views of the Sunday River Ski Area, Grafton Notch, and the distant Presidentials. The trail cuts back into the woods before climbing a steep boulder staircase with some mild rock scrambling. (Caution: The exposed granite areas are very slippery in wet weather.)

Reach the south summit of Puzzle Mountain, marked by a large rock cairn (3.2/3,080/44° 32.644′ N, 70° 47.624′ W). Excellent views open in all directions. The lower end of Woodsum Spur Trail enters from the right (see later, side trip not recommended from this direction). Ahead, the trail reaches the rocky ledge top of Puzzle Mountain (3.6/3,142/44° 32.802′ N, 70° 47.300′ W). Here, the upper end of Woodsum Spur Trail diverges to the right.

SIDE TRIP ON WOODSUM SPUR TRAIL

This 1.4-mile loop trail on the south side of Puzzle Mountain is part of the Stewart Family Preserve, a 485-acre parcel protected by a conservation easement. The trail is fairly rugged with significant elevation gains and losses for its relatively short length. Hiking the trail in a clockwise direction is recommended.

The northern end of the spur leaves Grafton Loop Trail and heads easterly below the true summit of Puzzle Mountain. Woodsum Spur Trail passes through a wet area, then descends to the col on the southeastern ridge. A short, steep pitch climbs to the southeast peak with limited views. The trail then drops off the peak to the south and west, descending through shrub and forest with occasional open ledges. The trail passes through a wet area before crossing a stream. Gradually ascending as it traverses westward, the trail turns sharply to the northeast and climbs steeply to a boulder field, where it rejoins Grafton Loop Trail on an open ledge.

Continue on Grafton Loop Trail and descend Puzzle Mountain to the north, following cairns. The route traverses rolling terrain with a few boulder scrambles and a steel ladder. Beyond, the trail descends gradually on stone steps. It reaches the junction with the 300-foot spur trail to Stewart Campsite (4.9/2,500), then makes a winding descent on switchbacks. The trail crosses an overgrown road before leveling out as it approaches Chase Hill Brook. Take care to follow only the blue trail blazes in this area.

Cross Chase Hill Brook (6.3/1,580), which may be difficult during times of high water. At the base of the mountain, the trail intersects an old road (6.7/1,720). Turn right, walk 0.25 mile, and reenter the woods at the cairn on the left side of the road. The trail winds up Long Mountain, crossing, following, and leaving the woods road several times.

The trail eventually leaves the woods road for good and continues through mature forest. It contours up a ridge on long, gradual switchbacks with occasional steep sections. As the trail gains altitude, gaps in the trees afford views of the Sunday River Ski Area and the summit of Mount Washington. The trail becomes steeper and uses a stone staircase and wooden staircase/ladder to assist with the ascent.

A short spur trail near the summit of Long Mountain leads north to a viewpoint shortly before Grafton Loop Trail reaches a highpoint on Long Mountain (9.5/3,021/44° 35.470′ N, 70° 49.012′ W). Beyond, the trail winds easily downhill, crossing several small streams. The trail reaches the 440-foot spur trail to Town Corner Campsite (10.4/2,420).

Continuing, the trail crosses a snowmobile trail and a log bridge, then descends along a brook to a former junction (11.9/1,840). Here a 400-foot spur trail once led to Knoll Campsite, which was permanently closed in 2013. Ahead, the trail follows Wight Brook through a level area, crossing it several times; the brook may be difficult to cross in high water.

Reach the junction with a spur trail leading 450 feet to Lane Campsite on Wight Brook (13.2/1,960). The spur continues beyond the campsite to a lovely waterfall and pool. Beyond the spur trail, the trail climbs steeply to reach a short spur to Lightning Ledge (14.2/2,600), where there are good views of Puzzle Mountain and the Bear River valley. The trail ascends next to the knob of Lightning Ledge (14.5/2,644), where there are good views of the Baldpates.

Head back into the woods and descend through a forest with rugged rock faces to the left. A short, moderate descent brings the trail back to and across Wight Brook (14.9/2,420). A short ascent leads to a 300-foot spur trail to East Baldpate Campsite (15.0/2,450). Grafton Loop Trail then continues on, passing a huge glacial erratic along the way. The hike next reaches the open summit of the East Peak of Baldpate (17.1/3,812/44° 36.557′ N, 70° 53.524′ W) and spectacular views of the mountains and lakes in all directions. (Take care to stay on the trail to avoid disturbing the fragile alpine vegetation.)

Grafton Loop Trail joins the AT on the summit for the descent 4.0 miles down to ME 26 and the Grafton Notch parking area (21.1/1,500).

Western Section

At the northern trailhead, from a kiosk on the north side of the parking area, follow the trail leading to the left (the right-hand trail goes to Baldpate Mountain). In 0.1 mile, Eyebrow Trail leaves right to circle over the top of an 800-foot cliff shaped like an eyebrow before rejoining Old Speck Trail.

The main trail crosses a brook and soon begins to climb, following a series of switchbacks with many rock steps to approach the falls on Cascade Brook. Above the falls, the trail, now heading more north, crosses the brook for the last time (last water until the Bull Run Campsite), turns left at a ledge with a view up to Old Speck, and passes the upper terminus of Eyebrow Trail on the right (22.2/2,560).

The main trail bears left and ascends gradually to the north ridge, where it swings toward the left. The ridge is ledgy, and the ascent is interspersed with numerous short descents. High up, the trail turns southeast toward the summit and reaches an outlook east from the top of a ledgy hump (24.1/3,320).

The trail descends again briefly, then ascends steadily to the south, passing the abandoned and closed Link Trail on the left. Old Speck Trail climbs a fairly steep and rough pitch and passes an excellent north outlook just before joining Mahoosuc Trail, where Old Speck Trail ends (24.6/4,031). The flat, wooded summit of Old Speck is 0.3 mile left (east); Speck Pond Campsite is 1.1 mile to the right.

Proceed to the summit (24.9/4,170/44° 34.269' N, 70° 57.217' W) for fine views northeast, and a full panorama from the observation tower. Continue on Grafton Loop Trail as it passes a trail sign and steadily descends. The footing gets rougher as the trail swings to the left and next passes an outlook southeast toward Sunday River Whitecap and Bear River valley.

Rocks, roots, and holes fill the trail as it angles the south slope of Old Speck. On its continuing descent, the trail passes through a blowdown patch with restricted views south. Easy switchbacks with good footing are a welcome change as the trail descends to a southeastern spur of Old Speck Mountain. The trail descends steadily off the ridge crest, enters conifer forest, and reaches a 0.1-mile spur path left to Bull Run Campsite (26.8/2,900), crossing a brook that is the water source.

Grafton Loop Trail then winds gradually down the east side of the valley, bears right to descend through a hardwood glade, and then swings left. Cross a small brook, and 35 yards later encounter a spur trail on the left that ascends 110 yards to Slide Mountain Campsite (27.8/2,600). Dropping gradually through mixed woods, the trail runs at easy grades through fine hardwood forest for some distance along the base of Slide Mountain. Pass a large boulder

**The rugged mountains of western Maine beckon the adventurous backpacker.
(Photo © Jerry and Marcy Monkman)**

on the right, then run southeast at easy grades, with minor ups and downs. The trail then descends briefly and swings east.

The trail reaches a low point then ascends through a boulder area with occasional rough footing. It then descends through partly logged areas and turns right (north) again. Here the trail runs nearly level for 0.1 mile across the broad floor of Miles Notch (29.9/2,350) before swinging right (north) and gently ascending through open woods. The trail passes beneath yellow blazes that remain from a former unofficial trail, then ascends steadily east. Next the trail encounters an open shoulder, swings right (east), and climbs into a belt of woods. Open ledges and patches of scrub soon provide excellent views of the peaks around Grafton Notch as the trail steeply climbs to the summit of Sunday River Whitecap (31.1/3,335/44° 32.946′ N, 70° 53.795′ W).

Cross the open summit area and follow the trail to two side paths. Both lead to designated viewing areas looking east and west, including fine views of the northern Mahoosucs and distant Presidential Range. Please stay on the defined trail and outlook areas to avoid damaging the fragile alpine vegetation. AMC trail crews have used innovative construction techniques on the open ledges here—including scree walls and raised wooden walkways—to protect this delicate ecosystem.

The trail descends from the ledges to a col, then follows the ridge over a hump to another small col. Here the trail descends moderately along the west slope of Sunday River Whitecap. It reaches a spur path (32.2/2,600) that descends 0.2 mile to Sargent Brook Campsite, crossing a small brook (reliable) en route.

The trail now traverses the southwestern slope of Sunday River Whitecap through open woods, with minor ups and downs, crossing several small, unreliable brooks. After rising at mostly easy grades, the trail swings south and follows a winding course through dense growth. The trail emerges on the semi-open ledges of the west knob of Stowe Mountain, where there are limited views. Marked by cairns, the trail runs across the ledges for 0.1 mile. Descending briefly, the trail crosses a small brook and reaches a minor col. Cross the flat, wooded crest of Stowe Mountain (33.7/2,730), then steeply descend over a series of wooden ladders and many rock steps. The gradient eases and the trail runs nearly level through a flat saddle to the left of a brushy logged area. Ascending moderately, the trail reaches a highpoint on Bald Mountain (35.0/2,070), crosses a small sag, and continues at easy grades across the plateau.

The trail eventually leaves the broad crest and steadily descends by switchbacks. The trail follows a brook at moderate grades, crossing it multiple times, as it cuts down the northeast slope of Bald Mountain.

The trail swings left away from the brook and encounters an old road, where the trail turns left (east). Marked by snowmobile trail arrows, the trail crosses two fields and then turns left to cross the Bear River on a snowmobile bridge. It then bears left, then right to follow a farm road along the edge of a field to reach ME 26 (37.6/730). Follow the road north for 0.6 mile to the trailhead parking area (38.2/720).

INFORMATION

Maine Appalachian Trail Club, P.O. Box 283, Augusta, Maine 04332, matc.org; Grafton Notch State Park, 1941 Bear River Road, Newry, ME 04261, 207-824-2912, 207-674-6080 (off-season), maine.gov/graftonnotch.

NEARBY

The towns of Gorham, New Hampshire, and Bethel and Newry, Maine, each offer a selection of amenities for pre- and post-hiking needs.

TRIP 32
BIGELOW RANGE

Location: Carrabasset Valley, ME; Bigelow Preserve Public Reserved Land
Difficulty: Challenging
Distance: 12.7 miles round-trip
Total Elevation Gain/Loss: 4,000 feet/4,000 feet
Trip Length: 2 days
Recommended Map: *AMC Maine Mountains Trail Map, Map 3: Bigelow Range* (AMC Books)
Highlight: A mountainous ridge with maple-cloaked flanks.

Bigelow Range creases the landscape of western Maine, a long, rocky ridge dotted with peaks and far-reaching views. At lower elevations, enriched soils create habitat for abundant sugar maples. In fall, they blaze in leaf-peeping glory. Come experience the full spectrum of 3,000 feet of elevation change, climbing from the mountain's base to its dramatic highpoint atop 4,145-foot West Peak.

HIKE OVERVIEW

The hike uses Fire Warden, Appalachian, and Horns Pond trails to loop up Bigelow Mountain's steep slopes and along the highest 4 miles of ridgeline. En route, the trail passes three designated camping areas and some of the best views in Maine. Dogs are permitted but must be leashed at designated campsites.

OVERNIGHT OPTIONS

Two of the three designated camping areas—Myron Avery Memorial Tentsite and Horns Pond Campsite—are located along the ridgeline and on the Appalachian Trail (AT). They consequently receive heavy use. (From midsummer until early fall, you'll generally need to reach Avery by midafternoon to secure a tent platform, which also provides time to do the side trip to Avery Peak and makes your second day's hike a much more comfortable length.)

To beat the crowds, the recommended overnight spot is Moose Falls Campsite, especially on weekends and during thru-hiker season (August and September), though staying there does make the second day longer and more strenuous. Less than a mile from the trailhead, there are several campsites that

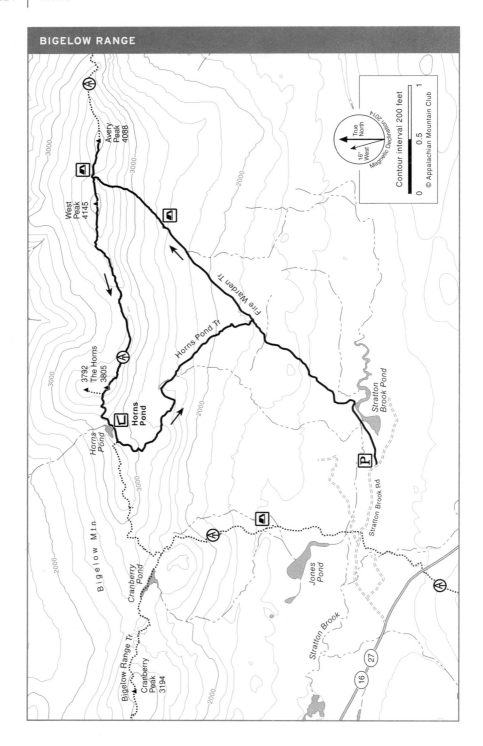

BIGELOW RANGE

are good options for a late-day arrival at the trailhead. Campfires are permitted at designated sites.

Moose Falls Campsite (3.6/2,470/45° 8.276′ N, 70° 17.317′ W) is located 1,300 feet below Bigelow Col and the AT and consequently receives minimal thru-hiker traffic. Two platforms and two other established sites spread along the slopes. Sugarloaf Mountain peeks through the trees; the lights of the ski resort are visible at night. Water is located a short distance uphill along Fire Warden Trail.

Myron Avery Tentsite (4.6/3,800/45° 8.791′ N, 70° 16.963′ W) hunkers down in Bigelow Col, a narrow cleft sandwiched between Avery and West peaks. Four tent platforms are tucked among balsam firs; one has a decent view south toward Sugarloaf and Crocker mountains. A larger group platform is also available. Two unreliable springs are located nearby; a filter is usually necessary to suck up any water.

Horns Pond Campsite (7.8/3,170/45° 8.668′ N, 70° 19.795′ W) nests atop the ridge near the shores of its namesake pond. It is one of the highest bodies of water in the state. The overnight area is a substantial complex that receives heavy use. Four tent platforms, two group tentsites, a general tenting area, two privies, a day-use lean-to, and two overnight lean-tos are all located here. Views to the south and east are available from a few spots, especially the privies. Water is readily accessible from the pond. Fishing is permitted, and the shallow pond is stocked annually with brook trout. Metal garbage cans are scattered around for food storage *only*; pack out all your trash.

TO REACH THE TRAILHEAD

Follow ME 27/16 north from Kingfield to the Sugarloaf Ski Area entrance on the left. Continue 3.2 miles farther to Stratton Brook Road, a small and easily-missed dirt road on the right. A small brown sign for Bigelow Preserve helps mark the turn-off. Stratton Brook Road is easily navigable for low-clearance vehicles and in 1.6 miles reaches a small parking area (45° 6.595′ N, 70° 20.227′ W). Coming from the north, Stratton Brook Road is located 4.6 miles south of the ME 27/16 split in central Stratton.

HIKE DESCRIPTION

From the trailhead (0.0/1,250), the blue-blazed route heads out past an information kiosk and down a wide woods road. Young forest surrounds you, highlighted by the fluttering leaves of quaking and big-tooth aspens. The white trunks of these trees superficially resemble the trunks of paper birch, but do

The open ridgeline of Bigelow Mountain offers dramatic views across central Maine. (Photo courtesy of Athena Lakri)

not peel in sheets. A pioneer species, aspen grows rapidly in disturbed areas with good sun exposure. Tell the two aspens apart by their leaf margins.

Continue on the road as it cruises atop a small levee, passes a small, two-car parking area, and then descends toward Stratton Brook Pond, intermittently visible to the right. The trail soon encounters an excellent view of Bigelow and Little Bigelow mountains. Above you to the north, the central spine of Bigelow Mountain can be spotted stretching from the Horns to West Peak—your upcoming hike. To the east, you can see the rocky cliffs of lower-elevation Little Bigelow Mountain, a peak along the AT's continuing route north.

The trail crosses an inflow to Stratton Pond, where you can take in a view of Bigelow Mountain's west front, stretching from Cranberry Peak to the Horns. The mass of 4,250-foot Sugarloaf Mountain bulges to the south. Though the shore is reedy, Stratton Pond has swimming potential. A designated campsite, complete with privy, is located by the lakeshore on the opposite side of the creek (0.5/1,230).

The route continues along the woods road, passing red spruces, balsam firs, and the occasional cedar. As the trail proceeds, keep an eye out for a big larch tree on the right near the water's edge. The only deciduous conifer in North America, larches are characterized by clusters of small, radiating needles, a fine pattern on its bark, and glowing yellow foliage in fall. A water-loving tree, it often grows near ponds, bogs, and other wet areas.

The trail reaches a fork by a designated trailside campsite and privy (0.7/1,240). Several other tenting areas are scattered among the nearby trees. Bear left at the fork, passing a beaver pond and a brief view toward the deep saddle overhead between West and Avery peaks. Sugar and striped maples start to appear, and you quickly come to a posted sign for Fire Warden Trail (1.0/1,240). Follow Fire Warden Trail as it slowly ascends through increasingly rocky terrain. Sugar maples and paper birches fill the deciduous forest. As the trail abruptly steepens, watch for some large red oaks growing here at the upper limits of their range.

The trail narrows and commences a steady ascent up rocky slopes, at times traveling over rock slabs. The path then levels, dances over sections of bog bridging, crosses a tiny stream, and reaches Horns Pond Trail on the left (2.3/1,740)—your return route. Remain on Fire Warden Trail, which stays level and crosses a few rivulets. Hobblebushes, yellow birches, and even a few large white pines appear in the forest mix.

Begin a rising traverse, aided by occasional rock steps, and cross a boulder-strewn brook. The ridgeline is palpable overhead and occasionally peeks through the trees. Sugar maples remain abundant as the trail climbs, eventually curving left to ascend a steep rock staircase, and reach the spur to Moose Falls Campsite (3.6/2,470/45° 8.276′ N, 70° 17.317′ W).

Water is scarce and at times unreliable between Moose Falls and Horns Pond Lean-to, a distance of 4.2 miles—fill up here before you start the ascent. The trail next climbs 1,300 feet in just under a mile. It's an ascent that keeps getting steeper . . . and steeper . . . and steeper.

Sugar maples accompany you to 2,800 feet, at which point the woods abruptly transition to spruce-fir forest. Mountain ashes and paper birches become common. Large boulders sprout from the slopes. The trail, aided by extensive rock staircases, eventually curves around to ascend almost directly up the mountainside. The gradient eases as you approach the saddle and curve right to make a gradual rise to the Myron Avery Memorial Tentsite, located to the right just below Bigelow Col. You then reach the col and junction with the AT (4.6/3,800).

SIDE TRIP TO AVERY PEAK

To tag the summit of 4,088-foot Avery Peak (300 feet up and 0.4 mile east from the trail), bear right (north) onto the AT. Initially level, the trail passes a caretaker's cabin (closed to the public) and then reaches a boulder field. Views north appear as you ascend the rocky slopes and reach the summit (45° 8.802′ N, 70° 16.523′ W), crowned by an abandoned fire tower.

The view looks north over landscape rolling in furrowed waves to the Canadian border. Flagstaff Lake spreads out below you, formed by the damming of the Dead River. Smaller Spring Lake is visible due north beyond it. Between Spring Lake and the northeast arm of Flagstaff Lake rises 2,225-foot Blanchard Mountain. Slightly to the left of Blanchard, prominent Coburn Mountain rises in the distance. The long ridge of Flagstaff Mountain rises west of Spring Lake. The Canadian border runs along the many peaks to the northwest; the low gap in the range marks the ME 27 border crossing. On a clear day, Katahdin is visible far to the northeast, 85 miles away as the crow flies and 180 miles on the AT. White Cap Mountain rises just to the right of Katahdin, near the center of the 100-Mile Wilderness (Trip 34).

Return to Bigelow Col (4.6/3,800) and head south along the AT. The white-blazed trail climbs steadily, remaining entirely within the trees until it nears the summit of West Peak. The trail bears left at some rock outcrops, revealing views across the col toward Avery Peak, and then traverses toward the summit, reaching the top among krummholz (4.9/4,145/45° 8.801′ N, 70° 17.300′ W). Savor sweeping views north one more time. Look west along the ridge, where you can see the approaching twin summits of the Horns. You can also pick out your starting point at Stratton Pond far below. Farther south, the more distant massif of Crocker Mountain neighbors Sugarloaf Mountain.

From the summit, the trail descends a narrow rocky ridge and quickly re-enters the trees. It then drops through dense fir forest, offering an occasional glimpse west toward the Horns. The trail then undulates along the ridgeline on a duff-covered track, providing intermittent views east toward West Peak and west toward the Horns ahead. The trail slowly descends to reach a low point, gradually rises, and then slowly steepens as it approaches the summit of South Horn (7.0/3,805/45° 8.696′ N, 70° 19.393′ W).

From the summit, look down at Horns Pond and its adjacent lean-tos. Farther west is the continuation of Bigelow Mountain, including Cranberry Peak and the isolated summit of East Nubble just beyond. Little Bigelow Mountain marches away to the east. Nearby is the slightly higher summit of North Horn, another worthwhile side trip. To visit it, remain on the AT as it descends South Horn and reaches the posted spur to North Horn (7.1/3,710). A steady ascent along the spur leads to the top (3,820/45° 8.869′ N, 70° 19.401′ W), where a nice boulder provides another 360-degree view.

Shimmering Horns Pond and its guardian cliffs intermittently appear as you continue south on the AT. Descend on a rocky trail and reach the col and the large covered awning of the site caretaker. After checking out the pond, privies, and other area sights, return to the AT, where a massive mileage sign indicates distances north and south. Next to the sign is the site's original shelter, a vintage lean-to built by the Civilian Conservation Corps in the 1930s. Briefly head south on the AT to reach Horns Pond Trail (7.9/3,170) on the left.

Follow blue-blazed Horns Pond Trail down staircases, past several boulder fortresses—including a huge 20-footer—and through stately spruce-fir forest. Glimpses of South Horn accompany you on the descent, which leads through an open grassy field (a filled-in bog) that offers full, and final, views of the Horn massif more than a thousand feet above. The trail becomes rockier. Red maples appear for the first time, followed shortly by sugar maples. The route parallels a pleasant brook for a period, then reaches a short spur that leads to a good view south of Sugarloaf and Crocker.

As you continue down, sugar maples once again burst forth in profusion, dominating a forest that also includes balsam firs, yellow birches, and big-tooth aspens. Beeches and the occasional large white pine appear farther down. A steady traversing descent takes you through this rustling broad-leaf forest and across several small brooks to return to the earlier junction with Fire Warden Trail (10.4/1,740). Bear right and retrace your route on Fire Warden Trail to the trailhead (12.7/1,250).

INFORMATION

Maine Bureau of Parks and Lands, Western Region Public Lands Office, P.O. Box 327, Farmington, ME 04938, 207-778-8231, maine.gov/doc/parks.

NEARBY

The small town of Kingfield makes for a good pre- or post-hike stop. Thanks to an influx of summer vacationers and winter Sugarloaf skiers, the town features several good restaurants and pubs, plus a few art galleries for browsing.

TRIP 33
CAMDEN HILLS STATE PARK

Location: Camden, ME
Difficulty: Easy for direct, moderate for scenic
Distance: 3.3 miles round-trip direct to shelter, 11.9 miles round-trip via a scenic route
Total Elevation Gain/Loss: Shelter Direct 800 feet/800 feet, Scenic Route 3,000 feet/3,000 feet
Trip Length: 1–2 days
Recommended Map: *AMC Maine Mountains Trail Map, Map 4: Camden Hills* (AMC Books)
Highlights: Coastal mountain views, forest diversity.

The lofty Camden Hills are the highest coastal promontories on the Eastern seaboard south of Acadia National Park. Most people summit 1,385-foot Mount Megunticook, the highest peak in the range, for its excellent ocean vistas. Far fewer explore the park's remaining network of trails, which tour a remarkably diverse forest and a handful of surprise views. Bald Rock Mountain hides out in the park's northern tier, offering two lean-tos near ocean panoramas.

HIKE OVERVIEW

The first variation of this hike provides direct access to the Bald Rock Mountain shelters from the northern corner of the park, a mini-loop on easy trails. The second tours many of the park highlights, including the views atop Mount Megunticook and sugar maple-cloaked Jack Williams Trail. Combine them by approaching from the north, setting up camp, and day-hiking from there.

The ecological diversity of 6,200-acre Camden Hills State Park is exceptional. Low-elevation, high-elevation, southern, northern, and coastal species all grow here. A short stroll around the park campground or trails passes more than a dozen tree species, including black cherry, choke cherry, yellow birch, paper birch, red maple, striped maple, white ash, balsam fir, red spruce, red oak, beech, white pine, basswood, dogwood, and quaking aspen.

OVERNIGHT OPTIONS

Backcountry camping is permitted only at the two shelters atop Bald Rock Mountain. Located just below the summit, the three-sided lean-tos have space

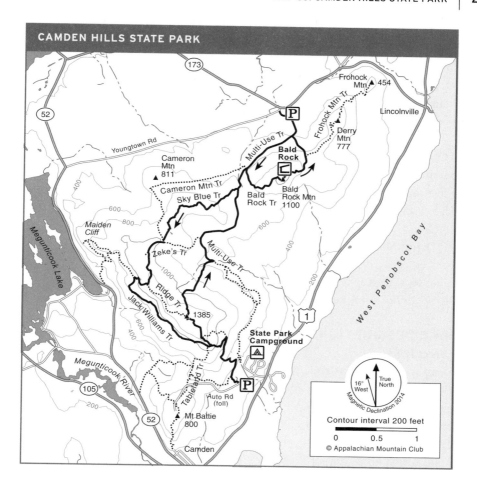

for up to six people. These free, first-come, first-served shelters are quite habitable, but have not been well maintained and both leak in the rain. The mileages in brackets note the distance from the trailhead on the scenic route.

The first shelter (2.0 [5.2]/1,100/44° 16.050′ N, 69° 2.600′ W), located just below the summit slabs, has a huge fire pit. Open views southeast over the ocean are a few steps away. The second (2.1 [5.2],/1,070/44° 16.067′ N, 69° 2.517′ W) is a short distance north of the summit, near some large boulders. Obtain water from the stream just past either trailhead or from Spring Brook at the junction of Multi-Use and Slope trails in the center of the park. Pit toilets are located near each lean-to. The shelters generally receive light use.

Megunticook Ski Shelter ([2.8]/560/44° 15.100′ N, 69° 3.117′ W) may be used on the scenic route in season. The enclosed cabin offers bunks for six, a woodstove and fireplace, picnic tables and chairs, and an adjacent privy. A nearby well and brook provide water; both sources must be treated. Reservations are required for overnight use, prepaid at least 10 days prior to your intended stay. Contact the park for more details.

A drive-in campground at the main park entrance offers hot showers, more than 100 sites, and easy access to trails. It is full many weekends in summer; to make reservations call 207-624-9950 or go online at campwithme.com.

TO REACH THE TRAILHEADS

Scenic Route Trailhead. From the junction of US 1 and ME 52 in Camden, travel north on US 1 for 1.5 miles to the signed entrance for Camden Hills State Park. Proceed to the entrance station, then make an immediate left to reach the hiker's parking lot (44° 13.733' N, 69° 3.267' W).

Direct Shelter Route Trailhead. Continue 4.1 miles on US 1 past the main park entrance to ME 173 in Lincolnville. Turn left and follow ME 173 for 2.3 miles to Youngtown Road and turn left. The trailhead parking lot (44° 16.821' N, 69° 2.686' W) is located on the left, immediately past the intersection.

HIKE DESCRIPTION

Direct Hike

From the trailhead (0.0/270), head down wide, well-graded, graveled Multi-Use Trail. Sensitive ferns, interrupted ferns, red oaks, white ashes, aspens, paper birches, beeches, white pines, sarsaparillas, and striped maples line the road. The trail rises, crosses a flowing stream, then passes Frohock Mountain Trail on the left (0.5/420)—your return route. Continue straight on Multi-Use Trail, which levels out, cruises past a few larger oaks, and reaches Bald Rock Trail on the left (1.2/610).

The longer scenic route joins here and unsigned Cameron Mountain Trail heads right (for the scenic route, see later), but you turn left on Bald Rock Trail and into a clearing shaded by white pines. Initially wide and root-laced, the trail soon narrows and becomes rockier, ascending by stone staircases. Dogwoods and maple leaf viburnums appear.

The trail curves up the mountain's southern flanks and climbs steeply among increasing softwoods and over abundant roots. The trail diverges just below the summit. Follow the blue-blazed trail left to the first shelter, or continue straight to the open summit slabs (2.0/1,100). From here, shimmering Penobscot Bay is 2.0 miles to the east. Dotted with islands, the bay bends and blends with the horizon on clear days.

From the shelter, continue north on blue-blazed Bald Rock Trail, which drops and reaches the second shelter. Red maples, choke cherries, and striped maples shade the lean-to. A jumble of adjacent rocks looks to the east and northeast.

From here, the trail drops steeply, then eases and slowly curves left to reach Frohock Mountain Trail (2.5/720), which leads 1.8 miles northeast over 777-foot Derry Mountain to its namesake peak (454 feet), a viewless and little-traveled side trail. To return to the trailhead, bear left to continue down Frohock Mountain Trail, which widens as it descends past nice oaks to the earlier junction with Multi-Use Trail (2.8/420). Bear right to return to the trailhead (3.3/270).

Scenic Hike

From the scenic route trailhead (0.0/270) under white pines, pass a No Camping sign (this does not refer to the shelters). The rocky, root-laced, heavily trod trail travels over bog bridging near an audible creek. The route reaches Nature Trail (0.1/310)—turn right toward Mount Megunticook. The trail crosses the small creek and treks beneath a canopy of oaks and beeches. Most of the beeches are badly diseased with the nectria fungus, as evidenced by the canker-like sores that dot their trunks. The path rises to reach Megunticook Trail on the left (0.3/440); follow it toward the Ocean Lookout.

The trail widens and passes extensive sarsaparillas and yellow *Clintonia*. Two gently curving switchbacks meet rock stairs, after which the trail curves right and levels to pass abundant maple-leaf viburnums.

The trail becomes rockier. Hobblebushes appear; catch glimpses of the ocean through the trees behind you. The path reaches Adam's Lookout Trail on the left (0.9/800). Follow it to open slabs with limited views southeast to Camden and a few islands in Penobscot Bay. The single-track trail then slabs upward to Tablelands Trail (1.2/1,020).

Go right on Tablelands Trail and ascend to a red oak–framed view of Camden Harbor and Mount Battie Auto Road. Above this point is a better view, overlooking Penobscot Bay. The large island mass of Vinalhaven is in the distance; Islesboro is closer. Glacial striations from the last Ice Age are evident in the rock underfoot, tracing the movement of the ice sheet to the south-southeast. Continue up Tablelands Trail, passing along the top of some cliffs with good views south to Camden, Battie, and the Megunticook River. Your return route—Jack Williams Trail—runs along the base of these cliffs.

Reach Megunticook Trail on the right (1.4/1,220) at the spectacular cliffs of Ocean Lookout, which offer great views over Camden Harbor and Mount Battie. Proceed straight to continue along the cliffs' edge. The path becomes Ridge Trail, which bears right into a forest of spruces, blueberry bushes, and laurels.

The trail slowly rises, crosses puncheon, and reaches Slope Trail on the right (1.8/1,380). Just past the junction, your route summits Mount Megunticook in a small viewless clearing.

Head right, down Slope Trail. The lightly used single-track trail drops past a pair of nice yellow birches, descends, and crosses several small brooks on little bridges. Halfway down, the trail widens and becomes wet and muddy. Enter a shady hemlock grove, where rushing Spring Brook appears to your left. The route parallels the stream then crosses it on a new bridge, emerging at Megunticook Ski Shelter, directly across graveled Multi-Use Trail (2.8/560).

From here, bear left and follow wide Multi-Use Trail through dense spruce-fir forest. The route rises, passes Zeke's Trail on the left (3.2/660), then levels out. Bald Rock Mountain peeks out ahead as the trail curves left near a swampy area and passes Sky Blue Trail (4.1/630)—your return route—on the left. To continue to the Bald Rock shelters, remain on Multi-Use Trail. It drops down across a flowing brook, briefly rises, and then reaches Cameron Mountain and Bald Rock trails (4.4/610). Bear right off Multi-Use Trail into the woods and proceed to the shelters (5.2/1,070).

To return to the park entrance, retrace your steps to the earlier junction with Sky Blue Trail (6.3/630). Follow Sky Blue Trail west on an old woods road; it splits right at a posted fork. Trillium and wintergreen are abundant. Lady's slippers appear as the path steadily rises through a forest of spruces, firs, and abundant beeches. Overgrown in spots, the trail appears lightly used. It undulates past prolific lady's slippers and blueberry bushes. Small cairns mark the route, which winds through several stone walls. The trail rolls to Cameron Mountain Trail on the right (7.8/980). Turn left to Zeke's Trail (7.9/960), where you turn right.

Zeke's Trail rises up a grassy corridor along an old woods roads buttressed by stone embankments. The path arrives at a side trail (8.2/1,150) on the right leading 100 yards to Zeke's Lookout. Ahead, the main trail crests briefly, becomes muddier and rockier, and then climbs to a clearing on the right with good blueberry potential before reaching Ridge Trail (8.7/1,160). Turn right; Ridge Trail steeply drops down across a creek and runs along its streambed for a short distance over roots and rocks. The gradient eases, and you traverse a slope with restricted views south-southwest. Resume the descent, curve left through a hemlock grove, and turn left on Jack Williams Trail (9.0/910).

Follow the single-track past continuing hemlocks. After a short drop, the trail encounters a spur on the right leading to a lookout. A bald eagle roosted here one June afternoon. There are views southwest over Megunticook Lake and to the Camden Snow Bowl Ski Area on Ragged Mountain and the surrounding hills.

From here, the trail descends across a boulder-lined creek and traverses through occasionally wet terrain. The woods abruptly transform to a lush forest of sugar maples. The trees thrive in the enriched soils that collect at the bottom of cliffs and talus fields, which are intermittently visible to the left. Some nice stands of white ash are interspersed.

The trail meanders through this exceptional forest, crossing a brook on a footbridge near a small pool. A younger forest then thickens around the trail. Softwoods reappear, and the cliffs become visible through the trees to your left. The route winds through denser forest closer to the looming cliffs. Reach Tablelands Trail (10.6/980).

Go left and follow Tablelands Trail up rock steps to reach the earlier junction with Adam's Lookout Trail (10.7/1,030). Turn right and retrace your steps to the trailhead via Adam's Lookout, Mount Megunticook, and Nature trails (11.9/270).

INFORMATION

Camden Hills State Park, 280 Belfast Road, Camden, ME 04843, 207-236-3109 (summer season), 207-236-0849 (winter season), maine.gov/camdenhills.

NEARBY

The nearby towns of Camden, Rockland, and Rockport offer dozens of restaurants, classic coastal scenery, and activities. To learn more, stop by an area visitor center or pick up one of the widely available free visitor brochures.

TRIP 34
THE 100-MILE WILDERNESS

Location: Appalachian Trail, northern Maine
Difficulty: Epic
Distance: 99.4 miles one-way
Total Elevation Gain/Loss: 18,000 feet/18,500 feet
Trip Length: 5–10 days
Recommended Maps: *Appalachian Trail Guide to Maine, Maps 1–3*
(Appalachian Trail Conservancy), *AMC Maine Mountains Trail Map,
Map 2: 100-Mile Wilderness* (AMC Books)
Highlight: The most remote section of the Appalachian Trail.

**The 100-Mile Wilderness encompasses the longest section of the
Appalachian Trail (AT) that does not cross a paved road. This rugged legendary stretch of trail offers a challenging adventure deep in
the Maine Woods. It is an endless parade of ever-changing scenery—rivers, streams, bogs, lakes, mountains, and more—and one of
New England's most challenging hikes.**

HIKE OVERVIEW

Follow the AT from the town of Monson to Abol Bridge on the edge of Baxter
State Park, a one-way 99.4-mile trip.

The hike travels through a lush, low-elevation hardwood forest and crosses
numerous streams and rivers that cut through wild terrain. The trail then
ascends the Barren–Chairback Range, traversing the mountain spine for 15
miles before crossing the West Branch of the Pleasant River and reaching the
slate gorge of Gulf Hagas. From here, the journey climbs White Cap Mountain's 3,654-foot alpine summit, the highest point on the hike.

After steeply descending White Cap, the AT treks toward Crawford Pond,
the hike's midpoint. The route follows Cooper Brook along an easy-cruising
section of trail past idyllic Cooper Brook Falls and enters the land of large
lakes and more level walking. Tour the shores of substantial Jo-Mary and
Pemadumcook lakes and walk alongside Nahmakanta Stream to emerge at
Nahmakanta Lake. After a steep climb over Nesuntabunt Mountain, the final
leg of the hike travels beside rushing Rainbow Stream and the long length of
Rainbow Lake. A final rise over the Rainbow Ledges leads to the hike's end at
the southwest edge of Baxter State Park.

Many people underestimate the rigors of this hike. The rugged trail is laced with roots and rocks, and occasionally boggy. There are no resupply points. The longer your trip, the more food you'll need to carry—and the slower you'll hike. Achieving the right balance of speed, pack weight, and enjoyment time is a challenge. AT thru-hikers often complete the 100-Mile Wilderness in only five days, an average of 20 miles per day. But keep in mind that thru-hikers are in top physical condition by this point in their journey, and inspired by their approaching endpoint atop Katahdin. Moving this quickly also allows little time for relaxing at the many beautiful locations on the way.

A seven- or eight-day itinerary sets a more relaxing, but still steady, pace covering an average of 12 to 14 miles per day. A trip of nine to ten days is a more leisurely journey, with plenty of time for fishing, swimming, and view-savoring, but you'll have to pack a lot of food. No matter how long you take, the trip requires a high degree of fitness. Dogs are allowed.

OVERNIGHT OPTIONS
Shelters and Tentsites
Thirteen shelters and three designated tenting sites line the route. Many other campsites are scattered throughout the hike as well. Campfires are permitted in fire rings at designated sites only.

Leeman Brook Lean-to (3.0/1,100/45° 21.094′ N, 69° 29.920′ W) perches on the slopes above rocky Leeman Brook and is surrounded by cedars and campsites.

Wilson Valley Lean-to (10.4/1,030/45° 23.928′ N, 69° 27.5513′ W) sits near a small brook. Two large hemlocks guard the eight-person shelter. Ample tent-sites are available uphill.

Long Pond Stream Lean-to (15.1/940/45° 25.270′ N, 69° 24.620′ W) is washed by the sounds of its namesake, boiling over rocks several hundred feet below. The adjacent water source can be thin at times; the next closest source is Long Pond Stream, 0.3 mile south on the AT. Several campsites are located uphill behind the shelter.

Cloud Pond Lean-to (19.7/2,440/45° 25.084′ N, 69° 21.235′ W) receives heavy use and is 0.4-mile off the AT. Cloud Pond is the highest body of water in the 100-Mile Wilderness and an excellent swimming hole. A thin spring is nearby, or you can collect water directly from the pond.

Chairback Gap Lean-to (26.0/1,980/45° 27.190′ N, 69° 15.745′) rests on the east (northern) end of the Barren–Chairback Range. The small shelter perches between Columbus and Chairback mountains; nice tentsites are nearby among

THE 100-MILE WILDERNESS (NORTH)

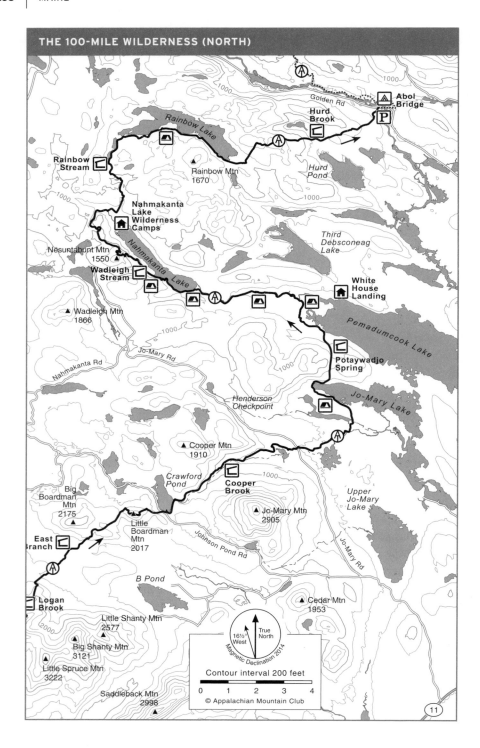

Contour interval 200 feet

0   1   2   3   4

© Appalachian Mountain Club

11

THE 100-MILE WILDERNESS (SOUTH)

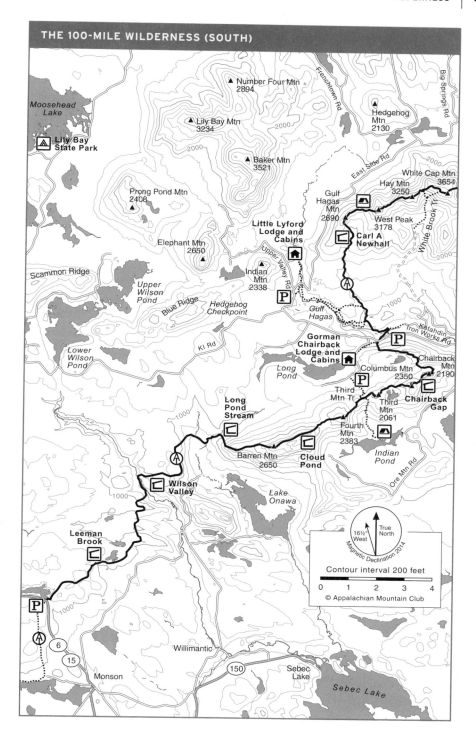

Moosehead Lake

Lily Bay State Park

▲ Number Four Mtn 2894

Frenchtown Rd

▲ Hedgehog Mtn 2130

Big Springs Rd

▲ Lily Bay Mtn 3234

East Side Rd

White Cap Mtn 3654

▲ Baker Mtn 3521

Hay Mtn 3250

Gulf Hagas Mtn 2690

West Peak 3178

White Brook Tr

Prong Pond Mtn 2408 ▲

Little Lyford Lodge and Cabins

Carl A Newhall

Elephant Mtn 2650 ▲

Upper Valley Rd

Scammon Ridge

Indian Mtn 2338 ▲

Upper Wilson Pond

Blue Ridge

Hedgehog Checkpoint

Gulf Hagas

Katahdin Iron Works Rd

KI Rd

Gorman Chairback Lodge and Cabins

Chairback Mtn 2190

Lower Wilson Pond

Long Pond

Columbus Mtn 2350

Chairback Gap

Long Pond Stream

Third Mtn Tr

Third Mtn 2061

Fourth Mtn 2383

Indian Pond

Barren Mtn 2650

Cloud Pond

Ore Mtn Rd

Wilson Valley

Lake Onawa

Leeman Brook

True North

16½ West

Magnetic Declination 2014

Contour interval 200 feet

0   1   2   3   4

© Appalachian Mountain Club

6

15

Willimantic

150

Sebec Lake

Monson

Sebec Lake

spruces and rocky outcrops. Water can be a problem here later in the season; a small spring in the saddle can get pretty thin and green during dry conditions.

Carl A. Newhall Lean-to (35.9/1,900/45° 40.737′ N, 69° 0.263′ W) sits on the flanks of Gulf Hagas Mountain, just above gurgling Gulf Hagas Brook. The small, basic shelter is popular because of the shortage of campsites to the south. (Camping is prohibited along the 2.0 miles of the AT north of the West Branch of the Pleasant River that lead to this lean-to.) A large, open clearing on the opposite side of the brook has room for multiple tents.

Sidney Tappan Campsite (37.7/2,450/45° 40.737′ N, 69° 0.263′ W) rests in the saddle between Gulf Hagas Mountain and West Peak. Several open, grassy tentsites provide a quieter respite from the shelter crowds. A good spring is a short distance down the slopes.

Logan Brook Lean-to (43.1/2,400/45° 40.737′ N, 69° 0.263′ W) nestles in a grove of paper birch on the eastern flanks of White Cap Mountain. Its namesake rushes adjacent to the shelter, its water splashing crystal clear. There are four or five established tentsites around the basic shelter, plus one more about 100 yards down the trail.

East Branch Lean-to (46.7/1,340/45° 40.737′ N, 69° 0.263′ W) features a new shelter and a basic picnic table and benches. The East Branch River flows audibly nearby and provides water. Spot Big Boardman Mountain from the riverbanks. Cedars, spruces, red maples, and a few white pines surround the camp. A few tentsites scatter among the trees.

Cooper Brook Falls Lean-to (54.8/980/45° 38.426′ N, 69° 5.248′ W), one of the more idyllic on the hike, sits at the bottom of its namesake waterfall and offers views of foaming sheets falling into a deep swimming hole. The rushing sound of water is omnipresent, boulders dot the area, numerous tentsites are tucked among them, and a diverse forest surrounds the site. The site's Full Moon privy boasts a luxurious padded seat.

Antlers Campsite (62.7/500/45° 40.737′ N, 69° 0.263′ W) rests on a small peninsula on Lower Jo-Mary Lake. The large camping area spreads out in a red pine grove. A few boulders protrude from the water. Lake breezes cool the site and help keep bugs at bay. Rock-lined paths lead to plentiful sites lake access points. Views from the peninsula look northwest toward the open slabs of Potaywadjo Ridge.

Potaywadjo Spring Lean-to (66.2/600/45° 42.398′ N, 69° 0.442′ W) tucks in the woods near its namesake spring, a large pool of crystal-clear water. Find extensive tenting areas near a log cabin–style shelter beneath hemlock and beech trees.

Nahmakanta Stream Campsite (70.5/600/45° 44.094′ N, 69° 03.290′ W) features an open tenting area under hemlocks, 50 to 75 yards from Nahmakanta Stream. The waters riffle pleasantly past numerous boulders, and there is easy access to the shore. Numerous sites dot the area, some well established. Fires are limited to the one central fire ring. Droves of mosquitoes frequent the area during the summer.

Wadleigh Stream Lean-to (76.3/690/45° 44.814′ N, 69° 08.670′ W) is a small shelter next to the trail, shaded by large sugar maples and adjacent to Wadleigh Stream. An old yellow birch stands sentinel on the opposite bank. Tenting areas are limited, though there is a small one near the brook, past the shelter on the right. A sandy beach on Nahmakanta Lake is a half-mile walk away.

Rainbow Stream Lean-to (84.4/980/45° 47.947′ N, 69° 10.229′ W) sits 20 feet from the riffling brook and features an uneven corduroy wood floor that can make for an uncomfortable night's sleep. Several tentsites rest in needle-covered clearings uphill—the best is above the stream, right behind the shelter on a big rock. A small totem pole next to the shelter keeps you company.

Rainbow Spring Campsite (88.2/1,070/45° 49.371′ N, 69° 08.162′ W) is located on the southern shore of massive Rainbow Lake, near its namesake spring. It offers several established sites in young hardwood forest. The refreshingly cool spring emerges right by the lake. Swimming opportunities in the lake are excellent.

Hurd Brook Lean-to (95.9/700/45° 49.109′ N, 69° 01.106′ W) is shaded by hemlocks and is within earshot of Hurd Brook, which flows through a rocky garden of roots and stones. The brook emerges from a big, marshy pond just upstream—be diligent about treating or filtering its water. The shelter features another uneven corduroy floor. Campsites are strewn about the area.

Lodges and Hostels

AMC's Little Lyford Lodge and Cabins (1,210/45° 31.019′ N, 69° 21.422′ W) are located beyond the head of Gulf Hagas on River Trail, accessed from the AT at mile 31.7 via Rim Trail (3.0 miles, one-way) or Pleasant River Tote Road (2.2 miles, one-way). The sporting camp features cabins and a bunkroom for overnight lodging, as well as hot showers and some basic supplies for purchase. Meals are included with an overnight stay. Little Lyford is not equipped to accommodate last-minute walk-in guests; reservations are required (603-466-2727, outdoors.org/lodging).

White House Landing is located a mile off the AT on the shores of Pemadumcook Lake. A muddy access road crosses the AT near mile 68 and leads to a boat landing and water shuttle to the camps; an airhorn and a signal flag at the landing allow you to alert the lodge to your presence. Cabins and a bunkroom are available for overnight lodging and supplies are available for sale. Hot food can also be purchased; their burgers are legendary in thru-hiker lore (207-745-5116, whitehouselanding.com, whlcamps@aol.com).

Nahmakanta Lake Wilderness Camps are located at the north end of Nahmakanta Lake; this is the most accessible sporting camp along the trail. Reach it via a short road walk that diverges from the AT at mile 83. Built in 1872, the camp's cabins and lodge are the only structures on the 4-mile-long lake and cater more toward affluent overnight visitors than thru-hikers. It is often booked solid during the summer; reservations are recommended (207-731-8888, nahmakanta.com).

TO REACH THE TRAILHEADS

To Reach the Ending/Northern Trailhead. Follow ME 11 west of Millinocket to the ME 11/157 junction by the First Congregational Church. Turn right and proceed 8.7 miles to a confusing intersection by the Big Moose Inn and a pool. Bear left here onto the Golden Road, and follow it 10.1 miles to the Abol Store (45° 50.125′ N, 68° 58.340′ W), located just before Abol Bridge. You can leave your car here, though there is a small per-day charge—touch base with store staff when you arrive.

To Reach the Starting/Southern Trailhead. From Pleasant Street in Monson, follow ME 15 north for 3.5 miles. The trailhead parking area (45° 19.880′ N, 69° 32.132′ W) is located on the right, by a significant curve in the road. A large AT parking sign indicates its location.

Shuttle Services. Shaw's Lodging in Monson offers a shuttle service throughout the 100-Mile Wilderness, though it can be pricey for small groups (207-997-3597, shawslodging.com).

Other Trailheads. Several major unpaved roads intersect the AT in the 100-Mile Wilderness and can provide alternate access points. Most of these roads lie within the KI Jo-Mary Multiple Use Forest, which charges a daily access fee to use the privately maintained road network. The KI Road crosses the AT at mile 29.9 and connects the towns of Greenville and Brownville. The West Branch Ponds Road intersects at mile 44.7 and approaches from the West Branch Ponds area to the northwest (a very confusing area to navigate). The Kokadjo-B Pond Road crosses at mile 51.6 and the Jo-Mary Road at mile 58.5; both are accessed from the Jo-Mary checkpoint on ME 11, located 15 miles south of Millinocket. The Jo-Mary Road also connects with access roads to Nahmakanta Lake, which cross the AT at miles 73.7, 79.4, and 83.1. You'll need a good map to navigate this network of confusing roads. Consult

DeLorme's *Maine Atlas & Gazetteer* or the *Southern Piscataquis Regional Recreation Map and Guide County Recreational Map* (AMC Books).

HIKE DESCRIPTION

The adventure begins from the edge of the parking area (0.0/1,220). Raspberry bushes grow to the left of the trailhead, identified by the white undersides of their leaves. The pointy leaves of red maples flutter overhead on both sides of the trail. The needles of aromatic balsam firs join the forest mosaic. To the right of the trailhead, spot the scaly bark of young black cherry trees in the understory.

Heading out, the AT immediately meets the trail to Goodell Falls, which leads in 0.3 mile to a pretty 10-foot cascade. Bear left on the AT, cross some wet sections, and meet the first bog bridging of the hike. Spot Spectacle Pond to the left through the trees, and cross the pond's flowing outlet on a bridge. Northern cedar trees line the lakeshore, though you can spot a larch tree across the inlet about 100 yards away; recognize it by its tall stature and droopy foliage.

The trail follows a root-laced track underlain by black shale. The dinner plate–sized leaves of hobblebush and five-needled clusters of white pine needles appear, joined by small blueberry bushes underfoot. As the trail slowly rises, the woods transition toward spruce-fir forest. The fluttering leaves of big-tooth aspens mix in with balsam firs and red spruces. The path intersects Old Stage Road (0.7/1,270), a woods road on the route stage coaches followed to Greenville in the nineteenth century.

Continuing, Bell Pond peeks through trees to the left. Several spur trails approach the water, but none provide good shore access. The AT curves right past the pond and crests a small rise. It then descends toward Lily Pond and passes some nice sugar maples. A spur goes down to the overgrown lakeshore (1.9/1,130).

Past the pond, the trail slowly rises through lush sugar maple forest. Diseased beeches afflicted with the nectria fungus join the forest—look for the canker-like sores on their otherwise smooth trunks. The route crests then heads downhill, providing the journey's first long-distance view of the upcoming Barren–Chairback Range. Notice the exposed rock faces of the Barren Ledges and Slide. To their right is Borestone Mountain, easily identified by its bald summit.

The path descends steeply and drops into the mini-gorge of Leeman Brook (3.0/1,080). The stream incises through solid slate here, leaving 20-foot-high cliffs and calving rock-bergs. Hemlocks shade the tumbling watercourse. Boulders fill the streambed—one large slab creates a grotto where you could sit under the showering water. The Leeman Brook Lean-to perches just above the brook.

Traveling onward through rocky terrain, the AT next reaches the shores of North Pond. The trail parallels the lake and offers good views, including glimpses of a tempting island nearby. Skirt the pond's small south arm, cross the outflow stream (3.8/1,030), and make a gradual ascent. The route crosses a woods road and passes restricted views northwest toward the rolling mountains. Begin an undulating descent to an open view of small Mud Pond, which is slowly filling in to become a bog.

The AT climbs past several mature spruces and crests atop Bear Pond Ledge. Banking left, the trail descends steeply through an older forest punctuated by large sugar maples, yellow birches, and hemlocks. At the bottom, cross trickling James Brook (6.3/990), lined by the lacy foliage of hemlock trees.

The dull roar of Little Wilson Falls becomes audible. Climb briefly, cross a woods road, and descend to this rushing landmark (6.6/880). The falls hiss down a staircase of fractured stone. Walls of cracked slate enclose the narrow ravine, precariously balanced like a deck of cards on its side. Above the falls, interrupted ferns line shallow placid pools.

Past the falls, the trail runs along the gorge's edge and passes a giant fin of slate protruding into space, plus nice hemlocks, white pines, and cedars. After rock-hopping Little Wilson Stream at a tranquil confluence (6.8/800), ascend a beech-covered hillside and reach a small, shallow pond. The trail crosses the outflow on puncheon and curves around the pond to a dirt road.

The AT turns left, follows the road for about 100 yards, then turns right and returns to single-track. Climb to open ledges with views southwest, and emerge atop an open and rocky prow. Borestone Mountain highlights the terrain to the southeast. A few red pines inhabit the thin soil here; recognize them by their needles in clusters of two.

The trail drops through spruce-fir forest, makes a slow U-turn, traverses steadily, and descends through a moss-carpeted forest and into the valley of Big Wilson Stream. Hardwoods reappear, the flowing stream becomes audible, and you encounter a wide woods road near the water's edge (8.9/620).

Turn left and follow the road as it parallels the river-like stream and reaches its confluence with Thompson Creek. This spot offers easy access to the creek. Moisture-loving white ashes and hemlocks line the riparian corridor. The AT rock-hops Thompson Creek and continues on the easy-walking road. Big Wilson Stream weaves in and out of sight; the route turns right to cross it by an obvious sign (9.7/620). The stream is wide here and usually deep enough to require a ford.

The view from Barren Slide looks out over Lake Onawa. (Photo courtesy of Hugh Coxe)

Once on the other side, the trail immediately climbs, passes some nice white pines, then crosses active railroad tracks. Beyond the tracks, the trail levels toward a small brook. Turn uphill to follow it to the junction for the Wilson Valley Lean-to (10.4/1,030) on the right.

Shortly past the shelter, the trail crosses the brook and parallels it before curving right to begin a long, level section. Cross another woods road, and make a gradual climb through hardwood forest, cresting atop an open outcrop (11.2/1,280) with tantalizing views of the fast-approaching Barren Mountains.

On the steep descent, Barren Slide, Barren Ledges, and substantial Lake Onawa appear intermittently through the foliage. The trail switchbacks twice, winds over talus, then crosses the base of a large rock slide. After hopping over a few small streams, the trail bends right and descends into the Bodfish Intervale.

Pass a grassy road just before Wilber Brook (13.5/630). The AT rock-hops the creek and reaches Vaughn Stream by a pretty 20-foot waterfall. A nice, waist-deep pool lies at the base of the falls, shaded by big-tooth aspens and cedars. Continuing, the muddy trail runs level and reaches a wide dirt road. Turn right, proceed 20 yards on the road, then turn left to remain on the AT. From here, the route descends to rocky Long Pond Stream (14.3/630). Rock-hop the river-like stream with care—be careful at high water. Resume your journey on the opposite bank by a large big-tooth aspen, but fill your water bottle before continuing—this is the last good source until Cloud Pond Lean-to 5.0 miles ahead. The trail climbs a rock staircase and winds above the rushing stream. The AT eventually turns steeply uphill and climbs to the spur for Long Pond Stream Lean-to (15.1/940).

Past the shelter, the trail ascends the Barren–Chairback Range. The route is gradual at first, crossing an overgrown woods road and slowly traversing upward. Then the trail abruptly steepens and becomes rockier as it climbs through spruce-fir forest. Traipse through a grassy clearing flush with pin cherries and restricted views west, then take a direct line up a rocky draw. The route bears left and the gradient eases. The trail crests onto the ridge but continues a slow rise to the spur for Barren Slide on the right (16.3/1,980).

The spur trail descends 60 feet into a jumble of giant rocks. Carefully scramble to the edge, and look down the tumble of talus stretching far down the mountainside. Lake Onawa is visible below. Borestone Mountain rises lumpily to the south. To the west and southwest, the broad valley of Bodfish Intervale is apparent; you will follow the ridge bordering the Intervale to the west.

Return to the trail, and continue a few hundred yards to the spur for Barren Ledges. The ledges offer large, flat areas better suited for lounging and view-savoring, and the vistas peer a bit farther west than from Barren Slide. Lake Sebec is visible in the distance beyond Lake Onawa to the southeast. Peaks dot the west horizon, including a prominent twin pyramid peak—the Bigelow Range (Trip 32), some 50 miles away. To the east, the rounded summit of 2,660-foot Barren Mountain is visible for the first time, crowned by the remains of an old fire tower. If you sit quietly, you may hear the call of loons wafting up 1,500 feet from the lake below.

Back on the AT, continue on the mellow path along the north side of the ridge. The trail slowly rises, cuts right, and steeply ascends the summit of Barren Mountain. This section is nicely maintained, and features a quality rock staircase. After climbing a final rocky gully, reach the summit of Barren Mountain (18.2/2,660/45° 24.944' N, 69° 22.232' W) and its all-encompassing views north. The rusting framework of the old tower still stands, but the rest is now just debris scattered on the ground. If you are feeling adventurous, clamber up the ladder to enjoy sweeping views north.

To the northwest is the long, prominent ridge of the White Cap Range—on your continuing route—topped by the bald summit of White Cap itself. Linear Long Pond is below to the north. Beyond its west arm is the low rise of Indian Mountain, in turn shadowed by Baker Mountain. Elephant Mountain is to the north-northwest, beyond the end of Long Pond. In the distance to the northwest, spot portions of Moosehead Lake and the distinctive profile of Mount Kineo.

Most of the immediate area to the north, including all of Long Pond and Indian Mountain, are part of the Katahdin Iron Works property, a 37,000-acre parcel purchased by AMC in December 2003 as part of its Maine Woods Initiative, a long-term effort to create a protected corridor of land from Moosehead Lake to Baxter State Park.

Continuing past the tower, gradually descend to the spur for Cloud Pond Lean-to (19.3/2,490), located 0.4 mile off the main route. To visit the shelter, bear right and follow the narrow and rough spur trail down toward the pond's edge. Shortly before the shelter, the trail passes a large tenting area on a small point near the shore. Spruce-fir forest surrounds the site; several nice specimens complement the bouldery landscape.

Back on the AT, continue along an almost perfectly level section of trail for the next half-mile. The trail then abruptly descends steeply, aided by a nice rock staircase. A small sag with a thin trickle provides a limited water source. The path continues down through mature spruce-fir forest. A few sugar maples and gnarled yellow birches join the forest mix shortly before the route bottoms out and crosses a more substantial brook (20.5/1,920).

After a short easy stretch, the trail reaches one of its ecological highlights: Fourth Mountain Bog in the saddle below Fourth Mountain. This wetland complex harbors many unusual plants, including two carnivorous species: pitcher plant and sundew. As the sign indicates, please stay on the bog bridging in this section. The spongy ground is easily damaged by boots.

As you proceed past abundant cedars, look for the meat-eating flora, including sundews' tiny red-haired globes. These sticky appendages trap flies, where they are slowly absorbed for their nitrogen—essential for survival in a nitrogen-poor soil environment. Pitcher plants grow in clusters and in season sport a wild and distinctive flower. The plant's "pitchers" are roughly 3 inches high, lined on the inside with downward-pointing hairs, and emit a smell similar to rotting flesh. Flies attracted to the odor crawl inside and are led inexorably downward. Eventually they tumble into a small pool of water at the bottom, where they drown and are absorbed by the plant.

After the bog, the AT returns to dry spruce-fir forest. Fourth Mountain's broad hump is visible ahead, and the trail ascends it directly. After cresting atop the summit plateau, pass a restricted view north to Baker Mountain to reach the signed summit (21.3/2,378/45° 25.948′ N, 69° 19.163′ W). Good views extend east to Columbus Mountain—on your continuing route—with Saddleback Mountain beyond. The full spine of the White Cap Range is visible to the northeast. The watershed of the West Branch of the Pleasant River watershed is visible north; Baker, Indian, and Elephant mountains are all visible.

The trail plummets down the opposite side. The gradient eases somewhat, but the descent is steady until the beech-filled saddle between Fourth and Third mountains.

Passing several gullies—some with the occasional trickle of water—the trail climbs again, reaching open slabs with views west to Fourth Mountain. Watch the rocks for parallel scratches, or striations, evidence of the ice sheet that once ground over these mountains. Top out on slabs offering views south toward Caribou Bog and the nearby east ridge of Mount Benson.

The trail drops along the northern flanks of Third Mountain, slowly curving to the right. After a gentle ascent, the route abruptly climbs very steeply to the summit of Third Mountain (23.6/2,060/45° 26.647′ N, 69° 17.826′ W). Views from open summit slabs stretch north, but continue briefly along the uneven summit plateau to another open pinnacle. This one looks west to Long Pond and along the spine of the Barren Range; the fire tower atop Barren Mountain is visible past Fourth Mountain. The best views are still to come at Monument Cliff, a flat ledge a short distance farther. Views of the White Cap Range and nearby Columbus Mountain sweep 180 degrees north across the landscape.

Continuing, the trail steadily traverses then drops to the outflow from West Chairback Pond and the posted junction for the lake (24.3/1,760). To visit the shore, turn right and follow the spur 0.1 mile to a heavily used area near the water. Spruces, firs, and white pines border the quiet lake. The fishing must be good here; local residents have hauled numerous small boats here and chained them to trees. Tenting areas are limited and close to each other. More than two groups would make the area feel crowded.

Back on the AT, cross the pond's rocky outflow stream, slowly ascend through dense forest, then climb steeply up the slopes of Columbus Mountain. The gradient eases, and you pass a posted viewpoint and a small spring by the trail. Fill up here if you are staying at Chairback Gap Lean-to, which often has a dry or stagnant water source. From here, a gradual ascent leads to the posted summit (25.6/2,342).

The level trail passes two restricted views north, then drops steeply to the Chairback Gap Lean-to (26.0/1,980). Continuing past the shelter, immediately reach the saddle below Chairback Mountain and come to a trail sign indicating your progress. The trail turns right to avoid a boggy morass, following a small stream for about 40 yards and stepping over it by a spring to steadily ascend the open ledges atop Chairback Mountain (26.5/2,180).

The summit provides another exceptional 180-degree view north. East Chairback Lake is visible below to the northwest. Katahdin Iron Works Road traces northwest across the landscape toward Greenville. Look up the watershed of the West Branch of the Pleasant River to the cleft of Gulf Hagas—your next destination. Spot Baker Mountain and its identifying slide on the northwest horizon. Due north is the round summit of White Cap. Big Spruce Mountain is closer, almost directly in line with White Cap, and Little Spruce Mountain rises to its right.

Views expand east as you descend from the summit, and Silver Lake can now be seen below Saddleback Mountain. The route drops over loose talus and heads diagonally to the left—watch for blazes—departing the talus before the bottom of the slide. After a steep drop, the trail mellows and undulates through several rocky clearings that offer views behind you of Chairback Mountain's steep cliffs.

The trail reenters taller spruce-fir forest and winds downward. The woods transition back to hardwoods. Sugar maples and beeches appear; steadily descend, ramble along a long undulating section, and reach the junction for East Chairback Pond (28.7/1,690).

To visit the pond, turn left onto the spur trail and proceed for 0.2 mile and descend 170 feet. With a rockier and more open shore, fewer boats, and pleasant tentsites, the pond is nicer than its eastern cousin. Spot Chairback Mountain's ledges from shore, as well as Columbus and Third mountains.

Back on the AT, drop quickly and gradually descend through mature spruce-fir woods. The forest slowly transitions to hardwoods, and large bigtooth aspens begin to predominate, easily identified by their platy bark and fluttering leaves. The abundance of big-tooth aspens—a fast-growing species that thrives in disturbed areas—indicates that a large-scale disturbance, most likely a clear-cut, took place on this hillside sometime in the past 100 years or so. Near the bottom, large white pines appear alongside hemlock trees shortly before wide KI Road (29.9/780).

The AT crosses the road and becomes a wide-track as it briefly parallels Henderson Brook. The stream joins the West Branch of the Pleasant River by a substantial camping area. The trail turns downriver, crowded by hazel and blackberry bushes, and reaches a major thoroughfare. A right turn leads to the Gulf Hagas parking area (30.4/650).

At this point, ford the wide, shallow river. It's an ankle- to shin-deep crossing in normal conditions, though heavy rains may make it more difficult or even dangerous. Red oaks shade the opposite bank. Note that there is no camping for the next 2.0 miles along the AT, because of the area's heavy visitation.

Past the crossing, the wide trail parallels the river and reaches KI Trail, which enters from the right. The AT next enters the Hermitage, a rare grove of old-growth white pines. Pass the first specimen—a large pine 3 feet in diameter—and look left into the stand of old-growth forest. Perfectly straight white pines dominate, with a younger understory of paper birches and striped and red maples.

The AT slowly ascends, curves right, and leaves the stand behind. The route runs parallel to the river, and water murmurs below. Chairback Range peeks through the trees. The trail becomes rockier as it turns uphill and continues to curve right, passing a restricted view into the deepening gorge below and crossing a flowing brook. The slow rise leads to Gulf Hagas Trail (31.7/930) on the left.

In Gulf Hagas, the West Branch of the Pleasant River tumbles over multiple waterfalls as it races through a narrow slate gorge. The scenery is striking and well worth the side trip. To see it all, follow Gulf Hagas Trail to Rim Trail, a rugged path that winds along the edge of the gorge for 3.0 miles. Return via easy-cruising Pleasant Valley Tote Road for a 5.2-mile round-trip. Alternatively, follow Rim Trail 0.9 mile to a short connector, and return along the Tote Road for a 1.5-mile round-trip that provides a good sample of the experience.

To reach AMC's Little Lyford Lodge and Cabins, located 2.2 miles past the end of Gulf Hagas, proceed to the farthest intersection of Rim Trail and Pleasant River Tote Road, where a single-track path, signed for Little Lyford, continues past the Gulf. About halfway to Little Lyford, you will encounter a dirt road. Turn left onto the road, cross the bridge, and take an immediate right to resume the single-track route to the camps.

Past Gulf Hagas Trail junction, the AT immediately narrows to single-track and becomes more overgrown. The trail steadily rises, then levels out in a maturing second-growth spruce-fir forest. Descend briefly, then traverse near audible Gulf Hagas Brook to Gulf Hagas Cutoff Trail on the left (32.4/1,060). This point marks the end of the no-camping zone.

The root-laced trail steadily climbs, running parallel to the invisible brook 30 feet below. The stream becomes intermittently visible as the route crosses several small tributaries and continues through diverse hardwoods. The path rises steadily through spruce-fir forest, and the gradient increases. The trail curves right, away from the brook, and levels out, offering glimpses east of lower Gulf Hagas Mountain. After a rough, level stretch, the trail bends back toward the creek, mellows, and passes a tenting area on the right, just before Gulf Hagas Brook. Rock-hop the clear water to the short spur to the Carl A. Newhall Lean-to (35.9/1,890).

Past the shelter, the trail rambles past a swampy beaver pond on the right; the rounded summit of West Peak—on your continuing route—is visible beyond. The gradient increases as the trail passes through spruce-fir forest and encounters an enriched site at the base of a cliff, where sugar maples proliferate and some nice, yellow birches grow in a mature canopy. The trail now steepens markedly, making half a dozen switchbacks as it climbs, traverses left, and becomes a grassy track lined with hay-scented ferns, blackberry canes, and hobblebushes. The route levels, curves right, and offers a few glimpses of White Cap Mountain ahead before the signed and viewless summit of Gulf Hagas Mountain (36.8/2,683/45° 32.427′ N, 69° 19.216′ W).

The trail undulates along the summit ridge, passing a large amount of bracken ferns and thick hobblebushes. As it descends, brief views to the north-northwest look toward Mount Baker. The trail winds along the north side of the ridge and drops steeply toward the saddle. After a momentary rise, descend through a dense, green tunnel to the Sidney Tappan Campsite (37.7/2,450). A nice flowing spring is available 200 yards down a posted blue-blazed trail.

Past the site, the path enters a young spruce corridor and widens on a steady, traversing rise. The trail switchbacks right and markedly steepens, ascending some nice rock stairs. Views behind peek west on the sustained climb, which ascends through dense spruce-fir woods. The gradient eases at 3,000 feet and makes a more gradual rise to the signed summit of West Peak among dense firs (38.4/3,181/45° 32.721′ N, 69° 17.747′ W).

The AT descends steeply through more thick forest. As the trail approaches the gap below Hay Mountain (which peeks out intermittently ahead), it curves right, levels, then makes a slower descent into the muddy saddle. Dense forest continues as the rocky trail climbs. Dead snags are abundant, likely caused by fir waves. Cresting at 3,000 feet, the trail mellows briefly, then steadily ascends to the broad summit plateau of Hay Mountain. The trail undulates along, entering a skeletal forest of snags just before the posted summit in dense woods (40.0/3,244).

The rocky trail descends once again. Watch for glimpses of White Cap Mountain ahead and Big Spruce and Chairback mountains to the south. The route levels out in a final saddle and encounters White Brook Trail on the right (40.6/2,960), a challenging backdoor access route to White Cap Mountain. The desperately thirsty can find water 0.6 mile down this side trail, though a much better source awaits 2.0 miles ahead, shortly before Logan Brook Lean-to.

Pass a small trailside tentsite just past the junction, and climb toward White Cap. The trail briefly eases near the summit ridge, then steadily ascends and curves slightly to the right. The route runs level for 0.2 mile to White Brook Trail Spur on the right (41.4/3,480), joining White Brook Trail a short distance down the mountain.

The trail rises slowly, enters a smaller forest with loose rocks and talus underfoot, and emerges atop the summit (41.7/3,644/45° 33.288′ N, 69° 14.757′ W). A broad field of talus composes the summit and offers expansive views south. (The rocky terrain makes pitching a tent here a lumpy proposition.) The rounded summit of Big Spruce Mountain is visible nearby, due south. Greenwood Pond sits in the bowl between Big Spruce and Little Spruce mountains. To the west are Hay Mountain and West Peak. Along the horizon, trace your previous route along the Barren–Chairback Range. Head to the north side of the summit for more views. Third West Branch Pond shimmers down below, and Big Boardman Mountain—near your continuing route—is apparent to the northeast. On a clear day, Katahdin is visible on the horizon 29 miles away.

Thick, diminutive firs crown the summit. Spot some alpine plant species, including cranberry, crowberry, and Labrador tea. Continuing north, the AT hops over talus and krummholz and descends the mountain's east ridge. Catch views east of large B Pond before the trail reenters the trees and descends via long sections of excellent rock steps. Just before dropping below 3,000 feet, you'll find the first water source since Sidney Tappan Campsite.

The trail levels out briefly on its continued descent, offering glimpses left into the deep drainage of Logan Brook, before a ledge opens views over the sheer drainage; water rushes down below, and White Cap rises above. To the northeast, your route heads across the East Branch River and toward Big Boardman Mountain. The trail banks left, leaves the ridge, and steadily side-hills. Enter an almost pure stand of paper birches just before the brook, and encounter the Logan Brook Lean-to (43.1/2,400).

Past the shelter, the trail cruises nicely and steadily. The nearby creek remains audible but inaccessible. The extensive paper birch stands continue, slowly joined by other hardwoods, including all the maples: red, striped, mountain, and sugar (at around 2,000 feet). The trail crosses a small tributary, curves right, then runs level for some time. Eventually, it drops steeply, curves left, and side-hills downward. Beeches appear and some mature sugar maples punctuate the forest. Just before West Branch Ponds Road, a major dirt thoroughfare (44.7/1,590), pass a small covered spring on the left. Cross the road and continue descending past granite boulders in an increasingly buggy area. The trail crosses a trickle and levels out in a hemlock-spruce forest loaded with pink lady's slippers. Cedars appear intermittently as the surroundings fill with nice spruce trees and occasional white pines. A long, level walk weaves through the dense lumpy woods and eventually slowly descends, abruptly enters dense foliage, and crosses a section of puncheon over ale-colored water. Alders and irises line the banks. The route winds across another flowing brook and reaches the spur for the East Branch Lean-to on the left (46.7/1,340). Boulders protrude from the ground all around, a living rock garden.

Past the shelter, the trail parallels the hidden East River then rock-hops across it. The route travels through a wet area then climbs the slopes of Big Boardman Mountain. Slowly gain elevation, crossing an old woods road in rocky spruce-fir woods. The gradient increases, switchbacks left, and ascends a remarkable tree talus field; tree roots seemingly hold the rocks in place. Switchback right, make a steady uphill traverse, and eventually curve left.

The trail continues to rise, bends right, and levels as it enters hardwood forest highlighted by nice sugar maples and yellow birches. The route undulates through an area of selective harvesting—only spruces remain—and drops back into hardwood forest and reaches Mountain View Pond (48.6/1,600). The AT crosses the pond outflow by an old beaver dam then parallels the placid, but inaccessible, shoreline. Just before the route turns away from the lake, an unposted spur on the left leads to a number of tentsites and chained-up canoes. A sign indicates that no campfires are permitted here.

The route follows the flowing pond outlet along a boggy creek bed and encounters a spring, located a short distance off the trail. Sweet, cold, and refreshing water pours out of the rocks here, an easy fill-up. Cruise on an overgrown woods road past young hardwoods and abundant diseased beeches. The trail eventually bears right off the old roadbed, drops briefly to cross a boggy area, and makes a quick rocky climb to a level section in dense spruce-fir forest. The route slowly rises, turns right to begin a more direct ascent, switchbacks left to gradually climb, then turns right again, straight up the slopes.

Catch a few tantalizing glimpses through the trees, and reach an open view west-southwest toward the White Cap Range and nearby Big Boardman Mountain. On White Cap, identify your route down and through the Logan Brook watershed. Past this vista, the trail curves to the top of Little Boardman (50.2/2,010). The trail runs level past red maples, sugar maples, and the occasional red oak before entering a rocky area full of blueberry bushes.

The descending route tours a magnificent sugar maple grove, full of mature, twisting trees, standing snags, and only a handful of beeches and yellow birches—one of the best groves of the hike. Beeches and yellow birches slowly increase and eventually the gradient eases. Crawford Pond becomes visible ahead through the trees. Pass some impressive spruces and a few final sugar maples, then emerge on Kokadjo-B Pond Road (51.6/1,260).

The AT crosses the road and a small wash gully, which leads to a small nearby beach (no camping allowed). The trail then rises and traverses the slopes past spruces and cedars, staying roughly 50 feet above the water, with little to no access. Drop to cross a small feeder brook, and encounter a posted sign for Sand Beach (52.0/1,240). A spur trail quickly leads to another small (no-camping) beach.

The AT merges with an old woods road for some easy walking, then leaves the road and parallels the lake, just visible through the trees. The trail rambles closer to the water, passes a few access spots, then crosses the lake outflow (Cooper Brook) over the remains of an old dam (52.5/1,220). Look for evidence of old beaver activity.

On the far side of the brook, the trail turns right and follows an old roadbed through a young forest of paper birches, firs, spruces, red maples, and beeches. This marks the start of the longest easy stretch in the entire 100-Mile Wilderness. Slowly descend parallel to nearby Cooper Brook, audible but seldom seen. The route travels over intermittent puncheon, crosses a few small streams, and passes a few nice white pines and hemlocks. Sugar maples and ashes slowly join the forest mosaic. The roadbed makes minor but pronounced drops. After crossing the largest tributary thus far, the trail widens and descends to Cooper Brook Falls Lean-to on the right (54.8/980).

Past the shelter, Cooper Brook once again disappears from sight as the AT remains on the old road and crosses a more substantial tributary. The delightfully easy walk rolls past lush and diverse hardwoods, slowly descends, and crosses another brook. Bugs increase, as does the diversity of trees—ashes and hickories appear in increasing numbers. The route slowly turns away from Cooper Brook, passes through stately hemlock groves, and enters increasingly soggy terrain; slippery puncheon increases. Cross another stream; Church Pond becomes faintly visible through the trees ahead. After a few brief rises, Cooper Brook reappears on the right, and the trail runs right alongside it, passing several good campsites in hemlock forest. Emerge on Jo-Mary Road (58.5/690).

The AT crosses the road and briefly parallels Cooper Brook in young woods, punctuated by the appearance of big-tooth aspens. The trail bends away from the brook, returns to dense spruce-fir forest, and reaches a signed, blue-blazed trail on the right leading to nearby Cooper Pond (59.3/660). The five-minute side trip passes a nice campsite en route to the lake's outflow, where there are good views south of nearby Jo-Mary Mountain.

The AT continues through spruce-fir forest and past occasional red pines, identified by their flaky scaly bark and distinctive branch structure. Cooper Brook reappears on the right, now a calm and wide waterway. The trail returns to single-track for the first time in many miles. Roots crisscross the path as it winds near placid Cooper Brook. After turning away briefly, the route returns to the brook, crosses a snowmobile corridor, and follows a wider trail across a smaller woods road. Enter a noticeably drier upland area populated by young conifers. Cross a small brook, a larger one on a puncheon bridge—the outflow from nearby Mud Pond (61.4/500)—and another small one via well-placed rocks. Now the route tours above the shore of Mud Pond; Jo-Mary Mountain is visible to the south.

Red pine forest is carpeted with needles and filled with abundant huckleberry bushes. The single-track trail passes through the hike's driest section before slowly curving to reenter a lusher environment. The woods transition back to mossy softwoods. Lower Jo-Mary Lake appears north through the trees, and the route is lined with evidence of an old communications line that was once strung through the trees.

The trail winds just inland from the lake, passing some nice white pines near the shore, and leads to the signed junction for Antlers Campsite (62.7/500). Turn left, away from the lake, to continue north on the AT. The single-track trail heads away from the lake through young forest then bends back toward the shore and crosses a small stream. The trail touches a tiny sandy beach at the far end of the lake, which offers a long view across the water. Continuing, cross another small stream, return inland to lush hardwood forest, and reach the posted junction for Potaywadjo Ridge on the left (64.2/540).

SIDE TRIP TO POTAYWADJO RIDGE

This detour is one of the hike's best, though it requires gaining 650 feet of elevation in less than a mile. From the junction, the blue-blazed trail steeply climbs to open slabs that offer views down the entire length of Lower Jo-Mary Lake. Mud and Cooper ponds are also visible; spot the White Cap Range in the distance. Nearby is the low hulking mass of Jo-Mary Mountain; Cooper Brook flows below it. But the best parts of this side trip are the prolific blueberries that cover the open ledges. They get lots of sunlight, ripen in mid- to late July, and produce more fruit than you'll have time to enjoy!

Back on the AT, follow a rocky path past enormous boulders, and reach a posted spur for Sand Beach (64.4/500), which looks across the lake toward the hump of Jo-Mary Mountain. The AT turns away from the lake, climbs, and quickly crosses a small stream. The route slowly rises and curves left through a young forest of birches, beeches, and big-tooth aspens. The trail steepens and parallels a rivulet, passing more giant rocks as it climbs.

The route levels, then gradually descends, passing extensive patches of Indian cucumber near the top. (Identify them by their two-tiered whorls of leaves and tiny flowers dangling beneath the upper whorl.) After a steady descent, the trail abruptly levels off among more abundant conifers and reaches the spur trail to Potaywadjo Spring Lean-to (66.2/600). Not far past the lean-to is its namesake spring—an impressive pool—cross a stream beneath abundant hemlocks.

The trail next crosses a dirt road, enters a hemlock-cedar forest, and reaches Twitchell Brook, crossing it on a puncheon bridge. Pemadumcook Lake appears ahead through the trees. A posted sign announces a view of Katahdin. The mountain is just visible from the lakeshore; scramble over nearby driftwood and rocks for better views.

Beyond this point, the AT follows extensive bog bridging over another stream and travels along an easy-walking path through dark forest. The trail becomes boggy near a swampy wetland on the left. The level trail runs over several long stretches of puncheon, crosses a muddy, seldom-used road, then enters the land of super bog.

The next section is extremely wet and washed out, requiring careful travel to avoid soaking your boots. The delicate bog-hopping act leads to a super-muddy road. (Head right here and hike about a mile to the landing for White House Lodge.) Navigate the muck and follow the AT north. A stream appears on the right. Rock-hop across Tumbledown Dick Stream, a moderately tricky crossing.

Nahmakanta Stream appears on the right, the trail quickly crosses another small tributary, and the path follows the broad, shallow, and quietly riffling stream. The route winds directly atop its steep-cut banks, a pleasant, level walk past many flat areas with good camping potential, though accessing the stream can be a challenge in many spots. A young forest of hemlocks, beeches, spruces, and firs surrounds the trail, which eventually leads to Nahmakanta Stream Campsite on the left (70.5/600).

Past the campsite, the trail passes another established tentsite then turns inland a short distance from the stream. Roots and mud increase, and both the trail and river become increasingly rocky. After more than a mile of steady, level progress, the stream widens into a broad, placid pool, and the slopes become perceptibly steeper. The trail crosses several small brooks and heads inland on an intensely root-laced path. Cross the largest tributary yet, rise briefly, begin a rising traverse along sheer slopes above the broad river visible below, and reach Woodrat Spring.

Head down a rock staircase and meet a dirt road and bridge (73.5/700). The AT crosses the road and returns along the river, passing a giant, knobby white pine. Pass a series of campsites by a small carry-in boat launch on the edge of Nahmakanta Lake (73.7/650). The trail turns left, quickly heads right off the area's wide main path, and cruises level past softwoods. The lake is nearby, just to the right through the trees.

The trail touches the shore at one point and offers views north of approaching Nesuntabunt Mountain—along your continuing route—on the left side of the lake. The route then crosses a small brook, runs directly along the rocky shore, and encounters a small, sandy beach. A short distance later, turn inland, climb briefly, then drop back to the lakeshore and rock-hop over Prentiss Brook. The trail now undulates near the shore through a young forest of cedars and yellow and paper birches.

The going is generally mellow; eventually the trail returns to the water by a small beach. Alder and small hickory trees line the lakeshore. The trail turns inland again, climbs around a small point, and rises nearly 200 feet. Drop quickly past some large granite boulders, then switchback left to descend among rock boulder chaos. Once near the lake again, the path cruises easily and reaches the water by a posted white-sand beach. A campsite and its thin water source are located just inland from here.

The trail heads inland again through lush deciduous flatlands, and crosses a seasonal stream emerging from the Wadleigh Valley. Several large sugar maples line the route as the trail continues inland; snags and downed trees indicate the age and maturity of this stand. The path passes Wadleigh Stream Lean-to on the left, located adjacent to the trail (76.3/690).

Past the shelter, the route climbs through hemlock forest on a soft and needle-covered path. The trail rises atop a steep outcrop with restricted views of the lake and swings right to easily traverse the slopes. Century-old white pines and fern-topped boulders accompany the traverse, which curves over a rise and descends. Abundant huckleberries line the trail as it passes good lake views, turns back inland, and visits a car-sized boulder balanced atop two others. The route briefly rises and descends past more large boulders as the forest transitions to a deciduous mix of sugar maples and beeches.

The trail crosses a flowing brook, rises slowly, then markedly steepens. Cross a trickling brook, and climb up a broad fissure in the bedrock alongside the trickling flow. The trail crosses the stream, banks left, and briefly levels. Curve right to ascend another broad cleft of large rocks. The route crosses the creek again, passes more cliffs, and continues its ascent through the rock fortress.

After a brief flat section, the trail climbs rock stairs; some have recently slid and may require some careful footwork. The route curves left at one point, then rises through a young sugar maple grove via another broad cleft in the mountainside. More rock steps lead to a saddle, where the trail curves right and continues its rise to finally crest in a stand of spruces (78.2/1,560).

From here, a short side trail leads 250 feet to an exceptional view from a small outcrop. The entire massif of Katahdin reveals itself. All of Nahmakanta Lake unfurls below; Nahmakanta Lake Wilderness Camps are visible at the lake's northern edge. The Rainbow Stream watershed—your continuing route—flows into the north end of the lake; your previous route past Pemadumcook Lake is visible south.

The trail drops steeply from the summit, traverses by more rock fortresses, descends more rock stairs, and curves left. The route levels, passes over a rock ledge with another view of Katahdin, then resumes a slow drop to a dirt road (79.4/1,000). Cross the road and follow the AT as it slowly rises and falls through younger hardwood forest. Crescent Pond appears through the trees. The trail wraps over to the far side of the pond, where smooth granite ledges slide into a perfect swimming opportunity (80.6/1,030). Good southern exposure here means lots of sun for drying out. Locals have tied up a few boats here.

The route winds around the shore, passes a nice, boat-free spot near the middle of the shoreline, then heads through spruce-fir forest. Curving right, descend toward Pollywog Stream—the outflow from Crescent Pond—and enter old-growth forest amid a chaotic garden of rock and deadfall. Take time to admire the massive white pines that punctuate the woods. Far below in a deep ravine, listen to Pollywog Stream rush downward.

Pass a posted spur to nearby Pollywog Gorge viewpoint, which overlooks the sheer slopes of the ravine. The trail briefly rises, traverses through dense woods, and heads slowly down. The gradient steepens, and footing is tricky at times, but eventually it bottoms out.

The route parallels wide Pollywog Stream, which riffles in a shallow streambed. The rough and rocky trail passes through a diverse forest then emerges on Nahmakanta Road (83.1/680). Turn left, cross the bridge, and curve slightly left on the road, past the NLC (Nahmakanta Lake Wilderness Camps) sign on the right. Fifty yards later, the AT bears to the right off the road and enters a young forest. Cross a suspect stream, and enter young forest (a few massive white pines still lurk by the trail).

Before long, rushing Rainbow Stream becomes audible. The trail reaches the racing stream and parallels it. The water rushes over solid rock—sheeting, sliding, and sluicing. As the trail ascends, it follows a small tributary to the left for a few hundred yards, then crosses it to return to the main stream.

The trail continues alongside Rainbow Stream's rapids and drops. Water chokes itself in raging chutes. Eventually the rapids end, and the trail levels out. Turn away from the stream, crossing Murphy Brook before returning to the now-placid brook a half-mile later. A level and easygoing stretch leads to Rainbow Stream Lean-to (84.4/980).

To continue, cross Rainbow Stream here. This may require either fording the shin- to knee-deep brook or delicately balancing across on thin logs, depending on conditions. Once on the other side, the trail parallels the stream and quickly reaches the first of the Rainbow Deadwaters. The trail runs just inland, passing through softwood forest before meeting the stream flow on the far side of the pond. The occasionally muddy trail runs close to the water on its way to the second Rainbow Deadwater. The path now becomes all roots and mini bogs, which makes it hard to develop a hiking rhythm.

The trail remains close to the second Rainbow Deadwater then turns inland near its far end. Rise briefly through increasing hardwoods to the unposted junction for Rainbow Dam (86.4/1,100). This easy five-minute detour leads to a small dam and two nice campsites at the end of massive Rainbow Lake, though only a small arm of the lake is visible from here. Katahdin looms ahead, looking closer than ever. Signs indicate that campfires are allowed here by permit only.

Back on the AT, descend momentarily to cross a tributary and begin a long level stretch through hardwood forest. The path is generally easygoing, though there are regular patches of mud and bogginess, and the bugs can be bad. Rainbow Lake is occasionally visible through the trees on the left on the way to Rainbow Spring Campsite (88.2/1,070) on the right. The spring is down by the lake's edge. Its cool waters bubble into a small, clear pool then immediately pour into the lake. Loons call from the lake, which is shallow for some distance from shore.

From here, the trail winds inland, climbs slowly, then winds back toward the water, crossing a few small brooks as it goes. Catch glimpses of the lake to the left through a young forest of ashes, red maples, sugar maples, and other hardwoods. You may hear the sound of boat motors and other human activity along this section, emanating from a nearby sporting camp. After hiking among softwoods for the first time in a while, pass posted Rainbow Mountain Trail on the right (90.2/1,120). The side trail leads 0.75 mile to the top of Rainbow Mountain and great views of Katahdin, the surrounding lake, and rumpled terrain—a worthwhile excursion.

The AT returns to the lake's edge and passes several nice spruce trees and good access points. Steeper slopes run upward to your right, populated by fern-topped granite boulders. The root-laced and rocky trail makes for slower going, though the forest is pleasantly mature; enjoy some nice sugar maples. The route rises among boulders and spruce-fir forest, passing a handful of 3-foot-plus diameter white pines before winding down to a shallow cove and a pair of nice campsites at the far end of the lake (91.6/1,050).

The AT crosses a small inflow stream and encounters the posted spur to Big Beaver Pond on the right (91.7/1,060). The side trail leads 0.7 mile to a big beaver pond, which is as exciting as it sounds.

Continuing, the AT passes through a mature forest of white pines, spruces, and paper birches. Leave this older stand, and enter thicker and younger woods with more red maples and beeches. The trail descends to cross a boggy area on rotting puncheon and steadily rises, entering young softwood forest. The ground underfoot becomes increasingly rocky, ascending toward Rainbow Ledges. Before long, the trail climbs a solid ribbon of bedrock. The forest diminishes on the sparse soil. Blueberries and lichens become common. Views southwest begin to peek out; see Jo-Mary Mountain and the White Cap Range in the distance. The trail crests at 1,500 feet and runs level along the ridge top, a pleasant stretch on solid rock. Huckleberry bushes become as prolific as blueberries.

The trail reaches a striking view of Katahdin, here only 9.0 miles away, before dropping back into a mossy and root-chocked spruce-fir forest. The path undulates through the dense woods, slowly rises, then descends into the Hurd Brook watershed. The route drops quickly at first, aided by rock stairs, then tapers off and descends more gradually. As it approaches the bottom, the needle-covered trail eases and winds among woods that become increasingly lush. The trail steeply descends to the valley floor and Hurd Brook in a maze of roots, rocks, yellow birches, and cedars. Hurd Brook Lean-to sits on the other side (95.9/700).

Past the shelter, the AT continues its rocky, root-hopping journey through softwood forest, passing a spring 0.3 mile beyond the shelter by some stone steps. The route slowly rises, drops, and passes over more roots and rocks in a hemlock forest. Mossy boulder humps are everywhere. The trail slowly rises through young beeches and descends along a very rocky section. Beeches, paper birches, and sugar maples eventually appear in green profusion as the trail begins its final descent.

The rocky drop leads through a mixed forest then eases a bit before an extended section of puncheon—the longest of the entire hike. The final section of trail cruises through thick spruce-fir forest to emerge onto paved Golden Road. Turn right to follow the road, cross Abol Bridge, and reach this long journey's end by the Abol Store (99.4/660).

INFORMATION

The Maine Appalachian Trail Club maintains the AT through the 100-Mile Wilderness and is your best source of information for current trail conditions. P.O. Box 283, Augusta, ME 04332, matc.org, info@matc.org. For more information on AMC's Maine Woods Initiative and additional recreation opportunities in the 100-Mile Wilderness region, visit outdoors.org/mwi.

NEARBY

At the southern end of the hike, the tiny town of Monson hosts a pair of long-standing, famous-among-thru-hikers destinations: Spring Creek Bar-B-Q, which dishes up some seriously hearty, protein-packed trail power, and Shaw's Lodging, which provides a range of amenities and services for thru-hikers.

At the northern end of the hike, eat up, fuel up, and gear up as needed in Millinocket. Once you leave town, you're on your own when it comes to supplies.

TRIP 35
CHIMNEY POND

$

Location: Baxter State Park
Difficulty: Moderate (climbing Katahdin: Epic)
Distance: 6.6 miles round-trip to Chimney Pond; 4.0 to 4.4 miles round-trip from Chimney Pond to climb Katahdin
Total Elevation Gain/Loss: 1,600 feet/1,600 feet to Chimney Pond; 2,500 feet/2,500 feet to climb Katahdin from Chimney Pond
Trip Length: 1–3 days
Recommended Maps: *AMC Maine Mountains Trail Map, Map 1: Baxter State Park–Katahdin* (AMC Books), *Katahdin Illustrated Map & Guide* (Wilderness Map Company)
Highlights: New England's grandest alpine amphitheater, base camp for climbing mile-high Katahdin.

Surrounded on three sides by soaring granite cliffs, Chimney Pond sits in the mountainous heart of Baxter State Park. Overhead looms mile-high Baxter Peak—northern terminus of the Appalachian Trail—which is connected to neighboring Pamola Peak by the mile-long arête, the Knife Edge. Together, this towering massif is commonly referred to by one name: Katahdin. From the pond and its adjacent campground, wild and adventurous trails scrape their way up the mountain flanks. Come enjoy the view and the challenge of Maine's mightiest mountain.

HIKE OVERVIEW

The out-and-back journey to Chimney Pond can be an easy day trip, or a longer multiday base-camping adventure for summiting Katahdin. Ascend well-trod Chimney Pond Trail through pleasant forest with occasional views. Crowds are common throughout summer. Dogs are prohibited in Baxter State Park. Park staff is vigilant; be sure to follow the rules.

The park's premier hike is the loop over Baxter Peak, the Knife Edge, and Pamola—the primary goal for most hikers heading beyond Chimney Pond. The Knife Edge is the only true arête in New England. Unlike all other peaks in New England, including Mount Washington, Katahdin was not overtopped by ice during the last Ice Age. Instead, glaciers scoured its lower flanks, gouging the mountain from both sides to create the narrow ridgeline along its crest:

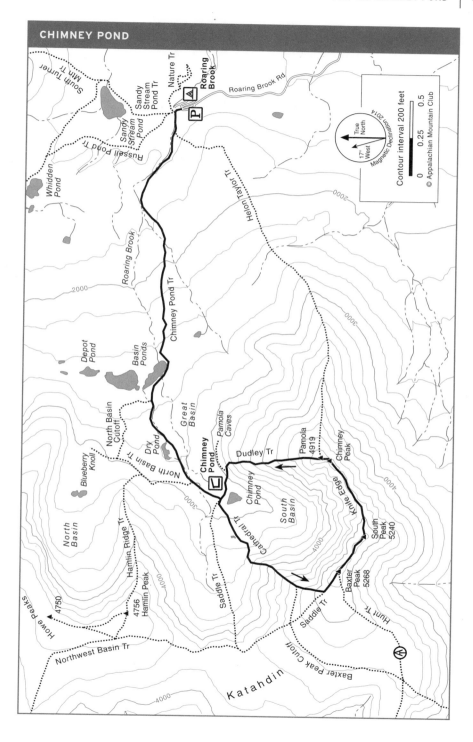

CHIMNEY POND

the Knife Edge. Hike across its entire length for a thrilling adventure requiring good footwear, balance, fitness, and agility. The crux of the Knife Edge is the Chimney, a cleft in the ridge just below Pamola that requires the route's most difficult scrambling.

The park has established specific cutoff times for hikers traveling to Chimney Pond, generally about three hours before sunset. You will not be allowed in after this point.

OVERNIGHT OPTIONS

Camping in Baxter State Park is permitted only in designated areas. Campsites are usually in high demand, especially those at Chimney Pond Campground. Reservations are required, an effort that takes some significant advance planning (see later).

Chimney Pond Campground (3.3/2,890/45° 54.979′ N, 68° 54.675′ W) consists of nine lean-tos on the east side of Chimney Pond and a recently rebuilt 10-person bunkhouse. Plan well in advance to secure a site in this extremely popular area, especially on weekends. Request a preferred lean-to when making a reservation. Lean-to 1 sits by the main trail and looks to Hamlin Ridge. Lean-to 2 rests on a side trail and offers an unobstructed view of Pamola. Lean-to 3 is larger with restricted views of Pamola and Katahdin's main headwall. Lean-to 4 also sits by the main path, offering limited views northeast down the valley. Lean-to 5, closest to the pond, has a view of Pamola, but is close to the main path. Lean-tos 6, 7, and 8 cluster together in the trees, offering no real views, but are removed from the campground bustle. Lean-to 6 is the smallest; lean-to 7 was recently rebuilt and offers good privacy. Lean-to 9 is the most isolated and offers glimpses of Pamola's cliffs through the trees. The lean-tos cost $20 per night; the bunkhouse is $11 per person. A maximum of four people are allowed per site. Chimney Pond campground is usually open from June 1 to October 15, though it may open later or close earlier depending on weather and road conditions.

Make online reservations on the park's website, baxterstateparkauthority.com, which shows current site availability and details the park's myriad rules and regulations. Make reservations up to four months in advance; if you're planning a weekend trip to Chimney Pond, reserve as early as possible. You can also make reservations by phone (207-723-5140) or in person at park headquarters in Millinocket. *Don't forget to bring your reservation with you when you come.* It might as well be your passport.

Kathadin's Knife Edge is a rugged icon of New England's wilderness.

TO REACH THE TRAILHEAD

From Millinocket, follow ME 11 west to the ME 11/157 junction by the First Congregational Church. Turn right onto Millinocket Road, and follow it to the park boundary, where the road becomes unpaved. At Togue Pond Gatehouse—the park's entrance—show your reservation form and pay an entrance fee. Bear right toward Roaring Brook and proceed 8.1 miles to the trailhead parking area (45° 55.253' N, 68° 51.476' W). Parking for overnight users is on the right.

HIKE DESCRIPTION

From the parking area, proceed to the Roaring Brook Ranger Station and trailhead (0.0/1,500). Sign in at the register. Past the ranger station, double-track Chimney Pond Trail immediately meets Russell Pond Trail on the right. Bear left to remain on Chimney Pond Trail, which quickly reaches crystalline Roaring Brook, a good spot for obtaining water. The trail initially parallels to the now-inaccessible brook, remaining double-track and very rocky. Some of the granite shows scars from early path-clearing efforts. The route reaches Helon Taylor Trail on the left (0.2/1,540).

A few sugar maples and yellow birches appear alongside the trail. Hobblebush becomes increasingly common. The trail touches Roaring Brook then crosses a small feeder stream on a plank bridge. The route follows some puncheon, curves away from the brook, and steepens. The rocky track steadily rises, crossing Pamola Brook on another plank bridge (1.0/1,800). Pamola itself peeks out upstream above its namesake waterway. Mountain ashes, yellow birches, and paper birches shade the burbling stream.

The trail ascends some nice rock stairs, eases somewhat, then steepens again to remain at a sustained grade. Occasional steps moderate the rocky route. The trail then passes Halfway Rock on the left in a small clearing (1.6/2,320), the midpoint of your journey to Chimney Pond. The route drops momentarily, offers a view down the trail corridor toward the North Basin, and reaches a posted spur on the right to a nearby viewpoint. Make the short side trip to a rocky clearing surrounded by wind-sheared spruces and firs. Views look west toward the North Basin and its headwall, topped by Hamlin Ridge. Spot the saddle between Hamlin Peak and Baxter Peak. There are two saddles actually—Saddle Trail ascends the slightly higher one to the right. South Turner Mountain is visible east behind you. Look for a few larch trees in a small bog below.

Back on Chimney Pond Trail, pass through a paper birch grove and briefly enjoy a level, stone-free path before rising to the posted spur to Lower Basin Pond (1.9/2,460). The short side trip leads to the pond's south shore. The water is clear and deep and is a good swimming spot. From here, views look toward the North Basin, Hamlin Peak, the Saddle, and Pamola. Chimney Pond is up ahead, just out-of-sight to the left.

Skirt the pond on Chimney Pond Trail, now rocky but level, and cross a stretch of puncheon. Keep an eye out for cedars, which appear for the first time. Mosey along a long boardwalk shaded by mountain ashes' curving branches. Cross above much-diminished Roaring Brook in a marshy area, resume climbing, and quickly encounter North Basin Cutoff Trail on the right (2.3/2,520).

Continue straight on Chimney Pond Trail, crossing a dry streambed on a guardrail-protected bridge. Looking down the gully, spot Lower and Upper Basin Ponds. The trail climbs again, but soon levels past diminutive Dry Pond on the right; the North Basin headwall is visible across the water. Cross Saddle Brook—the inflow to Dry Pond—on a plank bridge, and enjoy the easiest section yet. Katahdin's headwall looms over the trees ahead. Pass North Basin Trail on the right (3.0/2,820), cross a dry gully on a final plank bridge, and emerge at the Chimney Pond campground by a new group pavilion (3.3/2,890/ 45° 54.979′ N, 68° 54.675′ W).

SHORTER EXCURSIONS FROM CHIMNEY POND

NORTH BASIN (45° 55.689′ N, 68° 54.282′ W), 2.0 MILES ROUND-TRIP WITH 600 FEET OF ELEVATION GAIN/LOSS. Head to North Basin via North Basin Trail, which starts from Chimney Pond Trail 0.3 mile below Chimney Pond. The path ends at Blueberry Knoll with a 360-degree view of the bare alpine landscape. To the east, see Sandy Stream Pond, South Turner Mountain, and Katahdin Lake. Pamola and the Knife Edge are visible.

PAMOLA CAVES, 1.4 MILES ROUND-TRIP WITH 400 FEET OF ELEVATION GAIN/LOSS. Follow Dudley Trail toward Pamola for 0.3 mile, and then bear left on the posted 0.4-mile spur trail. These crevices provide opportunities for wriggling through small passages.

HAMLIN PEAK (45° 55.465′ N, 68° 55.665′ W), 4.0 MILES ROUND-TRIP WITH 2,000 FEET OF ELEVATION GAIN/LOSS. Follow North Basin Trail 0.4 mile past its junction with Chimney Pond Trail then take Hamlin Ridge Trail along a narrow, treeless ridge with superlative views of the North Basin and Katahdin massif. It is much less used than routes up Katahdin.

LOOP TO THE KNIFE EDGE

To complete the loop from Chimney Pond, hike counter-clockwise—up Baxter Peak, over the Knife Edge to Pamola, and then down Dudley Trail—or complete the loop clockwise by ascending Dudley Trail, crossing the Knife Edge to Baxter Peak, and then descending the Saddle Trail. Hiking counter-clockwise is the more popular (and recommended) option because Dudley Trail provides the least hair-raising descent. (Saddle Trail has a lot of scree and loose rock on its upper reaches. Cathedral Trail is extremely steep and not recommended for descent.)

On a counter-clockwise loop, ascent options include Saddle and Cathedral trails, which create loops of 4.6 and 4.0 miles, respectively. Saddle Trail is more popular, winding through forest to reach the Great Basin's headwall and then ascending the Saddle Slide—a scar of loose scree and talus—to attain the ridge at 4,300 feet. Baxter Peak is another mile and thousand feet of elevation gain beyond.

Cathedral Trail ascends the prominent ridge that divides the Great and South basins. Three large, bulging rock promontories protrude from the ridge. From bottom to top, they are dubbed First, Second, and Third Cathedral. The route scrambles steeply over talus and solid rock and is well marked by blue blazes. This exciting adventure provides the most direct route to the top, climbing 2,300 feet in just 1.4 miles. Only in New England would this route be called a trail—it is not for the faint of heart.

INFORMATION

Baxter State Park, 64 Balsam Drive, Millinocket, ME 04462, 207-723-5140, baxterstateparkauthority.com. For detailed route descriptions beyond Chimney Pond, consult AMC's *Maine Mountain Guide*, 10th Edition.

NEARBY

Eat up, fuel up, and gear up as needed in Millinocket. Once you leave town, you're on your own when it comes to supplies.

TRIP 36
KATAHDIN-RUSSELL POND LOOP

Location: Baxter State Park
Difficulty: Epic
Distance: 19.8 miles round-trip
Total Elevation Gain/Loss: 4,500 feet/4,500 feet, plus side trips
Trip Length: 2–4 days
Recommended Map: *AMC Maine Mountains Trail Map, Map 1: Baxter State Park–Katahdin* (AMC Books)
Highlights: Ponds, peaks, the grandeur of Maine.

Leave behind the trod and trammeled trails of Katahdin for a hauntingly wild landscape of alpine plateaus, remote ponds, rushing rivers, and hidden valleys. Explore Baxter State Park to the beat of your own drum.

HIKE OVERVIEW

The journey loops through the heart of Baxter, beginning from Roaring Brook Trailhead, where a short, well-traveled ascent leads to Chimney Pond and the sheer headwall of Katahdin. Scramble up the mountain on Saddle Trail and cross the Northwest Plateau, a little-visited alpine landscape. Descend steeply in the remote Northwest Basin, a small cirque occupied by cliffs, a waterfall, Davis Pond, and an overnight shelter.

From Davis Pond, the journey continues down Northwest Basin Trail and through the Wassataquoik Stream valley to reach boulder-studded Russell Pond. Adjacent Russell Pond Campground makes an ideal base camp for exploring the surrounding terrain; myriad day trips head off in all directions. Return to the trailhead via Russell Pond Trail, which fords substantial Wassataquoik Stream.

Dogs are prohibited in Baxter State Park. Crowds are common around Chimney Pond and Katahdin, but diminish once you reach the Northwest Plateau. There are good fishing opportunities at Russell Pond and the surrounding streams and ponds.

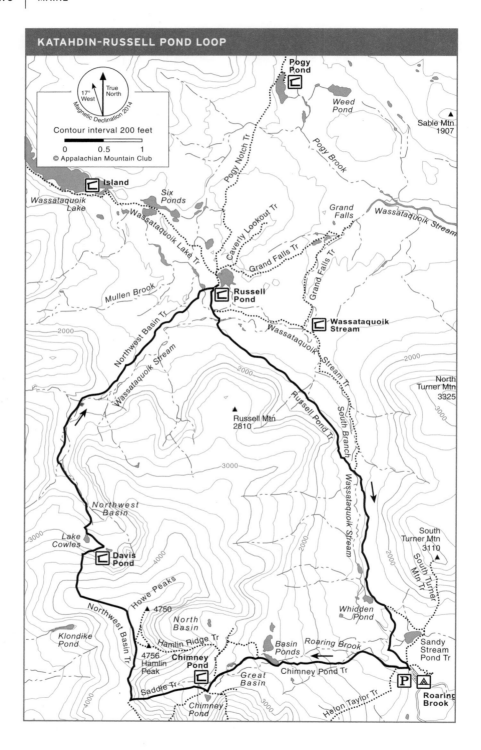

KATAHDIN-RUSSELL POND LOOP

OVERNIGHT OPTIONS

Camping is permitted only at designated overnight areas in Baxter State Park, and they are usually in high demand. Reserving a site requires some effort and advance planning (see later).

Make online reservations on the park's website, baxterstateparkauthority. com, which shows current site availability and details the park's myriad rules and regulations. Make reservations up to four months in advance; if you're planning a weekend trip to Chimney Pond, reserve as early as possible. You can also make reservations by phone (207-723-5140) or in person at park headquarters in Millinocket.

Backcountry lean-tos and tentsites cost $20 per night; a maximum of four people is allowed per site. The Chimney Pond bunkhouse is $11 per person per night. *Don't forget to bring your reservation with you when you come.* It might as well be your passport.

Chimney Pond Campground (3.3/2,890/45° 54.979′ N, 68° 54.675′ W) consists of nine lean-tos on the east side of Chimney Pond and a recently rebuilt 10-person bunkhouse. Plan well in advance to secure a site in this extremely popular area, especially on weekends. Request a preferred lean-to when making a reservation. Lean-to 1 sits by the main trail and looks to Hamlin Ridge. Lean-to 2 rests on a side trail and offers an unobstructed view of Pamola. Lean-to 3 is larger with restricted views of Pamola and Katahdin's main headwall. Lean-to 4 also sits by the main path, offering limited views northeast down the valley. Lean-to 5, closest to the pond, has a view of Pamola, but is close to the main path. Lean-tos 6, 7, and 8 cluster together in the trees, offering no real views, but are removed from the campground bustle. Lean-to 6 is the smallest; lean-to 7 was recently rebuilt and offers good privacy. Lean-to 9 is the most isolated and offers glimpses of Pamola's cliffs through the trees. A maximum of four people are allowed per site. Chimney Pond campground is usually open from June 1 to October 15, though it may open later or close earlier depending on weather and road conditions.

Davis Pond Lean-to (7.7/2,900/45° 56.592′ N, 68° 56.376′ W) is tucked away on the floor of the rugged Northwest Basin and a short distance from its namesake pond. There is only one site here—a single lean-to; once you book the spot you'll have it entirely to yourself. Per park regulations, if you want to overnight here, you must spend the previous night at Chimney Pond, Russell Pond, Wassataquoik Stream, Wassataquoik Lake Island, or Little Wassataquoik Lake. The lean-to is within 30 yards of the pond, but trees hide the water from sight. A small waterfall provides a soothing background murmur. Water is readily available from the pond's inflow stream, and a privy is located a short distance from the shelter. A maximum of four people can spend the night here. Tenting and campfires are prohibited.

   Russell Pond Campground (12.8/1,330/45° 59.676′ N, 68° 54.531′ W) lines three sides of Russell Pond, a circular lake ringed by boulders and low bluffs. There are five lean-tos and three tentsites. Lean-to 1, closest to the lakeshore, offers limited water views from the shade of a battered white pine. Lean-to 2 is the least private, located near the canoe racks, dock, and main trail. Lean-to 3, farthest from the lakeshore, is near the main path, but reasonably private. Lean-to 4 features decent lake views and water access from the pond's north-west corner. Lean-to 5 is the most isolated, located by the south shore in a bouldery landscape. Campsite 16 features a large, immaculate tent platform but no direct lake access. Campsite 17 has two small tent platforms located well away from the lake and is plainly visible from the main trail. Campsite 18 is the smallest, with one small platform and better privacy. Campfires are permitted at all sites, though you will need to travel far afield to find usable dead and downed wood. Canoes are available for rent by overnight guests ($1/hour, $8/day). Obtain water directly from the lake.

TO REACH THE TRAILHEAD

From Millinocket, follow ME 11 west to the ME 11/157 junction by the First Congregational Church. Turn right onto Millinocket Road, and follow it to the park boundary, where the road becomes unpaved. At Togue Pond Gate-house—the park's entrance—show your reservation form and pay an entrance fee. Bear right toward Roaring Brook and proceed 8.1 miles to the trailhead parking area (45° 55.253′ N, 68° 51.476′ W). Parking for overnight users is on the right.

HIKE DESCRIPTION

From the parking area (0.0/1,500), proceed to the Roaring Brook Ranger Station and trailhead and follow the Trip 35 directions to Chimney Pond (3.3/2,890). From Chimney Pond, strike out on Saddle Trail. A steady rocky climb leads past glimpses of the Katahdin headwall and Cathedral Trail but soon breaks out in more open terrain. Snags jut out of the forest, and the Saddle Slide appears ahead in the col to the left. The route eases and heads straight toward the slide, passing through a green corridor of spruce-fir forest.

   The trail crosses a brook (4.1/3,520) and then immediately transforms into a scrambling route up a narrow rockfall. Dense and scraggly paper birches line the path. Views of Pamola, the Chimney (the cleft in the ridge below Pamola), and Katahdin appear behind you. The route cuts directly up toward the left,

A hiker prepares to descend into the upper Wassataquoik Stream valley.

steepens further, and passes through a tunnel of birch branches growing horizontally from the hillside.

At the slide proper (4.3/3,810), the terrain becomes more open and views look down toward Chimney Pond and the trail corridor below. The slide widens over loose rocks and scree. The potential for rockfall is high—be aware of hikers above and below you. The slide returns to solid rock near the top, becoming more of a staircase for the final ascent to the top and Northwest Basin Trail (4.5/4,300).

To the south, the continuing route of Saddle Trail runs up the bare flanks of Baxter Peak. Chimney Pond shimmers below. Beyond it is Pamola's north ridge, also the route of Dudley Trail. To tag the summit of Baxter from here, drop your pack, and follow the Saddle Trail 1.0 mile and 1,000 feet up. Also at the junction, an unsigned path heads straight to reach Saddle Spring in less than a quarter-mile; this small, unreliable source is located in a rockpile near the edge of the krummholz.

Leave behind the trammeled trails, turn right (north), and follow Northwest Basin Trail. Descend briefly to reach the Saddle itself, and then proceed on a nice, level path through an open alpine tableland. Views peer westward to the cache of mountains in the park's west area, including (from north to south)

North and South Brother, Mount Coe, and Mount O-J-I, beyond which is the distinctive summit ridgeline of Doubletop Mountain.

Watch for crowberries, Labrador tea, dense clumps of diapensia, and other denizens of this harsh above-treeline environment. The trail cruises along, then makes a slow rise and enters a talus field; blazes and cairns mark the way through the boulders. The trail eases at 4,500 feet, levels off, and then drops slightly to Hamlin Ridge Trail on the right (5.5/4,630). Caribou Spring (45° 55.516′ N, 68° 55.883′ W) usually flows from nearby rocks, though it has become less reliable in recent years.

To ascend Hamlin (0.2 mile, round-trip) bear right on Hamlin Ridge Trail and talus-hop to the flat-topped, 4,756-foot summit. The vista encompasses the Knife Edge, Baxter Peak, most of the Katahdin massif, and the disk of Chimney Pond below. Dudley, Chimney Pond, and Saddle trails vein the mountain slopes. From Hamlin Peak, North Peaks Trail continues northeast above treeline to visit the Howe Peaks before continuing all the way to Russell Pond along a recently reopened section of trail.

Heading back north on Northwest Basin Trail, pass North Peaks Cutoff Trail on the right, and head toward the ridge. Beyond the open ridgeline are 4,151-foot North Brother (on the right) and 3,970-foot South Brother (left). Both peaks are lined by textbook fir waves, gray lines of dead trees that resemble arching eyebrows.

The path becomes fainter and less traveled; waving grass makes it seem almost prairie-like. Views of Baxter Peak continue behind. The route briefly passes through a section of head-high krummholz. Spot Saddle Trail snaking up the peak. The deep gouge of Witherle Ravine is apparent on Baxter's west flanks.

The trail reaches a knob at the end of the Northwest Plateau (6.6/4,410) with deep views into the Northwest Basin itself. Striking cliffs loom on the opposite side. To the north and northeast is the Wassataquoik Stream drainage—on your continuing route. The watershed leads toward adjoining Russell and Deep ponds, visible in the distance. The cliffs that hem in out-of-sight Wassataquoik Lake are apparent almost due north.

Descend toward Davis Pond; drop over loose scree and quickly enter waist-high krummholz. The route follows ankle-breaking talus down through thickening krummholz, a steep and rocky drop that soon travels through a corridor of trees. Intermittent views continue as the trail follows a flowing stream course and descends through taller forest. Follow the water down for nearly 300 feet, leave it briefly, and then recross it a short distance farther. Views of the vertical cliffs in the basin peek out before the trail abruptly steepens.

Lake Cowles, companion to Davis Pond, appears below. Davis Pond is just visible to the right. The next 300 feet are a steep, scrambling drop over roots and boulders of all sizes. The plummet finally ends, you bank right through a forested boulder field, and blueberry bushes proliferate. Views of the basin open up as the trail finally levels, curves left, passes a marshy area with larch trees, and reaches Davis Pond Lean-to. A path leads from the shelter down to the pond's inflow, where good views look over the pond and toward the upper headwall; a waterfall tumbles down the rock face.

Heading out, climb quickly to an open clearing, which offers expansive views of the Northwest Basin. To the northwest, peer down your continuing route, which runs through the narrow gap ahead. Nearby Fort Mountain earns its name from the rocky redoubt that crowns its summit. Larches populate the rocky bald and dot the surrounding cliffs. The trail travels over several rocky clearings with continued views down the U-shaped valley ahead. Lake Cowles briefly appears to the left, and the trail crosses extensive puncheon through a boggy area to reach the lake's north shore.

Cross the lake outflow on an abandoned beaver dam with a nice view of the water and surrounding ridges and cliffs. The route descends a narrow single-track path into the valley ahead of you. Rocks, roots, and a section of wet, sloping slabs make the descent tricky at times.

Approach the main stem of the stream that emerges from the basin—a tributary of Wassataquoik Stream—and hike parallel to it on rock slabs, boulders, and roots. The trail then reaches the rocky waterway by a small pool and travels directly along the streambed itself. The water disappears beneath the rocks underfoot and the trail crosses the streambed above a mossy slab. Enjoy the first level stretch of trail since the Northwest Plateau as the route parallels the stream.

Young paper birches and mountain ashes surround you as the trail passes intermittent views of the looming nameless cliffs overhead. The route crosses a small tributary, remains parallel to the main rushing watercourse, and winds gently through young forest. Though still rocky, the path is free of giant boulders and is a delightful contrast to sections preceding it. Cross another small tributary, pass a few cedar trees, and continue on a mostly level route to reach Wassataquoik Stream (9.2/2,120).

The trail rock-hops the 10- to 20-foot-wide stream over boulders. Once on the other side, enjoy nice views of the cliffs. Continuing, the trail passes through a boggy area on puncheon and widens to a level double-track corridor through spruce-fir forest. A large slope of talus peeks through the trees to your left as you pass near the stream again in a floodplain area. The route winds briefly through a boulder field and returns to the stream by massive car-sized boulders. A chest-deep swimming hole here may lengthen your stay. Parallel the extremely rocky stream, pass quaking aspens, bracken ferns, and blueberries, then cross Annis Brook (10.3/1,890) by a pile of rusty logging artifacts.

Past Annis Brook, the trail winds. The water soon disappears from sight, though it remains audible. The route cruises slowly and steadily downward through a forest of increasing hardwoods, especially yellow birches. Beeches appear in abundance as the environment rapidly transitions to northern hardwood forest. Sugar maples join the mosaic overhead, and hazel and elderberry bushes fill in the understory. A long level section leads to an abrupt transition back to spruce-fir forest, which slowly mixes with hardwoods as the easygoing trail continues.

The trail then steepens noticeably and curves left to pass a swampy boulder-studded pond. Views across the water look north to North and South Pogy mountains. At the outlet, views expand south to include the nearby massif of Russell Mountain. Cross the outlet on an easy rock-hop, then travel over puncheon to reach Russell Pond Trail (12.7/1,320). Bear left to visit Russell Pond Campground in 0.1 mile (12.8/1,320/45° 59.676′ N, 68° 54.531″ W).

A scale is located at the campground entrance and provides the opportunity for some pack-weighing diversion. Next to it, the outline of a moose has been painted on a nearby rock. A diversity of trees surrounds the lake, including larches, cedars, white pines, red pines, spruces, firs, red maples, and paper birches. Larches are particularly common along Ankle Knocker Bridge on the lake's west shore. A profusion of boulders dots the lake.

Explore the area as you can (see Excursions from Russell Pond); once you're done, start back for the trailhead by heading south along Russell Pond Trail. Russell Mountain occasionally peeks through the trees ahead; hike over a mix of dirt and rocks, drop briefly, and cross flowing Turner Brook on slippery puncheon. On the far side of the brook, reach Wassataquoik Stream Trail on the left (13.3/1,300). It follows the area's original logging route back to Roaring Brook and is a slightly longer and wetter return option, but it provides an alternate route if Wassataquoik Stream is unfordable on Russell Pond Trail.

Remain on Russell Pond Trail to quickly reach Wassataquoik Stream. This is the most difficult river crossing of the trip. The 10- to 20-feet-wide stream can easily reach above the knees (or higher during wet conditions). A walking stick or trekking poles are recommended. Return to and descend Wassataquoik Stream Trail if the stream cannot be safely forded.

EXCURSIONS FROM RUSSELL POND

Russell Pond sits at a nexus of trails. Nearly half a dozen routes emanate from here, making it a great base camp for exploring the landscape.

CAVERLY LOOKOUT TRAIL leads to good views south from the low hill north of the pond. Formerly Lookout Ledges Trail, it was renamed to honor long-time park director Buzz Caverly, who retired in 2005 after 24 years in the position. The 1.3-mile-one-way walk gains 400 feet of elevation through spruce-fir forest to a series of three viewpoints looking south to southeast, including Russell Mountain (right) and the Turner Mountains (left). Return via Roaring Brook, which traces between the two up the watershed of South Branch Wassataquoik Stream.

WASSATAQUOIK LAKE is a long, wild body of water located 2.2 miles from Russell Pond via Wassataquoik Lake Trail. To get there, gain 450 feet of elevation over undulating rocky terrain, passing Deep Pond at 0.5 mile and Six Ponds—where canoes are usually available for use—at 1.1 miles. Hemmed by steep bluffs, Wassataquoik Lake features a small boat launch at its east end, where canoes, paddles, and personal floatation devices are located for hiker use. Wassataquoik Lake Island Campsite hides on the small island just opposite the canoe launch. (Do not visit if the site is occupied.) Rushing Green Falls is located on the lake's south shore, near its midpoint, 1.1 miles past the boat launch on Wassataquoik Lake Trail.

GRAND FALLS is located 2.5 miles from Russell Pond via Grand Falls Trail, which splits off near the start of Lookout Caverly Trail. The substantial cascade chutes over naked granite walls near Inscription Rock, a massive boulder marked by loggers in the late nineteenth century. Make a 6.4-mile loop to the falls and back by returning via Ledge Falls and Wassataquoik Stream trails, which pass Ledge Falls and near the Wassataquoik Stream Campsite.

POGY POND is located in a broad, flat area 3.7 miles north of Russell Pond via Pogy Notch Trail. Isolation is the big attraction of this viewless and little-traveled hike, which descends slowly from Russell Pond and crosses the headwaters of Pogy Brook en route to the pond and adjoining campsite, located on the pond's northeast shore.

On the opposite bank, the trail rises and traverses the slopes of Russell Mountain. Sugar maples, beeches, and paper and yellow birches line the route; glimpses look east through them toward North Turner Mountain. The thin, single-track path crosses numerous small brooks and makes a slow, steady rise to rock-hop across a rushing tributary. The trail levels near a boulder field and several good-sized sugar maples.

The route descends a rocky staircase and passes glimpses of South Turner Mountain across the valley. Emerge before an RV-sized mega-boulder. The trail winds underneath an overhanging bulge of this "colossalith," which offers dry shelter in wet weather. This monster calved from the cliffs above you to the right. Beyond the rock, the trail gently descends, reenters spruce-fir forest, and crosses a clear-flowing brook.

The route takes a more direct line down the mountain, then curves right, levels, and descends to meet audible Wassataquoik Stream below (16.4/1,450). Recross the stream, here a bouldery rushing waterway approximately 20 feet wide. There is less water here than at the earlier ford, but crossing may still require a shin- to knee-deep ford or an exciting rock-hop.

Once on the other side, the trail turns right to head upstream and immediately reach Wassataquoik Stream Trail entering from the left (16.5/1,460). Continue on Russell Pond Trail, which parallels the creek. The route rises above it again and offers glimpses of Katahdin peeking out toward the southwest; the cliffs of Russell Mountain are visible beyond it.

The trail levels, crosses a tributary, rises briefly, and then winds over several small brooks in a young, diverse forest. The single-track path gently continues along, winds past another nice boulder, then enters denser spruce-fir woods, where views peek west toward Hamlin Ridge and Blueberry Knoll in Katahdin's North Basin. The trail crosses bog bridging and reaches a short puncheon spur down to the marshy shore of Whidden Pond on the right (18.4/1,640). Head to the water's edge for a final view of the Katahdin massif. From north to south (right to left), the distinctive features are the Little North Basin, Blueberry Knoll in the North Basin, Hamlin Ridge, and finally the Great and South basins, including Baxter Peak, Pamola, and Saddle Trail.

The trail crests the height-of-land and leaves the Wassataquoik Stream drainage. The path continues through dense spruce-fir and reaches Sandy Stream Pond Trail on the left (18.7/1,600). This marks the start of the popular Sandy Stream Pond Loop from Roaring Brook; the odds of encountering other hikers increase.

Remain on Russell Pond Trail as it slowly descends over roots, steepens, and becomes rockier. Leveling briefly and becoming muddy in spots, the trail crosses puncheon and passes a glimpse of nearby South Turner Mountain. Cross a stream on more bog bridging, then rise and drop briefly to rock-hop the rushing brook that feeds Sandy Stream. The trail runs level, then ascends briefly through a paper birch grove and attains a small ridge of beeches and other hardwoods. You can hear Roaring Brook ahead, and soon the route descends to reach Sandy Stream Trail and its rushing brook. Cross the bridge and return to the trailhead (19.8/1,500).

INFORMATION

Baxter State Park, 64 Balsam Drive, Millinocket, ME 04462, 207-723-5140, baxterstateparkauthority.com.

NEARBY

Eat up, fuel up, and gear up as needed in Millinocket. Once you leave town, you're on your own when it comes to supplies.

TRIP 37
CUTLER COAST PUBLIC RESERVED LAND

Location: Cutler, ME
Difficulty: Moderate
Distance: 9.2 miles round-trip
Total Elevation Gain/Loss: 1,600 feet/1,600 feet
Trip Length: 2 days
Recommended Map: *Cutler Coast Public Lands Guide & Map* (Maine Department of Agriculture, Conservation, and Forestry, Division of Parks and Lands)
Highlight: Coastal backpacking.

Located at the farthest end of Maine's coast, the Cutler Coast is often muddy, foggy, and wet. But it offers the opportunity to backpack through a spongy maritime forest along the rockbound hide of New England's northern coast.

HIKE OVERVIEW

The hike first follows Coastal Trail south along the ocean for 4.0 miles, passing cliffy promontories and pocket coves. It returns via Inland Trail, where a soggy cedar, spruce, and fir forest drapes the landscape. The trail is often muddy and travels across extensive sections of slick bog bridging. Available water sources are mostly brown and tannin-soaked. Carry a filter or bring all your water. Weekends in Cutler have become busy; weekdays generally see much less traffic and offer more solitude.

OVERNIGHT OPTIONS

Three primitive backcountry campsites are located midway through the hike, 4.3 to 4.6 miles from the trailhead. Perched in the forest immediately inland from the coast, the sites are available on a first-come, first-served basis. Camping is prohibited elsewhere. It may be hard to secure a site on weekends. If sites are all taken, look for a flat rock ledge near the ocean rather than establishing a higher-impact (and illegal) site inland. (The boggy, rooty, and mossy forest would make camping difficult anyway.) Campfires are prohibited. The sites are described in the order you encounter them (north–south). The closest water source for all three sites is located just past site 3, a funky brown-colored stream. Very primitive privies are available at all three sites.

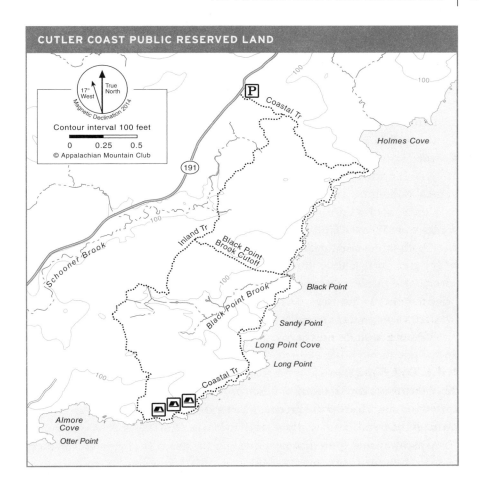

Site 1 is in a small clearing just inland from the coastal rocks, offering a lookout point over the water and space for two small tents.

Site 2 is sheltered in a larger clearing surrounded by spruces, with ready access to the rocks and good spots for cooking and lounging. Good views extend south along the coast to a classic lighthouse and its red-roofed buildings.

Site 3 is tucked farther back in the trees, provides more shelter in inclement weather, and has space for two tents. The site has a limited view. Nice open ledges are accessible down below, and there are several flat areas for cooking and relaxing.

TO REACH THE TRAILHEAD

From US 1 in East Machias, turn right onto ME 191 and follow it for 12.6 miles to the fishing village of Cutler. From the flagpole and bell in the town center, continue on ME 191 for 3.8 miles to reach the signed parking lot (44° 41.930′ N, 67° 9.478′ W) and trailhead on your right, where you'll find a pit toilet and information kiosk.

HIKE DESCRIPTION

From the trailhead (0.0/140), survey the surrounding trees. Yellow birches, spruces, red maples, and young black cherries ring the parking area. More interesting is the presence of Atlantic white cedar, a common tree along Maine's east coastline, but rare on most Northeast hiking trails. Recognize it by the vertical ribbons on its trunk and flat splays of needles.

Sign in at the information kiosk and head out on Coastal Trail, past a spruce tree. Yellow *Clintonia* grows below it. The route immediately encounters the first bog bridging, a slick, foot-sliding balance exercise, and crosses a boggy area on a small footbridge. Paper birches mix in with the surrounding spruce trees. A few roots and rocks protrude in the blue-blazed trail as it rises briefly, makes a slow drop, and reaches Inland Trail entering from the right (0.4/120)—your return route.

Continue straight on Coastal Trail, which passes a flowing water source and winds through increasingly dense woods. Understory plants fade away beneath the drunken stick forest. The trail undulates past a big, gnarly yellow birch on the left and travels over much bog bridging. It then widens and passes through a few clearings before noticeably descending. Ocean blue appears through the trees ahead, and you reach the coast (1.4/50).

A pathway and granite steps provide access to clifftops rising vertically from the ocean 75 feet below. Looking south, Black Point juts into the sea. Spot a gravelly cove to the north, but be aware that the coastline becomes private property only a few yards north of this access point. The long mass of Grand Manan Island in Canada is visible offshore to the east. In the water below, the tides are extreme, rising and falling between 12 and 20 feet twice each day.

Back on Coastal Trail, head south along the cliff's edge and past intermittent views. Alders and wood ferns line the single-track path as it navigates roots, climbs a rock staircase, and steeply descends. Pass views into a rocky cove. Ocean glimpses are intermittent but regular; peer down at whitewashed boulders littering the coast below.

The trail winds close to the cliff's edge, offers extensive views, and passes above a deep cove with small waterfalls. Slowly descend through a field of spruces and abundant laurels. The trail then drops to sea level, crosses flowing water, and runs along the coastal rocks. Blue paint and a few cairns mark the route. The seaweed-coated rocks are evocative of matted Chewbacca hair.

The remote and rocky coastline of the Cutler Coast offers a distinctive backcountry experience. (Photo courtesy of Carey Kish)

Raspberry bushes are common, and blueberries appear as well. The trail climbs briefly and then drops into the Black Point Brook watershed. Just before reaching the stream, the trail meets Black Point Brook Cutoff (2.8/20), which leads north to Inland Trail in 0.8 miles. Remain on Coastal Trail as it heads to the adjacent cobblestone beach on Black Point Cove.

Leaving the beach, climb a long ladder, reenter the forest, and curve away from the water to bypass Black Point. Winding through a spruce-cedar forest, the trail emerges at more views of the cliff-studded coast. The trail rambles along the clifftop, passes another small, cobbled beach, and then rises more than 100 feet over rocks and slabs. The route curves right and emerges by a broad valley dotted with stands of cedars and spruces.

The trail bends right and then left to meander above the meadow. Abundant blueberries line the path, which dips across the brook draining the valley. Descend to placid Long Point Cove and its cobblestone beach, accessed by a short flight of stairs. The trail climbs, switchbacks left, and makes a steep ascent via rock stairs. Then ramble downward along a rocky path and past an offshore mega-boulder. The route continues, crosses a bridge, and reemerges on the open coastline by a rocky outcrop. The trail returns inland, travels just above the cliffs, and then quickly drops back down next to the shoreline and returns to the rocks. Site 1 is just ahead, indicated by a small sign (4.3/30). A staircase and log steps lead up to it.

Past the site, the trail continues along the open rocks and then turns inland to climb up a small ravine and reach the posted junction for Site 2 (4.4/40), reached via log steps on the left. The route passes through a boggy section and returns to the shoreline rocks. Crest the sloping promontory of Fairy Head and look south toward a major antenna array poking above the hills. The U.S. Navy operates a very low frequency (VLF) radio transmitter station nearby, which consists of 26 1,000-foot high antennas spread over 2 square miles.

Purple irises, wild pea, and yarrow are common in the small patches of vegetation that dot the rocks. Turn a corner and reach the posted junction for Site 3 (4.6/30) in the woods to the right. Immediately past it is a meadow and small pond, fed by flowing brown water—the only nearby water source. The route passes one final cove with a nice view of Little River Lighthouse and then turns inland (4.8/30), leaving the coast behind for good.

The single-track trail returns to the sponge forest. After rising briefly, the route levels off and follows an easy-cruising, not-too-wet path. The trail curves back and forth up a slow rise, aided at times by small log steps, and then again winds downward. After encountering some puncheon, start up a rocky hill, enter a nice yellow birch grove, then cruise to the first of four posted over-looks. A short spur leads to a view southwest over a sea of conifers.

After a brief descent, reach a bench and posted fork in the trail. Go right to remain on Inland Trail, now an old woods road. The route slowly descends, crosses a tributary of Black Point Brook, and then passes through birch groves. Red maples mix in. Rise to the next posted overlook, this one peering north-east. A hundred yards farther, the third signed overlook leads to a bald rock with views east and southeast. The trail returns to single-track, drops again, and crosses more puncheon. Skirting a wet area, pass through a stand of red maples and begin a level section.

The hike next reaches the edge of a large pond, headwaters for Black Point Brook. Larch trees ring the shore, some of them substantial. Blackberries are abundant. The trail continues near the pond. A short spur trail climbs atop open boulders for the hike's final overlook, a spot that captures the essence of the region.

From here, the trail returns to spruce-fir sponge-land. The route is mostly level and then rises over open rocks to intersect Black Point Brook Cutoff (7.3/190), which reaches its inland end here; a cairn marks the spot.

Continue on Inland Trail and drop steeply over a talus-like section. The narrow path then levels and rambles past extensive spruces and firs. Cross an open boggy meadow; houses to your left indicate the approximate location of the highway. This section is particularly wet, and several portions of bog bridging almost float in the underlying water.

Wind for some distance through a small bog forest of aspens, alders, azaleas, laurels, and larches interspersed with a few dry rock outcrops. After crossing the hike's longest stretch of bog bridging, the trail reenters the matchstick forest of cedars, spruces, and firs. The final section of Inland Trail winds through a chaotic forest of leaning trees and deposits you at the earlier junction with Coastal Trail (8.8/120). Turn left and head back to the trailhead (9.2/140).

INFORMATION
Maine Department of Agriculture, Conservation, and Forestry, Division of Parks and Lands, 106 Hogan Road, Suite 5, Bangor, ME 04401, 207-941-4412, parksandlands.com, bpl@maine.gov.

NEARBY
Visit the easternmost point of land in the continental United States at Quoddy Head State Park, home to the iconic red-and-white striped West Quoddy Head Lighthouse. The park offers 5.0 miles of hiking trails, oceanside views across the water to Canada, and a visitor center and museum run by the West Quoddy Head Light Keepers Association, all located 11.0 miles east of the trailhead via ME 191 and Boot Cove Road.

INDEX

ABOUT THE AUTHOR
AND CONTRIBUTORS

MATT HEID is a former senior editor of *AMC Outdoors,* the member magazine of the Appalachian Mountain Club, and currently writes the magazine's Equipped column blog. He is also the author of *101 Hikes in Northern California* and *One Night Wilderness: San Francisco Bay Area,* a contributor to *Backpacking California,* and a researcher and writer for three *Let's Go* guides. Matt has hiked thousands of miles across New England, California, Alaska, and other wilderness destinations, and also cycles, climbs, and surfs. He leads trips and teaches classes in outdoor photography, natural history, and navigation.

Members of The Best Backpacking in New England Group each hiked one or more trips to ensure that every trip in this book features the most accurate and up-to-date information as verified in the field and on the trail. This updated edition would not have been possible without their dedicated efforts.

Wendy Almeida

Wendy is assistant features editor at the *Portland Press Herald/Maine Sunday Telegram* and has been writing about enjoying the outdoors with kids in her monthly Kid Tracks Outdoors column for more than 10 years. Her kids have grown up exploring the trails of Maine and New Hampshire on foot, skis, and bikes, as well as through the Geocaching and EarthCache games. They have found treasures of all sorts while out on the trail. Wendy lives in Standish, Maine.
Trip 29: Caribou-Speckled Mountain Wilderness

Hugh Coxe

Hugh works as a land use planner for the State of Maine and enjoys hiking, skiing, bicycling, kayaking, and microbrew beer. He has hiked, climbed, and

skied in Nepal, Switzerland, and throughout the Western U.S. and Canada but loves spending time in the White Mountains, Baxter State Park, and almost anywhere outdoors in Maine. He lives with his family in Falmouth, Maine.
Trip 34: 100-Mile Wilderness

Kristi Hobson Edmonston

Kristi works as an instructor for the REI Outdoor School and AMC Youth Opportunities Program and is an avid outdoor enthusiast, though backpacking and hiking are her first loves. She is already busy planning her next adventure with her husband, and favorite hiking partner, Bob. Raised in a rural area of Pennsylvania, Kristi currently lives in Watertown, Massachusetts.
Trips 22, 26: Pemigewasset Wilderness, Eastern Loop; King Ravine

Dan Eisner

Dan was AMC Books editor from 2007 to 2010 and is an occasional contributor to *AMC Outdoors* magazine. He bagged his first 4,000-footer, Mount Washington, in 2008 and needs only eight more to join the Four Thousand Footer Club. Every summer, he and six or seven friends meet in the Whites for a four-day hut-to-hut trip and wind down at the end of each day with overly competitive board-game playing.
Trip 28: The Kilkenny

Paul Gannon Jr.

Paul works as the senior instructor for REI Outdoor Programs in New England and is an avid hiker, climber, paddler, and teacher. Some of his favorite locales include the Icelandic interior and the woods and coastline of northern Maine. He's also a musician who can be seen slappin' da bass throughout Massachusetts. Paul lives in Shrewsbury, Massachusetts.
Trips 35, 36: Chimney Pond and Katahdin-Russell Pond Loop, Baxter State Park

Samantha Horn Olsen

Samantha has worked in Maine state natural resource agencies for more than 14 years and is passionate about natural resource science and policy. She enjoys hiking, camping, skiing, snowshoeing, canoeing, and learning new outdoor skills, and is presently having fun working her way through a list of hiking and skiing goals that give her a great excuse to plan lots of trips. Samantha lives with her family in Readfield, Maine.
Trip 34: 100-Mile Wilderness

Carey Michael Kish

Carey is the hiking and camping columnist for the *Portland Press Herald/ Maine Sunday Telegram* and editor of *AMC's Maine Mountain Guide*. An avid hiker and freelance outdoors and travel writer, Carey currently is working on a new book on classic Maine coast hikes for AMC's Best Day Hike Series. He lives in Bowdoin, Maine.
Trips 33, 37: Camden Hills State Park, Cutler Coast Public Reserved Land

René Laubach

René Laubach has been director of Mass Audubon's Berkshire Wildlife Sanctuaries since 1985. He is an avid hiker and highpointer and author of seven books including *AMC's Best Day Hikes in the Berkshires* and *Best Day Hikes in Connecticut* (with Charles W. G. Smith). René and his wife, Christyna, live in the Berkshire hilltown of Becket, Massachusetts.
Trips 3, 8, 10: Tunxis State Forest, The Taconics, Mount Greylock State Reservation

Colleen MacDonald

Colleen is the website manager for the Union of Concerned Scientists and enjoys hiking with her dog Hazel the Magnificent, a.k.a. the Über Goober. An amateur naturalist, she also enjoys exploring the New England outdoors by kayak and bicycle. Her favorite places in New England include the Maine coast and the peaks of the White Mountains. She lives in Hull, Massachusetts.
Trip 17: Mount Moosilauke

Kim Foley MacKinnon

Kim is a Boston-based travel journalist and author who loves exploring New England as much as she does globe-trotting. Her most recent book is AMC's *Outdoors with Kids Boston*. You can learn more about her at kfmwriter.com.
Trips 1, 2, 4, 6, 9: Arcadia Management Area, Pachaug State Forest, Sandy Neck, Tully Trail, Monroe State Forest

Jennifer Lamphere Roberts

Jennifer is the author of *AMC's Best Day Hikes in Vermont* and spent many seasons in the backcountry working for AMC and the Northern Forest Canoe Trail before turning that experience around to encourage other girls to get active and into the woods. She lives with her family in Montpelier, Vermont.
Trips 11-15: Glastenbury Mountain Wilderness, Lye Brook Wilderness, Breadloaf Wilderness, Camel's Hump State Park, Mount Mansfield

Jeff Ryan

Jeff Ryan calls South Portland, Maine, his base camp, but he is most often found exploring the trails and shoreline of New England and beyond. He has logged more than 10,000 hiking miles, including the Pacific Crest Trail, Appalachian Trail, and dozens of shorter-distance trails throughout North America. Jeff has also carved out a successful writing career specializing in promoting outdoor products and lifestyle.

Trips 16, 24: Wapack Trail, Montalban Ridge

James Vittetau

James is an avid outdoorsman and backpacker who has spent three seasons working in the Adirondacks and the White Mountains, including two seasons at AMC backcountry sites. James recently hiked the Arizona Trail and completed work for Alaska State Parks. He lives in Gorham, New Hampshire.

Trip 30: The Mahoosucs

Philip Werner

Philip is a four-season hiking and backpacking leader with the AMC Boston Chapter and the author of the popular backpacking blog SectionHiker.com. He bushwhacks, peak bags, and backpacks throughout Massachusetts, New Hampshire, Vermont, and Maine, and two of his trip reports about section hiking the Maine Appalachian Trail appear in *Hikers' Stories from the Appalachian Trail* (Stackpole Books, 2013). He lives in Boston, Massachusetts.

Trips 19, 25: Sandwich Range Wilderness, Eastern Loop; Great Gulf Wilderness

W. Cameron West

Cameron is an avid backpacker and adventurer who both works and plays in the woods of North America and has spent months solo and group trekking in various wilderness areas from Alaska to the White Mountains. He is an amateur photographer who seeks to capture people exploring and enjoying the natural world; his work has appeared in *Sierra* magazine and *USA Today Education,* among other places. He lives in New Britain, Connecticut.

Trip 21: Pemigewasset Wilderness, Western Loop

Additional thanks to **Bobby Haran and **Becky Huncilman,** who also field-checked sections of Trip 21, the Pemigewasset Wilderness, Western Loop hike.*

Appalachian Mountain Club

Founded in 1876, AMC is the nation's oldest outdoor recreation and conservation organization. AMC promotes the protection, enjoyment, and understanding of the mountains, forests, waters, and trails of the Northeast outdoors.

People

We are more than 150,000 members, advocates, and supporters, including 12 local chapters, more than 16,000 volunteers, and over 450 full-time and seasonal staff. Our chapters reach from Maine to Washington, D.C.

Outdoor Adventure and Fun

We offer more than 8,000 trips each year, from local chapter activities to adventure travel worldwide, for every ability level and outdoor interest— from hiking and climbing to paddling, snowshoeing, and skiing.

Great Places to Stay

We host more than 150,000 guests each year at our AMC lodges, huts, camps, shelters, and campgrounds. Each AMC destination is a model for environmental education and stewardship.

Opportunities for Learning

We teach people skills to safely enjoy the outdoors and to care for the natural world around us through programs for children, teens, and adults, as well as outdoor leadership training.

Caring for Trails

We maintain more than 1,800 miles of trails throughout the Northeast, including nearly 350 miles of the Appalachian Trail in five states.

Protecting Wild Places

We advocate for land and riverway conservation, monitor air quality, research climate change, and work to protect alpine and forest ecosystems throughout the Northern Forest and Mid-Atlantic Highlands regions.

Engaging the Public

We seek to educate and inform our own members and an additional 2 million people annually through the media, AMC Books, our website, our White Mountain visitor centers, and AMC destinations.

Join Us!

Members meet other like-minded people and support our mission while enjoying great AMC programs, our award-winning *AMC Outdoors* magazine, and special discounts. Visit outdoors.org or call 800-372-1758 for more information.

APPALACHIAN MOUNTAIN CLUB
Recreation • Education • Conservation
outdoors.org

AMC IN NEW ENGLAND

EACH YEAR, AMC'S EIGHT NEW ENGLAND CHAPTERS—Berkshire, Boston, Connecticut, Maine, Narragansett, New Hampshire, Southeastern Massachusetts, and Worcester—offer thousands of outdoor activities including hiking, backpacking, bicycling, paddling, and climbing trips, as well as social, family, and young member programs. Members also maintain local trails, lead outdoor skills workshops, and promote stewardship of the region's natural resources. To view a list of AMC activities in New England and across the Northeast, visit activities.outdoors.org.

AMC BOOK UPDATES

AMC BOOKS STRIVES TO KEEP OUR BOOKS AS UP-TO-DATE and accurate as possible. If after publishing a book we learn that trails have been relocated or route or contact information has changed, we will post the updated information online. Check for updates at outdoors.org/bookupdates.

If you find any errors in this book, please let us know by submitting them to amcbookupdates@outdoors.org or in writing to Books Editor, c/o AMC, 5 Joy Street, Boston, MA 02108. We will verify all submissions and post key updates each month. AMC Books is dedicated to being a recognized leader in outdoor publishing. Thank you for your participation.

AMC BOOKS & MAPS

EXPLORE THE
POSSIBILITIES

AMC Books

AMC's Best Backpacking in the Mid-Atlantic

Michael R. Martin

These 30 overnight trips range in difficulty from intermediate to expert and travel through forests of wild rhododendron at Dolly Sods, across the beaches of Assateague, and over the peaks of New York's Catskill Mountains.

$19.95 • 978-1-934028-86-5

Maine Mountain Guide, 10th Edition

Carey M. Kish

This is the definitive trail guide to the mountains of Maine. With options for every ability and interest level, the guide features updated descriptions of more than 450 trails, expert advice about trip planning and safety, and full-color, GPS-rendered maps with trail segment mileage.

$23.95 • 978-1-934028-30-8

White Mountain Guide, 29th Edition

Steven D. Smith

For over 100 years, hikers have relied on AMC's *White Mountain Guide,* the most trusted resource for the hiking trails in the region. This edition features accurate descriptions of more than 500 trails, topographic maps with trail segment mileage, trip planning and safety information, and a checklist of New England's Four-Thousand Footers.

$24.95 • 978-1-934028-44-5

AMC Guide to Winter Hiking and Camping

Lucas St. Clair and Yemaya Maurer

This comprehensive guide will help you plan a great trip with plenty of practical advice that emphasizes preparation, safety, outdoor stewardship, and fun. Learn when to go, what latest gear and clothing to bring, how to navigate, and the essentials of staying warm and dry.

$16.95 • 978-1-934028-12-4